MAUI REVEALED
The Ultimate Guidebook

5th Edition

Andrew Doughty

Photographs by Andrew Doughty & Leona Boyd

WIZARD
PUBLICATIONS
INC

MAUI REVEALED
The Ultimate Guidebook; 5th Edition

Published by Wizard Publications, Inc.
Post Office Box 991
Lihu'e, Hawai'i 96766–0991

ISBN 13: 978–0–9814610–3–8   6111
Library of Congress Control Number 2010920809
Printed in China

Cataloging–in–Publication Data

Doughty, Andrew
    Maui revealed : the ultimate guidebook / Andrew Doughty – 5th ed.
Lihue, HI : Wizard Publications, Inc., 2010.
    312 p. : col. illus., col. photos, col. maps ; 21 cm.
    Includes index.
    Summary : a complete traveler's reference to the Hawaiian island of Maui with full-color illustrations, maps, directions and candid advice by an author who resides in Hawaii.
    ISBN 978–0–9814610–3–8
    LCCN 2010920809

1. Maui (Hawaii) – Guidebooks. 2. Maui (Hawaii) – Description and travel.
    I. Title.

DU 628   919.6921__dc21

All photographs (except the cover) taken by Andrew Doughty and Leona Boyd.
Cartography by Andrew Doughty.
All artwork and illustrations by Andrew Doughty and Lisa Pollak.

Cover imagery courtesy of NASA. The image has been enhanced and is copyrighted.

Pages 2–3: Honolua Bay, right side, taken from the cliffs above.

We welcome any comments, questions, criticisms or contributions you may have, and have incorporated some of your suggestions into this edition. Please send to the address above or e-mail us at **aloha@wizardpub.com**.

Check out our website at **www.wizardpub.com** for up-to-the-minute changes.

Dedicated to Leo Doughty, whose love of flight and adventure has left its mark, and who has always paid his dues in silence.

(Continued...)

ACTIVITIES
170

ISLAND DINING
248

WHERE TO STAY
288

ADVENTURES
235

INDEX
306

Maui is the undisputed playground of Hawai'i. No other island has the range of activities and scenery available to you here. There's almost nothing you can't do on Maui: hike in pristine rain forests, snorkel in an extinct crater, coast a bicycle 10,000 feet down a volcano, walk along miles of beaches, frolic under a waterfall, dive into a natural freshwater pool, lie on a black or even red sand beach, or sip a drink as the sun sets over nearby islands. Whatever fantasy you have, Maui is bound to deliver.

Most travel publishers send a writer or writers to a given location for a few weeks to become "experts" and to compile information for guidebooks. To our knowledge, we at Wizard Publications are the only ones who actually *live* our books.

We hike the trails, ride the boats, eat in the restaurants, explore the reefs and do the things we write about. It takes us two *years*, full time, to do a first edition book, and we visit places *anonymously*. We marvel at writers who can do it all in a couple of weeks staying in a hotel. Wow, they must be *really* fast. Our method, though it takes much longer, gives us the ability to tell it like it is in a way no one else can. We put in many long hours, and doing all these activities is a burdensome grind. But we do it all for you—only for you. (Feel free to gag at this point.)

We have found many special places that people born and raised here didn't even know about because that's *all we do*—explore the island. Visitors will find the book as valuable as having a friend living on the island.

We recognize the effort people go through to visit Maui, and our goal is to expose you to as many options as possible so you can decide what you want to see and do. We took great pains to structure this book in such a way that it will

be fun, easy reading and loaded with useful information. This book is not a bland regurgitation of the facts arranged in textbook fashion. We feel strongly that guidebooks should present their information so that you don't have to look through every single page every time you want to find something.

If you are here on vacation, your time is extremely precious. You don't want to spend all your time flipping through a book looking for what you want. You need to be able to locate *what* you want, *when* you want it. You want to be able to access a comprehensive index, a thorough table of contents and refer to high-quality maps that were designed with you in mind. You want to know which helicopter, SCUBA, boat tour or lu'au is the best on the island. You want to find special hidden gems most people overlook. You want to be shown those things that will make this vacation the best of your life.

A quick look at this book will reveal features never before used in other guidebooks. Let's start with the maps. They are more detailed than any other maps you will find, and yet they omit extraneous information that can sometimes make a chore out of reading a map. We know that people in unfamiliar territory sometimes have a hard time determining where they are on a map, so we include landmarks. Most notable among these are mile markers. At every mile on main roads, the government has erected numbered markers to tell you where you are. We are the first to put these markers on a map so you can use them as reference points. In addition, we repeatedly drive or walk every inch of every road on the maps. This is important because many of the roads represented on existing maps have been shifted, moved or eliminated, making "current" maps obsolete. Where

ABOUT THIS BOOK

needed, we've drawn legal public beach access in yellow, so you'll *know* when you're legally entitled to cross someone's land. Most guidebooks have the infuriating habit of mentioning a particular place or sight but then fail to mention how to get there! You won't find that in our book. We tell you exactly how to find the hidden gems and use our own special maps to guide you.

One of the things unique to this book is the acceptance of change. We produce brand new editions of our books every two years, but during that time we are constantly incorporating changes into the text nearly every time we do a new printing. We also post many of these changes on our website. This allows us to make some modifications throughout the life of each edition. We don't have the luxury of making *every* change that happens on a weekly basis, but it does give us more flexibility than if we only acknowledged changes every two years.

As you read this book, you will also notice that we are very candid in assessing businesses. Unlike some other guidebooks that send out questionnaires asking a business if they are any good (gee, they *all* say they're good), we've had personal contact with the businesses listed in this book. One of the dirty little secrets about guidebook writers is that they sometimes make cozy little deals for good reviews. Well, you won't find that here. We accept no payment for our reviews, we make no deals with businesses for saying nice things, and there are no advertisements in our book. What we've seen and experienced is what you get. If we gush over a certain company, it comes from personal experience. If we rail against a business, it is for the same reason. All businesses mentioned in this book are here by *our* choosing. None has had any input into

what we say, and we have not received *a single cent* from any of them for their inclusion. (In fact, there are some who would probably pay to be left out, given our comments.) We always review businesses as anonymous visitors and only later as guidebook writers if we need more information. This ensures that we are treated the same as you. (Amazingly, most travel writers *announce* themselves.) What you get is our opinion on how they operate. Nothing more, nothing less.

Sometimes our candor gets us into trouble. More than once we've had our books pulled from shelves because our comments hit a little too close to home. And powerful local businesses that don't like our reviews and their friends in the media have stirred up lots of trouble for us on Maui. That's OK, because we don't work for the people who *sell* the book; we work for the people who *read* the book. It's also true that a handful of local residents have become upset because we've told readers about places that they'd rather keep for themselves. Ironically, it's usually not people born and raised here who have this selfish attitude, but rather the newcomers who have read about these places *in our book* (of all things), then adopted the *I'm here now—close the door* mentality.

Maui Revealed is intended to bring you independence in exploring Maui. We don't want to waste any of your precious time by giving you bad advice or bad directions. We want you to experience the best that the island has to offer. Our objective in writing this book is to give you the tools and information necessary to have the greatest Hawaiian experience possible.

We hope we succeeded.

Andrew Doughty

From the bottom of the ocean to their summits above the clouds, the Hawaiian Islands owe their existence to enormous volcanic and seismic pressures.

HOW IT BEGAN

Sometime around 70 million years ago an event of unimaginable violence occurred in the Earth's mantle, deep below the ocean floor. A hot spot of liquid rock blasted through the Pacific plate like a giant cutting torch, forcing liquid rock to the surface off the coast of Russia, forming the Emperor Seamounts. As the tectonic plate moved slowly over the hot spot, this torch cut a long scar along the plate, piling up mountains of rock, producing island after island. The oldest of these islands to have survived is Kure. Once a massive island with its own unique ecosystem, only its ghost remains in the form of a fringing coral reef, called an atoll.

As soon as the islands were born, a conspiracy of elements proceeded to dis-

mantle them. Ocean waves unmercifully battered the fragile and fractured rock. Abundant rain, especially on the northeastern sides of the mountains, easily carved up the rock surface, seeking faults in the rock and forming rivers and streams. In forming these channels, the water carried away the rock and soil, robbing the islands of their very essence. Additionally, the weight of the islands ensured their doom. Lava flows on top of other lava, and the union of these flows is always weak. This lava also contains countless air pockets and is crisscrossed with hollow lava tubes, making it inherently unstable. As these massive amounts of rock accumulated, their bases were crushed under the weight of subsequent

After their long journey across the sea, the islands' first life forms found nothing but stark rock to greet them.

lava flows, causing their summits to sink back into the sea.

What we call the Hawaiian Islands are simply the latest creation from this island-making machine. Kauaʻi and Niʻihau are the oldest of the eight major islands. Lush and deeply eroded, the last of Kauaʻi's fires died with its volcano a million years ago. Oʻahu, Molokaʻi, Lanaʻi, Kahoʻolawe—their growing days are over as well. Maui is in its twilight days as a growing island. After growing vigorously, Hawaiian volcanoes usually go to sleep for a million years or so before sputtering back to life for one last fling. Maui's volcano, Haleakala, awakened from its long sleep and is in its final eruptive stage. It *probably* last erupted around 1790 (see box on page 135 for an explanation) and will continue with sporadic eruptions for a (geologically) short time before drifting into eternal sleep.

The latest and newest star in this chain is the Big Island of Hawaiʻi. Born less than a million years ago, this youngster is still vigorously growing. Though none of its five volcanic mountains is considered truly dead, these days Mauna Loa and Kilauea are doing most of the work of making the Big Island bigger. Mauna Loa, the most massive mountain on Earth, consists of 10,000 *cubic miles* of rock. The quieter of the two active volcanoes, it last erupted in 1984. Kilauea is the most boisterous of the volcanoes and is the most active volcano on the planet. Kilauea's most recent eruption began in 1983 and was still going strong as we went to press. Up and coming onto the world stage is Loʻihi. This new volcano is still 3,200 feet below the ocean's surface, 20 miles off the southeastern coast of the island. Yet in a geologic heartbeat, the Hawaiian Islands will be richer with its ascension, sometime in the next 100,000 years.

These virgin islands were barren at birth. Consisting only of volcanic rock, the first life forms to appreciate these new islands were marine creatures. Fish, mammals and microscopic animals discovered this new underwater haven and made homes for themselves. Coral polyps attached themselves to the lava, and succeeding generations built upon these, creating what would become coral reefs.

Meanwhile, on land, seeds carried by the winds were struggling to colonize the rocky land, eking out a living and breaking down the lava rock. Storms brought the occasional bird, hopelessly blown off course. The lucky ones found the islands. The even luckier ones arrived with mates or were pregnant when they got here. Other animals, stranded on pieces of floating debris, washed ashore against all odds and went on to colonize the islands. These introductions of new species were rare events. It took an extraordinary set of circumstances for a new species to actually make it to the islands. Single specimens were destined to live out their lives in lonely solitude. On average, a new species was successfully deposited here only once every 20,000 years.

As with people, islands have a life cycle. After their violent birth, islands grow to their maximum size, get carved up by the elements, collapse in parts, and finally sink back into the sea. Someday, all the Hawaiian islands will be nothing more than geologic footnotes in the Earth's turbulent history. When a volcanic island is old, it is a sandy sliver called an atoll, devoid of mountains, merely a shadow of its former glory. When it's middle-aged, it can be a lush wonderland, a haven for anything green, like Kaua'i. And when it's young, it is dynamic and unpredictable, like the Big Island of Hawai'i, but lacking the scars of experience from its short battle with the elements. Maui is unique among the Hawaiian islands because it's in its prime—young enough to show the dynamism of its volcanic heritage, yet old enough for the elements to have carved lovely lines of character onto its face. The first people to occupy the island were blessed with riches beyond their wildest dreams.

Water and plants take turns converting lava into paradise.

The ancient Hawaiians went to great effort to create temples (heiaus) for their gods. The massive Pi'ilanihale Heiau near Hana, reclaimed from the jungle, is a particularly grand example.

THE FIRST SETTLERS

Sometime around the fourth or fifth century A.D., a large, double-hulled voyaging canoe, held together with flexible sennit lashings and propelled by sails made of woven pandanus, slid onto the sand on the Big Island of Hawai'i. These first intrepid adventurers, only a few dozen or so, encountered an island chain of unimaginable beauty.

They had left their home in the Marquesas Islands, 2,500 miles away, for reasons we will never know. Some say it was because of war, overpopulation, drought or just a sense of adventure. Whatever their reasons, these initial settlers took a big chance and surely must have been highly motivated. They left their homes and searched for a new world to colonize. Doubtless most of the first groups perished at sea. The Hawaiian Islands are the most isolated island chain in the world, and there was no way for them to know that there were islands in these waters. (Though some speculate that they were led here by the golden plover—see facing page.)

Those settlers who did arrive brought with them food staples from home: taro, breadfruit, pigs, dogs and several types of fowl. This was a pivotal decision. These first settlers found a land that contained almost no edible plants. With no land mammals other than the Hawaiian bat, the first settlers subsisted on fish until their crops matured. From then on, they lived on fish and taro. Although we associate throw-net fishing with Hawai'i, this practice was introduced by Japanese immigrants much later. The ancient Hawaiians used fishhooks and spears, for the most part, or drove fish into a net already placed in the water. They also had domesticated animals, which were used as ritual foods or reserved for chiefs.

Little is known about the initial culture. Archeologists speculate that a second wave of colonists, probably from Tahiti, may have subdued these initial inhabitants around 1000 A.D. Some may have resisted and fled into the forest, creating the legend of the Menehune.

Today Menehune are always thought of as being small in stature. The legend initially referred to their social stature, but evolved to mean that they were physically short and lived in the jungle away from the Hawaiians. (The ancient Hawaiians avoided living in the jungle, fearing that they held evil spirits, and instead settled on the coastal plains.) The Menehune were purported to build fabulous structures, always in one night. Their numbers were said to be vast, as many as 500,000. It is interesting to note that in a census taken of Kaua'i around 1800, some 65 people from a remote valley identified themselves as Menehune.

The second wave of settlers probably swept over the islands from the south, pushing the first inhabitants ever north. On a tiny island north of Kaua'i archeologists have found carvings, clearly not Hawaiian, that closely resemble Marquesan carvings, probably left by the doomed exiles.

This second culture was far more aggressive and developed into a highly class-conscious culture. The society was governed by chiefs, called Ali'i, who established a long list of taboos called kapu. These kapu were designed to keep order, and the penalty for breaking one was usually death by strangulation, club or fire. If the violation was serious enough, the guilty party's family might also be killed. It was kapu, for instance, for your shadow to fall across the shadow of the Ali'i. It was kapu to interrupt the chief if he was speaking. It was kapu to prepare men's food in the same container used for women's food. It was kapu for women to eat pork or bananas. It was kapu for men and women to eat together. It was kapu not to observe the days designated for the gods. Certain areas were kapu for fishing if they became depleted, allowing the area to replenish itself.

While harsh by our standards today, this system kept the order. Most Ali'i were

Hawai'i's First Tour Guide?

Given the remoteness of the Hawaiian Islands relative to the rest of Polynesia (or anywhere else for that matter), you'll be forgiven for wondering how the first settlers found these

Before they leave for Alaska.

islands in the first place. Many scientists think it might have been this little guy here. Called the kolea, or golden plover, this tiny bird flies over 2,500 miles nonstop to Alaska every year for the summer, returning to Hawai'i after mating. Some of these birds continue past Hawai'i and fly another 2,500 miles to Samoa and other South Pacific islands. The early Polynesians surely must have noticed this commute and concluded that there must be land in the

When they return.

direction that the bird was heading. They never would have dreamed that the birds leaving the South Pacific were heading to a land 5,000 miles away, and that Hawai'i was merely a stop in between, where the lazier birds wintered.

INTRODUCTION

Kalolopahu—Olowalu's Day of Infamy

In the first 20 years of Western contact, there were numerous incidents of Hawaiians killing westerners for weapons and westerners killing Hawaiians for revenge or to demonstrate superiority. But no skirmish between Hawaiians and westerners compares to the massacre of Kalolopahu.

A dozen years after Captain Cook was killed on the Big Island, a trading ship run by a vicious, contemptible captain named Simon Metcalfe stopped at the Big Island to trade goods. His ship was followed by a small, six-man sloop carrying the captain's son. A chief tried to climb on board Metcalfe's ship, and a crewman smacked him with a rope to prevent it. The chief was humiliated and vowed to take revenge on the next foreign vessel that came by. It was a vow that would change the destiny of the islands.

Metcalfe then went to Maui and began trading. One night, north of Lahaina, a Hawaiian sneaked over to the ship, cut loose the ship's cutter, killed the guard in the boat, then dragged the small boat to shore to break it up. (The Hawaiians didn't care about the boat; they wanted the iron.) When Metcalfe found out what happened, he fired his cannons into the nearest village in rage, then kidnapped some Hawaiians who told him that people from Olowalu did it (which was true). Metcalfe then moved his ship to Olowalu.

At this time, a high chieftess had declared the bay around Olowalu off limits. She was celebrating a family function, and the penalty for a commoner going into the water was to be burned alive. (Naturally, no one violated the kapu.) When she finally lifted the order three days later, commoners rushed in their canoes to begin trading with the foreign ship (Metcalfe's). Metcalfe told all the Hawaiians to line their canoes up on one side of the ship. When they were crowded around, Metcalfe unleashed his revenge. He opened fire with all his cannons (loaded with small shot) and muskets. More than 100 innocent Hawaiians were slaughtered (but not the one who had stolen the boat; he wasn't even there). The screaming and wailing went on for hours, and the natives named the place, Kalolopahu, meaning the place of spilt brains.

But remember the man who Metcalfe's crew had smacked with a rope? He got his revenge, too, beyond his wildest dreams. He didn't know about the Olowalu massacre, but as fate would have it, that first foreign vessel he found was the one carrying Metcalfe's son. The chief and some warriors went on board on the pretense of trade, seized the sloop, killed young Metcalfe and all but one of his crew, then stripped the boat of its weapons, including a cannon. The one person from the sloop he let live, along with a man from the senior Metcalfe's ship whom King Kamehameha had captured earlier, soon became Kamehameha's trusted advisers. They helped Kamehameha defeat his island neighbors using the stolen cannon and guns, starting with the battle at 'Iao Valley described on page 65. Kamehameha eventually became king of all the islands.

As for Simon Metcalfe, he was unable to find his son and eventually went back to the U.S. mainland. He had no idea that his presence had forever changed the politics of the islands.

sensitive to the disturbance their presence caused and often ventured outside only at night, or a scout was sent ahead to warn people that an Ali'i was on his way. All commoners were required to pay tribute to the Ali'i in the form of food and other items. Human sacrifices were common and war among rival chiefs the norm.

By the 1700s, the Hawaiians had lost all contact with Tahiti, and the Tahitians had lost all memory of Hawai'i. Hawaiian canoes had evolved into fishing and inter-island canoes and were no longer capable of long ocean voyages. The Hawaiians had forgotten how to explore the world.

OUTSIDE WORLD DISCOVERS HAWAI'I

In January 1778 an event occurred that would forever change Hawai'i. Captain James Cook, who usually had a genius for predicting where to find islands, stumbled upon Hawai'i. He had not expected the islands to be here. He was on his way to Alaska on his third great voyage of discovery, this time to search for the Northwest Passage linking the Atlantic and Pacific oceans. Cook approached the shores of Waimea, Kaua'i at night on January 19, 1778.

The next morning Kaua'i's inhabitants awoke to a wondrous sight and thought they were being visited by gods. Rushing aboard to greet their visitors, the Kauaians were fascinated by what they saw: pointy-headed beings (the British wore tricornered hats) breathing fire (smoking pipes) and possessing a death-dealing instrument identified as a water squirter (guns). The amount of iron on the ship was incredible. (They had seen iron before in the form of nails on driftwood but never knew where it originated.)

Cook left Kaua'i and briefly explored Ni'ihau before heading north for his mis-sion on February 2, 1778. When Cook returned to the islands in November after failing to find the Northwest Passage, he visited the Big Island of Hawai'i.

The Hawaiians had probably seen white men before. Local legend indicates that strange white people washed ashore on the Big Island sometime around the 1520s and integrated into society. This coincides with Spanish records of two ships lost in this part of the world in 1528. But a few weird-looking stragglers couldn't compare to the arrival of Cook's great ships and instruments.

Despite some recent rewriting of history, all evidence indicates that Cook, unlike some other exploring sea captains of his era, was a thoroughly decent man. Individuals need to be evaluated in the context of their time. Cook knew that his mere presence would have a profound impact on the cultures he encountered, but he also knew that change for these cultures was inevitable, with or without him. He tried, unsuccessfully, to keep the men known to be infected with venereal diseases from mixing with local women, and he frequently flogged infected men who tried to sneak ashore at night. He was greatly distressed when a party he sent to Ni'ihau was forced to stay overnight due to high surf, knowing that his men might transmit diseases to the women (which they did).

Cook arrived on the Big Island at a time of much upheaval. The mo'i, or king, of the Big Island had been militari-ly spanked during an earlier attempt to invade Maui and was now looting and raising hell throughout the islands as ret-ribution. Cook's arrival and his physical appearance (at 6-foot-4 he couldn't even stand up straight in his own quarters) almost guaranteed that the Hawaiians would think he was the god Lono. Lono was responsible for land fertility. Every year the ruling chiefs and their war god Ku went into abeyance, removing their power so that Lono could return to the land and make it fertile again, bringing back the spring rains. During this time all public works stopped, and the land was left alone. At the end of this *makahiki* season, man would again seize the land from Lono so he could grow crops and otherwise make a living upon it. Cook arrived at the beginning of the makahiki, and the Hawaiians naturally thought *he* was the god Lono coming to make the land fertile. Cook even sailed into the exact bay where the legend predicted Lono would arrive.

The Hawaiians went to great lengths to please their "god." All manner of supplies were made available. Eventually they became suspicious of the visitors. If they were gods, why did they accept the Hawaiian women? And if they were gods, why did one of them die?

Cook left at the right time. The British had used up the Hawaiians' hospitality (not to mention their supplies). But shortly after leaving the Big Island, the ship broke a mast, making it necessary to return to Kealakekua Bay for repairs. As they sailed back into the bay, the Hawaiians were nowhere to be seen. A chief had declared the area kapu to help replenish it. When Cook finally found the Hawaiians, they were polite but wary. *Why are you back? Didn't we please you enough already? What do you want now?*

As repair of the mast went along, things began to get tense. Eventually the Hawaiians stole a British rowboat (for the nails), and the normally calm Cook blew his cork. On the morning of February 14, 1779, he went ashore to trick the chief into coming aboard his ship where he would detain him until the rowboat was returned. As Cook and the chief were heading to the water, the chief's wife begged the chief not to go.

By now thousands of Hawaiians were crowding around Cook, and he ordered a retreat. A shot was heard from the other side of the bay, and someone shouted that the Englishmen had killed an important chief. A shielded warrior with a dagger came at Cook, who fired his pistol (loaded with small shot). The shield stopped the small shot, and the Hawaiians were emboldened. Other shots were fired. Standing in knee-deep water, Cook turned to call for a ceasefire and was struck in the head from behind with a club, then stabbed. Dozens of other Hawaiians pounced on him, stabbing his body repeatedly. The greatest explorer the world had ever known was dead at age 50 in a petty skirmish over a stolen rowboat.

KAMEHAMEHA THE GREAT

The most powerful and influential king in Hawaiian history lived during the time of Captain Cook and was born on the Big Island around 1758. Until his rule, the Hawaiian chain had never been ruled by a single person. He was the first to "unite" (i.e., conquer) all the islands.

Kamehameha was an extraordinary man by any standard. He possessed Herculean strength, a brilliant mind and boundless ambition. He was marked for death before he was even born. When Kamehameha's mother was pregnant with him, she developed a strange and overpowering craving—she wanted to *eat* the eyeball of a chief. The king of the Big Island, mindful of the rumor that the unborn child's real father was his bitter enemy, the king of Maui, asked his advisers to interpret. Their conclusion was unanimous: The child would grow to be a

*What rice is to Asians, taro is to Hawaiians—
their most important food.*

rebel, a killer of chiefs. The king decided that the child must die as soon as he was born, but the baby was instead whisked away to a remote valley to be raised.

In Hawaiian society, your role in life was governed by what class you were born into. The Hawaiians believed that breeding among family members produced superior offspring (except for the genetic misfortunes who were killed at birth), and the highest chiefs came from brother/sister combinations. Kamehameha was not of the highest class (his parents were merely cousins), so his future as a chief would not come easily.

As a young man Kamehameha was impressed by his experience with Captain Cook. He was among the small group that stayed overnight on Cook's ship during Cook's first pass of Maui. (Kamehameha was on Maui valiantly fighting a battle in which his side was getting badly whupped.) Kamehameha recognized that his world had forever changed, and he shrewdly used the knowledge and technology of westerners to his advantage.

Kamehameha participated in numerous battles. His side lost many of the early ones, but he learned from his mistakes and developed into a cunning tactician. When he finally consolidated his rule over the Big Island (by luring his enemy to be the inaugural sacrifice of a new temple), he fixed his sights on the entire island chain. In the 1790s his large company of troops, armed with some western armaments and advisers, swept across Maui, Moloka'i, Lana'i and O'ahu. After some delays in taking Kaua'i, the last of the holdouts, its king finally acquiesced to the inevitable and Kamehameha became the first ruler of all the islands. He spent his final years governing the islands peacefully from his Big Island capital and died in 1819.

MODERN HAWAI'I

During the 19th century, Hawai'i's character changed dramatically. Businessmen from all over the world came here to exploit Hawai'i's sandalwood, whales, land and people. Hawai'i's leaders, for their part, actively participated in these ventures and took a piece of much of the action for themselves. Workers were brought from many parts of the world, changing the racial makeup of the islands. Government corruption became the order of the day, and everyone seemed to be profiting, except the Hawaiian commoner. By the time Queen Lili'uokalani lost her throne to a group of American businessmen in 1893, Hawai'i had become directionless. It barely resembled the Hawai'i Captain Cook had encountered in the previous century. The kapu system had been abolished by the Hawaiians shortly after the death of Kamehameha the Great. The "Great Mahele," begun in 1848, had changed the relationship Hawaiians had with the land. Large tracts of land were sold by the Hawaiian government to royalty, government officials, commoners and foreigners, effectively stripping many Hawaiians of land they had lived on for generations.

The United States recognized the Republic of Hawai'i in 1894 with Sanford Dole as its president. It was annexed in 1898 and became an official territory in 1900. During the 19th and 20th centuries, sugar established itself as king. Pineapple was also heavily grown in the islands, with the island of Lana'i purchased in its entirety for the purpose of growing pineapple.

As the 20th century rolled on, Hawaiian sugar and pineapple workers found themselves in a lofty position—they became the highest paid workers for these crops in the world. As land prices rose and competition from other parts of the world increased, sugar and pineapple became less and less profitable. Today, these crops no longer hold the position they once had. The "pineapple island" of Lana'i has shifted away from pineapple growing and is focused on tourism. The sugar industry is now dead on the Big Island, O'ahu and for the most part Kaua'i, leaving only Maui to grow it commercially.

The story of Hawai'i is not a story of good versus evil. Nearly everyone shares in the blame for what happened to the Hawaiian people and their culture. Westerners certainly saw Hawai'i as a potential bonanza and easily exploitable. They knew what buttons to push and pushed them well. But the Hawaiians, for their part, were in a state of flux. The mere existence of westerners seemed to bring to the surface a discontent, or at least a weakness, with their system that had been lingering just below the surface.

In fact, in 1794, a mere 16 years after first encountering westerners and under no military duress from the West, Kamehameha the Great volunteered to cede his island over to Great Britain. He was hungry for western arms so he could defeat his neighbor island opponents. He even declared that as of that day, they were no longer people of Hawai'i, but rather people of Britain. (Britain declined the offer.) And in 1819, immediately after the death of the strong-willed Kamehameha, the Hawaiians, on their own accord, overthrew their own religion, dumped the kapu system and denied their gods. This was before any western missionaries ever came to Hawai'i.

Nonetheless, Hawai'i today is once again seeking guidance from her heritage. The echoes of the past seem to be getting louder with time, rather than diminishing. Interest in the Hawaiian language and culture is at a level not seen in many decades. All of us who live here are very aware of the issues and the complexities involved, but there is little agreement about where it will lead. As a result, you will be exposed to a more "Hawaiian" Hawai'i than those who might have visited the state a decade ago. This is an interesting time in Hawai'i. Enjoy it as observers, and savor the flavor of the islands.

If you fly directly into West Maui, you'll miss the spectacular shoreline highway.

In order to get to Maui, you've got to fly here. (You might be able to find a cruise to Hawai'i, but it's a pretty big and featureless piece of water to cross in a boat.)

GETTING HERE

When planning your trip, a travel agent can be helpful, though that method is becoming less and less common. The Internet has sites such as Orbitz, Expedia, Cheaptickets, Cheapair, Pandaonline, Priceline, Travelocity, Kayak, etc. If you don't want to or can't go through these sources, there are large wholesalers that can get you airfare, hotel and a rental car, often cheaper than you can get airfare on your own. **Pleasant Holidays** (800–742-9244) provides complete package tours.

The prices listed in the WHERE TO STAY section reflect the RACK rates, meaning the published rates before any discounts. Rates can be significantly lower if you go through a travel company or book online.

When you pick your travel source, be sure to shop around—the differences can be dramatic. A diligent effort can make the difference between affording a *one-week* vacation and a *two-week* vacation.

Though most visitors fly into Honolulu before arriving, there are some direct flights to Kahului. Not having to cool your heels while changing planes on O'ahu is a *big* plus since interisland flights aren't quite as convenient—or cheap—as they used to be. If you fly to Maui from Honolulu, the best views are *usually* on the left side (seats with an "A") coming in, and also the left side departing (for most routes). When flying to Honolulu from the mainland, sit on the left side coming in, the right going home. Interisland flights are done by **Hawaiian** (800–367–5320), **go!** (888–435–9462) and **Island Air** (800–652–6541). Flight attendants zip up and down the aisle hurling juice at you on most of the short interisland flights.

If you're staying in West Maui, it's tempting to look at a map and decide to fly into **Kapalua West Maui Airport** for the sake of convenience. Though it *is* nearby, we still recommend flying into Kahului. That's because the drive around the coastline into Lahaina during the day is dramatic and worth the extra time. It's during your drive along the coastline to either west or south Maui that you realize that this island, more than any other Hawaiian island, has an extremely intimate relationship with the water. No other Hawaiian island has highways that embrace the ocean so much.

If you're staying in Hana, **Pacific Wings** (888–575–4546) has pricey flights to Hana Airport from Honolulu and Kahului.

WHAT TO BRING

This list may assist you in planning what to bring. Obviously you won't need everything on the list, but it might make you think of a few things you may otherwise overlook:

- Waterproof sunblock (SPF 15 or higher)
- Hiking sticks (carbide-tipped ones are good for boulder-hopping hikes)
- Shoes—flip-flops, trashable sneakers, water shoes, hiking shoes
- Mask, snorkel and fins
- Camera with lots of memory or film
- Warm clothes (for Haleakala trips) and junk clothes for bikes, etc.
- Light rain jacket
- Small flashlight for Haleakala sunrise
- Mosquito repellent for some hikes (Lotions with at least 10% DEET seem to work best)
- Shorts and other cool cotton clothing
- Cheap, simple backpack—you don't need to go backpacking to use one; a 10-minute trek to a secluded waterfall is much easier if you bring a pack
- Hat or cap for sun protection

GETTING AROUND
Rental Cars

Rental car prices in Hawai'i *can be* (but aren't always) cheaper than almost anywhere else in the country, and the competition is ferocious. Nearly *every* visitor to Maui gets around in a rental car, and for good reason. Many of the island's best sights can only be reached if you have independent transportation.

At Kahului Airport, rental cars can be obtained from the booths to the right (as you look out) of baggage claim. It's a good idea to reserve your car in advance since companies can run out of cars during peak times. Cars are also available at the Kapalua and Hana airports.

Many hotels, condos and rental agents offer excellent room/car packages. Find out from your hotel or travel agent if one is available.

On the Hana Highway, a roadside shrine, ensconced in a natural lava cave, utilizes flowers from nearby.

Here's a list of rental car companies. The local area code is 808. Some have desks at various hotels.

The Big Guys

Alamo	**(877) 222–9075**
	Kahului: 871–6235
Avis	**(800) 321–3712**
	Kahului: 871–7575
	Kihei: 874–4077
	Ka'anapali: 661–4588
Budget	**(800) 527–0700**
	Locally: 871–8811
Dollar	**(800) 800–4000**
	Lahaina/Kahului/Hana:
	(866) 434–2226
Enterprise	**(800) 261–7331**
	Kahului: 871–1511
	Ka'anapali: 661–8804
Hertz	**(800) 654–3131**
	Kahului: 877–5167
	Lahaina: 661–7735
National	**(877) 222–9058**
	Kahului: 871–8851
	Ka'anapali: 667–9737
Thrifty	**(800) 367–5238**

The Little Guys

Kihei	**(800) 251–5288**
	Kihei: 879–7257
Maui Cruisers	**(877) 749–7889**
	Wailuku: 249–2319
Word of Mouth	**(800) 533–5929**
Bio-Beetle	**(877) 873–6121**
	Kahului: 873–6121
	(Rents bio-diesel cars)

4-Wheel Drive

On Kaua'i and especially the Big Island we've strongly recommended getting a 4WD vehicle, but it isn't as important on Maui. There aren't many off-road opportunities, and there are few places where access will require one. The drive past Hana doesn't require one, despite what you may read elsewhere. A few places in remote parts of West Maui will allow 4WDs to get *slightly* closer, but it's hard to justify the increased price here. Skip the 4WD. If you want to splurge, spring for a convertible instead. They can be fun, especially on the Hana drive.

Motorcycles & Scooters

If you think riding a HOG is something you do at a lu'au, you may want to skip this section. There's something about Harleys. Maybe it's the sound, or maybe the looks. But riding a Harley-Davidson around Maui is a blast. If you want to rent one to experience things on your own (freedom, after all, is what HOGs are all about), you can get them from **Hula Hogs** (875–7433) in Kihei and **Maui Harley-Davidson Rentals** (667–2800) in Lahaina. Expect to pay *(gulp!)* $120–$200 for 24 hours, about $100–$150 for 5–6 hours.

If you want to rent a scooter, try **Aloha Motorsports** (667–7000) in Ka'anapali and **Kihei Moped** (442–2770) in Kihei. Scooter rentals start at around $25–$75 and you need a driver's license.

Classic & Exotic Cars

Maui has a few opportunities to rent a flashy ride. If you want a fast car, **Hertz** (877–5167) in Kahului has Corvettes for around $240 per day. Bear in mind that there are no opportunities to open them up—we have no wide open highway straightaways—but if you just want to experience the thrill of driving a fast car and you have a wad burning a hole in your pocket, give it a shot.

Classic Cruisers of Maui (891–2474) is a small outfit that rents classic cars. They have a 1929 Ford Model A Woody Sedan and a 1955 Ford Thunderbird. You'll pay dearly for these—$200 to $500, but you won't have any trouble finding your car in the parking lot.

In East Maui, even the plants have plants.

It's best not to leave anything valuable in your car. There are teenagers here who pass the time by breaking into cars. It's not a *huge* problem, but it does happen. Thieving scum will work an area until the heat gets too hot, then move on to another area. When we park at a beach, waterfall or any other place frequented by visitors, we take all valuables with us, leave the windows up, and leave the doors unlocked. (Just in case someone is curious enough about the inside to smash a window.) There are plenty of stories about people walking 100 feet to a waterfall, coming back to their car and finding that their brand new video camera has walked away. And don't be gullible enough to think that trunks are safe. Someone who sees you put something in your trunk can probably get at it faster than you can with your key.

If you are between the ages of 21 and 25, **Maui Cruisers** and **Word of Mouth** don't charge you extra for the crime of being young and reckless. Enterprise charges $20 more per day, others tack on $25 and up. If you're under 21—rent a bicycle or scooter or take the bus.

A Few Driving Tips

Seat belt and **child restraint** use is required by law, and the police will pull you over for this alone. Open roads and frequently changing speed limits make it easy to accidentally speed here. Sobriety checkpoints are not an uncommon police tactic on Maui. And it's illegal for drivers to use a **cell phone** without a headset.

Buses

Maui doesn't have a typical public bus system. Our version is called the **Maui**

Bus (871–4838), mainly used for shopping. Fare is $1; call for schedules and routes or go to their website.

GETTING MARRIED ON MAUI

Maui is a wildly popular place to get married. Every romantic setting from a beach at sunset, a tropical garden or a waterfall is here for you to use as a background for your important day.

Finding a good person or company to help you isn't easy, and in this particular section we can't review the companies the way we normally would. (After all, it's not exactly practical to get married 25 times and rate the performance of a company.) That said, we *can* say that one particularly reputable source for your wedding planning is **Pacific Island Weddings** at (888) 824–4134 or (808) 874–9899.

Other full-service wedding coordinators that are available to contact for their wedding packages are listed below. Discuss your arrangements in detail with the coordinator to avoid misunderstandings over what your ceremony will be like and what it will cost.

A Dream Wedding Maui Style
(800) 743–2777 or (808) 661–1777
Romantic Maui Weddings
(800) 808–4144 or (808) 249–8484
A Paradise Dream Wedding
(888) 304–7750 or (808) 875–9503

Almost all the large resorts on Maui have wedding coordinators to help you arrange your wedding at their hotels. Be aware that site fees can be pretty high. Some of the more popular resorts for weddings are the **Four Seasons**, the **Grand Wailea**, the **Hyatt**, **Fairmont Kea Lani**, the **Westin**, the **Hotel Hana Maui**, and the **Ritz-Carlton**.

Getting married on Maui is a dream come true for lucky visitors.

Obtaining a License

Contact the State Department of Health (808) 984–8210 on Maui to obtain an application or to get the names of license agents on Maui. Both the bride and groom must be at least 18. No residency or blood tests are required. The fee is $60 *in cash,* and the license is good for 30 days. Both the bride and groom must be present with a photo ID at the time of the appointment with the marriage license agent.

WEATHER

How's the weather on Maui? A picture speaks a thousand words. The photo on the cover is very typical of the cloud and rain coverage on Maui and, to a practiced eye, tells you exactly what to expect around the island. You can see how the windward areas (meaning areas exposed to the trade winds out of the northeast) get most of the clouds and how Hana is dry, but farther uphill it's cloudy, feeding the waterfalls. Kihei and Lahaina (called *leeward* areas) are warmer, drier and sunnier than the rest of the island because they are shielded from the northeast trade winds. Notice how the clouds don't go all the way to the top of Haleakala, except where they are squeezed into the Koʻolau Gap; it's because of a temperature inversion at the 6,000 foot level. (The air actually gets warmer above that for a few thousand feet, causing the temperature-sensitive clouds to dissipate.) The top of West Maui Mountain is cloudy, as usual. The northeast trade winds build up along the bottom of Haleakala, heading southwest along the flank, and are directed off into the sea near La Pérouse Bay, leaving Kihei and Wailea calmer. This photo is quintessential Maui trade wind weather until about 1 p.m. Then more clouds will build as the island heats up, causing the air to rise, cool and condense into clouds. The summit of Haleakala may cloud up. Winds will increase all around the island as ocean air rushes in to replace the rising air.

To get **current weather forecasts,** call (866) 944–5025. Call 572–7873 for a **surf forecast**.

The Different Weather Regions

What does all this mean? It means the weather is radically different around the island. Many times we've been at the airport in Kahului and seen people coming off the plane looking gloomy and worried. "It's so windy and rainy here," they often say. Sometimes we wish the county would erect a sign at the airport saying, *"No worry, da weatha stay mo betta in Kihei and Lahaina."*

In the leeward area of **South Maui, Kihei** and **Wailea** will be warmer and drier. Winds that have just been squished between the two mountains will travel south along the Kihei coast, veering slightly offshore, so winds will be lighter the farther you go down the Kihei coast until you get to La Pérouse Bay. There the fierce wind from the bottom of the island meets calm air, creating a distinct wind line over the span of about 100 feet. That means mornings are usually calm from Makena to South Kihei. In the afternoon, however, onshore breezes will form to fill the void from the heated rising air, and the trade winds that have been absent along the coast at Makena and Wailea will start wrapping around the island parallel to the coast here. This means strong afternoon winds. Winters are less windy. The sunnier and hotter it is, the stronger the afternoon winds will be. If there's heavy cloud cover over much of Haleakala, the afternoon winds will diminish. (We're trying to avoid sounding like weather geeks, but if you understand the weather processes here, it helps you to plan your day.) High temperatures will average 80° in the winter, 86°

Rainfall Map

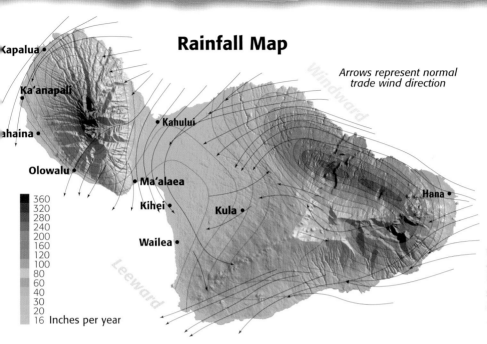

Arrows represent normal trade wind direction

Kapalua

Ka'anapali

Lahaina

Olowalu

Kahului

Ma'alaea

Kihei   Kula

Wailea

Hana

| 360 |
| 320 |
| 280 |
| 240 |
| 200 |
| 160 |
| 120 |
| 100 |
| 80 |
| 60 |
| 40 |
| 30 |
| 20 |
| 16 Inches per year |

Windward

Leeward

in the summer. South Maui nights can be cooler than in Lahaina because the air that has built up atop Haleakala during the day will tumble down to the bottom. If your condo has a skylight, you may notice puffs of cool air coming down from it at night.

Rainfall in leeward areas is light and variable. For instance, one year there were only seven days with rain in Kihei. It was going to total 4¾ inches for the year until New Years Eve brought *another* 4¾ inches, doubling the year's rainfall tally. Other years have seen 20 or more inches of rain.

In **Lahaina**, **Ka'anapali** and **Kapalua**, the exact direction of the trade winds are crucial. Lahaina is usually protected from the trades. There are fewer afternoon breezes in Lahaina than Kihei, making it warmer. High temperatures are 82° in January and 88° in August and September. As you head toward Ka'anapali, at some point the trade winds that you've been protected from in Lahaina will com-

plete their wrap-around from the other side, making wind a semi-constant companion. That's good if you like cool breezes, bad if you are trying to get a golf ball from Point A to Point B. It also means that the ocean is more susceptible to whitecaps and poor visibility north of Lahaina. **Kapalua**, farther north, is even windier, more drizzly and has the worst weather of any of the resort areas.

Just south of Lahaina, **Olowalu** would normally be protected from the trade winds, except for one slight detail. Its large, rain-cut valley leading to the center of West Maui Mountain connects with rain-cut 'Iao Valley on the windward side, cracking the mountain in two and making a natural diversion ditch for the wind to rip through, leaving Olowalu windy.

Kahului gets a concentration of winds deflected along the northern part of Haleakala that slither around the island here and are squeezed between the two mountains. So it's *almost* *always* windy in Kahului. This has made Kahului one of the greatest places on the planet for windsurfing and kiteboarding. Big-time riders from all over the world make pilgrimages here.

Ma'alaea at the south end of the valley gets a concentration of wind and dust that has been squeezed between the mountains, making it one of the windiest places on the island.

Hana is sunnier than most people think since the clouds usually form farther uphill, but it is more vulnerable to whatever the trade winds bring to the island. Most of the time Hana has beautiful weather, but sometimes systems can bring rain that can last for days, especially in the winter. The temperature is incredibly equitable. Average high in February is 78°, and the average high in September is only 84°. How's *that* for a change of season?

The summit of **Haleakala** has an average high of around 50° and low of 32° in February and reaches a scorching 58° and a low of 38° in August. It's *usually* not as windy *after sunrise*, but any wind on a cold morning can cut right through you.

Upcountry areas, such as **Kula** and **Pukalani**, are cooler due to their elevation and less windy.

Average humidity around the island ranges from 65%–75%.

In general, windward areas like Hana and Kahului get most of their rain at night and in the early morning. Leeward areas like Kihei and Lahaina get their

---

Maui is the only place we've ever seen where you can get waterfall fatigue. There are so many beautiful ones, like Wailua Falls here, that you start to take them for granted.

more sporadic rain in the late afternoon and early evening.

Ocean temperatures average 75° in February, 80° in September.

GEOGRAPHY

The island of Maui is made up of two large volcanoes called...well, that's a little confusing. The largest mountain, on the east side, is commonly referred to as Haleakala, meaning *house of the sun*. To the ancient Hawaiians, Haleakala referred only to a portion of the summit of the mountain, not the whole mountain. In fact, as far as we know, they had no name for either of the two large mountains that make up Maui. But the word Haleakala has been used so often in recent years to describe the entire mountain that it's now generally accepted. The other great mountain is topped by a small peak called Pu'u Kukui, or *hill of the candlenut tree.* A bit duller, huh? That name has never been used to describe the entire mountain, so it's commonly referred to by its less-than-exotic name, West Maui Mountain. Even scholarly geology books refer to them as Haleakala and West Maui Mountain. Annoyed at the western name, visitor bureaucrats are now pushing to refer to West Maui Mountain as Mauna Kahalawai, but that name was never accepted by Hawaiian linguists. We've also heard tour guides, such as boat captains, refer to West Maui as Halemahina, or *house of the moon.* Sounds so symmetric next to the *house of the sun*, but it's bogus.

West Maui is the oldest of the two. Streams have cut deeply into its slopes, and the results are lovely. Though you'd expect more erosion on the wet side, an accident of geology capped the wet side with more erosion-resistant lava, so big valleys aren't as prevalent as they normally would be.

Haleakala is the younger, still-active mountain. It's just over 10,000 feet high, but it wasn't always so. At one time it rose to 15,000 feet, making it the tallest mountain in the world at over 32,000 feet high (when measured from its base at the bottom of the ocean). But Haleakala is crushing itself under its own weight. Someday it will sink back into the sea. (But probably not before your trip here.) Its smoother slopes and 10,000-foot height hide an enormous volume of rock. The Hana side is a lush wonderland whose beauty is legendary. Kihei is in the dry rain shadow of the mountain, so there are few streams or eroded areas. The summit features the awesome Haleakala Crater. (Actually it's an erosion crater; see page 123.)

At one time, all the islands surrounding Maui formed one big island, which geologists called Maui Nui. (Meaning *Big Maui*—darned clever, those geologists.) In fact, if you'd visited here just 18,000 years ago, during a mini ice age that drastically lowered the sea level, you could have driven from Maui to Lana'i and on to Moloka'i. (Of course, finding a rental car might have been an issue.) As the volcanoes sank and the seas rose, the mountains separated, forming today's configuration. They continue to sink, and in about 15,000 years Maui will be two separate islands. We live in an era when Maui is perfectly arranged to easily explore the two sides. Enjoy our fortunate timing.

WHERE SHOULD I STAY?

The vast majority of visitors to Maui stay on the leeward side of the island—Lahaina to the Kapalua area in the west, or Kihei–Wailea in the south. This is the exact opposite of how things were 50 years ago. Back then all the major towns were on the windward side, where rain was abundant and crops grew vigorously. Few lived on the leeward side because it was harder to grow things there. (Lahaina has been around longer than most Hawaiian leeward towns because it was a good whaling port.) But the rain that makes everything so beautiful and lush also makes short-time visitors leery. So with the advent of jets and mass travel, the heretofore sparsely populated leeward sides of the islands became a magnet for travelers. Sure, the rain on the windward side makes things green, but it also means the ocean will have more runoff, the surf will be higher, and clouds will obscure the sun. On the leeward side you don't have the tropical lushness you may associate with Hawai'i, but you usually have clear weather, calm oceans, sparkling water and lots of sunshine. (And, after all, you can always *drive* to the lush areas.)

It's hard to decide *which* leeward side of the island to stay on, West or South. West Maui has more activities because it has a working harbor, and it doesn't get as windy off Lahaina in the afternoon as it does off South Maui, though they get plenty of wind north of Lahaina. Activities such as submarine rides, Jet Skis and dinner cruises are common there, but helicopter flights are more convenient from South Maui. West Maui is more remote, making drives to Hana, Haleakala or Kahului much longer. Parking in Lahaina is a mess. Also, it's hotter in Lahaina than in Kihei or Wailea, though northwest Maui (i.e., Ka'anapali and Kapalua) gets lots of cooling wind. South Maui has better access to Molokini, and South Maui reefs are better. West Maui has easier access to Lana'i and Moloka'i. Beaches are less crowded in South Maui, and its beach accesses don't fill up as often. Shopping is better in West Maui. West Maui's backdrop is more scenic, but it is also more densely developed. Food is better and more varied in West Maui, but South Maui has some of the most kickin' resorts. Golf

is better in South Maui, and so is the diving and snorkeling. If you're traveling with kids, West Maui is more popular with families, though South Maui has two parks that are very kid-friendly. West Maui has more cheap condos, but gas and grocery prices seem higher in West Maui. Both sides are hugely popular, but West Maui has a busier and more crowded feel.

So which is better? After living here and spending countless hours exploring and experiencing both sides, in our professional opinion, we'd have to say...we don't know. Each has advantages and disadvantages that sway us back and forth. Consider the pros and cons listed above, and the answer may become obvious to you.

IS MAUI TOO EXPENSIVE?

Maui has a reputation of being pricey. That's because...well, it *is* pricey. The truth is eating out costs more here than on the other islands. So do groceries and almost everything we can think of. Anyone who says otherwise hasn't lived on the different islands. Also, many of the activities available involve giving a company money to show you something, such as boat trips, SCUBA, aerial tours, lu'au and more. So spending time on Maui is synonymous with spending money. Some activities, like helicopters, cost more here than on other Hawaiian islands while others, like SCUBA diving, cost less.

This doesn't mean that Maui has to put you in hock for the next decade. There are *lots* of things to do that don't involve spending a fortune, and there are some tremendous values in restaurants—if you know where to look. Some of our favorite restaurants are some of the cheapest, and we point them out in DINING. The ACTIVITIES and ADVENTURES chapters have some delightful things that won't cost you a cent. Also, if you have a Costco membership or want to sign up for one, the Costco in Kahului near the airport is where most of us here buy lots of our groceries and other items. If you're here for a week or more, a Costco run can save you a bundle. Also consider the Walmart and Kmart in Kahului, both on the map on page 66.

That said, count on spending some dollars on this trip. Some of the paid activities are definitely worth the splurge. Others are a rip-off, and we'll try to point them out.

HAZARDS
The Sun

The hazard that by far affects the most people (excluding the accommodations tax) is the sun. Maui, at 20° latitude, receives sunlight more directly than anywhere on the mainland. (The more overhead the sunlight is, the less atmosphere it filters through.) If you want to enjoy your *entire* vacation, make sure that you wear a strong sunblock. We recommend a waterproof sunblock with at least an SPF of 15. Many visitors who get burned do so while snorkeling. You won't feel it coming because of the water. We *strongly* suggest you wear a T-shirt while snorkeling, or you may get a nasty surprise.

Try to avoid the sun between 11 a.m. and 2 p.m. when the sun's rays are particularly strong. If you are fair-skinned or unaccustomed to the sun and want to soak up some rays, 15–20 minutes per side is all you should consider the first day. You can increase it a bit each day. *Beware of the fact that our breezes will hide the symptoms of a burn until it's too late.* You might find that trying to get your tan as golden as possible isn't worth it. Tropical suntans are notoriously short-lived, whereas you are sure to remember a bad burn far longer. If, after all our warnings, you *still* get burned, aloe vera

gel works well to relieve the pain. Some gels come with lidocaine in them. Ask your hotel front desk if they have any aloe plants on the grounds. Peel the skin off a section and make several crisscross cuts in the meat, then rub the plant on your skin. *Oooo,* it'll feel so good!

Water Hazards

The most serious water hazard is the surf. Though more calm in the summer and on the leeward side, high surf can be found anywhere on the island at any time of the year. The sad fact is that more people drown in Hawai'i each year than anywhere else in the country. This isn't said to keep you from enjoying the ocean, but rather to instill in you a healthy respect for Hawaiian waters. See BEACHES for more information on this.

Ocean Critters

Hawaiian marine life, for the most part, is quite friendly. There are, however, a few notable exceptions. Below is a list of some critters that you should be aware of. This is not mentioned to frighten you out of the water. The odds are overwhelming that you won't have any trouble with any of the beasties listed below. But should you encounter one, this information should be of some help.

Sharks—Hawai'i does have sharks. Most are the essentially harmless white-tipped reef sharks, plus the occasional hammerhead or tiger shark. Contrary to what most people think, sharks are in every ocean and don't pose the level of danger people attribute to them. In the past 25 years there have been a few documented shark attacks off Maui, mostly tigers attacking surfers. But considering the number of people who swam in our waters during that time, you are statistically more likely to get mauled by a hungry timeshare salesman than be bitten by a shark. If you do happen to come upon a shark, however, swim away slowly. This kind of movement doesn't interest them. *Don't* splash about rapidly. By doing this you are imitating a fish in distress, and you don't want to do that. The one kind of water you want to avoid is murky water, such as that found in river mouths. Most shark attacks occur in murky water at dawn or dusk since sharks are basically cowards who like to sneak up on their prey. In general, don't go around worrying about sharks. *Any* animal can be threatening. (Even Jessica Alba was once rudely accosted by an overly affectionate male dolphin.)

Portuguese Man-of-War—These are related to jellyfish but are unable to swim.

They are instead propelled by a small sail and are at the mercy of the wind. Though small, they are capable of inflicting a painful sting. This occurs when the long, trailing tentacles are touched, triggering hundreds of thousands of spring-loaded stingers, called nematocysts, which inject venom. The resulting burning sensation is usually very unpleasant but not fatal. Fortunately, the Portuguese Man-of-War is not a common visitor to Maui. When they *do* come ashore, however, they usually do so in great numbers, jostled by a strong storm offshore, and usually land on north-facing beaches. If you see them on the beach, don't go in the water. If you do get stung, immediately remove the tentacles with a gloved hand, stick or whatever is handy. Rinse thoroughly with salt or fresh water to remove any adhering ne-

matocysts. Then apply ice for pain control. If the condition worsens, see a doctor. The old treatments of vinegar or baking soda are no longer recommended. The folk cure is urine, but you might look pretty silly applying it.

Sea Urchins—These are like living pin cushions. If you step on one or accidentally grab one, remove as much of the spine as possible with tweezers. *After* they are out, soak the wound in warm vinegar. See a physician if necessary.

Coral—Coral skeletons are very sharp and, since the skeleton is overlaid by millions of living coral polyps, a scrape can leave proteinaceous matter in the wound, causing infection. This is why coral cuts are frustratingly slow to heal. Immediate cleaning and disinfecting of coral cuts should speed up healing time. We don't have fire coral around Maui.

Sea Anemones—Related to the jellyfish, these also have stingers and are usually found attached to rocks or coral. It's best not to touch them with your bare hands. Treatment for a sting is similar to that of a Portuguese Man-of-War.

Bugs

Though we're devoid of the myriad hideous buggies found in other parts of the world, there are a few evil critters brought here from elsewhere that you should know about. The worst are **centipedes**. They can get to be six or more inches long and are aggressive predators. They shouldn't be messed with. You'll probably never see one, but if you get stung, even by a baby, the pain can range from a bad bee sting to a moderate gunshot blast. Some local doctors say the only cure is to stay drunk for three days. Others say to use meat tenderizer.

Cane spiders are big, dark and fast and they *look* horrifying, but they're not poisonous. (But they seem to *think* they are. I've had *them* chase *me* across the room when *I* had the broom in my hand.) We *don't* have no-see-ums, those irritating sand fleas common in the South Pacific and Caribbean.

Mosquitoes were unknown in the islands until the first stowaways arrived on Maui on the *Wellington* in 1826. Since then they have thrived. A good mosquito repellent containing at least 10% DEET will come in handy, especially if you plan to go hiking. Forget the guidebooks that tell you to take vitamin B12 to keep mosquitoes away; it just gives the little critters a healthier diet. If you find one dive-bombing you at night in your room, turn on your overhead fan to help keep them away.

Bees and wasps are more common on the drier leeward sides of the island and in Haleakala Crater. Usually, the only way you'll get stung is if you run into one. If you rent a scooter, beware; I received my first bee sting while singing *Come Sail Away* on a motorcycle. A bee sting in the mouth can definitely ruin one of your precious vacation days.

Regarding **cockroaches**, there's good news and bad news. The bad news is that here, some are bigger than your thumb and can fly. The good news is that you probably won't see one. One of their predators is the **gecko**. This small, lizard-like creature makes a surprisingly loud chirp at night. They are cute and considered good luck in the Islands (probably 'cause they eat mosquitoes and roaches).

There are no snakes in Hawai'i (other than some reporters). There is concern that the brown tree snake *might* have made its way onto the islands from Guam. Although mostly harmless to humans, these snakes can spell extinction for native birds. Government officials aren't allowed to tell you this, but we will: If you ever see one anywhere in Hawai'i, please *kill it*

and contact the **Pest Hotline** at 643–7378. At the very least, call them immediately. The entire bird population of Hawai'i will be grateful.

Swimming in Streams

Maui offers lots of opportunities to swim in streams and under waterfalls. It's the fulfillment of a fantasy for many people. But there are several hazards you need to know about.

Leptospirosis is a bacteria that is found in some of Hawai'i's fresh water. It is transmitted from animal urine and can enter the body through open cuts, eyes and by drinking. Around 100 people a year in Hawai'i are diagnosed with the bacteria, which is treated with antibiotics if caught relatively early. You should avoid swimming in streams if you have open cuts, and treat all water found in nature with treatment pills before drinking. (Many filters are ineffective for lepto.)

While swimming in freshwater streams, try to use your arms as much as possible. Kicking an unseen **rock** is easier than you think. Also, consider wearing water shoes or, better yet, tabis, while in streams. (Tabis are sort of fuzzy mittens for your feet that grab slippery rocks quite effectively. You can get them at Kmart in Kahului or any Longs Drugs.)

Though rare, **flash floods** can occur in any freshwater stream anywhere in the world, and it can happen when it's sunny where you are but raining up the mountain. Be alert for them.

Lastly, remember while lingering under waterfalls that not everything that comes over the top will be as soft as water. Rocks coming down from above could definitely shatter the moment—among other things.

Dehydration

Bring and drink lots of water when you are out and about, especially when you are hiking. Dehydration sneaks up on people. By the time you are thirsty, you're already dehydrated. It's a good idea to keep lots of water in your car. Our weather is almost certainly different than what you left behind, and you will probably find yourself thirstier than usual. Every time you think about it *suck 'em up* (as we say here).

Sugar Harvesting

When a cane field is ready to harvest, they cut off water for several weeks, then set the whole field on fire. A mushroom cloud of smoke and ash rises into the air, then travels downwind to harass South Maui. Once the cane has been gathered, machines plow the fields along central Maui, where trade winds are strongest, and huge clouds of dust can fill the air, looking more like Los Angeles than Hawai'i. The result for South Maui visitors (and residents) can be poor quality air when certain fields end their two-year growing cycle. We don't want to overstate it. During the winter, harvesting is suspended, and during the rest of the year you may have days with no harvesting, but you can't *count* on it. The only remaining Maui sugar company, HC&S, has 37,000 acres of sugar under cultivation, nearly all in the windswept valley between the two great mountains that make up Maui. Ironically, the same conglomerate that owns the sugar company (and the main shipping company to Hawai'i) also owns many of the resorts around the island. The resorts generate *far* more profit than sugar operations, but they still insist on burning the cane and filling the air with thousands of tons of smoke and dust. By the way, in case you're wondering where the county government is in all this, it's simple. They're in Wailuku—which is upwind of all the cane fires and dust storms. So as far as they're concerned, there's no problem.

Frogs

There are some irritating visitors that first arrived on Maui in the late '90s and won't leave. (Well, besides the in-laws.) They're small coqui tree frogs that emit a whistle all night long. Cute at first, like a bird. But incessant and ultimately irritating. Most of the resorts do their best to deal with them, but there's a chance that some errant froggies may occasionally give you a long night. West Maui seems to be slightly froggier (I *swear* that's a real word) than South Maui.

Traffic

Traffic can be a problem here. West Maui traffic between Lahaina and Kapalua is notoriously bad, especially at pau hana (quittin' time). Allow extra time during that part of the day. Road work also slows things down a great deal, and on Maui, road projects seem to be measured in decades rather than months or years. In South Maui, both South Kihei Road and Hwy 31 can be terrible during commute hours (and other times as well).

Grocery Stores

A decided hazard. Restaurants are expensive, but don't think you'll get off cheap in grocery stores. Though you'll certainly save money cooking your own food, a trip to the store here can be startling. Phrases like *they charge how much for milk?* echo throughout the stores. Even items *grown a mile from the store* may cost more here than you would pay for them on the mainland. Go figure. West Maui stores seem to be the worst, but Kihei stores aren't much better. If you're stocking up, consider buying groceries at Kahului stores and at the Costco, Kmart and Walmart there.

TRAVELING WITH CHILDREN (KEIKI)

Should we have put this under HAZARDS? It's been our observation that visitors with kids are far more numerous in West Maui than South Maui, perhaps because most of the Ka'anapali resorts have such good keiki infrastructure. If you want to stay in the south, the Grand Wailea seems the most keiki-friendly.

Baby's Away (344–2219) has the usual assortment of keiki paraphernalia for rent, such as car seats, strollers, cribs, bathtubs, etc. Wild Wheels Wentals (800–339–4743) has similar services (and a much cuter name).

Kalama Park in Kihei between Welakahao and Auhana on South Kihei Road has lots of lawn, a playground, a skateboard park, inline skating park, playground and a ball field. But stay out of the nasty water here. (See BEACHES on page 158.) Upcountry between Haiku and Makawao on Kokomo Road, the Fourth Marine Division Memorial Park has one of the coolest (and largest) wooden playgrounds we've ever seen, as well as a large lawn. See Upcountry map on page 115.

Maui Golf & Sports Park (242–7818) has mini golf, bumper boats climbing wall and a trampoline. A bit cramped (they pack a lot of stuff in a small area) but a viable keiki diversion. In Ma'alaea next to Maui Ocean Center on Hwy 330 near Hwy 310.

The accommodation reviews describe the resorts with good keiki programs. By the way, if your objective was to get *away* from the kids, then maybe these resorts won't be at the top of *your* list.

Hawai'i Nature Center (244–6500) has an interactive science arcade with lots of stuff to touch, but it's not open often. Good for kids 3–8. Entrance "by donation." They also have a 2-hour rain forest walk for $20 ($10 for kids.)

Surfing Goat Dairy (878–2870) is a goat dairy farm where your kids will be able to milk other kids (the four-legged kind) for $12. See Upcountry map on page 115.

Kids who want to try something more involved than snorkeling may want to try SNUBA. See page 227.

Lastly, you should know that it's a big fine plus a mandatory safety class if your keiki isn't buckled up. And booster seats are required for kids under 8.

SOME TERMS

A person of Hawaiian blood is Hawaiian. Only people of this race are called by this term. They are also called

When the sugar's ready to harvest, they set gigantic fields of it ablaze. The smoke and dust wafting from sugar operations help keep Maui cleaning people happy and employed.

Kanaka Maoli, but only another Hawaiian can use this term. Anybody who was born here, regardless of race (except whites), is called a local. If you were born elsewhere but have lived here a while, you are called a kama'aina. If you are white, you are a haole. It doesn't matter if you have been here a day or your family has been here for over a century, you will always be a haole. The term comes from the time when westerners first encountered these islands. Its precise meaning has been lost, but it is thought to refer to people with no background (since westerners could not chant kanaenae—praise—of their ancestors).

The continental United States is called the Mainland. If you are here and are returning, you are not "going back to the states" (we *are* a state). When somebody leaves the island, they are off-island.

HAWAIIAN TIME

One aspect of Hawaiian culture you may have heard of is Hawaiian Time. The stereotype is that everyone in Hawai'i moves just a little bit slower than on the mainland. Supposedly we are more laidback and don't let things get to us as easily as people on the mainland. This is the stereotype…OK, it's *not* a stereotype. It's real. Hopefully, during your visit, you will notice that this feeling infects *you* as well. You may find yourself letting another driver cut in front of you in circumstances that would incur your wrath back home. You may find yourself willing to wait at a red light without feeling like you're going to explode. The whole reason for coming to Hawai'i is to experience beauty and a sense of peace, so let it happen. If someone else is moving a bit slower than you want, just go with it.

SHAKA

One gesture you will see often and should not be offended by is the *shaka* sign. This is done by extending the pinkie and thumb while curling up the three middle fingers. Sometimes visitors think it is some kind of local gesture indicating *up yours* or some similarly unfriendly message. Actually it is a friendly act used as a sign of greeting, thanks or just to say, *Hey.* Its origin is thought to date back to the 1930s. A guard at the Kahuku Sugar Plantation on O'ahu used to patrol the plantation railroad to keep local kids from stealing cane from the slow-moving trains. This guard had lost his middle fingers in an accident, and his manner of waving off the youths became well known. Kids began to warn other kids that he was around by waving their hands in a way that looked like the guard's, and the custom took off.

THE HAWAIIAN LANGUAGE

The Hawaiian language is a beautiful, gentle and melodious language that flows smoothly off the tongue. Just the sounds of the words conjure up trees gently swaying in the breeze and the sound of the surf. Most Polynesian languages share the same roots and many have common words. Today, Hawaiian is spoken *as an everyday language* only on the privately owned island of Ni'ihau, 17 miles off the coast of Kaua'i (see Introduction chapter). Visitors are often intimidated by Hawaiian. With a few ground rules you'll come to realize that pronunciation is not as tough as you might think.

When missionaries discovered that the Hawaiians had no written language, they sat down and created an alphabet. This Hawaiian alphabet has only 12 letters. Five vowels: A, E, I, O and U, as well as seven consonants, H, K, L, M, N, P and W. The consonants are pronounced just as they are in English, with the exception of W. It is often pronounced as a V if it is in the middle of a word and comes after an E or I. Vowels are pronounced as follows:

A—pronounced as in *Ah* if stressed, or *above* if not stressed.

E—pronounced as in *say* if stressed, or *dent* if not stressed.

I—pronounced as in *bee*.

O—pronounced as in *no*.

U—pronounced as in *boo*.

One thing you will notice in this book are glottal stops. These are represented by an upside-down apostrophe ' and are meant to convey a hard stop in the pronunciation. So if we are talking about the type of lava called 'a'a, it is pronounced as two separate As (AH-AH).

Another feature you will encounter are diphthongs, where two letters glide together. They are ae, ai, ao, au, ei, eu, oi and ou. Unlike many English diphthongs, the second vowel is always pronounced. One word you will read in this book, referring to Hawaiian temples, is *heiau* (HEY-YOW). The e and i flow together as a single sound, then the a and u flow together as a single sound. The Y sound binds the two sounds, making the word flow together.

If you examine long Hawaiian words, you will see that most have repeating syllables, making them easier to remember and pronounce.

Let's take a word that might seem impossible to pronounce. When you see how easy this word is, the rest will seem like a snap. The Hawai'i state fish is the humuhumunukunukuapua'a. At first glance it seems like a nightmare. But if you read the word slowly, it is pronounced just like it looks and isn't nearly as horrifying as it appears. Try it. Humu (hoo-moo) is pronounced twice. Nuku (noo-koo) is pronounced twice. A (ah) is pronounced once. Pu (poo) is pronounced once. A'a (ah-ah) is the ah sound pronounced twice, the glottal stop indicating a hard stop between sounds. Now, you can try to pronounce it again. Humuhumunukunukuapua'a. Now, wasn't that easy? OK, so it's not easy, but it's not impossible either.

Below are some words that you might hear during your visit:

'Aina (EYE-na)—Land.

Akamai (AH-ka-MY)—Wise or shrewd.

Maui Ocean Center's aquarium in Ma'alaea is a hit with kids—and us not-so-kids.

Ahh, August in the tropics. These poor slobs nearly froze to death watching the sunrise from atop Haleakala. Make sure you are prepared, or you won't thaw out for a week.

Ali'i (ah-LEE-ee)—A Hawaiian chief; a member of the chiefly class.

Aloha (ah-LO-ha)—Hello, goodbye, or a feeling or the spirit of love, affection or kindness.

Hala (HA-la)—Pandanus tree.

Hale (HA-leh)—House or building.

Hana (HA-na)—Work.

Hana hou (HA-na-HO)—To do again.

Haole (HOW-leh)—Originally foreigner, now means Caucasian.

Heiau (HEY-YOW)—Hawaiian temple.

Hula (HOO-la)—The storytelling dance of Hawai'i.

Imu (EE-moo)—An underground oven.

'Iniki (ee-NEE-key)—Sharp and piercing wind (as in Hurricane 'Iniki).

Kahuna (ka-HOO-na)—A priest or minister; someone who is an expert in a profession.

Kai (kigh)—The sea.

Kalua (KA-LOO-ah)—Cooking food underground.

Kama'aina (KA-ma-EYE-na)—Long-time Hawai'i resident.

Kane (KA-neh)—Boy or man.

Kapu (KA-poo)—Forbidden, taboo; keep out.

Keiki (KAY-key)—Child or children.

Kokua (KO-KOO-ah)—Help.

Kona (KO-na)—Leeward side of the island; wind blowing from the south, southwest direction.

Kuleana (KOO-leh-AH-na)—Concern, responsibility or jurisdiction.

Lanai (LA-NIGH)—Porch, veranda, patio.

Lani (LA-nee)—Sky or heaven.

Lei (lay)—Necklace of flowers, shells or feathers.

Liliko'i (LEE-lee-KO-ee)—Passion fruit.

Limu (LEE-moo)—Edible seaweed.

Lomi (LOW-me)—To rub or massage; lomi salmon is raw salmon rubbed with salt and spices.

Lu'au (LOO-OW)—Hawaiian feast; literally means taro leaves.

Mahalo (ma-HA-low)—Thank you.

Makai (ma-KIGH)—Toward the sea.

Malihini (MA-lee-HEE-nee)—A new-comer, visitor or guest.

Mauka (MOW-ka)—Toward the mountain.

Moana (mo-AH-na)—Ocean.

Mo'o (MO-oh)—Lizard.

Nani (NA-nee)—Beautiful, pretty.

Nui (NEW-ee)—Big, important, great.

'Ohana (oh-HA-na)—Family.

'Okole (OH-KO-leh)—Derrière.

'Ono (OH-no)—Delicious, the best.

Pakalolo (pa-ka-LO-LO)—Marijuana.

Pali (PA-lee)—A cliff.

Paniolo (PA-nee-OH-lo)—Hawaiian cowboy.

Pau (pow)—Finish, end; *pau hana* means quitting time from work.

Poi (poy)—Pounded kalo (taro) root that forms a paste.

Pono (PO-no)—Goodness, excellence, correct, proper.

Pua (POO-ah)—Flower.

Puka (POO-ka)—Hole.

Pupu (POO-POO)—Appetizer, snacks or finger food.

Wahine (vah-HEE-neh)—Woman.

Wai (why)—Fresh water.

Wikiwiki (WEE-kee-WEE-kee)—To hurry up, very quick.

Quick Pidgin Lesson

Hawaiian pidgin is fun to listen to. It's like ear candy. It is colorful, rhythmic and sways in the wind. Below is a list of some of the words and phrases you might hear on your visit. It's tempting to read some of these and try to use them. If you do, the odds are you will simply look foolish. These words and phrases are used in certain ways and with certain inflections. People who have spent years living in the islands still feel uncomfortable using them. Thick pidgin can be incomprehensible to the untrained ear (that's the idea). If you are someplace and hear two people engaged in a discussion in pidgin, stop and eavesdrop for a bit. You won't forget it.

Pidgin Words & Phrases

An' den—And then? So?

Any kine—Anything; any kind.

Ass right—That's right.

Ass why—That's why.

Beef—Fight.

Brah—Bruddah; friend; brother.

Brok' da mouf—Delicious.

Buggah—That's the one; it is difficult.

Bus laugh—To laugh out loud.

Bus nose—How one reacts to a bad smell.

Chicken skin kine—Something that gives you goosebumps.

Choke—Plenty; a lot.

Cockaroach—Steal; rip off.

Da kine—A noun or verb used in place of whatever the speaker wishes. Heard constantly.

Fo Days—plenty; "He got hair fo days."

Geevum—Go for it! Give 'em hell!

Grind—To eat.

Grinds—Food.

Hold ass—A close call when driving your new car.

How you figga?—How do you figure that? It makes no sense.

Howzit?—How is it going? How are you? Also, Howzit o wot?

I owe you money or wot?—What to say when someone is staring at you.

Mek ass—Make a fool of yourself.

Mek house—Make yourself at home.

Mek plate—Grab some food.

Mo' bettah—This is better.

Moke—A large, tough local male. (Don't say it unless you *like beef*.)

No can—Cannot; I cannot do it.

No mek lidat—Stop doing that.

No, yeah?—No, or is "no" correct?

'Okole squeezer—Something that suddenly frightens you ('okole meaning derrière).

O wot?—Or what?

Pau hana—Quit work. (A time of daily, intense celebration in the islands.)

Poi dog—A mutt.

Shahkbait—Shark bait, meaning pale, untanned people.

Shaka—Great! All right!

Shredding—Riding a gnarly wave.

Sleepahs—Flip-flops, thongs, zoris.

Stink eye—Dirty looks; facial expression denoting displeasure.

Suck rocks—Buzz off, or pound sand.

Talk stink—Speak bad about somebody.

Talk story—Shooting the breeze; to rap.

Tanks eh?—Thank you.

Tita—A female moke. Same *beef* results.

Yeah?—Used at the end of sentences.

MUSIC

Hawaiian music is far more diverse than most people think. Many people picture Hawaiian music as someone twanging away on an 'ukulele with their voice slipping and sliding all over the place like they have an ice cube down their back. In reality, the music here can be outstanding. There is the melodic sound of the more traditional music. There are young local bands putting out modern music with a Hawaiian beat. There is even Hawaiian reggae. Hawaiian Style Band, the late Israel Kamakawiwo'ole (known locally as Bruddah Iz) and Willie K are excellent examples of the local sound. Even if you don't always agree with the all the messages in the songs, there's no denying the talent of these entertainers. If you get a chance, stop by **Barnes & Noble** (662–1300) in the Lahaina Gateway Shopping Center. They have a good selection. **Request** (244–9315) in Wailuku on Market Street is a local music store with *pleny kine* music, new and used.

THE HULA

The hula evolved as a means of worship, later becoming a forum for telling a story with chants (called mele), hands and body movement. It can be fascinating to watch. When most people think of the hula, they picture a woman in a grass skirt swinging her hips to the beat of an 'ukulele. But in reality there are two types of hula. The modern hula, or hula 'auana, uses musical instruments and vocals to augment the dancer. It came about after westerners first encountered the Islands. Missionaries found the hula distasteful, and the old style was driven underground. The modern type came about as a form of entertainment and was practiced in places where missionaries had no influence. Ancient Hawaiians didn't even use grass skirts. They were brought later by Gilbert Islanders.

The old style of hula is called hula 'olapa or hula kahiko. It consists of chants and is accompanied only by percussion and takes years of training. It can be exciting to watch as performers work together in a synchronous harmony. Both men and women participate, with women's hula being softer (though no less disciplined) and men's hula being more active. This type of hula is physically demanding, requiring strong concentration. Keiki (children's) hula can be charming to watch, as well.

FARMERS' MARKETS

Maui isn't the best island for farmers' markets. In fact, you'll probably pass a few roadside fruit stands on your way to the market with deals just as good. We suggest shopping at the Central Maui markets for their abundant selection and convenient locations.

West Maui—In the Farmers' Market parking lot across from Honokowai

Beach Park, Mon., Wed. and Fri. from 7 a.m. to 11 a.m.

Central Maui—Inside both the Queen Ka'ahumanu Center and the Kahului Shopping Center on Tues., Wed. and Fri. from 7 a.m. to 4 p.m.

Upcountry—In Makawao at 3654 Baldwin Ave. Wednesdays from 10 a.m. to around 5 p.m.

South Maui—Next to the ABC parking lot at the corner of Uwapo and South Kihei Road Mon.–Fri. 8 a.m. to 4 p.m.

BOOKS

There is an astonishing variety of books available about Hawai'i and Maui. Everything from history, legends, geology, children's stories and just plain ol' novels. **Barnes & Noble** (662–1300) in the Lahaina Gateway Shopping Center has a dazzling selection. Walk in and lose yourself in Hawai'i's richness.

THE INTERNET

Our website, **www.wizardpub.com** has recent changes, links to cool sites, the latest satellite weather shots, calendar of events and more. We also show our own aerial photos of most places to stay on Maui, so you'll know if oceanfront *really* means oceanfront. It has links to every company listed in the book that has a site—both those we like and those we don't recommend. For the record we don't charge a cent for links (it would be a conflict of interest), and there are *no advertisements* on the site. (Well…except for our own books, of course.) We've been asked why we don't list websites and e-mail addresses in the book. Linking from the site makes more sense. Nothing is more mind-numbing than seeing URL addresses in print.

If you're on-island and need Web access (and a computer), most of the big resorts have business services available for around $20 an hour. In West Maui try **Maui Swiss Café** (661–6776). In South Maui try **Café @ La Plage** (875–7668). **Green Banana Café** in Pa'ia (579–9130) is in Central Maui.

If you brought your own computer—then shame on you, you're on vacation. You'll find that hot spots are numerous and fairly easy to find.

A NOTE ABOUT ACCESS

If a lawful landowner posts a NO TRESPASSING sign on their land, you need to respect their wishes. That seems simple enough. But here's where it gets tricky.

It's common in Hawai'i for someone who doesn't own or control land to erect their own NO TRESPASSING, KEEP OUT and ROAD CLOSED signs. Picture a shoreline fisherman who doesn't want anyone else near his cherished spot, putting up a store-bought sign to protect his solitude. Or a neighbor on a dirt road who hates the dust from cars driving by, so he puts up a sign that he knows locals will ignore, but it might dissuade unwary visitors.

In the past we did our best to try to ferret out when NO TRESPASSING signs were valid, and when they were not and we took *a lot* of heat from residents who thought we were encouraging trespassing when we weren't. But the current environment doesn't permit us to do that anymore. So if you're heading to one of the places we describe and you encounter a NO TRESPASSING sign, even if you think it's not authorized by the landowner (and even if it's on *public* land), we have to advise you to turn around and heed the sign. All descriptions in our book come with the explicit assumption that you have obtained the permission of the legal landowner, and unfortunately it'll usually be up to you to determine who that is and how to get it. But please, under no circumstances are we suggesting that you trespass. Plain and clear. Don't trespass…ever…for any reason…period.

A NOTE ON PERSONAL RESPONSIBILITY

In past editions we've had the sad task of removing places that you can no longer visit. The reason, universally cited, is *liability*. Although Hawai'i has a statute indemnifying landowners, the mere threat is often enough to get something closed. Because we, more than any other publication, have exposed heretofore unknown attractions, we feel the need to pass this along.

You need to assess what kind of traveler you are. We've been accused of leaning a bit toward the adventurous side, so you should take that into account when deciding if something's right for you. To paraphrase from the movie *Top Gun*, "Don't let your ego write checks your body can't cash."

Please remember that this isn't Disneyland—it's nature. Mother Nature is hard, slippery, sharp and unpredictable. If you go exploring and get into trouble, whether it's your ego that's bruised or something more tangible, please remember that neither the state, the private land owner nor this publication *told* you to go. You *chose* to explore, which is what life, and this book, are all about. And if you complain to or threaten someone controlling land, they'll rarely fix the problem you identified. They'll simply close it…and it will be gone for good.

Sometimes even good intentions can lead to disaster. At one adventure, a trailhead led hikers to the base of a wonderful waterfall. There was only *one* trail, to the left at the parking lot, that a person could take. Neither we, other guides nor websites ever said, "stay on the trail to the left" because at the time there was only one trail to take. The state (in their zeal to protect themselves from liability at an unmaintained trail) came along and put up a DANGER KEEP OUT sign at the trailhead. Travelers encountering the sign assumed they were on the wrong trail and started to beat a path to the right instead. But that direction started sloping downward and ended abruptly at a 150-foot-high cliff. Hikers retreated and in a short time a previously non-existent trail to the right became as prominent as the correct (and heretofore *only*) path to the left. Not long after the state's well-intentioned sign went up, an unwitting pair of hikers took the new incorrect trail to the right and fell to their deaths. They probably died because they had been dissuaded from taking the correct trail by a state sign theoretically erected to keep people safe.

Our point is that nothing is static and nothing can take the place of your own observations and good judgment. If you're doing one of the activities you read about in our book or someplace else and your instinct tells you something is wrong, *trust your judgment* and go do another activity. There are lots of wonderful things to do on the island, and we want to keep you safe and happy.

And also remember to always leave the island the same way you found it.

MISCELLANEOUS INFORMATION

Traveler's checks are usually accepted, but you should be aware that some merchants might look at you like you just tried to offer them Mongolian money. You should also know that Discover Cards seem to be less welcome here than other destinations. *Many* places will not accept them.

It is customary here for *everyone* to remove their shoes upon entering someone's house (sometimes their office). If you are going to spend any time at the beach, woven bamboo beach mats can be found all over the island for about $3. Some roll up; some can be folded. The sand comes off these easier than it comes off towels.

If you're looking for a church to attend, the Saturday *Maui News* has complete listings and times.

Around the island you'll see signs saying VISITOR INFORMATION or something similar. Allow me to translate. That's usually code for WE WANT TO SELL YOU SOMETHING.

If you want to arrange a lei greeting for you or your honey when you disembark at Kahului Airport, **Aliʻi Leis** (800) 575–4443 and **Greeters of Hawaiʻi** (800) 366–8559 can make the arrangements for around $25. Nice way to kick off a romantic trip, huh?

The local hospital, **Maui Memorial Medical Center** (244–9056) is at 221 Mahalani St. in Wailuku and is shown on the map on page 66.

A WORD ABOUT DRIVING TOURS

Maui is split into geographic regions. We are well aware that for some regions, our chapter names such as SOUTH MAUI SIGHTS, aren't geographically accurate. Hey, don't blame us; we didn't invent these names. Other regions, like the "North Shore" are also strangely worded, since it's not where you'd think. It refers to the Hana Highway coastline, not the real north shore of the island. But this is how people here refer to the areas, so who are we to argue? The inside *front* cover shows how the tours are labeled.

Most main roads have mile markers erected every mile. Since Hawaiʻi is mostly devoid of other identification signs, these little green signs can be a big help in knowing where you are at a given time. Therefore, we have placed them on the maps represented as a number inside a small box ⑯ . We will often describe a certain feature or unmarked road as being "⁴⁄₁₀ miles past the 22 mile mark." We hope this helps.

For directions, locals usually describe things as being on the *mauka* (MOW-ka) side of the road—toward the mountains— or *makai* (ma-KIGH)—toward the ocean.

Beaches, activities and adventures are mentioned briefly but are described in detail in their own chapters.

Found nowhere else in the world...Maui is home to many endemic species, such as this silversword. All three stages of its life are shown here.

Little known Olivine Pools are proof that there is still much to discover in West Maui.

West Maui—playground of the rich and famous? Those are the words that could have described this area hundreds of years ago, when Hawaiian royalty spent considerable time frolicking in West Maui waters and sampling its delights. Today, West Maui serves as a playground for the rest of us. Calm waters, some great beaches, limitless activities and an exciting, dynamic town: West Maui delivers on its legacy of fun.

Whether you're staying in West Maui or just passing through, there's only one road in and out—Hwy 30, which changes its name to Hwy 340 once you get past the populated areas. We'll describe it as most see it, coming from Central or South Maui going clockwise.

MA'ALAEA TO LAHAINA

Between the 7 and 8 mile markers you'll see a road on the left leading to **Mc-Gregor Point and Lighthouse** (actually a beacon). This is a good place to watch a sunset or look at whales during the season (mid-December through mid-May). Past the 8 mile marker is the more popular **scenic lookout**. In addition to a beautiful view of South Maui, it's a well-known whale-spotting place. In fact, there must be an underwater sign for the whales, because they seem to approach this area a lot. Maybe it's a scenic lookout for them, too, where they can come and observe us humans in our natural habitat. Morning and early afternoon bring more spottings, since the light winds produce less choppy seas, making the behemoths easier to spot.

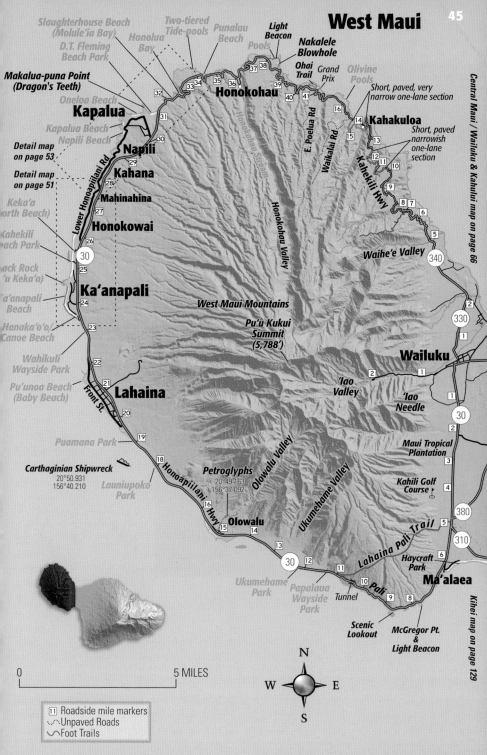

West Maui

Slaughterhouse Beach
(Moluleʻia Bay)
Honolua Bay
Two-tiered Tide-pools
Punalau Beach
Light Beacon
Nakalele Blowhole

D.T. Fleming Beach Park
Pools
Ohai Trail
Grand Prix
Olivine Pools

Makalua-puna Point (Dragon's Teeth)
Oneloa Beach
Short, paved, very narrow one-lane section

Kapalua
Honokohau
Kahakuloa
Short, paved narrowish one-lane section

Kapalua Beach
Napili Beach
E. Poelua Rd
Waikalai Rd.
Kahekili Hwy

Detail map on page 53
Napili

Detail map on page 51
Kahana

Mahinahina

Kekaʻa (North Beach)
Honokowai

Honokohau Stream

Kahekili Beach Park
Honokohau Valley

lack Rock (ʻu Kekaʻa)
Kaʻanapali

Waiheʻe Valley

ʻanapali Beach
West Maui Mountains

Hanakaʻoʻo/ Canoe Beach
Puʻu Kukui Summit (5,788')

Wahikuli Wayside Park
ʻIao Valley

Puʻunoa Beach (Baby Beach)
Wailuku

Lahaina
ʻIao Needle

Front St.
Maui Tropical Plantation

Puamana Park

Carthaginian Shipwreck
20°50.931
156°40.210
Launiupoko Park

Honoapiilani Hwy
Petroglyphs
20°49.163
156°37.092
Olowalu Valley
Kahili Golf Course

Olowalu
Ukumehame Valley

Lahaina Pali Trail

Haycraft Park

Ukumehame Park
Papalaua Wayside Park
Pali
Tunnel
Maʻalaea

Scenic Lookout
McGregor Pt. & Light Beacon

Central Maui / Wailuku & Kahului map on page 66

Kihei map on page 129

0   5 MILES

N
W   E
S

Roadside mile markers
Unpaved Roads
Foot Trails

© 2010 Wizard Publications, Inc.

From the shoreline highway, it's easy to pull off the road and lose yourself in an idyllic setting.

still visible in places, such as near the tunnel. It's possible to awkwardly scramble up to the old road and walk along it (if you're so inclined). You get an idea of how something as "permanent" as a road can be quickly consumed by nature, even on this dry side of the island. This part of West Maui is called the **Pali** (cliffs) and soon gives way to a shoreline highway.

In ancient times there was a legendary female robber named Kaiaupe. She would lure men to get friendly with her at the edge of the pali, then kick them over the cliff and rifle their body for valuables (a practice that was named Ka-ai-a-Kaiaupe in her honor). So if you see a woman hitchhiker with a big K embroidered on her clothes...you might want to pass.

Descending to sea level, you'll find yourself constantly stealing glances toward the water. Views up the mountain are also scrumptious, and you'll probably want to pull over around the 13 mile marker and take them in.

Less known is the good snorkeling and diving below the lookout. See BEACHES on page 157 for more.

Highway 30 is a modern, two-lane highway. In the old days (which anthropologists define as any time before TVs had remote controls) there was a narrow, winding road along West Maui. Parts are

At the **14 mile marker** you'll see lots of cars. This area is listed in virtually all visitor information as having some of the best snorkeling on the island. Don't waste your time. That's *way* out of date. Runoff (perhaps from the old sugar operations) has created cloudy water with terrible visibility. Farther offshore it's good, but the shoreline snorkeling usually stinks. See BEACHES for more.

At the 15 mile marker is the pea-sized town of **Olowalu**, the site of the massacre described on page 16. It's also here that you'll find Maui's best **petroglyphs**. (See map on page 45.) In an era before pen and paper, the best way to record your thoughts was to scratch them on lava rock. At this site, pre- and post-contact Hawaiians left their artistic impressions in the smooth lava. (These have been augmented recently by mindless mutts leaving behind their more modern thoughts.) To get there, enter at the 15 mile marker, drive past the Olowalu General Store, then right, left and right. The latter is marked by a water tank. There is a gate there granting access to this private land. It's ½ mile along the dirt road to the metal railings protecting the glyphs. Beware of wasps nesting in the area.

Back on the highway, more ribbons of beach come and go. Parks like **Launiupoko** dot the shoreline. Though the valleys up mauka are beautiful, there are no roads to the center of West Maui, and only a few private subdivision roads penetrate a short distance. The farthest inland you can go up is on Lahainaluna Road in Lahaina. From there the view of Lahaina is peaceful and broad.

LAHAINA TOWN

Lahaina is the only town in all of leeward Maui with a *real* downtown. If someone told you to meet them in downtown Kihei, you wouldn't have any idea where they meant. Same goes for Wailea, Kapalua, Ka'anapali or Napili. Though it's only 1½ miles long, downtown Lahaina is well-defined and bursting with things to see and do.

NOT TO BE MISSED!

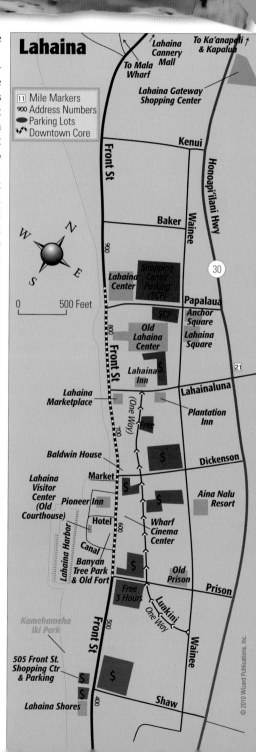

Lahaina

- 11 Mile Markers
- 900 Address Numbers
- Parking Lots
- Downtown Core

To Mala Wharf
Lahaina Cannery Mall
To Ka'anapali & Kapalua
Lahaina Gateway Shopping Center

Front St
Kenui
Honoapi'ilani Hwy
Baker
Wainee
30
Lahaina Center
Shopping Center Parking (SCP)
Papalaua
Anchor Square
Old Lahaina Center
Lahaina Square
21
Lahaina Inn
Front St
Lahaina Marketplace
(One Way)
Lahainaluna
Plantation Inn
Baldwin House
Dickenson
Market
Lahaina Visitor Center (Old Courthouse)
Pioneer Inn
Hotel
Wharf Cinema Center
Aina Nalu Resort
Lahaina Harbor
Canal
Banyan Tree Park & Old Fort
Old Prison
Free 3 Hours
Prison
Luakini One Way
Kamehameha Iki Park
Front St
Wainee
505 Front St. Shopping Ctr & Parking
Shaw
Lahaina Shores

0   500 Feet

© 2010 Wizard Publications, Inc.

The biggest problem with Lahaina is that it's crowded. And even when it's not crowded...*it's crowded.* A secluded stroll along Front Street is about as likely as a snowy day in Miami. But Front Street has an electricity that defies explanation. No matter how much you curse its popularity, you can't deny Lahaina's charm. It's busy, tacky, weird and wonderful. It's full of old world character and new world annoyances. It manages to energize and relax at the same time. If you visit West Maui without strolling along Front Street (abiding by that old Yogi Berra axiom, "*Nobody* goes there anymore; it's too crowded"), then you missed out on more than you think. Because for all its faults, Lahaina works.

Lahaina should be viewed as an event, not a place. You *do* Lahaina. You go there to eat, shop, walk and gawk. Lots of activities, especially boating-related, are centered around Lahaina. (This was, after all, an old whaling port.)

Ironically, as a place to stay, Lahaina lacks many of the things that make West Maui special. Namely good, clean beaches, cool breezes and a slow pace. Plus, there are relatively few places to stay in town. (Nearly all West Maui accommodations are north of Lahaina, in Ka'anapali, Honokowai, Kahana, Napili and Kapalua.) Of course, what it lacks in some areas, it makes up for by having a better nightlife, tons of restaurants and a more happenin' feel.

Lahaina means *cruel sun.* According to one legend, there was a chief named Hua many generations ago who, in a huff, killed all his priests. Drought soon followed, and villagers referred to the area as the land of the cruel sun. Today, that ever-present sun is the very thing that attracts people from all over the world, though it can get pretty hot in the summer.

Parking in Lahaina is a *buggah!* If anything can bring on that old-fashioned

Believe it or not, this is one single tree. Banyan Tree Park in Lahaina seems to go on forever. But you gotta wake up pretty early in the morning to find—and photograph—it this empty.

mainland road rage, this is it. Lahaina is woefully under-equipped in the parking department (though fully staffed in the *enforcement* department). The county makes a tidy sum from unsuspecting visitor naïveté, and parking fees have created a cash bonanza for the ever-hungry county coffers. Even at night, big brother is watching. An example: There's a three-hour lot near the harbor, but if you park there at 5 p.m. for a sunset cruise and return at 8:10, you may find that the ever-efficient parking paratroopers have targeted you for a fee. Be very careful, or you'll end up paying for some new carpet at City Hall. Here are a few tips.

Parking is free on Front Street for three hours if you can get a stall, and yes, they *do* keep an eye on your car. There are several pay lots marked on the map. If you're having a hard time finding *any* spots in Lahaina, the pay lot on Dickenson near Wainee seems to fill up later than other lots. Don't forget to try the free lots shown on the map. They're usually full, but you may get lucky. (I don't mean it *that* way.) If you're doing an early morning boat trip, look at the free Luakini Street lot first.

Your best parking opportunities are in the morning. Arrive in Lahaina between 9 and 10 a.m., and you stand a reasonable chance of getting a street-side stall. You'll also find the shops and street much less crowded.

There is a huge, four-hour lot at Lahaina Center. It's free if you buy something at the center. We guess that technically means that you could park there and walk the town, picking up a bottle of water at the ABC store before you leave. But we *know* you'd never do anything so sneaky.

While strolling around town, your personal tastes will dictate which shops and attractions work for you. Additional attractions, all labeled on the map, include the **old courthouse** (where they have a detailed brochure describing all historic sites in town), **Banyan Tree Park** (an incredible must-see tree that encompasses an entire park), **Baldwin House** (the oldest house on the island) and the **old prison** (called Hale Pa'ahao, or "stuck in irons house"). It's kind of interesting to visit this last site, made with coral walls, to get an idea of the kind of crimes that people were imprisoned for in the 1850s. They include "profanity, furious riding, adultery and fornication (the second most common offense), refusing to work on the road, giving birth to bastard children, lewd conversation, and affray." (We had to look up that last one; it basically means disturbing the peace.)

Offshore the Lahaina Marketplace you *may* (if it's still there) see a 22-ton steel hull sailboat named the *Dolfijn* washed up on the reef. How it got there is fairly boring. (An unexpected halloween swell in 2004 shook it from its sand anchor.) Personally, we like asking locals such as waiters how it got there. Stories range from renegade fugitives running from the law in South Africa to a local hiding from a $100,000 per day fine.

While strolling Front Street, you'll notice that activity salesmen are unusually aggressive. Lines like, *You folks have any questions? Ya need some coupons? Want to make a free phone call?* or *Interested in any activities?* are sales speak for *I want to sell you something* or *Want to see a timeshare presentation?* See ACTIVITIES on page 171 for more on activity brokers.

You'll also find the **Lahaina Ka'anapali Railroad.** *(Yawn to all but very young keiki.)* See page 207 for more on that thrilling *(not)* trip of a lifetime.

And the best show we've ever seen in Hawai'i, **Warren and Annabelle's** (see Nightlife on page 285), is on Front Street near Papalaua.

KA'ANAPALI TO KAPALUA

Ka'anapali was part of a large sugar plantation when the sugar company's board met in 1956 and hatched a plan that would soon be repeated around the globe—the master planned destination resort, the first in Hawai'i. The large land owners had their pick of where to put the resort, and they chose the fantastic **Ka'anapali Beach** here as their showcase to the world. (If *you'd* owned the entire island back then, you too, probably would have chosen this beach.) It opened in 1962 and has been admired ever since.

Half a dozen fancy resorts line the beach. There's a wonderful paved **beachside path** that runs along all the resorts. It's an excellent place to stroll at sunset and can take an hour or more. Beach accesses are shown on the map. You can also park at the Whalers Village Shopping Center. Any shop will validate if you spend around $20. (Heck, you can practically knock that out with a scoop from Häagen-Daz.)

Separating the two halves of the great beach is **Black Rock**. As mentioned earlier, Hawaiian volcanoes fall asleep for up to a million years before awakening for a last series of eruptions. West Maui had only four small eruptions during its final days. Black Rock was one. (Another is the rock where the Olowalu petroglyphs are located.)

The ancient Hawaiians believed Black Rock, which they called Pu'u Keka'a, was the jumping off point for their spirits or souls, called 'uhane, leaving this world. Each island had such a point. When Hawaiians died, it was here that their souls would leave this life and join their ancestors forever. If there were no 'aumakua, or family spirits, to receive them, they would wander around the area, attaching themselves to rocks and generally causing mischief. That's why it's considered unwise to take any rocks from this area. You may bring back a spirit itching to get back home.

The snorkeling around Black Rock is excellent. See page 154 for more.

The sunset torch lighting ceremony at Black Rock is followed by a plunge into the ocean.

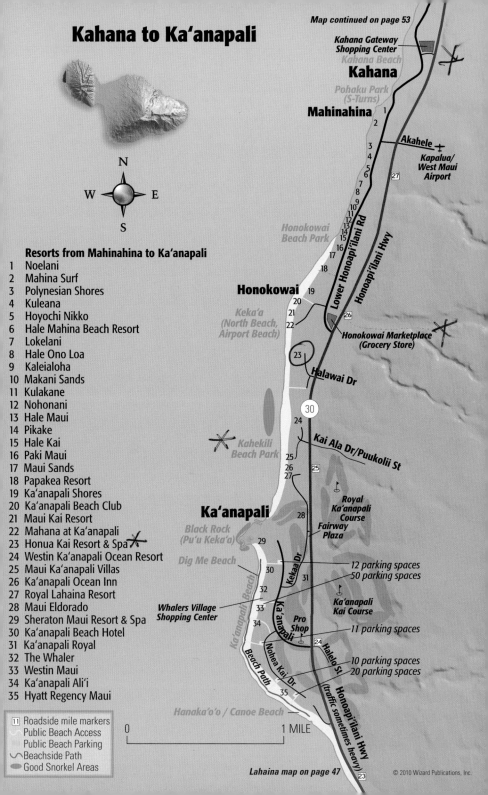

Kahana to Ka'anapali

Map continued on page 53

Kahana Gateway
Shopping Center
Kahana Beach

Kahana

Pohaku Park
(S-Turns)

Mahinahina

Akahele

Kapalua/
West Maui
Airport

Honokowai
Beach Park

Honokowai

Keka'a
(North Beach,
Airport Beach)

Honokowai Marketplace
(Grocery Store)

Halawai Dr

Kai Ala Dr/Puukolii St

Kahekili
Beach Park

Royal
Ka'anapali
Course
Fairway
Plaza

Ka'anapali

Black Rock
(Pu'u Keka'a)

Dig Me Beach

12 parking spaces
50 parking spaces

Ka'anapali
Kai Course

Whalers Village
Shopping Center

Pro
Shop

11 parking spaces

10 parking spaces
20 parking spaces

Hanaka'o'o / Canoe Beach

Lower Honoapi'ilani Rd

Honoapi'ilani Hwy

Keka'a Dr

Ka'anapali Beach

Beach Path

Nohea Kai Dr

Ka'anapali

Halelo St

Honoapi'ilani Hwy
(traffic sometimes heavy)

Resorts from Mahinahina to Ka'anapali

1 Noelani
2 Mahina Surf
3 Polynesian Shores
4 Kuleana
5 Hoyochi Nikko
6 Hale Mahina Beach Resort
7 Lokelani
8 Hale Ono Loa
9 Kaleialoha
10 Makani Sands
11 Kulakane
12 Nohonani
13 Hale Maui
14 Pikake
15 Hale Kai
16 Paki Maui
17 Maui Sands
18 Papakea Resort
19 Ka'anapali Shores
20 Ka'anapali Beach Club
21 Maui Kai Resort
22 Mahana at Ka'anapali
23 Honua Kai Resort & Spa
24 Westin Ka'anapali Ocean Resort
25 Maui Ka'anapali Villas
26 Ka'anapali Ocean Inn
27 Royal Lahaina Resort
28 Maui Eldorado
29 Sheraton Maui Resort & Spa
30 Ka'anapali Beach Hotel
31 Ka'anapali Royal
32 The Whaler
33 Westin Maui
34 Ka'anapali Ali'i
35 Hyatt Regency Maui

11 Roadside mile markers
Public Beach Access
Public Beach Parking
Beachside Path
Good Snorkel Areas

0   1 MILE

Lahaina map on page 47

© 2010 Wizard Publications, Inc.

Kahekili was the last king of Maui. He was utterly fearsome looking, with tattoos almost blackening one side of his body from head to foot, but completely clean on the other. He loved the sport of lele kawa (cliff diving), and legend states that he had once jumped from as high as 350 feet. Though terrifying to look at (even Captain Cook made reference to his scary appearance in his logs), he had a tiny, weak voice (sort of an ancient version of boxer Mike Tyson). This is the man that Kamehameha fought so hard to defeat when he conquered all the islands. It was only years later that Kamehameha learned Kahekili was actually his father. **Kahekili Beach Park**, a great beach north of the 25 mile marker, is one way islanders remember him.

We should alert you that grocery stores in West Maui are renowned for their *hurt me* prices. Prepare for the stomping of your life the first time you go in for some milk here (which they may have run out of!).

Also, allow for traffic when driving to Lahaina in the afternoon from Ka'anapali or Kapalua. Pau hana (end of work) traffic can be a problem, at its worst between Ka'anapali and Lahaina.

There are dozens of condos north of Ka'anapali. This is where the more reasonably priced West Maui accommodations are found. Unfortunately, a few of the beaches north of Ka'anapali can be unpleasant for the same reasons listed for north Kihei on page 158. The first great beach after Kahekili Beach is **Napili Bay**, described under BEACHES on page 152. (Ah, and what a wonderful beach it is…)

Sugar has been the symbol of West Maui since before the American Civil War. All who grew up here lived their lives in its shadow. A single company dominated all commerce here. Surprisingly, it was a German company that ran the sugar operations until WWI, when an irritated U.S. government seized the company and sold it to Americans. (In an *eat this* gesture to the Germans, they named it

Some say that West Maui beaches are getting a bit crowded. This couple at Kahekili Beach Park knows better.

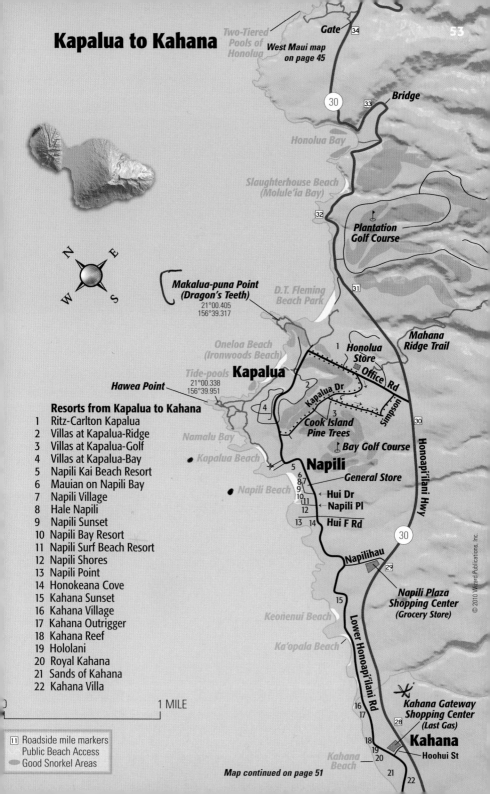

Kapalua to Kahana

Two-Tiered Pools of Honolua

Gate 34

West Maui map on page 45

30

33 **Bridge**

Honolua Bay

Slaughterhouse Beach (Molule'ia Bay)

32

Plantation Golf Course

31

Mahana Ridge Trail

Makalua-puna Point (Dragon's Teeth)
21°00.405
156°39.317

D.T. Fleming Beach Park

Oneloa Beach (Ironwoods Beach)

Tide-pools **Kapalua**
21°00.338
156°39.951

1 **Honolua Store**

Office Rd

Hawea Point

2

Kapalua Dr

Simpson

3

30

Resorts from Kapalua to Kahana

1 Ritz-Carlton Kapalua
2 Villas at Kapalua-Ridge
3 Villas at Kapalua-Golf
4 Villas at Kapalua-Bay
5 Napili Kai Beach Resort
6 Mauian on Napili Bay
7 Napili Village
8 Hale Napili
9 Napili Sunset
10 Napili Bay Resort
11 Napili Surf Beach Resort
12 Napili Shores
13 Napili Point
14 Honokeana Cove
15 Kahana Sunset
16 Kahana Village
17 Kahana Outrigger
18 Kahana Reef
19 Hololani
20 Royal Kahana
21 Sands of Kahana
22 Kahana Villa

4

Cook Island Pine Trees

Namalu Bay

Kapalua Beach

Bay Golf Course

5 **Napili**

6 **General Store**
8 7
9
10 **Hui Dr**
11 **Napili Pl**
12
13 14 **Hui F Rd**

Napili Beach

Napilihau

29

Honoapi'ilani Hwy

30

Napili Plaza Shopping Center (Grocery Store)

15

Keonenui Beach

Ka'opala Beach

Lower Honoapi'ilani Rd

© 2010 Wizard Publications, Inc.

0 _____ 1 MILE

16
17

28

Kahana Gateway Shopping Center (Last Gas)

18 **Kahana**
19
20 **Hoohui St**
21
22

Kahana Beach

11 Roadside mile markers
   Public Beach Access
   Good Snorkel Areas

Map continued on page 51

Dragon's Teeth at Kapalua is a bizarre lava formation that owes its existence to the wind and sea.

American Factors, and their retail stores were named Liberty House.)

The waning days of the 20th century brought an end to sugar in West Maui. Even after a decade, nobody still really knows how the previously sugar-laced slopes will look in the years to come. Longtime sugar workers have moved on to other industries. The large mill off the highway is idle. Ironically, pineapple contributed to the demise of sugar here. Sugar is an intensely thirsty crop, and the sugar company was never able to get as much water as they needed, in sharp contrast to HC&S's water bounty in Central Maui. Their single best source of water dried up when their water supplier decided to start growing pineapple and cut them off from their source.

Farther north, **Kapalua** is an incredibly manicured oasis of green in this wind-swept part of the island. The gardening bill must be immense because no dead leaf goes unpunished. *Expensive* is the operative word at these resorts. Some of the beaches, such as Kapalua Bay, are excellent. The wind tends to be strong here, and it's also more prone to drizzle than any other leeward resort area.

Where Lower Honoapiilani Road becomes Office Road, there's a little road turnout with a parking lot. Walk toward the shoreline along the golf course next to the short hedge to a long point of lava that separates two large beaches. Called **Makalua-puna Point**, it's worth the 5-minute stroll. The lava here is different than most Hawaiian lavas. Light-colored, dense and fine grained, bleached white in some areas, it flowed during the dying days of the West Maui volcano. Salt spray on the upwind side has etched the lava into thrusting shapes known as **Dragon's Teeth**. Other areas on the point have other types of lava objects embedded in them. In some places the ocean has eroded holes completely through the lava rocks. Walk over to the left (west) side and look at Oneloa Bay, often calm and protected on the nearest side. You'll also spot a strange maze on the ground. Please make sure you don't move or disturb any rocks around the point as the land here is sacred to the Hawaiians.

The huge **lawn** in front of Dragon's Teeth has a tumultuous history. The Ritz-Carlton Hotel inland was *supposed* to be an oceanfront hotel. The lawn was to be its location. The only things standing in their way were approximately 2,000 ancient Hawaiians buried in the area. The developers began digging up the graves and, when the Hawaiian community learned of it, they began a series of emotional protests. Nearly 900 remains were dug up before common sense prevailed, and the hotel decided to relocate the buildings and reinter the bones in 1990. A state law was enacted after this to prevent such a thing from ever happening again.

PAST KAPALUA; OVER THE TOP

Like the highway past Hana along the bottom of Haleakala, the drive along the top of West Maui suffers from a long out-of-date reputation. Chances are you'll read that the road is not passable in a rental car or the ridiculous statement that you need 4WD. Free tourist brochures need to update their write-ups. Years ago the road was nearly impossible to drive. Poor pavement gave way to no pavement, and the narrow spots would make a stunt driver sweat. But today the road is much better. The real caveats are the two sections where it is one-lane. About 1½ miles of the highway are a *very* narrow paved one-lane road, and another 2½ miles a narrow*ish* one lane. There are some turnouts on these stretches, and

The Green Flash

Ever heard of the green flash? No, it's not a superhero. We'd heard of the green flash for years before we moved to Hawai'i. We assumed that it was an urban myth, or perhaps something seen through the bottom of a beer bottle. But now we know it to be a real phenomenon, complete with a scientific explanation. You may hear other ways to experience the green flash—but this is the only true way.

On days when the horizon is crisp and clear with no clouds in the way of the sun as it sets, you stand a reasonable chance of seeing it. Avoid looking directly at the sun until the very last part of the disk is about to slip below the horizon. Looking at it beforehand will burn a greenish image onto your retina, creating a "fool's flash" (and possibly wrecking your eyes). The instant before the last part of the sun's disk disappears, a vivid flash of green is often seen. This is because the sun's rays are passing through the thickest part of the atmosphere, and the light is bent and split into its different components the way it is in a rainbow. The light that is bent the most is the green and blue light, but the blue is less vivid and is overwhelmed by the flash of green, which lingers for the briefest of moments as the very last of the sun sets.

For a variety of reasons, including our latitude, Hawai'i is one of the best places in the world to observe the green flash. But if you aren't successful in seeing the real green flash, try the beer bottle method—at least it's better than nothing.

timid drivers may want to evaluate if this is for them. (If two cars meet where there's no turnout, etiquette dictates that the *uphill* driver needs to back up.) Just drive the one-lane portions very slowly.

For what it's worth, we think this is one of the least appreciated drives on the island. It's like the Hana Highway without the traffic. Though nowhere *near* as lush as the Hana drive (nor as long), the windswept charm of this almost forgotten piece of Maui makes it worth the drive—if you can stand the curviness and the narrow sections. Along the way are some unforgettable sights, including one we discovered that amazed us with its perfection.

Our description assumes you will be driving this section from west to east, in a clockwise direction. We strongly suggest you do it this way for several reasons: The sights are better from that direction. Also, drivers rarely discover the road from the Wailuku side, so most traffic, sparse when compared to Hana traffic, will be flowing *with* you. Blind corners seem more blind when driving from Wailuku. Lastly, when on a narrow road, it's more comforting to be on the *inside* lane. Passengers can get uncomfortable when you're on the outside lane as you would if you came from Wailuku.

There are still some popular attractions past Kapalua. There's the *lovely sounding* **Slaughterhouse Beach**, after the easy-to-miss 32 mile marker, with its concrete steps down to the shoreline and, before the 33 mile marker, **Honolua Bay** with its outrageous snorkeling in the summer and monstrous waves in the winter. Both are worth stopping for if your destination is the water. Both are described further under BEACHES. A dirt road along the sea cliffs after you've climbed above Honolua Bay past the 33 mile mark offers a tremendous view of Honolua. Try to ignore the

voluminous black plastic embedded in the ground there. It's one of the less glamorous legacies of growing pineapple. It was used to reduce the amount of water and pesticides needed. Pretty ironic, isn't it? That plastic litter is all over the place *to protect the environment.* (Gee, thanks guys.)

At times you'll see a yellow/orange stripe in the lava cut by the road or erosion. These are deposits of ash from the island's youth. At that time huge volcanic explosions covered much of the mountain in ash that was then covered with lava flows. Though quiet now, West Maui was very violent in its younger days.

Still one last beach remains along this stretch, though you'd have a hard time finding many visitors or even locals who know about it. Called **Punalau Beach**, the access is 7/10 mile past the 34 mile marker. It's always uncrowded during the week. Past here you won't find any sand beaches until you reach the other side of West Maui Mountain at Wailuku. There's a nice view of Punalau and the coastline in general from the top of the turnout just past the 34 mile marker.

The road begins its sinuous 25-mile trek to central Maui from here. Dynamite coastal views are common. Now, 25 miles might not *seem* very far, but you're likely to drive slow and stop often, so don't assume you'll be there in an hour. There are countless places to pull over and gawk at the untamed shoreline— sometimes from cliffs above, sometimes from along the shore. And don't count on cell phone coverage here; it's sparse.

Past the 36 mile marker is the village of **Honokohau**. There's a road that leads to the back of the valley, but expect plenty of stink eye if you try to go. They don't seem too neighborly there.

Drive ½ mile past the parking lot at the 38 mile marker to a wide turnout backed by rounded boulders. About

Like a jet engine firing into the sky, Nakalele Blowhole rocks when the ocean rolls.

1,200 feet from the road (and 205 feet below you) is one of the more spectacular sights in West Maui. Called the Nakalele Blowhole, the ocean here has undercut the shoreline, pounding under-neath the lava shelf, where it **A REAL GEM** spits through a man-sized hole in the lava. The blowhole varies *tremendously* with the tide and size of the surf. We were here once when the blowhole wasn't blowing a thing. Zero water was issuing from the hole. Four hours later we returned and found the blowhole shooting 70 feet into the air every few seconds with such vicious, explosive force that it made the ground tremble, and we were convinced the earth was going to split beneath our feet. It was like a jet engine rocketing sea-water into the air with amazing fury. High tide is your best bet, and high surf adds to the fury. The local newspaper has tide information on page 2.

Remember, this is wilderness. There's no guard-rail to stop you from shrinking the gene pool should you use bad judg-ment and fall into the hole. If the blow-hole is pumping (which is quite common

in the winter), get as close as common sense dictates. It's hard to predict which waves will make it scream. Huge waves sometimes produce nothing, while wimpy-looking waves sometimes surprise you. The area to the left (west) of the blowhole is some of the most amazing-looking landscape you'll ever see. It looks like an alien war zone where combatants fought with acid. Over countless eons, bil-lions of tons of sea spray have shot through the blowhole and been blown on the wind. The spray attacks the fracturous rocks on contact, literally eating the land, and the results are never to be forgotten. Rock hounds will enjoy seeing how the elements have tortured the rocks into var-ious bizarre and jagged formations.

If the blowhole isn't overly angry while you're there, you'll notice a whole community of life living off this phenom-enon. Crabs tempt the ocean by lining the steamy hole during pauses, eating algae growing on the sides, in constant danger of being swept away from a wave. Primitive-looking blennies (also called rockskippers since they can leap from pool to pool) live their whole lives in the 3 inches of water that remain from the splashes that shoot out of the hole. There's a natural lava viewing ledge above the blowhole, but you are still in the potential wet zone there.

The trail starts at the turnout men-tioned above and goes down toward the ocean slightly to the left. (It's not the more obvious-looking road cut slightly to the right; see map.) While on the trail, take note of the huge amount of olivine encrusted in much of the lava rock. We've found dime-sized specimens of this semiprecious gem in the area. If you're interested in a longer, more beau-tiful hike to the blowhole, see page 193.

This is probably a good time to warn you of the mindless cows that often wan-der onto the road. Cows aren't known

Nakalele Blowhole

2 pools Light Beacon
Parking Lot
38 Trail
Several dirt roads are along here
Blowhole
21°01.621
156°35.314
30
Rounded Boulders Trail
N W E S
0   1/4 Mi.
39

© 2010 Wizard Publications, Inc.

When you reach the mushroom rock, you've reached a spectacular place to watch the ocean's fury.

for their smarts, but they seem especially clueless along this route, so be on the lookout for them. We've also seen a couple of donkeys on the road—and they're very friendly—so watch for them.

At ³/₁₀ mile past the 40 mile marker is a small turnout on the ocean side. It presents a truly kickin' view along the coast. If the blowhole is pumping, you'll see the results from here. The ocean is directly beneath you, and you don't need to go more than 10 feet from your car. Another ²/₁₀ mile along the highway is a parking area. There's a concrete path leading to an unimpressive lookout. Even better is a 20+-minute hike called the **Ohai Trail**. We called it "remarkably dull" in a previous edition. We were right...yet we got it dead wrong. We discovered it's important to do this trail counter-clockwise. See HIKING on page 194.

At ⁹/₁₀ mile past the 40 mile marker the road opens up around a corner exposing the peak of majestic 636-foot high **Kahakuloa Head** off in the distance. More on that later. At that corner there's small pull-out and a 5-minute trail to the left that leads to a point with a commanding view. (There's a cattle fence near the end of the trail that most people just climb over since it's not private land; it belongs to the state.) The real oddity on

this point is the crumbling remains of an old **Pontiac Grand Prix**. Its presence seems inconceivable here. There's no way it could have been driven or rolled out onto the point. Let us know if you figure out how it got here.

If you notice a strange feeling in your lungs about now, there's a technical reason for it. It's called *perfectly clean air*. The air here has drifted over the landless Pacific for many weeks. Skies are often crystal clear along this part of the island. So when you're at a sea cliff, suck in a deep breath; this is as clean as air can get.

Shortly after the sign saying END OF STATE ROAD, you'll find a turnout and trails leading toward the shoreline. One leads to a **mushroom-shaped rock**. From there, you'll find one of the best places in West Maui from which to observe the beautiful ferocity of the ocean during high seas. The unchecked pounding violence has tortured and scarred the helpless lava into a fantastic array of grotesque and wonderful shapes and textures. It's mesmerizing from this secluded spot to watch the creation and destruction happening at the shoreline. Be careful on the trail down; it's slippery when wet. The ocean is 175 feet below you. 4WDs can go much of the way.

This area has some very nice hiking, though less structured and often trailless. Just stop at any particularly inviting piece of shoreline and dig in. One very nice hike from here is described under HIKING on page 194.

Now that you're on a county road the mile markers will start at 16. At ½ mile past the END OF STATE ROAD but *before* the 16 mile marker, on the mauka side of the road, is the **Bellstone**. This large, round boulder *can* make a mildly metallic clank if you hit it at the right spot on the mountain side. Odds are, however, you'll simply look like some fool mindlessly whacking on a rock.

Right after the Bellstone is a dirt road on the ocean side. (It's almost kitty-corner to a dirt road on the mauka side with a gate leading inland.) A curious, unattributed sign advising you not to go beyond the point confuses us since this is public land, and the sign says the whole ocean is dangerous under *all* conditions. If you walk the short distance toward the ocean (veering to the right at the second intersection), you'll come to some nicely placed rock platforms 150 feet above the shoreline. (See map on page 62.) People occasionally go there and then turn around because some maps erroneously label the area as containing the Nakalele Blowhole. Until we revealed this site, however, few, if any, realized what they were missing below.

When you write guidebooks for a living and actually *do* and experience the things you write about, you get used to discovering exciting new things. But we were unprepared for the grand perfection of this totally unexpected oasis, which had never appeared in print. Judging by its pristine appearance when we found it, we'd say that not more than a handful of people on the island even knew about it, even though it's on public land.

We called it the **Olivine Pools** because of its gem-like quality, the color of the 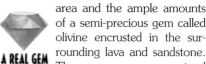 area and the ample amounts of a semi-precious gem called olivine encrusted in the surrounding lava and sandstone.

A REAL GEM They are numerous natural lava swimming pools ensconced in an ancient lava shelf, offering an outrageous and often very safe place to swim with the restless ocean pounding at you on three sides. It's reminiscent of the Queen's Bath on Kaua'i but far more grand and with more pools. The setting is as idyllic as any we can imagine. One of the pools is extremely deep and cool with a natural step to enter and exit. From this pool, your vantage point to the ocean cauldron beyond makes you feel snug and smug. Another pool is just deep enough to sit in, which makes it shallow enough for the afternoon sun to occasionally heat it to about 90 degrees in the summer. Another pool has only one way in and out. Water shoes are fine, but we've walked around barefoot and not had

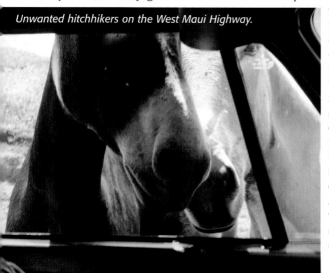

Unwanted hitchhikers on the West Maui Highway.

Some deep, some shallow, the Olivine Pools can be a calm playground in a restless sea.

a problem since the lava is pretty smooth, and there are no nasty sea urchins to kill your feet. It can be slippery, however. Perched above the pools is an amazingly flat platform, a perfect place to stretch out your towel to sun yourself. Natural lava steps lead to the pools themselves.

As the tide rises, splashes from the ocean may trickle into some of the pools and flow from one to another, sometimes forming small waterfalls. As far as we've observed, only high surf or prolonged heavy rain seems to ruin the area. (Big waves could make it—and any part of the shoreline—dangerous.) Big rains *occasionally* cause the pools to form one large silty pond that you'd never recognize from our above description. When spoiled like this, nature usually cleans it up within a week. *Rarely*, long periods of south winds and low surf may cause it to get a bit stagnant. Observe for yourself to see if conditions are good. Very high surf, above 10 feet, could spoil it during *all* tides. And don't get too close to the unpredictable ocean,

which could always send a large wave to pick you off. People standing at the water's edge instead of in the pools can *and have* been killed by large waves. And we've even heard of people getting scraped up *in the pools* when large waves came crashing ashore. Bottom line: Use common sense and stay out if the ocean appears threatening.

There's a small blowhole off to the side that rarely does much, and next to it is the hole where most of the water drains to return to the ocean. (Be careful around the hole; falling into it would be a *big* problem!) This area tends to be windy, though it's partially blocked by some lava. Sometimes, especially during the summer, it can get so windy that you'll want to blow off this attraction (so to speak).

Since we revealed the Olivine Pools in our first edition, we no longer find it empty all the time like we used to. *Great!* You can't imagine how good it makes us feel to share this discovery with people. It seems tailor-made for recreation *if* the ocean's cooperating.

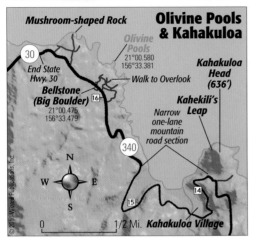

Olivine Pools & Kahakuloa

Mushroom-shaped Rock

Olivine Pools
21°00.580
156°33.381

30
End State Hwy. 30

Walk to Overlook

Bellstone (Big Boulder)
21°00.475
156°33.479

16

340

Kahakuloa Head (636')

Kahekili's Leap

Narrow one-lane mountain road section

N W E S

15

14

0   1/2 Mi.   **Kahakuloa Village**

© 2010 Wizard Publications, Inc.

From the pools, take a look at the unusually intriguing lava formations around you. Some look like lava chessmen sentries. Above the pool is one formation that looks like a lava admiral's chair facing the ocean.

To get to the Olivine Pools from the rock platform overlook, look down the cliff and to your left for a lava bench below you. You should see a heart-shaped pool on the lava bench. There is faint trail leading down to the bench. Footing can be awkward, rocky and a bit slippery. Flip-flops are not advised for the trail. Please be certain to bring everything out that you bring in. Also, it's easy to sunburn in the placid pools, but we're worried that too much suntan lotion may harm the pools. Try to refrain if you can while in the water. Though it's tempting to bring back rock souvenirs, you should know that Hawaiians strongly believe that any rocks that leave the islands bring bad luck due to a curse from the volcano goddess Pele. True or not, we can tell you that readers often mail rocks to us after they've returned home and experienced a string of bad luck. So it's up to you, but we advise you to leave everything where you find it.

Soon the highway gets narrow—*very* narrow—as it descends along the side of the mountain. Skittish passengers may *hate* this 1½ mile part. (We've seen some who had expressions as if they had just unexpectedly bungee-jumped into hell.) Soon their nightmare is over as they descend into **Kahakuloa Village**.

Kahakuloa is a tight-knit community isolated from the rest of the island, though some locals commute to work out in the "real world." In the village on the left side is **Panini Pua Kea Fruit Stand**. They have an unusual handmade coconut candy that's pretty addictive. As you are leaving Kahakuloa and the road is just beginning to ascend, **Julia's** is a stand on the left next to a wet-looking taro patch that makes the best **banana bread** on the planet. Makes my mouth hurt just writing about it. (Hmm, raising the bar pretty high, aren't we?) When they're closed, Panini Pua Kea (above) often becomes their outlet.

As you're leaving Kahakuloa town, you ascend the valley walls on the narrow road. At the top of the road is a turnout, if your nerves are shot and you want a nice view of the village and bay. After this the road widens, and you'll see a fence and gate with a path through a cattlestop leading down between the 636-foot high **Kahakuloa Head** (which means *the tall lord)* and a 547-foot high hill to the right called Pu'u Kahuli-'anapa. The short trail between the hills offers some good views of the back side of Kahakuloa Head towering above you.

If you're feeling adventurous, from near the cattlestop you could make your way to the top of the hill to the right. It's fairly steep, and you won't pick up the cattle trails until toward the top. We've hiked to the top, and the views are second to...well, one, actually. You see, the much steeper Kahakuloa Head to your left has a summit that can only be reached by a death-defying, 'okole-squeezing, nail-biting scaling of the crumbly rock wall. Thanks, but no thanks. But while exploring this area from the air in an ultralight I discovered something quite impressive. At the peak of the mountain were *two folding lawn chairs*. Someone apparently loved nothing better than to climb this beast in order to relax at the top while enjoying the views. Whoever you are, *bruddah*, you've earned it!

Part of Kahakuloa Head used to be called **Kahekili's Leap**. Why? Because the 18th-century Maui King Kahekili used to sometimes reside up here, according to legend. At a place part of the way down (but over 200 feet above the ocean) he would regularly dive into the water, then climb back up the cliff face for his breakfast.

After Kahakuloa Head you'll pass **Kaukini Gallery**. They have a nice selection of Maui-made jewelry, art and furniture (plus a restroom). Prices are expensive. (This is the place to buy that $14,000 koa wood rocking chair you've been looking for.)

After the 11 mile marker is the sharpest **hairpin turn** we've ever seen. Look as you're approaching it, and you'll see that the upper road is almost literally on top of the lower road. (We've tried photographing it but can't get a good vantage point.)

Just after the 10 mile marker is the **Bruce Turnbull Studio and Sculpture Garden**, an apt description. Open weekdays only, the area is replete with wood and bronze sculptures, and it's worth a stop.

Around the 8 mile marker is something you probably haven't seen on this side of the island—*a waterfall* below the road. **Lower Makamakaʻole Falls** is visible from several turnouts; keep an eye out for it. It is a multi-tiered falls and is refreshing after all the dryness you've seen. Its name means *without friends*. (How sad.)

One last thing. For some odd reason, as you're pulling into Wailuku after the long drive, the last 1/10 mile of this road is one way—the *wrong* way—at the Vineyard intersection, and you're given no warning. We've seen some terribly close calls here as tired drivers plunge into oncoming traffic.

WEST MAUI SHOPPING

West Maui, or more specifically **Lahaina**, has the most extensive shopping on the island. The prime areas are along **Front Street** and at **Lahaina Cannery Mall**, but other intriguing options exist on side streets or down small alleys, so don't be afraid to explore.

At **Lahaina Cannery Mall**, some notable stores are **Footprints Maui** for a large selection of sandals at less staggering prices than seen elsewhere on the island. One of our favorite stores there is **Banana Wind**. They have fine products made from natural materials—bamboo, sea grass, beach glass, etc. for your home. **Maui Water Wear** is a great place to pick up a new swimsuit. **Maui Toy Works** will wow kids of every age. **Hats Galore** has...uh, hats galore. Check out surf gear and clothes at **Big Daddy Surf Shop**. There's a **Longs Drugs** here and a 24-hour **Safeway** supermarket.

Across the highway at **Lahaina Gateway Mall**, there is a large **Barnes & Noble** for Hawaiiana books and music, and **Lahaina Farms** supermarket, which has a wide selection of freshly prepared foods and sandwiches, if you are looking to picnic on the beach.

For shopping on **Front Street** in downtown Lahaina, park at south end (see map), enjoy lunch at the north end and start back again. On some weekends there are locally made products for sale under the **Banyan Tree**. The Visitors' Center and the **Museum Store** in the Old Courthouse Building have a good selection of Maui souvenirs.

There are way too many shops along or just off Front Street to list here, but some stand-outs include **Dan's Green House** on Lahainaluna Road at Wainee Street. They'll ship (or you can carry back) plants that are grown on lava rock. (The birds they sell there are pretty entertaining, too.) **Glass Mango Designs** has outstanding glass jewelry. **Karina's Boutique** carries really unique women's clothing and fantastic accessories from Israel, South America and Europe. **Honolulu Cookie Company** has yummy shortbread cookies in flavors like lilikoi, mango and Kona coffee.

For clothing, try **T-shirt Factory**, **Moonbow Tropics, Honolua Surf Co.**, **Aunty Panty's Lingerie, Aloha Shirt Museum** and **Hilo Hattie**. **Homegrown Tropix** and **Volcom** are two of our favorite surfwear shops in town.

There are tons of **galleries** on or near Front Street and some of the best (though hardly the least expensive) shopping can be found there. We suggest you leave plenty of time to peruse them.

In **Ka'anapali**, there is **Whalers Village** (3-hour free parking if you buy something), a beachside shopping mall with a small museum. You'll also find upscale and local chain stores here. Some shops worth a look are **Martin & MacArthur** for koa wood items, **Sandal Tree** is for the woman who can't get enough...*sandals*, that is. **Maui Toy Works** has tons of items for little kids (and big ones, too), **Totally Hawaiian** has mostly (not "totally") Hawaiian-made products for your home, and **Lahaina Printsellers** has antique maps.

WEST MAUI BEST BETS

Best Hike—Blowhole thru Acid Warzone

Best Hidden Gem—Olivine Pools

Best Sunset Stroll with Your Shoes On—Ka'anapali Beachside Path

Best Sunset Stroll with Your Shoes Off—Ka'anapali Beach

Best Beach to Start Your Day—Kahekili Beach Park

Best Place to Watch a Guy Jump off a Rock—Black Rock from Sheraton at Sunset

Best Place to See the Ocean Explode— Nakalele Blowhole

Best Banana Bread (on the Planet)— Last Stand in Kahakuloa

Best Place to Find Golf Balls While Snorkeling—Oneloa Beach

Best Place to Kiss off Snorkeling—14 Mile Marker

Best Place to Waste Your Money— Lahaina Ka'anapali Railroad

Best Beach to Frolic—Napili Bay

Best Protected Beach—Kapalua

Best Place to See Just How Narrow a Road Can Be—Hwy 340 Segment Going Toward Kahakuloa

Best Snorkeling—Right Side of Honolua Bay When Calm, or Black Rock from Sheraton Side

Best Parking Job—Abandoned Grand Prix on Cliff mentioned on page 59

Best Way to Recapture Mainland Road Rage—Trying to Park in Lahaina

Best Place to Sandblast Your Da Kines—D.T. Fleming Beach in Wind

Best Swimming Pool—Hyatt

Best Place to Lose Your Voice—Yelling at the Person Next to You at the Waterfall Grotto Bar at the Hyatt

Best Tree—Banyan Tree Park

Best Evening Show—Warren & Annabelle's

Central Maui and its patchwork of big city and agriculture is where you'll start your journey.

Central Maui is your introduction to the island. You'll land here. You'll shop here. You'll also come through here when you head to Hana, up to the top of Haleakala or after circling West Maui. But with all that exposure, few people come to Central Maui just to see Central Maui. It's like the *Denver Airport* of Maui. Everyone passes through, yet few look around. But don't blow it off completely. Central Maui does have some reasons to stop and stay a while.

Since there's no logical way to organize this area, we're going to describe it in a scattershot manner.

WAILUKU

The county seat, center of power and, most importantly, home to a few good restaurant bargains. (How's *that* for a reason to come here?)

Think of it as a once-grand hub of island activity that's now in the shadow of Kahului, often forgotten and showing its age. There is a certain charm to Wailuku, but not enough to lure many visitors. Too bad. In its day, Wailuku was quite a place: where sugar barons wined and dined, island leaders made important proclamations, and people came from all over to be entertained. One part of town is known as Happy Valley, even to this day. The origin is uncertain, but the age-old rumor says it's related to the fact that the area was known for its collection of bordellos. (Hard to imagine in sleepy little Wailuku.)

Most people simply drive through Wailuku on their way to 'Iao Valley and the 'Iao Needle. This was a sacred burying place for chiefs and the location of Maui's last giant battle for supremacy.

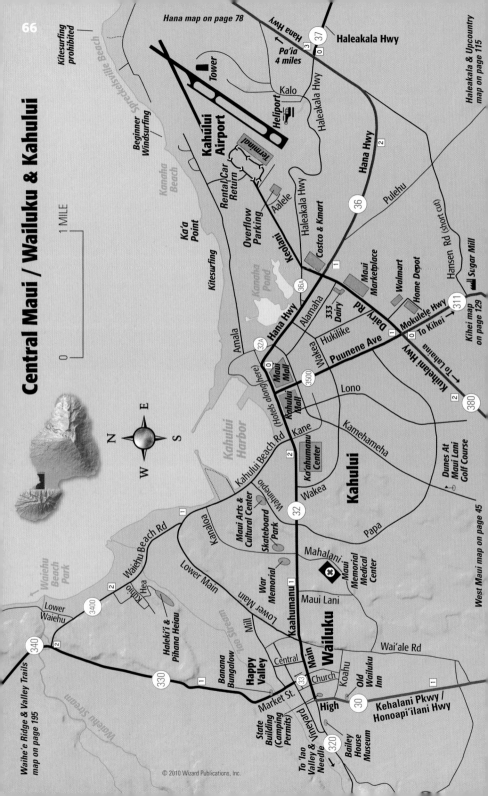

The king of the Big Island was Kamehameha the Great. In 1790 he decided that the time was right to invade Maui (again). After he had personally killed the leading chief of Maui, his forces swept into Kahului and Wailuku. The two sides were fairly equal except for one thing: The cannon Kamehameha had nabbed from the seized sloop belonging to Metcalfe's son. (See page 16.) With this cannon, which the natives affectionately nicknamed Lopaka (Robert), and some captured (though now happily compliant) westerners as advisers, Kamehameha was able to utterly annihilate the Maui forces.

They steadily rolled Lopaka along the rocky trails into 'Iao Valley, backing the troops into a corner, and proceeded to murder almost everyone. Many of the women and children had been moved higher up the cliffs and saw their loved ones die as Robert, loaded with shells and sometimes rocks, blasted away. The carnage was so great that the bodies clogged up the stream. Even by Hawaiian standards of the time, the killing was appalling. The natives called the battle Ka'uwa'u-pali (clawed off the cliff) and Kapaniwai (damming of the waters).

Today 'Iao is a peaceful, beautiful valley. It seems impossible to imagine the death that once permeated the area. The valley stream is lovely, and there are short trails looping around the bottom. The 'Iao Needle is a prominent point sticking up from the valley. It's actually the end of a long, winding knife-edge ridge. (If you saw it from the side, you'd probably call it the 'Iao Plate.) This valley is what remains of the central caldera (crater) of the West Maui volcano. See map at left.

NOT TO BE MISSED!

The 'Iao Needle and stream make a splendid diversion in Central Maui.

Also nearby, the Hawai'i Nature Center on your left on Hwy 320 may appeal to kids. See page 36 for more.

For the cerebral-oriented, the Bailey House Museum (244–3326) is the former mid-19th century home of missionary Edward Bailey. His home, now a museum, is a good place to check out artifacts from the past—such as a century-old surfboard, Hawaiian stone tools, spinning wheel, Hawaiian Bible, quilts, dresses almost two centuries old and even more surprising items, such as an opium scale and pipe. Bailey was also a painter, and his renditions of Maui in the 1800s are interesting. Entry fee is $7, $2 for kids. On Main Street on your way to 'Iao Valley. Closed Sunday.

Also in Wailuku are the remains of the Haleki'i and Pihana heiau. These are former luakini temples (places of human sacrifice). The view from this strategic hill is impressive. You can see all of Wailuku and Kahului. As you gaze from the top of the heiau, your views of the mountains are mixed with views of the surrounding houses, creeping close to the heiau. Instead of houses, what would the ancient priests have seen when they looked out from here? Houses…and taro. This area was called Na Wai Eha, or Four Waters, and was one of the largest taro-growing areas in the state. The streams around here provided abundant water, so it would have looked similar to rice fields but with broad-leafed taro instead of rice. Thousands of Hawaiians lived here. Instead of shingles, they had thatch. Instead of a two-car garage, they had a two-canoe shed. But this area has always been home to lots of people.

The heiau park is not well maintained by the state, which is surprising, given how few ancient relics there are on Maui. (Well, except in the state government.)

To get there, take Waiehu Beach Road to Kuhio to Hea. (See map on page 66.) You'll have to park at the bottom of the parking lot access road and walk up "due to land dispute issues," we were told.

KAHULUI

People who live on Maui find themselves coming to Kahului all the time. What do they come for? Malls, movies, restaurants and—most important on an island where things cost a lot—*Costco*.

Kahului is where people come to take care of business. The biggest mall, Queen Ka'ahumanu Center on Hwy 32, is a big draw. And Maui Marketplace on Dairy Road is where you'll find Borders Books and the island's biggest sporting goods store.

Finding someplace in Kahului is easy if you know one thing: Midas Mufflers is on Wakea and Hukilike. Why in the heck are we telling you this? Because every small town has a place like this. The *thing* that everything is relative to. Call up a business in Kahului and ask where they are, and, if it's not on a main street, invariably the response will be, *"You know where Midas is? Well, you take a left…"* We don't know why; it's just the way it is.

Kahului is nearly always windy. And on those few occasions that it's not windy—it's *real breezy.* If you rent a large vehicle, like a minivan, it'll often feel like someone's outside rocking your car.

THE VALLEY OF SUGAR

This is the reason Maui is called the Valley Isle—the large flatland separating East and West Maui. This area is dominated by only one thing—*sugar*. A single company—HC&S—is growing all that sugar you see—all 37,000 acres of it. Before people came to these islands, a thin, dryland forest existed here. The

Hawaiians quickly cut down the trees when they discovered the island, and the area became a barren desert, after which the Hawaiians had little to do with it. When western man arrived, he saw an opportunity to grow sugar in this unused region and began building ditches to bring water to this thirsty land. Today, the broad valley between the two great volcanoes is an ever-waving field of green trisected by the three highways. This is the last sugar plantation in Hawai'i and its days seemed numbered at press time.

At one time, all of the islands surrounding Maui formed a single large island. Then the ocean rose and the land sank to isolate each of the volcanoes into different islands. The valley separating East and West Maui is the last land bridge remaining, and its days are numbered, too. Given the present sinking rate, East and West Maui will be separate islands in about 15,000 years when this landbridge disappears. (Gives the realtors something to worry about, huh?)

On Honoapi'ilani Hwy (30) heading toward the west side, you'll find Maui

Tropical Plantation (244–7643) between the 2 and 3 mile markers—60 acres of assorted tropical fruits and plants. It's a classic tourist trap, and it'll cost you $15 to ride the tram to see the gardens. (No walkers.) The place seems more geared to tour buses. The tour can be marginally interesting, but it's definitely *not* a must-see. The Moloka'i coffee company that owns a piece of it is growing coffee on the slopes above the plantation. Also, the best zipline in the state cuts across the land above this part of the West Maui Mountains. See ACTIVITIES on page 233.

If you drive along Hwy 311 on your way toward South Maui, you'll pass Maui's ugliest sight (except for the line at the rental car counter when you're late for your flight home). A sugar mill looking like it belongs more in the 19th century (which is when it was built) belches steam and sometimes black smoke into the air. The smoke is from the burning of bagasse, the fiber remaining after sugar

Sugar, sugar everywhere. This tall grass requires one ton of water to make one pound of sugar.

has been removed from sugarcane. They produce all of their electricity that way and sell the excess to the local electric company. At the corner of Hwy 311 and Hansen Road you'll find the Sugar Museum (871–8058). It has everything you ever wanted to know about sugar harvesting and refining, but were afraid to ask. It's $7 for admission, and they have lots of relics and artifacts. You'll feel hot and stuffy just *looking* at the outfits that field workers used to wear in the hot sun.

PA'IA

If you're heading in the direction of Hana, the last town you'll visit is Pa'ia. This town has accomplished something few Hawai'i towns can claim: It has become an attraction without any attractions other than itself. No great views, no waterfalls, no scenery, no big institutions like an aquarium. Pa'ia's sights lie in its character—and characters. The odd and bizarre add color to Pa'ia like no other Maui town. An example—one morning we saw the following: A guy with a feather stuck in the top of his head (not his hat), a 90-year-old couple on a Harley (she was driving), a woman whose entire body was covered with tattoos, one gentleman with more dirt in his dreadlocks than a medium-sized canefield, a guy having a serious argument with himself (and losing), and a man in a hard hat carrying a full-sized cross. (Unfortunately, we *just missed* the naked woman painted green doing her Christmas shopping at the various shops.) Welcome to Pa'ia, where it's *still* the Age of Aquarius, and shoes are always optional in the streets. It's not a quiet town (even the name means *noisy* in Hawaiian), but it's unique.

Residents along these windward towns are so used to the frequent, short, passing showers that they don't even seem to notice when it starts to rain. They often just go about doing exactly what they were doing, oblivious to the falling drops.

In addition to people-watching, Pa'ia is a great place to do some shopping. Though not as large as Lahaina, the selection is varied. Stores like Alice in Hulaland and Hemp House are situated near surf shops and *lots* of coffee shops. Every shop has its own flavor. Even men, who normally don't like shopping, may like wandering around Pa'ia. And the town has some surprisingly good restaurants.

If you're looking to stock up on foods and want to see the best health food store *in the state*, stop by Mana Foods just up Baldwin Avenue. It's a strange experience: It looks tiny and dumpy from the outside. Then you walk in, and you'll be *blown away* by the size and selection. (Good prices, too.)

Up Baldwin Avenue, Holy Rosary Church, across from Pa'ia School, is a beautiful birch and glass building. They also have a nice memorial to Father Damien of Moloka'i, the priest (and now saint) who worked at the leprosy settlement described on page 144.

While in Pa'ia, wave bye-bye to that last stoplight. If you're heading toward Hana, you won't see another light until you've almost completely circumnavigated Haleakala to Kula, 100 miles around.

Leaving Pa'ia, the Ho'okipa Lookout just before the 9 mile marker is a perfect place to watch the surf. When it's pounding, there's no better place to be than along this shoreline. Breakers can pound with such ferocity in the winter that it makes the ground tremble. Much of the year, expert windsurfers (see page 231) ride the waves after 11 a.m., often streaking faster than the wind, and it's quite a sight to see. Wind is so predictable here—and it runs almost parallel to the shore—that it's considered the single best beach in the United States to windsurf.

CENTRAL MAUI SHOPPING

Kahului is where residents do much of their shopping. The largest mall here is Queen Ka'ahumanu Center on Hwy 32. You'll find department stores, such as Macy's and Sears, well-known chain stores and local business-es that offer island-made gifts and clothing.

Also on Hwy 32, Maui Mall has a cou-ple of reasons to stop—a sherbet-type treat called Guri Guri at Tasaka's and an organic kids clothing and toy store called Wild Creatures. There is also a Longs Drugs and a Whole Foods here.

If you enjoy big outdoor swap meets, Maui's biggest is on Saturdays from 7 a.m. to 1 p.m. Located in the parking lot of Maui Community College off Kahului Beach and Wahinepio roads, they have lots of fresh fruits, baked goods and flowers, as well as coffees, T-shirts and other locally made items—50¢ admis-sion charge.

Costco and Kmart are at the corner of Hwy 380 and Dairy Road (see map). You'll want to stop here to stock up on food if you're here for a few days or more. Kmart sells inexpensive sunblock, T-shirts and water shoes. Walmart is kind of hidden behind Maui Market-place. You'll see it to the left of Home Depot off Dairy Road.

The town of Pa'ia is one of the most eclectic places to shop on the island. There are many small boutiques offering amazing variety. If you can't find parking on the street, there is a parking lot on the mauka side as you enter town. Not all of Pa'ia's business owners are early

risers, so you may find some shops that don't open until 10 or 11 a.m.

Some clothing shops to look for are Mandala Ethnic Arts, Tamara Katz, Jaggers, Moonbow Tropics, Maui Girl & Co., Hemp House, Aloha Shirt Museum and Biasa Rose Boutique. For your keiki, be sure and stop in at Tropikidz, which also has toys. For surf gear, try Simmer Surf, Hi-Tech Surf Sports or Hana Hwy Surf. Don't miss Wings Hawai'i, which started as a school art project and has *very* unusual, locally-made clothes with Hawaiian and nature patterns and one-of-a-kind jewel-ry. Lilikoi Passionate Beauty is a good stop for locally made and other spa-type beauty products.

The Wine Corner has an outstanding selection of beers (and wine, of course), and we think Mana Foods is one of the most reasonable and extensive whole food grocery stores in the state. Indigo is a great place to check out home acces-sories, as is Sand & Sea. If you like antiques, stop by the Pa'ia Trading Co. Maui Hands is found at several locations around the island, but this one is by far the best for its diverse selection of local artists' works for sale. There are some good galleries here, such as Avi Kiriaty and Pa'ia Contemporary Gallery.

CENTRAL MAUI BEST BETS

Best Restaurant View—Mama's Fish House
Best Place to Watch Windsurfers Race the Wind—Ho'okipa Beach Park
Best Place to Find Weird People Doing Odd Things in a Strange Way—Pa'ia
Best Place to Pick Up Healthy Food— Mana Foods in Pa'ia
Best Pizza—Flatbread Company
Best Signs to Ignore—Any Sign That Says LAST FOOD BEFORE HANA

If heaven had a highway…

The road to Hana is without question the most famous and desired drive in all Hawai'i, the crown jewel of driving. It's been compared to driving through the garden of Eden: a slow, winding road through a lush paradise that you always knew existed—somewhere.

If you're in a hurry to get to Hana, you're missing the point. Unless you're staying the night in Hana, you probably won't spend much time there. You're heading somewhere else. (Those who spend the night in Hana will have more time to sample its delights.) At the risk of sounding like a Chinese fortune cookie, fulfillment lies in the journey, not the destination. The whole reason to drive this route is to see the Hawai'i of your dreams, the tropical fantasy that becomes reality along the way. This is a drive through wonderland, and the only

thing at the end—is the end of your discovery. As you drive, don't feel the need to hurry up to get "there," because you may find that there is no there there.

If you're going to be staying in Hana for a couple of days (which we *highly* recommend), then you'll have a chance to see and do much of what the following two chapters present. But if you'll be seeing this part of the island on a one-day tour (as most do), then you won't have a chance to experience even a third of the things we've discovered on the road around Haleakala. If you're a one-dayer, we suggest you read through the following two chapters before you leave so you can prioritize the things that interest you most. For instance, if you're looking for a once-in-a-lifetime photo op of you at the top of a waterfall, check out the Infinity Pool on page 107. Maybe you want to do some bodysurfing at the best beach on the island for it. Then Hamoa Beach on page 97 is what you want. If you want to see a drop dead gorgeous view of the coast, make sure you take Nahiku Road on page 88. If you want to dig your toes in a genuine volcanic black sand beach, then Wai'anapanapa on page 91 is a must-see. Maybe you'd like to swim in a freshwater cave. Page 92 is where you'll find it. Want to see crazy fools make daring leaps into the water? Gotta check out page 84. Want to take a powered hang gliding flight along the coast? You need to see Armin on page 184. This is just a small portion of what's available. The point is, you can't do it all, so decide which adventure is most important to you.

The road to Hana is two lanes with lots of one-lane bridges. Tourist literature says there are 600 turns, though I don't know exactly how they classify a turn since the road is never straight. (Your steering wheel *certainly* changes direction more than that.) Whether you find the Hana Highway wild or tame depends on your experience. We've noticed that people who have lived most of their lives in flat areas—where a straight line *really is* the closest distance between two points and you can always see what's a mile in front of you—find the constant winding road and blind turns unnerving. Those of us who grew up with crooked roads find it a joy. We once met some visitors from the midwest who were highly adventurous. They skydived, flew ultralights and thought nothing about jumping off the 60-foot bridge over 'Ohe'o Gulch into the water. But they refused to drive the Hana Highway again because it "made us nervous." Ironically, they were traveling with timid couch potatoes who grew up in Northern California and loved the "relaxing feel" of the highway. So I guess it depends on what you're used to.

CAN A RENTAL CAR GO ALL THE WAY?

There are many myths associated with the Hana Highway. Let's dispense with the biggest and most entrenched.

Myth—You can't drive a regular car all the way around Haleakala; you need a 4WD vehicle and high clearance past Hana, and even if you could, it would violate your rental car agreement.

Fact—The road past Hana is nearly always perfectly driveable and *may* not violate your rental car agreement. You *don't* need high clearance or 4WD. Years ago, the road to Hana was a tortuous drive. The sadistic pavement was full of potholes and ill-conceived pothole fills beating you and your car up along the way. But today, the road to Hana is smooth, though a winding and narrow two lanes much of the way. *Yeah, but what about the part past Hana?* Well, 14 miles past Hana, after the 39 mile marker (the number sequence is altered at Hana), the road goes from pavement to gravel that is graded regularly. After a few miles of bumpy gravel (its bumpiness depends on when you catch it during the maintenance cycle) it becomes blacktop again, textured rough from countless poor patch jobs. After six miles of bumpy blacktop the smooth highway returns. *Very* rarely, extremely heavy rains may close the road at one point where a normally dry stream crosses the road, but it is usually reopened as soon as they can get a crew out there.

Most rental car contracts we've seen restrict you from using the car on "unpaved" or sometimes "unimproved" roads and don't mention the road to Hana specifically. In the past that language certainly covered the latter part of the road. But now those terms don't sound as if they apply. After all, the paved portion would seem to be legitimate, and the gravel portion is certainly "improved" constantly. Besides, if it's so bad, how come large tour buses are able to drive all the way around? The fact is, the second half of the road has a very out-of-date reputation, and all the free magazines and maps that tell you otherwise need to have their people drive it for themselves. Even if you are violating your rental car agreement, what does that mean? According to the rental car companies we contacted, it means the extra insurance you took out *may* not cover you there (and you may not want to pay for that anyway because your own personal car insurance may cover you), and it means they won't come get you if you get into trouble.

Driving all the way to Hana and then turning around (which the vast majority of visitors do) means missing the windswept back of Haleakala in the late afternoon. The way the light casts deep shadows in the water-scoured gulches, the incredibly expansive views of the coastline, the impossibly blue sky against the brown and red upper slopes of the volcano, the angry, wind-ravaged seas, and the utter lack of civilized development—these are the things that make a drive along the bottom part of the island worthwhile. It won't look like the Hana drive; you just *saw* that. But it will pass from Eden-like lushness to the land of sun and wind. It's hard to believe that the backside is part of the same mountain.

DRIVING THE ROAD

You *definitely* want to drive in a clockwise direction so you can take advantage of the sun. The Hana side is sunny in the morning, shady in the afternoon, and its waterfalls are best before 11 a.m.

It's best to start the road to Hana *early,* so you'll have time to see and experience as much as possible. Unfortunately, we're not the only ones who give this advice, so everyone else seems to be leaving early, too. On average, between 1,500 and 2,000 cars per day drive the road to Hana. Most leave Kahului between 8:30 a.m. and 10 a.m. I know, I know. You're supposed to be here on vacation, and we *really* hate to suggest something as regimented as a timetable, but let us make one recommendation. If you're not going to be staying in Hana overnight, we strongly suggest you leave early enough to be passing Kahului by 8 a.m. This lets you avoid the crowds and see the sights in good light and allows you to take your time. If you're staying in Hana, leave after 10:30 a.m. when the road's more empty.

Both of these scenarios allow you to avoid being in a procession of cars. This can take away *much* for the driver. *We can't emphasize this enough.* Whether they realize it or not, drivers focus almost constantly on the car ahead. You can't help it; it's instinctive. But when no one's ahead of you, your eyes tend to sweep and record the road ahead and then fall onto the delicious scenery. That's why we're more than happy to pull over repeatedly to allow cars to get far enough ahead so that we can drive to Hana and enjoy ourselves. We've done informal surveys and found that people who drove behind another car didn't think the drive was *nearly* as nice as those who drove it with no one in front of them. And if you notice a long line behind you, pull over to allow the faster ones to get by. There's virtually no place for them to pass on this highway.

WATERFALLS

Everybody loves **waterfalls**. They seem to universally affect people with a peaceful, soothing feeling. On this drive, waterfalls near the road are easy to find. This part of Maui was tailor-made for waterfall production because it has the two necessary ingredients—constant elevation changes and lots of rain up the mountain. But many of the lovelier ones are off the road, often accessible from trails. We have identified many with this symbol.

WATERFALL ALERT!

We tried to photograph most of the waterfalls flowing about halfway between abnormally pumping and abnormally light. The only exceptions are Hanawi (we just *had* to show you what it looks like when it's really going) and Lower Puohokamoa. The others are fairly typical middle-of-the-road; sometimes higher (usually winter), sometimes lower (usually summer).

One thing you need to understand is the extremely variable nature of waterfalls. At different times, the same falls can be an unimpressive trickle, a world-class waterfall in a lovely setting, or a brown, swollen mass of water and mud after a heavy rain. We have found most of these falls in all three states at different times. During some wet winter months, you may find more waterfalls than we mention. Sometimes, during dry months, some of our favorites may shrivel to a pathetic dribble, but you'll never see fewer than six falls between Kahului and Hana, *if* you know when and where to look.

A FEW BASICS

East Maui Irrigation Company (EMI) has ditches that run most of the way to Hana. At times, they will turn off various falls as they divert the water to feed the thirsty cane fields in Central Maui and for some residential use. Be aware that some of these falls may be on land controlled by EMI. Much of the land here is *state-owned* forest reserve, not private. EMI merely leases the water rights on a revocable month-to-month lease. Here and under HIKING we describe several awesome hikes in this area. It's mandatory that you contact EMI in advance to get a waiver to hike to some of the falls. Don't expect to be able to get permission while at the falls themselves

There are a lot of waterfalls. Some you'll never even see as you zigzag your way along the Hana Highway.

Serious jungle action, brah.

because you'll rarely find any EMI person-nel around at the falls to ask. You'll need to go to their office. EMI has been stingy with hiking permits in the past, but with sugar operations reportedly losing $25 million in a single year, local farmers fight-ing them for water rights and considering EMI's reported short-term grasp on the leased land, who's to know if, by the time you read this, they have a lease on the land or not? You'll need a waiver or you'll have to participate with one of the hiking groups that EMI allows accesss to. Our descriptions are not meant to encourage you to trespass. (See page 41 for more on that.) They are merely so you'll know which hikes you want to request from EMI or one of their authorized groups.

Car break-ins can occur at scenic spots, such as waterfalls. Though not exactly common along the Hana road, all it takes is one or two scumbags smashing windows to create a problem. So avoid leaving valuables in the car, especially vis-ible on the seat.

Many of the businesses along this road are closed on Sundays.

Start the trip with a full tank of gas.

The car of choice for the Hana High-way is the convertible. There are many times that you'll see striking greenery above you that others will miss.

The **weather** on the Hana Highway is notoriously difficult to predict. Parts of it get a *lot* of rain; that's why it's so beau-tiful and the waterfalls so plentiful. You can call (866) 944–5025 for a weather update. One thing that Hana road veter-ans know is that as you start the drive, if you observe bad weather, it usually (but not always) gets better past Nahiku, so don't turn around assuming it will be rain-ing the whole drive. More times than we can count, we've hit heavy rain much of the way only to have it disappear just before the Hana Airport.

This stretch of road, more than any other in the state, suffers from the lem-ming effect. (Lemmings are rodents known for going over cliffs *en masse* because the ones in front of them are doing it.) The drive is so special that everyone's afraid of missing something, so when you pull over, you'll likely see others pulling up behind you to see what they might be missing. We are well aware that many of the sights that we've discov-ered—some of them never mentioned anywhere else—attract others who pull in behind our readers. But at least *you* know what to look for, and *they* are the lemmings. And just because you see others on the side of the road, don't think they know something you don't. Odds are they don't.

A WORD ABOUT ALOHA

We noticed for this edition (and voluminous reader e-mail confirms) that a conspicuous few East Maui residents have forgotten what aloha means, permeating their area with unfriendly signs and rude behavior. We promise you, most Maui residents *aren't* like that and would be embarrassed by it. If you do run into any unfriendly people or attitudes, we strongly request that you simply smile and wave at them. Maybe, in some way, you'll help them get their aloha back. And please make sure you leave the areas you visit just as you found them.

PA'IA TO HIGHWAY 360

The first part of the drive starts on Hwy 36 after you've passed Pa'ia. (That town is described in CENTRAL MAUI SIGHTS.) The map on page 115 covers this first part. As you pass the 10 mile marker, you'll cross **Maliko Gulch**. An older bridge and train trestle were erected ½ mile up mauka (toward the mountain) in 1913. The sugar company that built it had lots of trouble getting people to work on the foundations. It required swinging into the 300-foot gulch on ropes, and nervous workers kept refusing to go. Finally the boss/owner of the sugar company grabbed the rope and swung into the ravine. None of the other workers *ever* refused again. You see, the boss, Henry Baldwin, did it while recovering from a recent accident—where he had *lost an arm.* Baldwin had swung into the gulch armed with only...well, you know. After that, no worker had the nerve to refuse to do something with two arms that the

boss man had done with one. The bridge was eventually torn down to prevent indestructible teenagers from repeating the feat.

While still on Hwy 36, you'll come upon the **Maui Grown Market** past the 14 mile marker with their sign saying, "Last Stop Before Hana." Don't you believe it! There are better places 20 miles ahead.

ON HIGHWAY 360

Soon the highway changes its name to 360 (now it's a county road), and the mile markers start at 0. The map on the next page starts here. You should reset your odometer so you'll always have a general idea where you are, but bear in mind that the mile markers aren't always placed a mile apart as they should be. We refer to their *actual* location, not where they're *supposed* to be. So if we say something is ³/₁₀ past the 8 mile marker, check again at the 8 mile marker to see what the odometer reads.

The first half of the drive is more tightly enclosed by vegetation, so you won't get too many expansive views. There's a fruit stand and lots of people just past the 2 mile marker. A series of roads and trails leads to **Twin Falls**, actually six or seven waterfalls, none very spectacular compared to what's ahead. People tend to spend too much time here because it's the first available falls and then rush by better opportunities. You should avoid them for the nicer, less-mobbed waterfalls later. But the fruit stand itself, when it's there, is pretty good with lots of fresh fruits and decent banana bread.

Little more than a half mile past the 3 mile marker is a road which leads to **Kaulanapueo Church.** Built in 1853, it's still in use and is an excellent example of 19th-century churches, though it will probably be locked when you visit.

Hana Highway

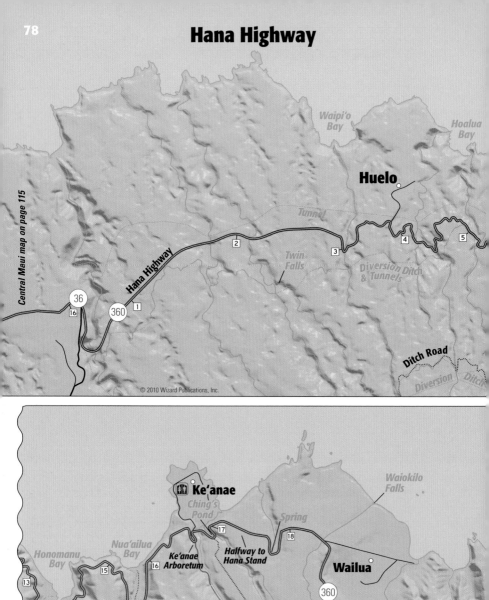

Waipi'o Bay

Hoalua Bay

Huelo

Tunnel

Central Maui map on page 115

Hana Highway

Twin Falls

Diversion Ditch & Tunnels

2

3

4

5

36

360

1

16

Ditch Road

Diversion Ditch

© 2010 Wizard Publications, Inc.

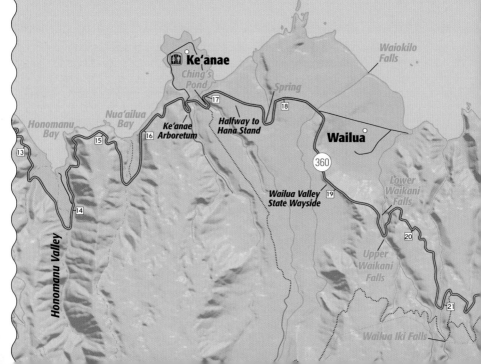

Waiokilo Falls

Ke'anae

Ching's Pond

Spring

Honomanu Bay

Nua'ailua Bay

Ke'anae Arboretum

Halfway to Hana Stand

17

18

Wailua

360

13

15

16

14

Wailua Valley State Wayside

19

Lower Waikani Falls

20

Honomanu Valley

Upper Waikani Falls

21

Wailua Iki Falls

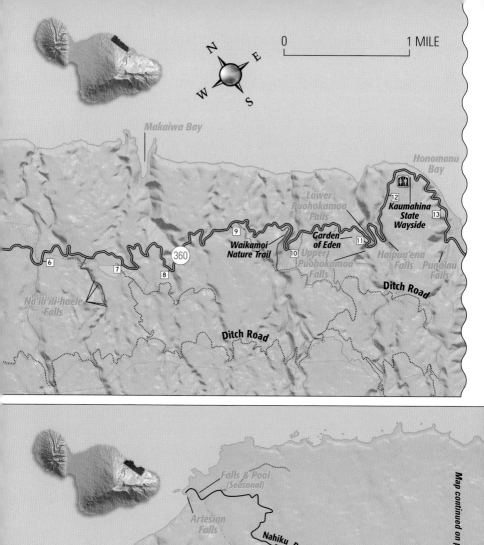

N
W—E
S

0 ——— 1 MILE

Makaiwa Bay

Honomanu Bay

Lower Puohokamoa Falls

Kaumahina State Wayside

12

13

9

Waikamoi Nature Trail

Garden of Eden

11

360

10

Upper Puohokamoa Falls

Haipua'ena Falls

Punalau Falls

6

7

8

Ditch Road

Na'ili'ili-haele Falls

Ditch Road

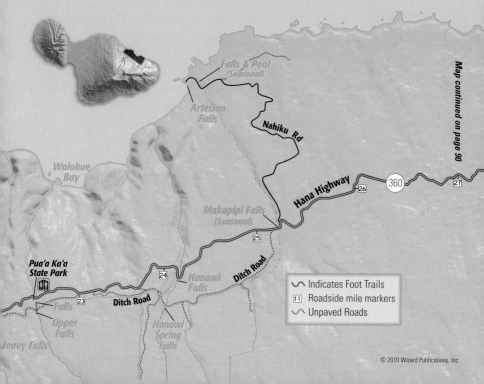

Falls & Pool (Seasonal)

Artesian Falls

Nahiku Rd

Waiohue Bay

Map continued on page 90

Hana Highway

360

27

26

Makapipi Falls (Seasonal)

25

Pua'a Ka'a State Park

24

Hanawi Falls

Ditch Road

23

Falls

Ditch Road

Upper Falls

Hanawi Spring Falls

Heavy Falls

⌇ Indicates Foot Trails
11 Roadside mile markers
⋯ Unpaved Roads

© 2010 Wizard Publications, Inc.

At ⁶⁄₁₀ mile past the 6 mile marker (it's one of the few on the *left* side of the road) is a dirt turnout. A trail leads to *four waterfalls.* Many of the waterfall trails along the highway are in this section. But this one's harder to get to and is in ADVENTURES on page 237.

Between the 9 and 10 mile markers on the Hana Highway is the Waikamoi Nature Trail. Two nature loops—one about 10 minutes, the other about 30—make a pleasant place to stretch your legs a bit, but it's not a hugely compelling hike. It's good for families, and you gain,

at most, 200 feet. If you venture past the main trail, a pretty waterfall awaits. See HIKING on page 202 for more. No restrooms here.

Waikamoi Stream just before the 10 mile marker is usually dry, but after a heavy rain it can be a giant cauldron with a large waterfall up the mountain and a slippery trail to a smaller one. You'll know whether to bother by the amount of water flowing under the bridge.

Soon you come to the Garden of Eden (572–9899). Pretty tough name to live up to; it's an arboretum and botanical

Kamehameha Fights to the Death

Just before Holokai Road between the 15 & 16 mile markers (on Hwy 36) there is a hill visible a mile up mauka. This hill became famous during the time of Kamehameha, the only king to conquer all the islands. While he was here battling for Maui in the late 1700s, the Maui king's top warrior was sent with troops to repel Kamehameha. One night Kamehameha camped at that hill and paraded his war god Ku around the camp to see how the feathers on the head of the god would look. It was believed that the more erect the top feathers bristled, the better the battle would go. The feathers cooperated. The next day a fierce battle was fought beyond the hill at a place called Kokomo. Though most battles were fought by lower ranking soldiers, here Kamehameha himself fought in a battle to the death with Maui's top warrior. Kamehameha had practiced making war since he was a child, even going so far as to have some of his top men surprise him from time to time by throwing spears at him when he wasn't looking, just to keep him sharp. (He prided himself on being able to dodge or catch as many as five spears thrown at once.) The battle was begun as most Hawaiian battles were—both leaders on opposite sides of the battle-field hurled insults back and forth to stir up each other. When the Maui warrior land-ed a particularly cruel blow (accusing Kamehameha of having no royal blood, but rather descending from slaves—yes, the Hawaiians did keep slaves), Kamehameha roared. Both leaders shot sling stones at each other. Then they charged each other with spears. Hand to hand, Kamehameha landed a vicious blow with his leiomanu, a club studded with shark's teeth, opening the Maui warrior's chest. The Maui warrior stabbed Kamehameha with a wooden dagger, but Hawai'i's future king finished off his opponent with his club. Maui's top warrior was slaughtered on the field of battle in front of the Maui troops who were so demoralized that the taking of Maui became inevitable.

garden. The $15 per person entrance fee seems a little high at first, but you soon realize that this is a meticulously maintained and very beautiful garden. Everything is scrupulously labeled. You can either drive it or walk a separate path. They have a picnic area with good views down the coast, if you're looking for a place to eat that sandwich you brought with you, and there's a restroom.

At $\frac{8}{10}$ mile past the 10 mile marker on the ocean side of the road is a turnout with a telephone pole. There's a well-worn path to the right. Take it for a couple of minutes, and you'll be treated to a view of a particularly large waterfall that the vast majority of drivers miss. Plunging about 200 feet, Lower Puohokamoa Falls drops into a large pool as drivers, blissfully unaware of its existence below, rush along on their way to Hana. The trail continues and gets steeper as it meanders into the valley, but the latter part is treacherous.

Just past the 11 mile marker is a path to Upper Puohokamoa Falls. The landowner (Garden of Eden) has erected a wall and won't allow people to access it from the near side. Perhaps they simply want you to visit their garden and view the falls from their property instead. Fortunately, they don't own the land on the far side (the state does), and from there you'll find a trail to the falls.

A half mile past the 11 mile marker there's a small turnout on the far side of the bridge and a trail that leads 30 seconds or so to a pool and small waterfall

Most drivers (top) have no idea that they are passing Lower Puohokamoa Falls. A short trail takes you to this vantage point.

WATERFALL ALERT!

called Haipua'ena Falls. It's worth a stop. There's another, larger falls just upstream, but the trail to the second falls, even on a dry day, has a short stretch where it's easy to fall. (An ugly fall at that.) Not worth it; stay at the first waterfall.

WATERFALL ALERT!

Past the 12 mile marker you come across the Kaumahina State Wayside with its restrooms. The restrooms at Ke'anae 5 miles ahead are usually less crowded, even though there are fewer of

The ocean along the raw, younger Ke'anae coastline is often bathed in beautiful, violent chaos.

them. The wayside also has a series of short nature loops heading uphill from the ocean overlook.

There's a place on the right side past the 12 mile marker where the road opens up, exposing the very scenic **Ke'anae Peninsula**, but there's no place to pull over. You'll get a chance to pull over at the 13 mile marker. What a view!

As you cruise along, consider that cars couldn't make it to Hana from central Maui until an unpaved road was cut in 1926. Before that, Hana was isolated and quiet. Even with the new road, driving was only for the brave and the well insured. It remained unpaved until 1962. The paving job was awful, and the paved Hana Highway deteriorated until it was almost worse than the old unpaved road it replaced. The state finally did it right in the 1980s, creating the smooth (though still narrow) ride you enjoy today.

If you've been itching for your very own private waterfall, you *may* be in

luck. One quarter mile past the 13 mile marker there's a tiny turnout on the far side of the bridge and another one kitty-corner up the road. Even when it looks dry, there *may* (or may not) be more water flowing unseen under the rocks near the highway, so it's hard to gauge the flow here. About 800 or so feet upstream is a pretty and lacy unnamed falls on the Punalau stream. (We'll call it

Punalau Falls.) This is one of the few falls along the way that you can visit and have a reasonable chance of having it to yourself for three reasons: You can't see it from the road, it's never been written about, as far as we know, and you'll have to walk on the (usually) dry stream boulders nearly the whole way. (When the boulders are wet, they're pretty slippery.) It'll take between 10 and 25 minutes to get there (depending on your rock-hopping aptitude). A pair of walking sticks is invaluable for stream walking; you'll go from being a two-legged animal to a four-legged one. Even if the falls are a trickle (EMI has a ditch upstream), the area around the falls is an impossibly narrow vertical-walled chasm bursting with ferns and moss and a cool pool to swim.

On the highway just past the 14 mile marker there's a dirt road that leads to Honomanu Bay. The beach here is gravelly and the swimming poor, but in the early morning or late afternoon, the sun creates a magnificent golden green on the gouged-out valley walls, reminding you why you came to Hawai'i.

The present government road to Hana is by no means the first. Back in the 1500s a king named Kihapi'ilani decided that trips around the island were too perilous. Many of the gulches you have passed along the way were well known places for robberies, since the thieves could easily get away. So the king had trails cut and paved with smooth stream stones all around Haleakala—quite a feat at the time. It took years (though probably less time than the current county government seems to take these days when they repave it). It was said that the king didn't want to be forgotten when he died. His public works project succeeded, because five centuries later he is still remembered fondly, and another public works project, Pi'ilani Highway, bears his name and the name of a 17th-century governor. His 500-year-old stone road was still visible in places until the jungle consumed the last of it in the early 1900s.

After the 14 mile marker there are several pullouts, but the county has let vegetation block most of them. Just over ½ mile past the 14 mile marker is your best shot of seeing the highway ribbon draped across the mountain. Of the three pullouts, the middle one has a trail to the left that sports an overlook with an amazingly tranquil view of Honomanu Bay and Valley and of the zig-zagging Hana Highway working its way up the cliffs. Take your time here and savor the smashing scene. The upper part of the valley you're looking at is full of burial sites. The old Hawaiians refused to walk there at night, believing that the spirits of chiefs buried there roamed the valley.

Off the highway just before the road into Ke'anae Peninsula is the Ke'anae Arboretum. Neglected for years, the state rarely puts any effort into maintaining it. On our last visit the taro field was weed-infested, and the signs were covered with mold and hard to read. The paved and unpaved path is a 25–30 minute stroll. Bring mosquito repellent unless you're a practiced bloodletter.

KE'ANAE TO NAHIKU

Next comes the road into Ke'anae Peninsula and village. (The YMCA camp you just passed has cabins for rent; see page 176.) The road hugs the coastline for a time, and at one place there's an excellent photo op with the ocean tearing through some jagged lava boulders. Very striking, especially at high tide. The impossibly blue water against the rich lushness of the Hana coast is a feast for the eyes. Farther ahead are some restrooms near the ballpark. (Before the ballpark, a stand called Aunty Sandy's on the right sells banana bread and snacks.) The coastline across from the restrooms is a good place to watch the waves beat up the shoreline. The land here is younger than the rest of the island, and it shows.

There's an extraordinary legend about the origin of the taro fields at Ke'anae that can't be confirmed but ties in nicely with what we know about the geology of the land. The legend states that in ancient times there was a chief who was constantly at war with the neighboring village of Wailua. At that time Ke'anae was mostly a barren lava field. The chief decided that he needed more taro-growing land and more people living in the area. So he decreed

DIVERSION ALERT!

that every man, woman and child would go to the upper valley, gather soil in baskets and fill the peninsula with enough soil to grow taro. In time, the peninsula became a prime taro-growing area. True story? Who knows? It's a legend. But what a task it would have been. Imagine hiking miles up the valley, hauling a basket of heavy dirt back, dumping it on the lava rock and heading back uphill. The definition of a thankless, Dilbert-like job!

Keʻanae was nearly wiped out by the tsunami (tidal wave) of 1946. Nearly every building was destroyed, leaving only the immovable stone church.

Back on the highway, just before the 17 mile marker, is a bridge and pullout. The path about 75 feet to the left leads down to a marvelous pool, known locally as Ching's Pond. The swimming is particularly good, and most drivers never even see this pond. Above the narrow stream portion (just before it opens up to the pool) there's a concrete platform on the right side. We've seen daring young locals *diving* out and away from the cliff into the tiny part they claim is deep enough so you don't hit rocks. We're talking about a 25 foot or so drop with *zero* margin for error. *That's* what we call an ʻokole squeezer. (We'll let you guess what an ʻokole is.) Obviously you shouldn't do this unless you name us as beneficiaries on your life insurance.

About ⅓ mile past the 17 mile marker is a stand generally known as Halfway to Hana. (Actually, you're ⅔ of the way from Kahului.) We review theirs and *Aunty Sandy's* banana bread every time we travel the road. (Just to be thorough, you understand. We do it for you, only for you.) Currently they are neck and neck (but completely outshined by *Julia's* in Kahakuloa, West Maui and *Haiku General Store* upcountry). Halfway to Hana also has fruits, beverages, some sandwiches and so-so burgers, and other snacks. If you're hungry, consider stocking up here for snacks. Hana has relatively few food options. By the way, take a peek at the house behind the stand to see if they still have all those pigs' heads hanging on the wall.

About ⅔ mile past the 17 mile mark, pull over and walk to the white concrete bridge. Look down on the

A cliff diver at Ching's Pond lands in the only space deep enough.

ocean side of the bridge, and you'll see water gushing out of the mountain, surrounded by flowers and some huge elephant ears (called 'ape) in a garden setting tailor-made for a postcard (though they sometimes let the jungle overgrow the area). This is a spring-fed gusher, originating here. Any pipes you see under the flowers are tapping the water, not feeding it. When they keep it well-tended, it's a lovely sight, but it's been overgrown on our last few visits.

You may see Uncle Harry's stand on the left side. Snacks, burgers and banana bread; unfortunately, none of it tasty.

The tiny settlement of Wailua is off the road not long past the 18 mile marker. This community is mostly built around taro growing. (Taro is the plant Hawaiians use to make poi, the purple, less-than-tasty paste you may try—once—at a lu'au.) That road is dead-on straight. (Bowlers may get sweaty palms imagining the possibilities. It's strange to be driving on straight pavement again; your hands are searching for something to do.) Keep an eye on your right for a glimpse of the enormous, multi-tiered Waikani Falls, which drop 1,000 feet in several stages just under the highway. (You can't see the large lower falls from the highway.) For what it's worth, we (and readers) seem to get more stink eye here than just about any other place on the island.

Just before the 19 mile marker, most people blow by without even noticing the Wailua Valley State Wayside on the mauka (mountain) side. Take the stairs to the right to the top, and on the ocean side you'll see the village of Wailua with its fields of taro beneath you. Turn around and look up mauka. You'll see (clouds permitting) the Ko'olau Gap at the top of the mountain. Notice how steep the valley walls are, yet the floor is so broad and flat. This valley used to be thousands of feet deep, cutting into the very core of the vol-

cano. It was filled in at the same time as the Kaupo Gap on the other side of the volcano. (See page 111 for the full story.) The relatively new lands of Wailua and the Ke'anae Peninsula were formed by the same flows that filled the gaps.

Many of the one-lane bridges along here are close to 100 years old. The county wants to replace them, but there's a hitch. In order to get federal (meaning your) dollars, the bridges usually need to be two-lane. (The feds don't like paying for one-lane bridges.) The problem is that Hana residents don't *want* two-lane bridges. Since the county is perpetually short of funds, it's a safe bet that some two-lane bridges are on their way. In fact, in Kaupo on the bottom of the island before the 27 mile marker you'll notice two nice, expensive concrete two-lane bridges—connecting two halves of a one-lane road. We Maui residents thank you for your support.

Between the 19 and 20 mile markers there's a very popular waterfall to photograph called Upper Waikani Falls, sometimes called Three Bears Falls (the upper cousin to the huge falls partially visible from Wailua village). These falls vary dramatically, depending on flow. In case you're wondering, yes, you *can* get to the falls themselves. At the far side of the bridge (on the mauka side) is a fairly easy, short path—it's just the first step that's pretty ugly. Standing near the falls, you'll realize that they're a lot bigger than you thought. At press time NO PARKING signs forced you to drive about 800 feet past the falls to an inadequate parking area and walk the road back. Police were ticketing those who ignored the signs.

Remember, the secret to shooting waterfalls is a long exposure. If your camera has adjustable shutter speeds, the longer the exposure (say around $\frac{1}{10}$

second), the better the shot looks—if you can hold the camera still enough. If you flunked out of surgeon school because your hands shake, use a tripod or prop the camera on a rock. Also, see page 33 for precautions on swimming in streams. This is probably a good time to tell you that, while swimming in natural pools, use your hands as much as possible to avoid kicking unseen rocks. (Voice of experience with the stubbed toes to prove it.)

The stream just before the 21 mile marker is sometimes almost dry. That's because most of the water is diverted less than a ½ mile upstream. But ²/₁₀ mile past the 21 mile marker is a hunters' road called **Wailua Iki**. A 10-minute walk from there (at the top of the dirt road turn right) leads to a very nice waterfall and pool, as well as a *gorgeous* valley.

WATERFALL ALERT!

(See page 75 for hiking in this EMI area.) There are two more falls farther up the stream, but they're harder to reach. By the way, *if* there's water flowing at the highway, the real view is from about 250 feet up the highway (there's a one-car turnout just up the hill), where the water that flows under the highway plunges off the cliff in a very dramatic fashion.

At ⁹/₁₀ mile past the 21 mile marker is one of the heavier-flowing falls along the coast. (It's heavy because there's no ditch upstream robbing its water.) Unfortunately, it's just barely out of sight (except maybe the top as you're driving up) 500 feet inland. This whole area is part of the Ko'olau Forest Reserve, but EMI, which has the water rights, has infrastructure there that dissuades you from visiting the falls. Assuming they give you their blessing to hike to it, you'll find a trail on the right

Most people seem to think that the heavier the water flow, the prettier the waterfall. These two shots of Waikani Falls (AKA the Three Bears) are an example of how sometimes less is more.

side of the stream leading most of the way to the falls. You'll have to find a way to scramble up the rock wall in front of you to get to it, which looks sketchy. If you're willing to get your feet wet and the stream flow isn't too high, consider the far side of the bridge and crossing the stream in front of the ditch.

Between the 22 and 23 mile markers is **Pua'a Ka'a State Park**. (*That's* a hard one to say.) Two easily visited small waterfalls make good photo ops, and there are (sometimes crowded) **restrooms**. The falls are often fairly light, but it's not for lack of water. If you're adventurous, we have a surprise for you. There's an awkward trail on the right side of the upper falls. It first leads to a short path to the top of the falls, but if you go past it for 5–10 squishy minutes (it's usually muddy), there's a much heavier untapped falls and pool just above the diversion ditch that's taking much of the lower falls' water. When the trail gets to the elevated waterway (viaduct), you have to walk along it (which those afraid of heights will *hate*), then across. Only 100 more feet upstream is your prize. The falls make an ideal photo op—you know, the *me under a waterfall* shot, if the flow's not too heavy—and it's a pretty dependable waterfall, even during the driest times. (But it's pretty cold, indicating spring water.) The trail goes around a hill and narrows as it goes down to the pool.

By the way, there are boreholes in the Pua'a Ka'a highway bridge to answer that question that's troubled you all your life—how thick are these bridges anyway?

Two turnouts after the 23 mile mark (left side) you see a cave on the mauka side of the road. If you have a flashlight (and are willing to do some stooping), the cave loops to the right and emerges in an ethe-

real green scene guarded by banyan tree roots next to a babbling stream. It's short, but sweet. To be precise, it's 140 feet long—we measured it. (*Yeah*, we can be a bit too detail-oriented at times.) Climb out of the cave there or retreat back to your car. These caves are **lava tubes**, created when lava from volcanic vents forms a river that crusts over on top. These tubes can transport the lava for over 20 miles, losing a mere 20°F along the way. Lava tubes tend to collapse over time, so young islands like the Big Island are loaded with them, whereas older islands, like Kaua'i have relatively few.

After the 24 mile marker, yet another pretty waterfall called **Hanawi Falls** awaits. It's particularly attractive. If you take a photo from the bridge, be careful. The guard-rail is shorter than it looks. There have been people who have sat on the rail for a photo, only to careen backward onto the rocks. When the flow is heavy, this becomes one of the nicest waterfalls on the whole coast. It splits around the rocks, and the portion on the left adds to the portion on the right, making it a dream.

OK, OK. I know you've probably seen a number of nice waterfalls by now. Been there, done that. But *when it's flowing,* this next one is different. Pull over on the far side of the bridge shortly past the 25 mile marker. If you walk out to the bridge (there's no walkway for you), from the middle of the ocean side, look straight down. (Be *really* careful not to topple over.) You'll see something you don't normally get to see. You are *directly* above the spot where **Makapipi Falls** plunges unfettered into a large pool. Enjoy the excellent vantage point as you follow the stream with your eyes as it burrows through the vegetation on its way to the

Hanawi Falls, when it's really pumping as it is here, is glorious even when you don't get out of your car. At other times, only the right side flows.

ocean. Makapipi is more seasonal than most falls and is dry about half the time.

NAHIKU

Next to the falls, Nahiku Road leads 2½ miles down through the luxuriant community of Nahiku. If you think the road to Hana looked lush and beautiful, wait till you see Nahiku. When plants go to heaven, Nahiku must be their destination. Everything green seems so happy and healthy, you can almost hear them giggling. Life bursts from every corner at the bottom half of the road. Nahiku was formed in 1905 as a rubber tree plantation, but the effort went flat a decade later.

Drive slowly; children play in the streets. Several honor-system fruit stands are often present. Near the end of the road is a series of conflicting signs that might turn you around. Here's the deal: The ROAD CLOSED sign dates from when the bridge needed repairs. (It was fixed at press time.) The PRIVATE ROAD—PROCEED AT YOUR OWN RISK part is true. The short stretch from the bridge to the ocean is not a county road. The landowners have traditionally allowed *everyone* to drive to the end. The RESIDENTS ONLY sign does not appear to be officially sanctioned, as far as we could determine.

Once at the bottom of Nahiku Road, you're in for a treat—a jaw-dropping view of the shoreline all the way back to Keʻanae. There's a little path on the left that leads to a variable but charming little artesian waterfall and pool, right next to the ocean. What a spot! As you stand there in your own private heaven, you can't help but wonder if there's a more beautiful place in the world. Perhaps you can't see forever, but you can see all the way to paradise. This is one of our favorite spots to sit and gaze along the Hana coast. Miles of coastline are revealed as the sounds of the surf and the small falls make everything just perfect. A grassy area near the ocean makes a good place to have lunch.

As you depart and the road leaves the shoreline, you may think that Nahiku has delivered everything it can. But during rainy times there's one surprise left. Pull the car over about 150 feet uphill from the shoreline guard-rail. The stream to your left forms a big pool with a small waterfall. (It can dry up in the summertime.) The whole setting is ensconced in an area packed with more shades of green than you ever knew existed. The scene is as wholesome and idyllic as any you may encounter. It's a flawlessly sculpted natural setting. Only the mosquitoes remind you that it's still the real world. There's a short path down to the pool.

DINING OUTSIDE OF HANA

Before the 27 mile marker, you'll start to see pre-Hana dining opportunities. Hours are squirrelly (and some may be temporary businesses), but stand-outs include the small but light banana bread at Nahiku Roadside and the banana fudge dairy-free ice cream (made from coconut milk) at Coconut Glen's (past the 27 mile marker).

At Nahiku Marketplace (before 29 mile marker) they have good, slow-baked coconut candy, generous fish tacos at Island Style Tacos, reasonably good fish and chips at the Chinese vendor and good tropical coconut cake (when they have it) at the Nahiku Cafe.

Ake has good BBQ chicken on left side of the road at the 33 mile marker.

Hana Fresh often has incredible cherry tomatoes and unusual smoothies after the 34 mile marker. (They are right in front of the health dept., which is comforting.)

Past Hana town and past Hasegawa General Store, Braddah Hutts BBQ Grill has excellent BBQ pork strips as well as great shrimp pasta with big portions. The pasta is big enough for two to share.

NAHIKU TO HANA

Back on the highway, you'll notice that the terrain is changing. It's less eroded because the land is relatively new here.

Near the 31 mile marker is 'Ula'ino Road. Drive a couple miles down 'Ula'ino and you come to Kahanu Garden (248–8912), part of the National Tropical Botanical Garden. They have self-guided tours (which take around 30 minutes) between 10 a.m. and 2 p.m. for $10, Mon–Fri. The garden is set among spacious grounds, and the emphasis is on native and Polynesian-introduced plants, not ornamental flowers. The love and care is evident. They take good care of

Nahiku Road is heaven for anything green.

this place, and the plants are well labeled. The most extraordinary feature is not a plant at all, but rather the **Pi'ilanihale Heiau** (shown on page 14). This massive temple, the largest in the state, was largely forgotten and buried under vegetation until the garden restored it in the late '90s. The first time we saw it, we were unprepared for its immensity. When you first spot it, it looks enormous. But after you get close and go around a corner, you realize how utterly colossal it really is. It covers almost *three acres* and took an estimated 128,000 man-days to build, starting in the late 1200s A.D. The second phase was completed around 1570. You won't be allowed to walk on it, and your vantage point isn't as good as our aerial photo, but you'll get a feel for its sheer size.

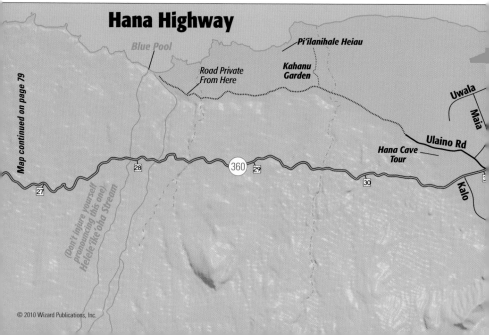

A REAL GEM

There are some nice coastal views from parts of the garden, as well as some Hawaiian stone implements and tools. Begin your walk at exhibit #4.

Near Kahanu Garden is **Maui Cave Adventures** (248–7308). See page 241 for more on that.

Past here the road eventually becomes private, ending at a stream crossing. You may read about a lovely waterfall past the crossing called **Blue Pool**. It's a fantastic site with a tall, delicious waterfall on one side of the pool and the ocean on the other. Unfortunately, access has become a tangled mess. It's on a single large parcel with dozens of owners. Some of the owners of this single parcel are inviting you onto their land, evidenced by their signs near the end of the road saying you can park for $2. At least one of their fellow owners apparently *doesn't* want you there, evidenced by a purportedly grumpy greeting at the end of the road and sometimes even threats, according to numerous e-mails we've gotten from readers. We're very concerned about someone getting hurt and can't recommend going to Blue Pool any longer.

Back on the highway, you'll pass the tiny **Hana Airport**. If you want a thrilling

Hana Highway

Map continued on page 79

Blue Pool

Pi'ilanihale Heiau

Road Private From Here

Kahanu Garden

Uwala

Maia

Ulaino Rd

Hana Cave Tour

Kalo

28

360

29

27

30

(Don't injure yourself pronouncing this one)
Helele'ike'oha Stream

© 2010 Wizard Publications, Inc.

An idyllic Nahiku pond that looks so perfect it can't possibly be real.

adventure, consider a **powered hang glider flight** in a seated ultralight along the Hana coast. The views along the coast are unreal. See page 184 for more.

WAI'ANAPANAPA
BLACK SAND BEACH

Just past the 32 mile marker is the road to **Wai'anapanapa Park**. (Gee,

that really rolls off the tongue, huh? Blew a gasket in the old spellchecker on *that* one. It sounds like WHY-A-NAH-PAH NAH-PAH.) The park is clean and well maintained. They even have cabins for rent. Other facilities include restrooms, showers, picnic tables and camping. It's got two other things going for it. One, there is a freshwater cave that makes a

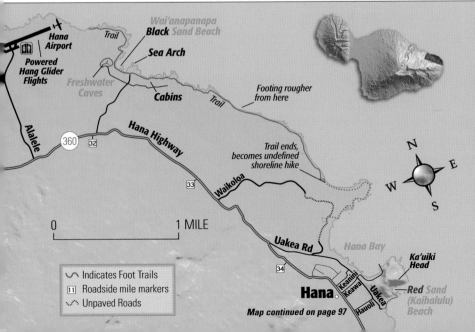

Map continued on page 97

Wai'anapanapa State Park has the only volcanic black sand beach (created from a lava flow) on Maui. Good facilities, freshwater caves; the only thing difficult about this park is pronouncing it.

great place for a dip. Two, it has a volcanic black sand beach.

First, the **spring-fed freshwater caves**: These are probably the remnants of lava tubes. There are two, though only one is suitable for swimming. The water level rises and falls each day with the tide, on which the fresh water floats. A little sea water mixes with the fresh water, meaning the water is slightly brackish but crystal clear. The temperature is very cool, though not painfully so. There are two small chambers that snake their way back a bit. A short loop trail drops three stories and circles the two caves. There's a Hawaiian legend posted on a sign near the loop trail. Occasionally, prolonged dry spells combine with low tide translating to little water in the cave.

If you've heard of **volcanic black sand beaches**, you may have thought they were all on the Big Island. *Au contraire.* **Pa'iloa Beach** here at Wai'anapanapa Park is 100 or so feet wide and attests to

the newness of the land here. The beach was formed when lava flowed and fountained into the sea near here, shattering on contact with the ocean. Fragments smashed against each other and formed the sand you see.

A REAL GEM

(Don't believe books that tell you that the beach was formed by cliff erosion.) Maybe Rome wasn't built in a day, but this beach may have been, because these type of beaches are often formed in days or weeks. We've watched black sand beaches being created on the Big Island, and it's an awesome sight. They usually have a short life span since the source of the sand stops as soon as the lava stops flowing. Usually within a few hundred to a thousand years they vanish as the ocean gradually sweeps the precious sand away. (White sand beaches have organic sources like coral and shells, which are renewed.) Occasionally the sand is deposited in a perfectly shaped bay like this one, which allows it to stay a little longer. Some lava flows nearby are 500 years old according to a dated sample taken a mile south of here. There's a pretty coastal hike that leads to the source of all this sand. It's described under HIKING on page 200.

Older islands like Kaua'i and O'ahu have no volcanic black sand beaches. (They can sometimes have the other type of black sand beach, like the one at Hana Bay, caused when water chips flecks of lava from stream beds and piles them up onshore.) Since the sand supply here is finite, please try to refrain from taking samples back home with you, except the stowaways lodged in your bathing suit. Don't swim during high surf as currents can form in the bay.

HANA

Hana doesn't hit you, it seeps into you. Living on Maui, we had driven through Hana many times and thought we knew it well. But it wasn't until the first time we spent a week in Hana that we truly connected with it. The peace that Hana exudes can only penetrate when you're here at leisure, not on a mission. Today, Hana is one of our favorite places to go to get away from the hellacious rigors of guidebook writing. (You have no idea how hard it was to write that last sentence with a straight face.) If you're on Maui for a week or more, we strongly suggest you consider spending the last couple of days in Hana.

Hana has the reputation of being a rainy place. In fact, they get just over 80 inches of rain per year at the Hana Airport, though it varies quite a bit. That may sound like a lot (actually it *is* a lot), but hidden in that number are two things you need to know. First, it's *way* less rain than what they get farther up the mountain (which is what feeds the waterfalls), and it's less than what they get to the northwest, around Nahiku. This is

because Hana is relatively flat and the orographic rain engine that waters most of Hawai'i misses Hana more than most people think. (The photo on the cover is typical. Notice how Hana itself is sunny, with the clouds starting farther uphill?) Second, the great majority of the rain falls at night and early mornings due to the same effect. During the day, heavy five-minute showers also contribute to those rain stats. Don't get us wrong. You can still come for a week and have it rain every day. They occasionally get monstrous rains, especially in the winter. It can happen anywhere in Hawai'i. But it's much less likely in Hana than you may guess by simply looking at raw stats.

Things move slowly in Hana, and if you try to rush, you'll only end up frustrated. Businesses may close for any reason. The only bank is open 1½ hours a day. (How's *that* for bankers' hours?)

Here are some of the things you'll want to check out near Hana.

HANA BAY

Hana Bay has a large, black sand beach. The sand source is lava eroded from a nearby stream. This is usually the safest place to swim along the coast. You can grab something to eat here (see Tutu's, page 98) and eat it at the shore.

On the north (left) side of the bay you may spot an area where the waves come in and seem to die at a certain place. Called Ke'anini, Hawaiian legend says there was once a visiting Tahitian chief who wanted to go surfing there. He asked the gods to give him waves, and this they did. As he was surfing, two beautiful local girls saw the handsome chief from shore and fell in love with him. Competing with each other for his attention, they both removed their pa'us—skirts—the only things they wore. The chief saw them and was so startled by the sight that he stopped right there in the water, and the

Little gems, like this tiny red sand pocket beach near Hana Bay (not the larger, more famous Red Sand Beach), are here to be discovered for those not in a hurry to get to the "Seven Sacred Pools."

wave went no farther. That is why the waves always stop at that surf site today.

On the right side of the bay is the **Hana Pier**. Nearby, there is a trail that leads 200 or so yards along **Ka'uiki Head**. There's a plaque at the end of the trail marking the spot near a cave where Ka'ahumanu (King Kamehameha the Great's "favorite" wife) was born. The real reasons to take the trail are to visit a small but unknown **red sand pocket beach** that varies seasonally (not *the* Red Sand Beach mentioned later) and to get up close and personal with the geology of this part of the island a little farther along. This hill was formed in geologically recent times when a volcanic vent sprayed lava high into the air. The hill came into being as airborne, gas-frothed lava was caught by the trade winds and piled up here. Near the plaque area you see places where globs of lava plopped and piled up. The deep burgundy color (especially at the small

beach) is from iron in the lava. It's literally rusting before your eyes. There's an isthmus connecting the end of the trail to a small islet that houses a light beacon. During real calm seas you can cross it. One caveat: The beginning part of the trail near the pier was faint to non-existent at press time thanks to a small landslide, so be careful there. The cove below the end of the trail is an excellent snorkel spot, and it's common to see kayakers there.

If you ever decide that you need to make a stand somewhere, this hill is the place to do it. For generations invaders from the Big Island would capture this hill and were nearly impossible to dislodge due to the hill's easy defense. From up top they could harass area residents and plan general mischief.

RED SAND BEACH

Though we usually describe all beaches in the BEACHES chapter, Hana is so far that you'd never come here simply for a day at the beach. So we're deviating from our usual format and describing Hana's beaches here. The far side of Ka'uiki Hill hides one the area's more exotic looking beaches, **Red Sand Beach** (Hawaiian name is **Kaihalulu**). There's a photo on page 169. It's made from the same crumbling red and black cinders that make up the hill. The swimming is often poor except during calm seas. There's a strip of jagged lava that forms a semi-pool at the head of the beach, but it sometimes has the perverse effect during high seas and high tide of making the water more chaotic and disorienting, like swimming in a washing machine. The snorkeling opportunities are usually marginal. To make matters worse, the trail is on the side of the hill, with loose cinders making the footing awkward in several spots. (And you wouldn't want to slip and fall down the side of the hill—regular shoes are preferred over beach shoes). And one part of the trail is along the shoreline, exposing you to rogue waves.

In the past the landowner, Hana Ranch, had NO TRESPASSING signs to dissuade you. We're *thrilled* that they finally saw the light and now allow access under a Hawai'i law that clears them of liability. (So don't complain to them if you get hurt; *you* are legally responsible for your own safety.) So we often have marginal swimming much of the time, marginal snorkeling and an awkward, potentially injurious five-minute walk. Is it worth going to? To us, it sure is! This is a striking beach, at least worth a look. The rainbow of colors in the lava cinders along the way, the electric blue waters outside the cove, the menacing-looking lava rock inside the bay, the ironwood trees, the layered cinder walls and the untouched beauty make this a memorable place to visit. It's popular and sometimes used by nudists, though nudity is particularly resented by the Hana community and

Gobs of life, gobs of color. The Hana Highway rarely disappoints.

locals sometimes make their displeasure known in a big way, so you might want to take your bare *da kines* elsewhere.

To get there, park on Uakea near Hauoli. (See map on page 97.) Even though it's a dead-end street, make sure you park facing the correct direction. Furiously *under*worked Hana cops will give tickets for this heinous crime. Just before the Sea Ranch Cottages there's a large lawn area owned by the county. Look past the second lamp post on the right for a path leading downhill. Continue straight down, taking a left just near the shore. It's easier to navigate than it sounds. Don't hike if the trail is muddy, and be careful on the slippery cinders. All told, it's about a five-minute walk.

KOKI BEACH

This beach is a mixture of black sand (from the nearby crumbling hill) along with white sand from pulverized coral. It's a good place to sit and observe the ocean under the nearby trees with a dramatic view of the red hill behind you, a sea arch off to the left and the coconut tree-topped 'Alau Island off to the right. Swimming is unprotected and can be hazardous, except when calm. Boogie boarding can be good here. The shape and direction the beach faces make it a good place for beach-combing. Fishing nets, Japanese net glass floats and other flotsam often wash ashore. Local residents have made strong efforts to keep down the litter that once plagued Koki. Be careful not to leave anything valuable in your car here or at Hamoa as we've seen the beach cased many times by young thieves looking for an opportunity.

The large hill next to the beach is called Ka Iwi o Pele, said to contain the bones of the volcano goddess Pele, left

Hamoa Beach, in the early morning, is where you'll find the best bodysurfing on the island.

behind after she had a battle with her sister. The hill and adjacent land is currently owned by Oprah Winfrey.

HAMOA BEACH

A great beach! Tons and tons of fine salt and pepper sand, some shade, showers, clear water and the best bodysurfing on the island make this one of the island's primo beaches. The thickness of the sand toward the middle **A REAL GEM** is so great that you don't have to worry as much about stubbing your toe on rocks as at most north- or east-facing Hawai'i beaches. (Though it's always possible.) Toward the center of the beach the sand drops abruptly a little way offshore, meaning that the waves tend to break at the same spot each time—exactly what you want for bodysurfing. If you've never done this before, be real careful and only do it on small waves. The ocean is unprotected here—no reef to break things up—so the waves have more power here and can drill you into the sand if you're not cautious.

To bodysurf, you simply stand in place, wait for a wave to break right about where you are, and jump forward with your arms extended, turning yourself into a surfboard. I use a mask and snorkel while doing it to keep the salt out of my eyes since I wear contacts. (The mask sometimes gets torn off, so to keep from losing it, I bite down harder on the snorkel when I feel the wave coming.) Many an hour we've spent bodysurfing this beach. Don't try it during high surf; it's too dangerous. Snorkeling is marginal, and there are currents at the two ends of the beach; best to stay in the middle. Located at the south end of Haneo'o Road, there's a paved path leading down. Make sure you park facing the right way. There are other facilities that are for guests of Hotel Hana Maui, but the showers and restrooms are used by all.

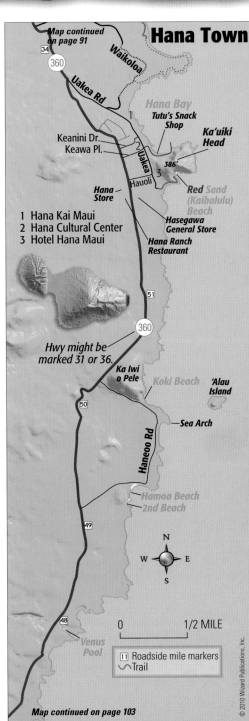

Hana Town

Map continued on page 91

Tutu's Snack Shop

Ka'uiki Head

Keanini Dr.
Keawa Pl.

386'

Hana Bay

Red Sand (Kaihalulu) Beach

Hana Store

Hauoli

1 Hana Kai Maui
2 Hana Cultural Center
3 Hotel Hana Maui

Hasegawa General Store

Hana Ranch Restaurant

Hwy might be marked 31 or 36.

Ka Iwi o Pele

Koki Beach

'Alau Island

Sea Arch

Haneoo Rd

Hamoa Beach
2nd Beach

N
W · E
S

Venus Pool

0   1/2 MILE

11 Roadside mile markers
Trail

© 2010 Wizard Publications, Inc.

Map continued on page 103

Hana's offshore 'Alau Island.

Around the rocks to the right (south) is another beach, which is usually deserted. Best to swim to it as the rock scrambling may be difficult.

DINING IN HANA

We normally put dining reviews in the DINING chapter, but we're putting them here for the same reason we put beaches here. Hana is so far out, *nobody* drives there just for the food.

Hana Ranch Restaurant (248–8255)

Arguably, this used to be the worst restaurant on Maui, and our criticism, however harsh, was understated (in our opinion) but became notorious on Maui. (OK, perhaps we were a bit over the top when we begged *don't eat lunch here, don't eat lunch here, don't eat lunch here* at the beginning of the review.) Anyway there were only two places to eat lunch in Hana at the time, and this place had the luxury to be as bad as they wanted and still get away with it. We're pleased to report, however, that they have improved *a lot* since then. The menu is mostly ½-pound burgers, some

sandwiches and salads inside; add some local-style items and shave off a few bucks at the outside window. The burgers aren't great, but hey…they're just burgers. And their salads are downright decent and usually fresh-tasting. The setting at the restaurant outdoor tables is quite nice. $14–$20 for lunch or early dinner. Open from 11:30 a.m.–8 p.m. daily. No bathing suits allowed.

Tutu's Snack Shop (248–8224)

Though essentially a burger shack, it's right on Hana Bay, which is its only redeeming quality. When we first started reviewing Tutu's, the service was slow but they had great breakfast sandwiches. And each year it seems to get slower and slower, and the breakfast sandwiches are now bad. Open 9 a.m.–4 p.m. (*roughly*), they have burgers, good fries (when they don't overcook them), hot dogs, chili, plate lunches, sometimes teriyaki chicken, etc. The place is pretty disheveled…and did we mention that they are *slooow?* $5–$10. By the way, the dark cliff just before Tutu's at the base of the hill was used as a bake-oven to cook the warriors taken captive here during a battle for the hill in 1782. No, they weren't eaten, and let's not hear any cracks about what the special of the day at Tutu's is, huh?

Travaasa Hana (248-8211)

This is Hana's version of fine dining. The food is quite excellent, though expensive. Breakfast prices are confiscatory with $18 oatmeal and $19 pancakes. Dinner is a small but well-chosen menu of steak and seafood utilizing local ingredients for $35-$45. Presentation is nice and it's soothing and relaxing, but service can be *slooow* at dinner. Is it overpriced? Yeah...so? *Whaddaya-gonnado?* It's Hana and this may be your only choice for dinner. Dress code is enforced. Collared shirts and slacks or nice shorts for men and a similar caliber of clothing for women. Otherwise, you'll have to eat at the adjacent bar. Reservations are *required* (even when things are slow).

As an alternative, if you're staying in Hana, you can always pick up something cookable at Hasegawa's Store and fix it back at your hotel/condo/house.

ALSO IN HANA

The Hana Cultural Center (248-8622) is a tiny museum on Ke'anini Street with a small display of Hawaiian stone tools, quilts, shells, Chinese and Japanese bottles as well as re-creations of thatched huts and a canoe shed. (Dugout canoes required serious labor, and the ancients always built a garage for them.) The museum is somewhat interesting but expendable if your time is precious.

Hina Malailena's Hana Village Marketplace is a series of market stalls built years ago but never occupied. There are rumblings that, after more than a decade of the bureaucratic two-step, it'll finally be opening, but that rumbling has been going on for a long time.

Hana-Maui Kayak & Snorkel Reef Watch (248-7711) has short, fun kayak/snorkel trips at Hana Bay. For $89 you take a 3-hour tour of Hana Bay and/or some nearby areas. Depending on seas you may get some nice snorkeling, and owner Kevin is a good guide. Extras include Rx masks, rash guards, digital photos of you, and for a bit extra you can try their under-water scooter.

Hasegawa General Store (248-8231) has the most widely diverse assortment of...stuff we've ever seen. That's the only word that describes it. Stuff. Where would you find men's dress socks? Next to the shower curtain rings, of course. And the aloha shirts? To the right of the epoxy. How about fishing spears? Across from the movie rentals. Really need some muffler tape? Turn right when you see the red cabbage; it's between the dried cuttlefish and the lawn mowers. By the way, they also have tabis, great for walking on wet rocks. (They're next to the galvanized pipe.) Some items are a decent deal. Milk was actually cheaper here than at the confiscatory Safeway in Kahului. Other items can be breathtakingly expensive. (I remember going in for a few items once. When I checked out, the total came to $68. I was convinced that this must be a running total from the last few customers...*it wasn't*.)

HANA HIGHWAY BEST BETS

Best View of Coastline—End Nahiku Rd.
Best Bodysurfing—Hamoa Beach
Best Exotic Beach—Red Sand Beach
Best Place for a Cool Dip—Cave #1 at Wai'anapanapa
Best Place to see Every Shade of Green—Nahiku
Best Place to See a Cliff Diver—Ching's Pond
Best Attraction to Skip—Twin Falls
Best Breakfast on the Way—Charley's, or Anthony's in Pa'ia

What a difference from the wet, windward side. The dry mountaintop above Kaupo is 9,000 feet high.

After the inspiring drive to Hana, what else can there be? *Plenty!* Past Hana the road goes through beautiful Kipahulu, past the 'Ohe'o Gulch (formerly called the Seven Sacred Pools) and along the bottom of the island, where jungly forest is replaced with wide open expansiveness. The road to the pools is good. Past that you have a decision to make. To go around the bottom...or not to go? The answer is on page 73.

KIPAHULU

If you've driven the entire Hana Highway today, it's easy to fall into a sort of beauty fatigue by now. In fact, it wasn't until we stayed in Hana the first time and drove this part of the road in the morning that we realized how utterly gorgeous it was. Only when we were fresh and had allowed Hana to melt our bones did Kipahulu seep in.

The mountains are so stunning and the waterfalls unspoiled; it's hard to believe that the highway can still deliver after all these miles. Those making the all-day drive are now getting tired. It's after noon and they are looking for the payoff at 'Ohe'o Gulch, AKA Seven Sacred Pools. But if you're lucky enough to be in Kipahulu in the morning, when the light is best, you have the highway pretty much to yourself, and any waterfalls you find are yours and yours alone.

The mile markers have changed and are now counting down. (Until 15, then they jump back to 20 and start going down again—*go figga*.) Leaving Hana, there is a surprise waiting for you if you have time to venture to it. It's one of the largest and nicest freshwater pools on the island. Called **Waioka** by the Hawaiians, its physical appearance has spawned a new age name that seems to have stuck— **Venus Pool**. It looks like a painting that you would normally dismiss as being too contrived, too perfect, yet **A REAL GEM** here it is. It's located next to the ocean with a hala tree-capped ball of lava symmetrically dividing the sea view. There you'll find numerous places that people jump from, deep water in several spots, the pounding ocean just on the other side of the gravel and some perfect areas on the mountain side from which to sit and cogitate. The aura is unforgettable. If you go in the morning or late afternoon, you'll sometimes have it to yourself. The water is slightly brackish (salty) from the ocean but usually very clean since it is partially spring-fed and not dependent on the seasonal stream it resides in. During whale season we've seen the leviathans breaching close to shore. All told, it's a fifteen-minute hike from your car. If you're look-

ing for a unique place to swim or ponder, this will definitely ring your WOW meter.

To get there, park on the side of the highway just past the 48 mile marker. Near the Hana side of the bridge is a trail toward the ocean near a sign erected by Hana Ranch reminding you that a state law protects them if you hurt yourself on their land while recreating. (Which is true; *you* are responsible for your own safety in this case.) After years of denying access here, this is a giant and gracious move on Hana Ranch's part, which we applaud. As a cattle ranch they understandably don't want you messing with their barbed-wire fence, and the land in the gulch itself is state land, so you can start the trail that way without hurting the fence. Just before the path hits a weird, large, round concrete…thing (it's actually an old Portuguese bread oven), veer to the right toward the stream. Be careful of slippery rocks, and don't jump unless you've checked out what's below. (Look around to find the best

Sunrise at Venus Pool. Could anything be more surreal?

place to get in and out of the water.) Avoid if the flow is too heavy from the stream. Occasionally, very long dry spells make the water a bit stagnant.

Weather permitting, look for the Big Island peeking above the clouds. Its massive mountains, over 13,000 feet tall, are impressive to see.

Back on the highway, there may be a small waterfall at the 46 mile marker. Then, before the 45 mile marker, you'll notice a **cross** erected in memory of Helio Koaeloa, one of the earliest Hawaiian Catholic priests. The trail lead-

ing to the bottom is treacherous and not worth the bother. There's sometimes a pretty little waterfall near the sign called **Paihi Falls**.

After you cross the Wailua Stream, yet another *(sigh)* sweet waterfall called **Wailua Falls** on the next stream awaits. (Why isn't Wailua Falls on the nearby Wailua Stream?) Wailua is best in the morning when the sun shines on it. The flow varies *a lot*. (There's a photo of it on page 28.) Its water pattern can be exceptionally idyllic—even for

WATERFALL ALERT!

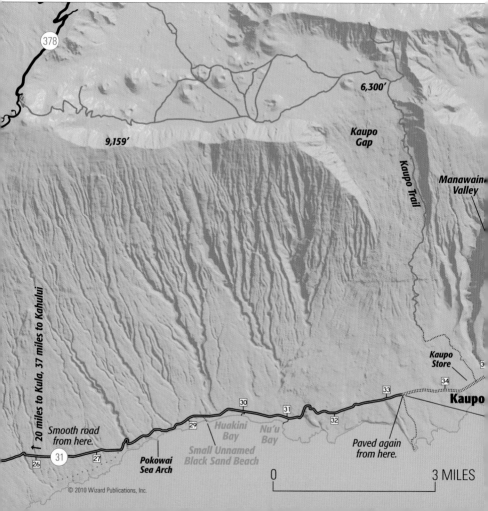

© 2010 Wizard Publications, Inc.

Maui—or a light, pathetic trickle. Later in the day vendors sometimes congregate there, selling handmade souvenirs.

Are we at the Seven Sacred Pools yet? No, sorry. You'll have to endure yet another falls called **Pua'a-lu'u Falls** just past here. We apologize for the inconvenience. The falls are to the left of the bridge and also fall under it. Driving past these falls, look for a **Blessed Mother Shrine** in a remnant from an old lava tube. It's lovingly maintained by a retired woman in the area. A priest chose

WATERFALL ALERT!

this location because Pua'a-lu'u Falls always flows, so there's always water available nearby for blessings and for cleaning the statue.

Those Seven Sacred Pools are just ahead before the 42 mile marker.

'OHE'O GULCH— AKA SEVEN SACRED POOLS

OK, enough of these single waterfall scenes; now comes the big daddy. This series of waterfalls and pools at the shoreline is the most popular attraction in all of east Maui. Why? Because the old name,

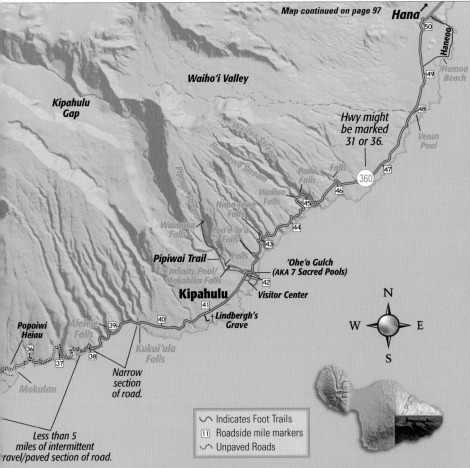

Map continued on page 97

Hana

Waiho'i Valley

Kipahulu Gap

Hwy might be marked 31 or 36.

Hamoa Beach

Venus Pool

Paihi Falls

Wailua Falls

Haha-'awe Falls

Waimoku Falls

Pua'a-lu'u Falls

Pipiwai Trail

Infinity Pool/ Makahiku Falls

'Ohe'o Gulch (AKA 7 Sacred Pools)

Visitor Center

Kipahulu

Lindbergh's Grave

Popoiwi Heiau

Alelele Falls

Kukui'ula Falls

Narrow section of road.

Mokulau

Less than 5 miles of intermittent travel/paved section of road.

N / W / E / S

⌣ Indicates Foot Trails
11 Roadside mile markers
⁙ Unpaved Roads

Southeast Maui/Kipahulu & Kaupo

Seven Sacred Pools, sounds so appealing you just gotta check 'em out. Also because the swimming is usually so good and the setting so beautiful. What's not to love? Back when nobody had ever **A REAL GEM** heard of Hana, the owner of the Hotel Hana Maui wanted desperately to attract people here. He had a choice: Tell people they could visit the fabulous 'Ohe'o Gulch or the wondrous *Seven Sacred Pools* (which he made up). Which do *you* think looked better on a brochure? (For the record, there are not seven of them, and they never were sacred.)

When a retired airline executive from the mainland named Sam Pryor planned to build a house right near the pools back in 1960, articles began to appear in local papers warning that access to the pools would become a thing of the past. Pryor realized that the pools were so beloved by residents that he contacted the people who sold him the land and insisted that they trade it for land elsewhere, saying the pools should belong to everyone. He later contacted his old friend Laurance Rockefeller and convinced him and others to buy 52 acres around the pools and eventually donate it to Haleakala National Park. So today, the pools are protected forever.

The park became one of the best places in the world to jump off waterfalls because they were so user-friendly, and for decades people came from all over the world to do just that. Falls, pool, falls, pool, falls, pool. It's an ideal playground where visitors jumped for joy into deep pools till their hearts content. But an accident, lawsuit and subsequent giant settlement in 2009 changed all that. Park officials responded by banning jumping off anything, plastered the area with warning signs, and rangers vigorously patrol the pools. You will be fined and perhaps even arrested if you jump off anything. Their message is quite clear: *We want to save you from yourself...and we want to save ourselves from your lawyer.*

They will let you swim in the lower pools—*sometimes*. But they'll often close them off to public access at the mere hint of rain up in the mountains (which happens more days than not). Over the course of months, they were closed more times than they were open for "safety reasons."

When you can swim here, it's absolutely great. And even if you can't swim, it's still drop dead gorgeous. Whether you want to swim, hike or just watch, the park is a great place to polish off a day. People *staying* in Hana have it best, because they can get here before the crowds do. There is often nobody at the falls in the morning. In the afternoon, expect *a lot* of people to join you in the fun.

Park at the lot past the 42 mile marker. The lot sometimes fills up around peak time (2 p.m.). The loop trail from the lot to the pools and back is just over ½ mile.

Part of Haleakala National Park, it's $10 per car for entrance here, sometimes on a quasi-honor system. This fee also gets you into the park at Haleakala's summit and vice versa, so save your receipt.

Camping is available; see page 175. There are restrooms at the park *but no water*. At the visitor center there are opportunities to learn about the Hawaiian culture and their relationship with the land. You can also go on guided hikes or visit a taro-farming area. Check with park personnel to find out what's available.

The huge valley above the pools, stretching all the way up the mountain to Haleakala Crater, is a wondrous area. Called **Kipahulu Gap**, it has resisted the introduction of most foreign plants brought by man, making it one of

Whether you get to swim in them or not, the pools at 'Ohe'o Gulch are some of the most scenic on the island.

The Infinity Pool rests at the top of a 200-foot waterfall. Just make sure you stay at the right end.

the more pristine forests in the state. Endemic birds and plants, found nowhere else in the world, thrive in the waterlogged rain forest above you. It has been designated a biological reserve, and entry past the end of the Pipiwai Trail is closed. Park officials are in a never-ending battle with pigs in this valley. Despite their best efforts, pigs abound here and can wreak havoc with endemic plants.

PIPIWAI TRAIL

Above the pools lies one of the best hikes on the island. You certainly won't have it to yourself, but you get more *wowie* views and settings per mile on this trail than almost any other. All told, it's almost 2 miles each way and you gain 650 feet (not 800, as the park brochure says) from the highway, though the grade is fairly gentle. (The first part is the steepest, and it's not that steep.) Called the Pipiwai Trail, it's smashing and takes anywhere from 2½–5 hours, depending on how much of a hurry you're in.

Trails are usually described in HIKING, but we deviate here to make things sim-

pler because there's no chance you woke up, decided you wanted a good hike and drove way over to these-here parts to do it. The trailhead is down the highway toward the 'Ohe'o Bridge near the 42 mile marker. (See map on page 103.)

The trail basically follows the stream. You'll want mosquito repellent in places if you deviate from the main path. Early into the hike you see a concrete derrick with a pulley on top. Another is on the far side of the bridge. Back when sugar was king, they were used to haul sugar cane across the gorge on its way to the mill down the road. Around ⅔ mile into the hike you come to the Makahiku Falls overlook. This massive falls drops 200 feet.

Shortly past this you have an opportunity to deviate onto a side path to the right of the main trail. The park doesn't seem to be encouraging people to take this side trail much anymore because of liability concerns. If you take it anyway and if conditions are right, it makes for the kind of photo that you can put on your desk and be assured that people walking by will stop and exclaim, *My*

God, where is that?! If you've ever seen an infinity pool at a resort—the kind that have no lip to give the impression while inside that it goes on forever—imagine that very same pool at the top of a 200-foot waterfall! This **Infinity Pool** has a row of thick rocks to the right that keeps you from going over

DIVERSION ALERT!

during normal flows. To the left is where water cascades over during normal flows (so don't go there!). Needless to say, you need to evaluate the setting for yourself. Too much water flow would be ugly, and you always need to be aware in any stream of the potential for flash floods. While in the pool, all you see is the ocean beyond as you hear the water cascading beneath you. We've seen airplanes dip below the field of view—flying below us—and white-tailed tropic birds soar in the valley beyond the falls. What a scene!

Sometimes the flow grinds to a trickle, making it less dramatic. Behind the pool is a surreal, plant-draped bend in the stream. If you're feeling adventurous, you can scramble over the rockface on the right side, swim across a pool, then scramble over another rockface, and you'll find a large, pretty waterfall that flows even when the Infinity Pool doesn't. (Much of its water percolates under the rocks and gurgles out at the base of the falls below the Infinity Pool.)

Back on the trail, you'll go through a gate, and in a few minutes there's an intersection. Check out the wise-looking banyan tree with its aerial roots along the way. Without a doubt, banyans are the most ancient-looking trees you'll ever see.

A hundred yards after the banyan you can take a side trail to one of the louder waterfalls you'll find. It free falls and smacks onto rocks, then runs into a particularly emerald green pool that has under-

cut the mountain, forming a cave. You can see more of the falls by following the rock steps to the right.

More diversions await, including a pool at least a football field long. Then a pair of bridges soon enable you to cross the magnificent stream you've been following. (And yes, foolhardy buggahs jump off the first one here, too.) The vantage point from the bridge is tongue-wagging.

What next? Why, a beautiful, thick, vigorous bamboo forest, of course. (Bamboo, which is a grass, makes an excellent walking stick.) After the long, impressive boardwalk—constructed to keep you out of the perpetually muddy areas—you eventually come to the end of the line. (Well, you still have to go back, of course.) Slicing 400 feet down the back of a three-way sheer wall of lava, **Waimoku Falls** marks the instantaneous beginning of this canyon. What a way to end a trail! You could walk under the falls, but remember that any debris falling from above will feel like getting hit by a meteorite. Did you bring your hard hat? Best to view it from a little distance. During abnormally dry times in the summer the water flow can diminish somewhat, but it's mostly spring-fed, so its flow is not as rain-dependent.

PAST THE PARK

Back on the highway, about $\frac{1}{10}$ mile past the 41 mile marker is an easy-to-miss paved road that leads to **Palapala**

DIVERSION ALERT!

Ho'omau Church where the world's greatest aviator, **Charles Lindbergh**, is buried. See box on the page 109. Lindbergh's grave is through the cement post openings, and straight past the older graves on the corner. Just past the grave is a tiny park. Walk to the far end for a scrumptious view of the jagged coastline, or munch on a snack at the shaded picnic tables.

Towering Waimoku Falls dwarfs a lowly hiker.

At ³/₁₀ mile past the 41 mile marker you'll see the **Laulima Fruit Stand**. They use a bicycle to power their blender. That's kind of misleading because *you* have to do the peddling. Makes you wonder where they hide the team of cyclists that must be necessary to power their refrigerator and coffee machine. The smoothies aren't that great, even after you work up a sweat to grind them up.

At ⁶/₁₀ mile past the 40 mile marker there's a small one-car pullout. If you walk across the street, there's an utterly glorious view of the Kipahulu coastline. The road's about to get narrower for a few miles with many blind turns, so be alert for oncoming cars.

At the bottom of this first valley, pull over past the second set of guard-rails into the short gravel driveway to the ocean. Looking back the way you came, you'll *usually* see **Kukui'ula Falls** plunging into the ocean. (You can't reach the falls by land, and we have the scars to prove it.) It only occasionally runs dry.

OK, here's your last chance to frolic at a waterfall, and it's a sweet one. About ⅓ mile past the 39 mile marker is a white bridge with the word ALELELE on it. There are several trails, all leading 5–10 minutes inland. It's fairly easy (though you'll have to cross the stream at one point, usually keeping your feet dry). **WATERFALL ALERT! Alelele Falls** is around 40–50 feet high and has the cleanest, clearest and coldest water you'll find. We believe that it's partially spring-fed, which accounts for its clarity. The lower pool is lined with lots of pebbles, making entry easy on your feet. The pool's about 6 feet deep. Bring your camera; you'll really like this one. It occasionally slows to a trickle, but not often.

At ¼ past the 36 mile marker at a grassy corner up on the hill in front of you are the barely visible remains of the

Where Legends Come to Die

Kipahulu will be forever distinguished as the final resting place of aviation great Charles Lindbergh. Most of those from our generation know very little about Lindbergh, and that's a shame. In 1927 the world held its collective breath as this 25-year-old airmail carrier fought weather and fatigue-induced hallucinations for $33^1/2$ hours to become the first man to cross the Atlantic solo in an airplane. One of the greatest feats of his time, it was celebrated as much in its day as the moonshot was years later. Lindbergh hadn't been able to sleep the night before his flight left New York, so when he landed in Paris, he had been awake for nearly 60 hours. Some 150,000 screaming well-wishers met his plane when it landed in France. (More than 4 million later turned out for him when he returned to New York.) He had no idea when he landed in Paris that he had the world in the palm of his hand. All he wanted was to take a nap.

After the flight, Charles Lindbergh became the century's first media superstar. His life was followed with more interest than any man alive at the time. He represented the very heart and soul of aviation and was a worldwide hero. When his baby was kidnapped a few years later, the ransom demands went on for $2^1/2$ months, and the baby was eventually found dead just a few miles from his house. (The infant never even made it out of the house alive; he died when the kidnapper's ladder broke on the way out the window.) The Lindbergh baby kidnapping trial was called the trial of the century (before anybody had ever heard of O.J.).

In later life, when Lindbergh's old friend Sam Pryor told him, "I have found heaven on earth, and it is at Kipahulu, Maui," Lindbergh visited his friend and was immediately smitten with this part of Maui. He built a home here and spent the last six years of his life in East Maui.

In 1972 Lindbergh was diagnosed with lymphosarcoma. Over time he tried various treatments in New York, but the cancer eventually spread to his lungs. His doctors told him his time was very short. He phoned his physician in Hawai'i and told him, "I have eight to ten days to live, and I want to come back home to die. I would rather spend two days alive on Maui than two months alive here in New York." Against his New York doctors' wishes, he was flown on a stretcher in a commercial 747 (the other passengers had no idea who was behind the curtain in first class) back to his beloved Maui. He spent the next week meticulously planning all facets of his funeral, even designing his coffin and picking the lining. Lindbergh wanted the wild plum tree next to his grave removed, but his grave digger convinced him to let it live there with him. Just over a week later, on August 26, 1974, he died. As the small funeral procession passed the tourists visiting the "Seven Sacred Pools," none had any idea who it was for. Fewer than 15 people were invited to attend, and Lindbergh had asked that his pallbearers wear their work clothes. A Hawaiian hymn was sung as the casket was lowered into the ground, and one of his sons said the hymn "just soared out and away with the wind and the crashing of the waves below us."

A short distance from Lindbergh are the graves of Sam Pryor (the friend who lured Lindbergh to Maui) and Pryor's wife. Between Pryor's and Lindbergh's graves you'll find six small graves. These were Sam's "children," including Keiki, George, Lani, and his favorite, Kippy. None have last names because his "children" (as he always referred to them) were actually Asian gibbons. Sam took these apes with him wherever he went. Townsfolk rarely saw him without one of his children.

The inscription on Lindbergh's grave, from the 139th Psalm, reads, "If I take the wings of the morning, and dwell in the uttermost parts of the sea." The rest of that passage, not on the stone, is, "Even there would Thy hand lead me. And Thy right hand would hold me."

In remote and sparsely populated Kaupo, St. Joseph's Church, built in 1862, only holds services if there's a fifth Sunday in a month.

Popoiwi Heiau, a religious structure. They aren't visually interesting. What's unusual about it is that it wasn't made by the Hawaiians. It was made by the people who were here *before* them. You see, when the first people arrived here from the Marquesas Islands around 300 A.D., they lived untouched for about 700 years. Then another group came, this time from Tahiti. They killed and subdued the first inhabitants, driving them ever farther northwest. (The first inhabitants were called Menehune by the second arrivals, a derogatory term denoting small in class and stature. The legend was later distorted by westerners who didn't understand, and Menehunes became the Hawaiian equivalent of elves.) The last remnants the Menehunes left behind are some decidedly un-Hawaiian carvings on tiny islands northwest of the main Hawaiian Islands.

Before the 35 mile marker there's a road on your left that angles back toward the ocean and leads to a church and cemetery. It's a dirt road, but 2WD vehicles are usually OK unless it's been raining.

DIVERSION ALERT! Drive to the end and you'll see why it's called **Mokulau**, or "many islets." Dozens of lava outcroppings in the water defying the relentless waves make a dramatic photo op as the water pounds and twists to get past them. Keep an eye out for Hawaiian monk seals that sometimes beach themselves here. The church at Mokulau has restrooms. If you see signs saying the road is private (or a chain blocking access), it's not true. County records show (and the church owner confirms) that the road and the parcel at the end of the road are *state* land. The church and Kaupo community put up the signs and unlocked chain to "prevent casual visitors" because some unsavory residents were abusing the area at night. If you go, please pack out anything you bring in to help their efforts.

Kaupo Store past the 35 mile marker is your last chance to pick up snacks. Mostly sodas, chips, ice cream and candy mixed with an interesting collection of antique cameras, clocks and assorted knickknacks. There's also a restroom out back. Check the dates on any food here as freshness this far out can be hard to maintain.

We were once at the Kaupo Store when a visitor noted to the woman behind the counter how much Kaupo had *grown* in the 30 years since her last visit. "How has it grown?" asked the woman behind the counter. Lots of new buildings, the visitor replied. The counter woman and I exchanged confused glances, and then she patiently explained to the visitor that the only thing that had changed in Kaupo in the last 30 years was that so-and-so had added a new room to his house and Auntie Jane opened a lunch wagon (which is now gone). That's it! The moral of the story: *Nothing* ever changes in Kaupo.

Looking around in this part of the island, it's easy to think that nothing important ever happened along here. Actually, this area was subject to a vicious invasion in 1775 by the king of the Big Island. He occupied the area and treated his captives so badly that they called it the war of Kalaehohoa (meaning, roughly, *the war where they beat our brains out with*

clubs). When Maui's king responded, he routed the Big Island king along the shoreline below the 33 mile marker. One of his Big Island lieutenants in this defeat was Kamehameha, who would later become king of all the islands. Kamehameha barely escaped with his life.

At 1½ miles past the 33 mile marker (32 is missing) just before the road zigzags is one of our favorite spots to pull over and enjoy the views of Haleakala and the broad expanse of shoreline in the late afternoon. The deep gorges, formed by sporadic but intense rain, show up well in the afternoon. Look to the top of the mountain and you'll see the **Kaupo Gap**, the large, wide opening at the top of the mountain. At one time the gap, caused by erosion, was at least 5,000 feet deep, perhaps deeper, and cut into the very core of the mountain. (There's a similar gap on the other side of the mountain, meaning the volcano was essentially cut into two halves.) Later, lava again poured from the summit, filling the great Kaupo canyon to the shallow level you see now. If you look

Even in the harsh waters off Kaupo, a net fisherman has to eat. This one was knocked down several times before he successfully caught his dinner.

at the left side of the gap, it's not hard to imagine how the lava dammed up against the side of the older mountain and flooded the canyon and the plains below.

Wind is almost always present along here as the trade winds pile up along the flank of the great mountain. We once saw three helicopters struggling to land on a barren, grassy field next to the road. We soon learned that a wedding coordinator had convinced a group of Germans that this would be an ideal place for a wedding reception, so they chartered the expensive helicopters to fly everyone in. We can still picture them standing there, with the wind blowing champagne all over their shirts, as they looked around asking each other, "Whose *stupid* idea was this?"

At the 31 mile marker there's a gate. This leads to Nu'u Bay, the only decent ocean swimming area along this entire

Dry and desolate. Nothing in common with Hana, on the other side of the mountain, except the beauty.

stretch of coastline. You can open the gate and proceed, but you'll either need 4WD for the ²/10 mile road or you'll have to walk it. The road terminates at the spotty remains of an old cement landing. The snorkeling is fairly good to the left (away from the shore), but don't venture beyond the protected point where the water is rougher and there's a current. The only thing marring the plentiful coral scenery is an unusually large number of fishing nets. Local fishermen thoughtlessly abandon them when they become entangled on coral heads, which creates a permanent hazard for sea life. We once found a dead reef shark (a normally docile animal) entangled on the bottom here. That's not a sight we'd like to see again.

If the surf is up, the short dirt road just before the 30 mile marker leads to a great

DIVERSION ALERT! place to listen to the surf. Huakini Bay is lined with small- and medium-sized rounded stones. When large waves rake at the shoreline, these stones make a deep rumbling sound that you won't soon forget. The bigger the waves, the better. Just don't get too close to the water. The cliffs behind the bay are said to contain ancient Hawaiian petroglyphs, according to a 19th-century archeological report we read, but we must confess we haven't been able to find them. Let us know if you're more successful. Be careful of the wicked kiawe (mesquite) thorns.

Modern man is not the first to traverse the island along this route. The ancient Hawaiians built a highway centuries ago, paved with lava stones and wide enough for two. This was how they went from east to west. Keep an eye out on the right side for remnants of it.

At ⅔ mile past the 30 mile marker, a dirt road angles back to the shoreline. This is it—the *last* beach on the island. It's a small, **unnamed black sand beach** about 60 feet wide. Its sand source is a nearby intermittent stream patiently dismantling its lava streambed. Cloudy water, but the sand has an exotic look. Sometimes storms remove the sand for months at a time.

Past the 29 mile marker you'll spot the **Pokowai Sea Arch**, but don't pull over until the road descends to the shoreline. From there you can get out and get a closer look at the arch and shoreline. Though the ocean is almost always whipped and frothed here, we've seen throw-net fishermen braving the water for their catch.

Soon you'll find a brand new two-lane bridge on this one-lane road. (As with Hana Highway bridges, federal dollars will only pay for two-lane bridges, even if they are on one-lane roads.) The gulch that the bridge spans is beautiful, showing the layers of the different lava flows.

As the road leaves the sea on its way up to the 3,000-foot level, you may wonder what you are missing with all that land and shoreline below that you won't get to see. The answer is you're missing *nothing!* The land below the highway past here is the most wretched you'll find on Maui. Harsh and unforgiving lava fields, sparse and scrubby brown grass—there is nothing visually pleasing about this area other than some marginally interesting lava rock ruins. (Even paradise has to have an ugly side—this is it.) The shoreline, though rich in fish, is lashed by heavy seas, making it hazardous. Many maps show a trail that goes from South Maui all the way to where the highway started leaving the shoreline. Yeah, the trail's there, but it's sporadic, miserable and ugly and passes almost nothing of interest.

Surprisingly, this area used to be heavily populated by Hawaiians. Thousands took advantage of the fishing area and the good sweet potato growing conditions in some pockets where there was soil. There was even a forest in those days, before cattle were introduced. Hawaiian ruins are scattered about the rocky fields. Today, native Hawaiians are in the process of trying to repopulate the higher elevation areas. Over 100 families are working as a group to rebuild this part of Maui, called **Kahikinui**. It won't be easy. Life was always difficult in this land of little rain and ever-present winds. Easier life elsewhere lured their grandfathers away for a reason and they abandoned the land. Even today the homesteaders live with no power or running water and only time will tell if they are successful.

Past the 15 mile marker (the 18–15 markers are only visible to traffic coming the other way) you see the **Tedeschi Winery**. They have a nice wine-tasting room and gift shop (albeit with fairly unremarkable wine, some made from pineapple), and it's worth a stop. The grounds are pretty and serene. Across the street is the **Ranch Store**, a deli/grill if you're hungry.

SOUTHEAST MAUI BEST BETS

Best Surreal Sunrise—Venus Pool
Best Hike—Pipiwai Trail
Best 'Okole Squeezing View—Infinity Pool
Best Place to Pay Homage to an Aviation Legend—Lindbergh's Grave
Best Isolated Waterfall—Alelele Falls
Best Place to Hear the Ocean—Huakini Bay if the Surf's Up
Best Place to Loosen a Filling—On the Bumpy Road Past 'Ohe'o Gulch
Best Place to Build a Windfarm—On the Scrubby Land Below the Highway Past the Pokowai Sea Arch

Sunrise from Haleakala Crater can be a surreal, ethereal experience.

People come to Maui for the ocean, palm trees and balmy weather. So why on earth would you want to use up one of your precious vacation days in the center of the island where you won't find *any* of that? Simple. This part of the island has green, rolling hills, switchback roads, cool mountain air and a *lump-in-your-throat* crater. It may not be typical Hawai'i, but it's definitely worth visiting.

UPCOUNTRY

Upcountry refers to the cluster of towns located 2,000–4,000 feet up the slope of Haleakala. They aren't pointing directly into the trade winds, so rain is less frequent. Drought happens on occasion, sparking water rationing. Since temperatures fall almost 3° with every thousand feet, it's cooler up here than at the shore. It's popular with people who want to work or play in the tropics but don't want to *live* there.

Don't tell people who live upcountry this, but in ancient times, Kula residents were considered dim-witted and dense and were the butt of jokes throughout the islands. It stems from the fact that they lived so far from the water that they possessed little sea knowledge, and were thought of as stupid and backward. Sort of the ancient equivalent of *how many Kulans does it take to pound poi? Five! One to hold the pounder and four to raise the bowl over and over. Ha, ha, ha…*

To get upcountry, most people head up the Haleakala Highway on 37. (The term *Haleakala Highway* and the signs

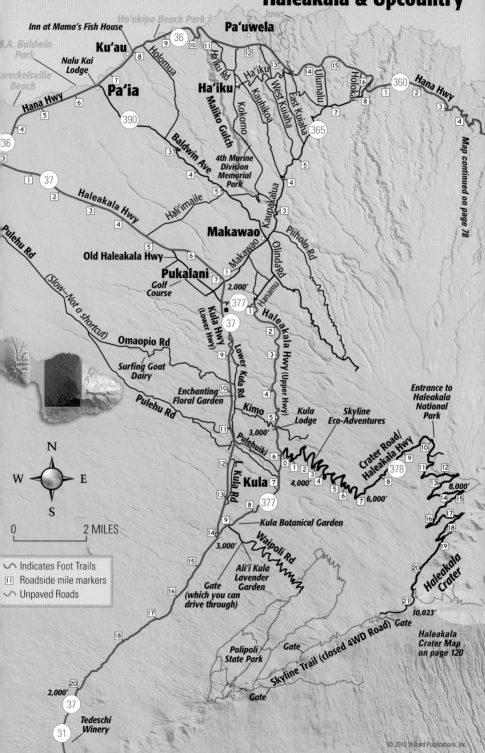

Haleakala & Upcountry

Ho'okipa Beach Park

Jaws

Inn at Mama's Fish House

Pa'uwela

36

M.A. Baldwin Park

Nalu Kai Lodge

Ku'au

Breckelsville Beach

Holomua

9

10

11

Ha'iku Rd

12

Ha'iku

13

14 Ulumalu

15

Holokai

16

360

Hana Hwy

8

7 Paia

Hana Hwy

6

Pa'ia

Ha'iku

Kauhikoa

West Kuiaha

East Kuiaha

Holokai

2

3

Kokomo

8

365

Map continued on page 78

5

Hana Hwy

4

390

Maliko Gulch

4th Marine Division Memorial Park

Kaupakalua

5

1

Baldwin Ave

4

36

3

37

1

Haleakala Hwy

Hali'imaile

5

Piiholo Rd

2

3

4

Makawao

3

Olinda Rd

4

Old Haleakala Hwy

5

6

Makawao

1

2,000'

Entrance to Haleakala National Park

Pukalani

7

Golf Course

377

37

Hanamu

Haleakala Hwy (Upper Hwy)

3

Crater Road/ Haleakala Hwy

9

10

11

12

Pulehu Rd

9

Kula Hwy (Lower Hwy)

Lower Kula Rd

9

3

Kula Lodge

Skyline Eco-Adventures

13

8,000'

14

15

378

(Slow—Not a shortcut)

Omaopio Rd

Surfing Goat Dairy

Enchanting Floral Garden

10

Kimo

5

6

0

1

2

3

4

8

6,000'

8

16

17

19

20

Haleakala Crater

Pulehu Rd

11

Pulehuiki

3,000'

4,000'

5

6

7

21

10,023'

Gate

12

L. Kula Rd

Kula

7

377

13

8

Kula Botanical Garden

Haleakala Crater Map on page 120

9

14

Waipoli Rd

3,000'

Ali'i Kula Lavender Garden

15

16

Gate (which you can drive through)

Polipoli State Park

Gate

17

Skyline Trail (closed 4WD Road)

Gate

18

Gate

N
W E
S

0   2 MILES

Indicates Foot Trails

11 **Roadside mile markers**

Unpaved Roads

20

2,000'

37

Tedeschi Winery

31

© 2010 Wizard Publications, Inc.

are misleading because it is actually composed of segments from *three different highways, 37 to 377 to 378.*) If it's clear, between the 4 and 5 mile markers you get a perspective of just how *big* this mountain really is. It's over 10,000 feet high, and from here you can tell by the width that this single mountain hides a monstrous amount of rock.

There are areas mentioned in this chapter that you won't pass by coming up Hwy 37, the most notable being Ha'iku and Makawao.

Why are the Days 24 Hours Long? Thank Maui.

The Hawaiians believed that in ancient times there was a demigod named Maui. (A demigod is the offspring of a god and a mortal.) Maui noticed that his mother used to complain that the days were too short for her to dry her tapa cloth. So young Maui set his mind to lasso the sun as it streaked across the sky. He went to Hana to watch the sun rise, then tried to catch it at Haleakala but failed. Later, near Kahului, Maui cut down all the coconuts he could find and made a long fiber rope. He climbed Haleakala and hid at a place across the crater called Hanakauhi. When the sun streaked by, he lassoed many of the sun's rays, weakening it. Maui told the sun, "Now I will kill you for hurrying so fast." The sun answered, "Let me live, and I promise that from now on I'll walk instead of run across the sky." Maui agreed and the sun kept his promise. Today the days are 24 hours long as a result of this agreement. (Weekends were apparently exempt from the deal because they seem much shorter.)

HA'IKU

Ha'iku is just below the area normally considered upcountry and is probably the least discovered town in Maui. The population is around 10,000, consisting of a mix of old-time locals, hippie-turned-farmers, wealthy mainlanders, Maui business owners and computer commuters. Green, wet and quiet is what they come for, and they're not disappointed. Their higher-elevation neighbors sometimes look longingly at Ha'iku's abundance of water. The roads here tend to be narrow. Twenty feet was considered wide enough in the horse and buggy days, and parts of some roads have maintained that width. There's usually very little traffic on Ha'iku roads during the week. Look at the map on page 115 if you're interested in driving (for no particular reason) some of these pretty roads like Ha'iku or Ulumalu roads. The town is worth visiting if you're in a wandering mood or want a treat from the Ha'iku Marketplace. The Ha'iku Grocery Store makes some excellent banana bread labeled Pa'ia General Store.

MAKAWAO

Makawao is a major upcountry hub. It's supposed to be the island's cowboy town. Most visitor information conveys the impression that you'll see old cowpokes riding horses through town. Not likely. If you see anybody on a horse, it'll probably be a teenage girl picking up some brie for her mom's get-together. But it's a pretty cool and interesting place to wander and shop, with some unusual finds. For instance, the Rodeo General Store sells "island coconut-flavored gourmet kosher Maui-grown coffee." (You know, it's kind of hard to picture a grizzled old Hawaiian cowboy saying, *Hey,*

The mystic forest along the upper part of Waipoli Road.

Kimo, pass the gourmet kosher coffee, will ya?) Around town you'll also find Hot Island Glass, which blows their own glass art works, and Supernatural with their vast selection of crystals and lots of treats. The absolute best is **Komoda Bakery** on Baldwin Avenue. Unimpressive on the outside, but unreal baked goods at reasonable prices. Makawao is where people with dreadlocks, backpacks and bare feet share the streets with the well-groomed, iPad-toting business crowd.

Galleries are also common here and they're friendly. Not like a few years ago when they took themselves pretty seriously saying they were for "peace and the enrichment of humankind with their visions" and they "accept the aloneness in the creative process and celebrate the aloha with their togetherness." Well, damn, that's really good to know. But hey, do you folks sell that velvet painting of the dogs playing poker?

Be aware that mornings can be busy in Makawao since the downhill bicycle tours race through town. You'll want to check your gas in Makawao or Pukalani. You've got a lot of climbing ahead and there's no gas on the way to Haleakala. Also, if you're trying to park and find all those two-hour stalls filled, look across from Ai Street off Makawao Avenue for a free lot.

By the way, no self-respecting Hawaiian cowboy (called paniolo) would ever be caught dead saying, *Get along, little dogie.* Here he would say, *hele makai* (go to the ocean). Other local cowboy terminology are:

Hemo kapuka—open the gate
Pipi—cattle
Lio—horse
Oni—let's move out
Kau ka lio—mount your horses
Waha!—yeehaa!

KULA

Think of Kula as everything past **Pukalani** (which itself offers little other than golfing). Kula has some downright tasty views of the central valley as well as restaurants and flower farms. Overall, it's not huge on the visitor hit parade, but you may want to consider some of these attractions:

Kula Lodge (878–1535) is the most renowned landmark up here. In addition to its accommodations, it has a beautiful (though pricey) restaurant with great views, a pretty garden terrace and a confiscatory gift shop.

Though there are numerous flower farm and gardens, not all are worth stopping for. The best is probably the **Kula Botanical Garden** (878–1715) on Hwy 377 between the 8 and 9 mile markers. It's well maintained, well marked and there's a nice assortment of tropical plants scattered over 6 acres. Well worth the $10 if you're into gardens. Another garden, **Enchanting Floral Gardens** (878–2531), has a setting that isn't as pretty as Kula Botanical. It's $7.50 and is just past the 10 mile marker on Hwy 37. **Sunrise Market and Protea Farm** (269–4080) just up Hwy 378 is a small but well-tended collection of proteas with a gift shop and snack bar.

Polipoli State Park is at the end of that *other* winding road (Waipoli Road) working its way up Haleakala. It's the road few people ever take. (See map.) At the end is an unexpected redwood forest in the middle of this tropical island. The trails are described under HIKING on page 198. It's cool and misty and would seem to belong more to Northern California than the center of Maui.

Also on Waipoli Road just before a gate and cattle guard is **Ali'i Kula Lavender** (878–3004). You never knew you could do so much with lavender until you come here. They sell lavender chocolates, sherbet (yummy), scones (also yummy), coffee, lotions, lemonade (not so good), candles, face pillows and more. The staff is exceptionally nice and they are generous with samples, so it's hard not to buy something at their gift shop. They have 30-minute guided tours for $12. For $25 you can ride with staff on a golf cart—certain days. Overall, they do a good job.

Past main Kula on your way toward the bottom of the island, the **Sun Yat-sen Park** is not far from the 18 mile marker on Hwy 37. History buffs will remember that Sun lived in Hawai'i, attended school here where he learned about democracy, and went back to China to overthrow its last emperor in 1912. If you drive down the road next to the park, you'll (literally) find yourself on EASY STREET.

Past the park, the last thing between you and the vast lands of Kaupo is the **Tedeschi Winery**, described on page 113.

HALEAKALA NATIONAL PARK

From Hwy 37 you took 377 then 378, right? (See map on page 115.) You now begin the endless switchbacks necessary to scale the steep slopes of Haleakala. A donut **A REAL GEM** ring of clouds often forms part of the way up, fooling people into thinking the summit's socked in. Most of the time the clouds clear before the summit. Watch for mindless, wayward cows on this stretch. It's an open ranch, and the witless bovines often wander onto the road. They're occasionally turned into hamburger prematurely by cars traveling too fast in the fog. You will be afforded many outstanding views of West Maui and the valley between the mountains. (Unless you're heading here for the sunrise; then you'll have to see many of the sights mentioned here on your way down.)

If you ever want to *see* what **turbulence** looks like, take a look at the cloud formations as you drive up and down Haleakala. As a pilot, this is the only place I know of on the island where I can come to and *see* turbulence (as opposed to feeling it) close up as the clouds roil and boil in all directions. While coming *down*, after the 8 mile marker is often a good place to see it.

After the 10 mile marker you'll pay your $10 per car entrance fee and enter

Sunrise From Haleakala—Is it *Really* That Good?

Sunrises from atop Haleakala have taken on legendary status. They are said to be comparable to a religious experience, that they will heal your soul, rejuvenate your spirit and perhaps even fix that ingrown toenail you've had lately. In short, they are said to be the best in the world. As a result, sunrises from up here are considered must-dos.

The first time we came to watch the sunrise up here, we thought it was the most overrated, overhyped event we'd seen. Pleasant, yes, but hardly *worth the effort*. Those around us seemed to agree. Also, the first time we were so wretchedly cold that we couldn't have appreciated winning the lottery, much less seeing a sunrise. The second time we did it, however, we were blown away by its majesty. Wouldn't have missed it for the world. What's the difference between pleasant and wow? Multiple trips have cemented a theory. It's simple—clouds. A sea of clouds (especially broken clouds) below you with the sun rising from beneath makes a glorious canvas for the sun to paint. It's like nothing you've seen, and when it's good, it's as good as a sunrise can get. Other times, when it's too clear, it's simply...nice...and cold. And for nice it's hard to justify the hardship. Fortunately, having clouds below you is fairly common.

To get the time of sunrise and a weather forecast, call (866) 944–5025. You'll want to get there at least half an hour before sunrise. However, if you don't arrive about an hour before, you run the real risk of not getting a parking spot at the actual summit. You'll have to park at the upper visitor center instead. If you try to park in the dirt, you may get a monstrous ticket. If you park at the visitor center, consider walking the short distance to the Sliding Sands trailhead. (See map on the next page.) It's less crowded, and you may find the wind partially blocked by White Hill next to you. Allow just under two hours from Kihei, a bit over two hours from Ka'anapali. If you don't allow enough time, you'll be one of the poor saps who woke up at 3 a.m. and still missed the good stuff. Bring a small flashlight, if possible; it's easy to fall down in the dark and numbing cold. If you get here while it's still inky dark, you'll probably see more stars than you've ever seen in your life. No matter how warmly you think you need to dress, dress warmer. Bring every piece of clothing you brought from the mainland, if necessary. If you rented an open-air JEEP, here's where you pay the piper. You'll freeze your nuggies off. (In fact, look on the side of the road and you'll see mounds of nuggies frozen off from past visitors.) If the wind's blowing at that high altitude (which it often is), it'll make a penguin scream. We bring our ski clothes, gloves and a wool cap, and even still, we sometimes get cold. The temperature rises quickly when the sun does, but few visitors are properly prepared for the morning cold, even in summer. At the summit there's an enclosed viewing area, but it's usually crowded and noisy in there, and the views are more restricted. If properly prepared, consider toughing it outside.

the park. Try to smile at the poor slob at the entrance gate freezing his/her ʻokole off in the booth. For years admittance was often free because (only the government could come up with this kind of logic) they "didn't have the budget for someone to collect money all the time." Can you imagine Disneyland making that policy? Now they've installed an honor system pay box when personnel are absent. Anyway, the visitor center and campground are the first things you pass. The visitor center has restrooms and the only phone available. This is where you make camping arrangements. Save your receipt and you won't have to pay again at the Seven Sacred Pools at Kipahulu within the next three days.

Camping is allowed at several places in the park, including the coveted cabins at the bottom of the crater. See CAMPING on page 175 for more. The campsite at **Hosmer Grove** as you entered the park has a 25-minute **nature loop**, though it seems more neglected than the rest of the park. Consider it dispensable. This campsite is a good place to see **moonbows**, when the full moon's rising in the east and it's raining toward the west.

As you've ascended the mountain, note how much the vegetation has changed. You're not in Hawaiʻi anymore; you're in Alaska. Cold, windy and arid conditions favor plants with needles and very small leaves. One plant that looks like a whisk broom has powder-filled spore casings. Ancient Hawaiians used to come up here and gather the powder to rub into their *da kines* to prevent chafing on long walks.

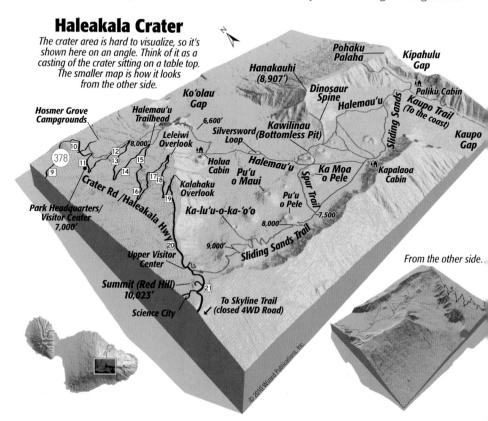

Haleakala Crater

The crater area is hard to visualize, so it's shown here on an angle. Think of it as a casting of the crater sitting on a table top. The smaller map is how it looks from the other side.

Pohaku Palaha — Kipahulu Gap

Hanakauhi (8,907')

Koʻolau Gap

Dinosaur Spine

Paliku Cabin

Halemauʻu

Kaupo Trail (To the coast)

Hosmer Grove Campgrounds

Halemauʻu Trailhead

6,600'

Kawilinau (Bottomless Pit)

Silversword Loop

Kaupo Gap

Leleiwi Overlook

8,000'

Holua Cabin

Puʻu o Maui

Halemauʻu

Ka Moa o Pele

Kapalaoa Cabin

Crater Rd / Haleakala Hwy

Kalahaku Overlook

Spur Trail

Puʻu o Pele

Park Headquarters / Visitor Center 7,000'

Ka-luʻu-o-ka-ʻoʻo

8,000'

7,500'

9,000'

Sliding Sands Trail

Upper Visitor Center

Summit (Red Hill) 10,023'

To Skyline Trail (closed 4WD Road)

Science City

From the other side.

© 2010 Wizard Publications, Inc.

The visitor center at 7,000 feet has an average high temperature of 59° and low of 41° in February. In August it averages a high of just 66° and a low of 47°. It's about 10° colder at the summit, and every few years they even get a light dusting of snow or ice. Most of the rain at the summit falls in the winter months, but it's still not nearly as rainy as the lower elevations can be with 54 inches at the 7,000 foot level and much drier at the summit. (If you have computer access, our website, wizardpub.com, has a link to current weather readings on Haleakala, including temperature and wind speed.)

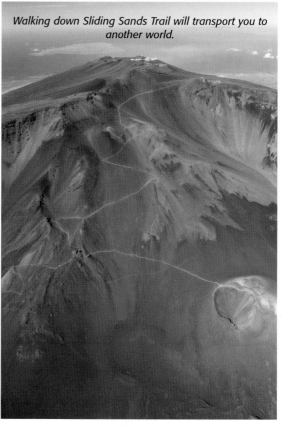

Walking down Sliding Sands Trail will transport you to another world.

HALEAKALA SUMMIT

After the 17 mile mark you'll see a parking lot for the **Leleiwi Lookout**. Most people blow right by in their frenzy to get to the summit, assuming Leleiwi merely gives them another nice view down the mountain to the coast. Too bad, because Leleiwi is nothing of the sort. Walk five minutes to the end, and the crater itself suddenly explodes into view. What a startling sight! It looks very different than the more traditional view at the top and is well worth the diversion. A small shelter protects you from any wind that may be present. This is a good alternative to the summit for less crowded sunrises.

DIVERSION ALERT!

As you near the summit, keep an eye out for **silverswords** ('ahinahina). You'll know them when you see them. This plant, unique to Hawai'i, first arrived as a California tarweed seed in the feathers of a wayward bird a million years ago and evolved into this striking round silver wonder. They developed their dense covering of silver hairs to live in this difficult environment. It allows them to retain water and ward off the intense sun at this altitude. If you see one blooming with a large stalk of flowers, pay your respects. Silverswords may live up to 50 years, but, like salmon, they only reproduce once then die. At one time silverswords were endangered when thoughtless people plucked them out of the ground for all sorts of ornamental purposes. Today they are protected and their numbers have rebounded. Be careful walking around them, however, as the fine for damaging them is more than the cost of your whole vacation. For the ancient Hawaiians, there was nothing silver in their universe until they met this plant. Their name for it, 'ahinahina, literally means *gray gray.* That's as close as they could get.

There are several trails that are supposed to highlight silverswords, like the one at the **Kalahaku Overlook** up ahead. But you're more likely to see them from the side of the road nearer the summit. While at Kalahaku, take the time to enjoy the view of the crater, which already looks a bit different than at Leleiwi.

There aren't many types of birds that can live up here. Flying in thin 30 mph winds, which is common, is not a very efficient means of transportation. So they walk most of the time. The three most successful are the native **nene** and the imported **chukar** and **ring-necked pheasant**. A nene is what results when you take wayward geese from Canada and stick them on an island for a few million years. They've left the water and adapted to high, arid lands, losing much of the webbing on their feet in the process. They were almost extinct at the beginning of

Though perfectly adapted to live their life above the clouds, the endemic nene is one of the world's most accomplished beggars. Try to resist their charm.

this century. Today they are protected, but are often accidentally killed because of their laid-back attitude toward cars. They just don't seem impressed with an auto's size, like frogs at night looking into your headlights as they're squashed. People often accidentally back over them. As a result, it's more important than usual not to feed them, or they'll get even cozier with cars. They'll likely come up and beg if they see you, and they're hard to resist, but try. They're often visible at the **Halemau'u Trailhead** between the 14 and 15 mile markers.

Most visitor information refers to **Haleakala Crater** as the *largest extinct volcanic crater in the world.* Cool! Too bad none of that statement is true. It's not the largest, it's not extinct, and the crater is not volcanic in origin. (In fact, the park now prefers to call this a *basin, valley* or *wilderness area,* but we refer to it as a *crater* because people will look at you funny if you mention *Haleakala Valley.*)

After Haleakala built itself up, it went to sleep for several hundred thousand years as most Hawaiian volcanoes do. During its snooze, two great valleys formed on either side due to erosion. These valleys cut at least 5,000 feet deep, into the very core of the volcano. They worked their way up the mountain until they met at the summit, back to back. Now the mountain was essentially cracked down the middle, separating the east and west sides, with only a thin ridge between the two great canyons. Then Haleakala awoke for one last series of eruptions before falling forever silent and eventually sinking under its weight back into the sea. That's what will happen to all of the Hawaiian Islands. (This last series of eruptions is in its final phase, having last erupted around 1790.)

When it awoke, it did so from the summit, filling the enormous canyons with lava and raising the summit floor you see before you. So, you see, Haleakala Crater is an *erosion* crater that was partially filled with lava and gravel from the crumbling sides, not a volcanic crater like those on the Big Island. When you drive around the bottom of the island, you'll be able to see, from around the 32 mile marker, where and how the lava flowed through the Kaupo Gap and flooded the plains below in an ever-widening flow of molten rock hitting the sea between the 30 and 35 mile markers.

As you approach the top of the mountain, you may find yourself a bit breathless. You've gone from sea level to almost 2 miles high with no time to acclimate. Take it easy and drink plenty of water. You dehydrate very quickly without noticing at this altitude. If you've been SCUBA diving in the last 24 hours and your blood feels a bit carbonated up here, remember—as far as your body's concerned, you may as well be flying. *You got da bends, brah; go back down.*

The upper visitor center after the 20 mile marker has kickin' views, a place to park and restrooms. (Though the latter are inadequate for the number of bikers and tour buses that come up here. Expect lines. There's also a restroom at Kalahaku Overlook and at the Halemau'u Trailhead.) If you brought a bike for the 38-mile downhill ride, this is the best place to launch. (Commercial tours are banned from the park, and have to start way down at the 6,500-foot level.) See BIKING on page 171 for more.

The way the clouds race by, clawing at some of the nearby peaks, you could be looking at Mt. Everest instead of a Hawaiian peak across the crater. The beauty is hard to describe, but it's unlike any **A REAL GEM** other place we've seen. Adjectives that

describe it include *desolate, wondrous, arid, majestic, colorful, harsh, peaceful, vast, spiritual, exciting, scary, ancient...* all of these and more can be applied to Haleakala Crater. If you were smart enough to dress warmly and can concentrate on things other than the temperature, you'll come up with your own adjectives.

If you're here in late afternoon to see the **sunset** (which can be fantastic and not nearly as crowded as a sunrise), you may be treated to something available in only a few places in the world. It happens as you're standing at the crater's edge, and there's cloud below and in front of you (and relatively close) while the sun is low and directly behind you. (Leleiwi Lookout is a good place to see it since it's close to the Ko'olau Gap's clouds.) Called **Spectre of the Brocken** or **akaku anuenue** in Hawaiian, it's when you see your own shadow on the clouds with a rainbow surrounding your shadow. It's an *incredible* sight. The Hawaiians felt blessed to experience it because they believed that what they were seeing was their actual soul, and the rainbow was a promise from heaven that their souls would be taken care of. If you're lucky, maybe you'll be blessed, too.

The ancient Hawaiians never lived up here, but they did visit for religious purposes and to hunt birds. Many artifacts have been found in the crater. The Hawaiian historian Kamakau says that commoners used to come up here to toss the remains of their loved ones into a pit at the bottom they called Ka'a'awa, now called **Bottomless Pit** or **Kawi-linau**. (Hawaiians were always fearful that others would desecrate the bones of their ancestors, so this bottomless pit was a perfect place to assure that their remains wouldn't be tampered with.) People who lived at the bottom of the mountain in Kaupo believed that their water came from Haleakala Crater, and

Sharp contrasts, impossibly blue skies and a myriad of colors; your eyes will be dining on a feast.

they used to bitterly complain that the reason their water tasted so insipid was because of this practice. (Hmm, sort of makes you want *bottled* water while driving through Kaupo.)

Hawaiians also came for the rock. Most lava rock is relatively soft. There are several deposits of harder stone that the Hawaiians used to make adzes (a stone ax) for shaping other tools.

Lastly, Hawaiians came to Haleakala to hide the umbilical cords of their newborns. Hawaiians strongly felt that if rats, notorious thieves, were to steal a baby's umbilical cord, the child would grow up to be a thief. So they hiked to some of the smaller volcanic pits in Haleakala to keep the cords from rats (which aren't native—the Hawaiians brought the Polynesian rat with them from the South Pacific).

At one time imported goats were a huge problem in the crater, eating everything in sight and tearing up the ground with their hooves. When they eradicated them, they purposely left a few sterilized males marked with radio transmitters to roam the wilderness. Referred to affectionately as *Judas Goats,* the theory was that lonely males were *far* more effective

(and motivated) at locating any unaccounted-for female goats than park personnel could ever hope to be. It worked and the crater is now goat-free.

Past the upper visitor center parking lot, the road leads to the actual summit itself at 10,023 feet. Winds can be strong up here and can cause windburn if you're exposed to them for an extended period. If it's not windy, as is often the case later in the morning and afternoon, it's tempting to shed your warm clothes. You should know that sunburn happens very quickly up here since the light filters through a thinner atmosphere. (OK, OK, no more nagging.) The peak directly southeast of the summit is called **Magnetic Peak**. Can't find southeast? That's because the iron in Magnetic Peak is messing with your compass.

At the 21 mile marker, if you avoid the turnoff up to the summit and instead stay to your left, you're heading to **Science City**. The Air Force and the University of Hawai'i have astronomical observatories up here, but they're not open to the public. The Air Force uses their 12-foot diameter scope to optically sweep space, tracking space junk that could collide with existing satellites. The optics alone for this cost $40 million, and it can spot items the size of golf balls in space. (The space shuttle reportedly lost very few golf balls, but the Air Force *is* tracking a wayward glove.) Astronomers also bounce laser beams off retro-reflectors left on the moon by the Apollo astronauts in the '70s. By timing the reflection, they can measure the speed of continental drift. Maui's Pacific plate moves northwest at the same rate that your fingernails grow. (Apparently, their procurement office moves at about the same speed. It wasn't until this millennium that they finally replaced their '70s-era 4mhz computers with newer ones that were only five years out of date. Now *that's* progress!)

We came up here once in the middle of the night to watch a meteor shower, but the shower was mostly a bust. After dozing for a few minutes in the car, we awoke and thought we were hallucinating. *How can this be?* It looked like thousands of shooting stars in line with each other, like a special effect from a *Star Wars* movie. It took a minute to realize it was a pulsating laser shooting all the way to the horizon from one of the university's many science experiments.

On this road to Science City, at the next intersection, the FAA has a sign (and sometimes a locked gate) saying that trespassers will be tortured and maimed, or something to that effect. It's apparently incorrect, unauthorized and contradicted by the fact that the state has established a *public access* to Skyline Road (mentioned below). Few people have been to this part of the summit in the past because of the sign. Too bad. We did a little digging and found that the FAA erected the sign to prevent *tour buses* from using the narrow washboard road

DIVERSION ALERT!

for (c'mon, everybody, you know the words to this song) *liability reasons*. The FAA doesn't have a problem with hikers (and smaller vehicles) if the gate is open using the road since it's necessary to access **Skyline Road**, a fantastic and lightly used dirt road that meanders down the spine of Haleakala, ending at Poli-poli Park. (See BIKING in ADVENTURES or HIKING in ACTIVITIES.)

If you take the federal road (the sign may vanish since the state's considering taking over the road), you'll come to a dirt road on your left. That's Skyline, and if you walk on it around the corner for a few minutes, you're treated to a magnificent view of most of Kahoʻolawe. Though you're almost 10,000 feet up, the ocean is only 6 miles away. What a sweeping vista! The Big Island—at 4,000 square miles it's almost as big as Connecticut— lives up to its name. It looks positively *huge* from up here.

After all these beautiful sights, it's (literally) all downhill from here. Remember to use a lower gear driving back down; the slope will burn your brakes.

INSIDE THE CRATER

On the other side of the hill next to the upper visitor center is **Sliding Sands Trail**. If you're only going to do one hike at Haleakala, this is the one. The trail descends 2,400 feet fairly evenly over a span of almost 4 miles (it's hard on the knees) to the crater floor, but you don't need to go that far to see some of the gorgeous views from your slow but constant descent. Just go as far as you want, and you'll see how much larger and grander the crater looks from inside. At times it looks big enough to hold another island. The colors inside are amazing. Everything from green, yellow, red, brown, grey and blue are represented. If you don't want to hike it, there's a company that takes people down on horseback, all the way to the bottom. It's an *outstanding* ride, showcasing the crater at its best, and is the coolest horseback ride we've done in Hawai'i. See HORSEBACK RIDING on page 203. The trail leading into the crater is far less windy than up above. The **A REAL GEM** weather is usually sunny, especially in the morning. Clouds will push up from the Ko'olau and Kipahulu gaps as the day progresses. From inside you'll often see the clouds roiling at the head of the Kipahulu Gap at the far end, like a white waterfall, but passing no farther. Quiet prevails inside the crater, and the ever-eroding walls provide endless gravel. In fact, it's been necessary to dig up the horse hitch at the bottom of the crater several times. Erosion from the sides of the crater keeps raising the basin floor, creating the illusion that the hitch is sinking.

Inside are numerous hiking trails described under HIKING. Though Haleakala's most recent eruption in 1790 was at the coast, the crater is far from dead. Lava flowed in the crater 900 years ago while Hawaiians occupied the island, and perhaps even more recently. And it probably will erupt again.

There are cabins in the crater for the lucky lottery winners. If you get one, enjoy that complimentary firewood. It'll make the most expensive stove fire you've ever had because the park service gets it there by helicopter. Other maintenance is done by rangers on horse and mule.

HALEAKALA & UPCOUNTRY SHOPPING

An often-overlooked shopping destination is Makawao. There are many small locally-owned galleries, shops and clothing boutiques to browse, and in some ways it's even better than Pa'ia. Park in the free lot as you enter town behind Stopwatch Bar & Grill.

One of the premier showcases for Maui contemporary artists is **Viewpoints Gallery**. This gallery shines for its diversity, quality and originality. Other galleries worth noting are **Kirsten Bunney Gallery**, **Julie Galeeva Fine Art**, **Bernardo & Blakk Fine Art** and **Randy Jay Braun Gallery**. **Hot Island Glass** is a glass gallery where you can watch the stuff being created in their workshop.

Women's clothing boutiques are plentiful, and some of our favorites are **The Merchantile**, **Pink by Nature**, **Gecko Trading Co.**, **Jewels of the White Tara** for ethnic fashions and **Altitude** for sophisticated clothing.

Paniolo still roam these parts, and you'll find shops catering to cowboy fashion, gear and accessories at **Aloha Cowboy** and **Piiholo Ranch Store**.

For jewelry, check out **Maui Master Jewelers**, which showcases Hawaiian and Pacific Island pieces. **Little Tibet** breathes new life to antique pieces and designs originals around unique stones.

HALEAKALA & UPCOUNTRY BEST BETS

Best Tour—Horseback Ride Down
  Sliding Sands into the Crater
Best Hike—Sliding Sands as Far as
  Your Heart Takes You
Best Coup—Getting a Cabin in the Crater
Best Decadent Treat—Komoda's
  Bakery in Makawao
Best Sign to Ignore—FAA Sign to Skyline
Best Place to See Someone Shoot at
  Klingons—From Science City at Night
Best Way to Freeze Your Da Kines Off—
  Wear Shorts to Watch the Sunrise
Best Place to Get a Glimpse of Your
  Soul—Leleiwi Overlook

Calm water, luscious beaches like Ulua and swanky resorts are why people love South Maui.

Ahh, South Maui. Land of sun and beaches and visions of offshore islands.

Until the mid-1900s, there were few people living in South Maui. Lack of water made it difficult to grow things, and, after all, what else was land good for? Today we know it's good for growing Hawai'i's most important cash crop—*visitors!* South Maui gets so little rain (many years it may only rain three or four times), and its beaches are so extraordinary that it's a mecca for anyone looking for a dreamy, dependable tropical vacation.

If you look at the graphic above, the first thing you notice is that the term *South Maui* is not very geographically correct. *South Central Maui* seems more accurate. But South Maui is what the region has been historically called, so who are we to quibble?

We're going to describe it from Ma'alaea at the top of Hwy 31 heading south as far as you can go.

MA'ALAEA

At the intersection of Hwys 30 and 31, Ma'alaea was feared and despised by early airborne visitors. Because it was here, where the Kealia Pond now exists, that clueless aviation officials chose to place Maui's first airport in 1929. (It looked geographically convenient on a map to early planners.) It didn't last long because this is the windiest spot in Hawai'i. The scouring wind ensured that the inbound flight experience would be as terrifying as possible. There are cows born and raised on the slopes north of Ma'alaea. If the winds stops, they'd probably fall over.

Ma'alaea is still a transportation hub, only now it's for boats. If you take a snorkel or whale watching trip, odds are very good you'll leave from here.

Maui Ocean Center (270–7000) is the other big attraction here and is definitely worth a stop. Opened in 1998, this is a relatively small (compared to some mainland aquariums) but extremely well-done aquarium. The living reef exhibit has a fantastic collection of fish found around the Hawaiian islands, and the sealife seems remarkably well cared for. Turtle Lagoon has lots of turtles roaming around that you can view from above or from a glass wall below the surface. Elsewhere there is a glass tunnel that passes right through a large tank, complete with sharks. Stop in the tunnel's center, and the sharks pass right beneath the glass floor. The gift shop has a surprisingly fine and vast assortment of gift items, many locally made. It's one of the more impressive gift shops we've seen on the island. The aquarium is more crowded when the weather is bad. The $26 entrance fee may seem excessive

due to the small size, but the quality shines. (Kids are $19.)

Ma'alaea's greatest natural asset is its 3-mile long Ma'alaea Beach, stretching all the way to north Kihei. If you're looking for a great walking or jogging beach, this is the one. Early mornings and early evenings are best, as winds punish the area during the day. You won't have it to yourself, but you will have an amazingly peaceful stroll. Start at Haycraft Park at the end of Hauoli St. in Ma'alaea, and you won't see another building for 2½ miles.

While *you* may have come to Maui for the beaches, *birds* visit us for Kealia Pond. This important wetland is home to several species of native birds. There's a turnout and boardwalk trail between the 1 and 2 mile markers on Hwy 31. (Also labeled as Hwy 310 as some signs are marked.) This is a good place to birdwatch. During the summer the ponds dry up.

In the past we were pretty tough on Ma'alaea. The astonishing winds and dust

Though it may dry up in the summer, the existence of Kealia Pond, a wetland in perennially dry South Maui, is a surprise to everyone except the birds.

from sugar operations convinced us that staying here was a bad idea. (You'll be forgiven if you think *Ma'alaea* must be Hawaiian for *bad hair day.*) So before we went to press on this edition, we spent five months living in Ma'alaea and came away with this conclusion—if you want to experience life in *both* South Maui and West Maui, Ma'alaea can be pretty darned convenient. See the WHERE TO STAY chapter.

Until that fence lining the shoreline was installed, hawksbill turtles would occasionally cross the road here in late spring/early summer to lay eggs in the Kealia Pond. Today they lay their eggs on the beach. But that's the only time you're likely to see them. They live and feed in deeper waters, far from shore. The turtles you see while snorkeling are usually green sea turtles, which rarely nest here, preferring French Frigate Shoals, 700 miles away. (Like restless teenagers, sea creatures rarely want to hang around the place they were born.)

As you're entering Kihei, you have a choice of either taking South Kihei Road along the shore or staying on the highway. The latter you'll use when you're simply interested in getting farther south. Though you won't take it every time, we'll describe South Kihei Road from here

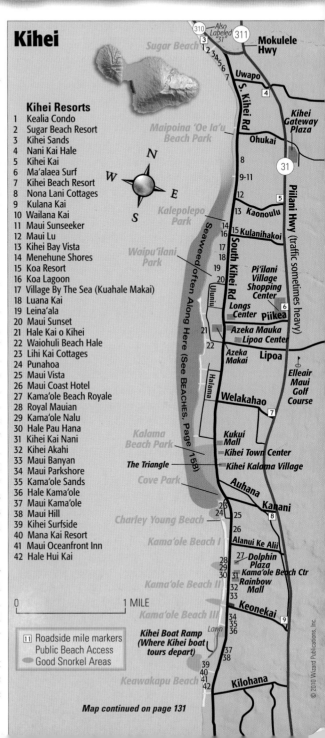

Kihei

Kihei Resorts
1 Kealia Condo
2 Sugar Beach Resort
3 Kihei Sands
4 Nani Kai Hale
5 Kihei Kai
6 Ma'alaea Surf
7 Kihei Beach Resort
8 Nona Lani Cottages
9 Kulana Kai
10 Wailana Kai
11 Maui Sunseeker
12 Maui Lu
13 Kihei Bay Vista
14 Menehune Shores
15 Koa Resort
16 Koa Lagoon
17 Village By The Sea (Kuahale Makai)
18 Luana Kai
19 Leina'ala
20 Maui Sunset
21 Hale Kai o Kihei
22 Waiohuli Beach Hale
23 Lihi Kai Cottages
24 Punahoa
25 Maui Vista
26 Maui Coast Hotel
27 Kama'ole Beach Royale
28 Royal Mauian
29 Kama'ole Nalu
30 Hale Pau Hana
31 Kihei Kai Nani
32 Kihei Akahi
33 Maui Banyan
34 Maui Parkshore
35 Kama'ole Sands
36 Hale Kama'ole
37 Maui Kama'ole
38 Maui Hill
39 Kihei Surfside
40 Mana Kai Resort
41 Maui Oceanfront Inn
42 Hale Hui Kai

0   1 MILE

11 Roadside mile markers
Public Beach Access
Good Snorkel Areas

Kihei Boat Ramp (Where Kihei boat tours depart)

© 2010 Wizard Publications, Inc.

Map continued on page 131

because that's where all the goodies are. The maps show all the connecting roads.

KIHEI

Kihei is the unplanned outcome of South Maui's explosion of popularity during the 1970s and '80s. It's a linear collection of condos and strip malls. While it certainly lacks the old world charm of Lahaina, Kihei doesn't try to be anything other than what it is—a beach town—where everything is water-related. As for downtown Kihei, there is no such animal. The closest you could come to defining the town center is the shopping center area near Lipoa and South Kihei Road. And that's a stretch.

Before it was developed, Kihei looked like what you see up the mountain: dry, scrubby and not overly attractive. Water was scarce. With no water to tap from this dry side of Haleakala, planners drilled wells over in water-rich West Maui and piped it in under the central plain. Most people who live here don't even know this, and when Upcountry experiences its occasional droughts, residents look resentfully down the hill at the green of Kihei and Wailea and wonder where *they* seem to get all their water.

South Kihei Road is quite a sight for first-timers. It's so close to the ocean and beaches, you recognize immediately how important the sea is to this town.

When the Big Island's King Kamehameha invaded Maui for the last (and ultimately successful) time, he came ashore in Kihei at one point. The fighting was fierce with Maui warriors employing a novel weapon—*heated* sling-stones. Kamehameha's forces were a bit intimidated by the hot rocks and contemplated retreating. So Kamehameha ordered all of their canoes destroyed. The message was simple—win or die. With newfound motivation, his troops eventually won (with the help of some western cannons) and went on to conquer all the islands.

Though south Kihei and Wailea have some of the *best* beaches on the island, north Kihei has some of the *worst*. In short, you probably won't want to swim in most of the water from just south of the intersection of South Kihei Road and Ohukai down to Cove Park, 3 miles south. We explain the gory details in BEACHES on page 158. Simply put, the water is often yucky. (The scientific term is HAB, or harmful algal blooms.) Not as bad as it was in the early 2000s, but still a problem.

As you pass Cove Park, note the color of the water. Brownish, right? Less than 200 yards south the water will get clean and clear again, and the next beach, Kama'ole Beach I, offers fine swimming. From here on, it's nothing but great beach after great beach. All are described under BEACHES. Outstanding Keawakapu is the last beach you pass on South Kihei Road. Here the road veers away from the shoreline. You'll take a right on Wailea Alanui Road to continue your southward journey.

Breezes usually stiffen into winds in the afternoon in South Maui. (See WEATHER on page 26.) Most beach activities are best in the morning or late afternoon just before sunset.

If you're watching a sunset from South Maui and the sky is clear of clouds, take a look behind you as soon as the sun sets. If Haleakala's free of clouds, too, you'll see that the sun still shines there. It's so tall that the sun sets several minutes later on Haleakala, bathing it in sunlight when the sun has vanished from your eyes.

WAILEA

This is the premier resort area on the island (Kapalua's and Ka'anapali's claims notwithstanding). Expensive resorts line its heavenly beaches. Some, like the Fairmont Kea Lani, are so posh and exotic, you'll weep when you finally have to go back to the *real* world. While Kihei was an *every man for himself* development, the Wailea area had a single owner with a single vision: grand, green, groomed and golf. With splendid weather (cooler than Kihei and with lighter afternoon winds), phenomenal beaches, clean water and kickin' views of Molokini and Kaho'olawe, Wailea is a grand success.

A REAL GEM

There are no mile markers here, and some places don't have signs. If you reset your odometer at the corner of Wailea Ike and Wailea Alanui, we've marked distances on the maps.

Many of the best beaches on the island are found right here. In addition to its beaches, Wailea has a glorious beachside path. Though not as long or as well known as Ka'anapali's path, it stretches between Mokapu and Polo Beaches and is a perfect way for visitors at one Wailea resort to dine at another without messing with cars. It also makes a great place for a sunset stroll or a sunrise jogging path.

Wailea Alanui becomes Makena Alanui past the Fairmont Kea Lani. (That's the goofy-looking, though very luxurious, resort past the Four Seasons—someone was reading *Arabian Nights* when they designed *that* one.) Segments of the old Makena Road visit less known beaches, such as Palauea and Makena, as well as snorkeling and diving areas like Five Graves. Kayakers often launch at Makena Landing.

One sound that's common in South Maui is the call of the gray francolin. This bird starts every morning with a surprisingly vigorous call, which sounds something like a car alarm.

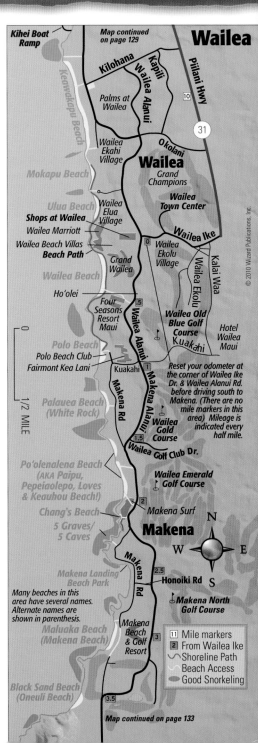

Map continued on page 129

Wailea

Kihei Boat Ramp

Kilohana · Kapili · Wailea Alanui · Piilani Hwy

Palms at Wailea

Keawakapu Beach

Wailea Ekahi Village

Okolani

Wailea
Grand Champions

Mokapu Beach

Wailea Town Center

Ulua Beach · Wailea Elua Village

Shops at Wailea
Wailea Marriott

Wailea Ike

Wailea Beach Villas
Beach Path

Wailea Ekolu Village

Grand Wailea

Wailea Beach

Ho'olei

Four Seasons Resort Maui

Wailea Ekolu

Kalai Waa

Wailea Old Blue Golf Course
Kuakahi

Hotel Wailea Maui

Polo Beach
Polo Beach Club
Fairmont Kea Lani

Kuakahi

Reset your odometer at the corner of Wailea Ike Dr. & Wailea Alanui Rd. before driving south to Makena. (There are no mile markers in this area) Mileage is indicated every half mile.

1/2 MILE

Palauea Beach (White Rock)

Wailea Gold Golf Course

Wailea Golf Club Dr.

Po'olenalena Beach (AKA Paipu, Pepeiaolepo, Loves & Keauhou Beach!)

Wailea Emerald Golf Course

Chang's Beach
5 Graves/ 5 Caves

Makena Surf

Makena

N · W · E · S

Makena Landing Beach Park

Honoiki Rd

Many beaches in this area have several names. Alternate names are shown in parenthesis.

Makena Rd

Makena North Golf Course

Maluaka Beach (Makena Beach)

Makena Beach & Golf Resort

11 Mile markers
2 From Wailea Ike
Shoreline Path
Beach Access
Good Snorkeling

Black Sand Beach (Oneuli Beach)

© 2010 Wizard Publications, Inc.

Map continued on page 133

Stand up paddleboarding is all the rage in South Maui, although some people seem to have developed their own unique style.

MAKENA

Leaving Wailea and passing the Maui Prince, as you round the corner you'll notice a large hill near the ocean. The drama that created that hill was probably witnessed by the ancient Hawaiians.

Haleakala is in its twilight years as an active volcano. Its time is almost up. The typical life cycle for a Hawaiian volcano is to grow slowly beneath the sea through sporadic eruptions. It then begins vigorous, near-constant growth, building an island. Later it falls asleep for 500,000 to 1 million years and then awakens for its last hurrah before dying and eventually sinking beneath the sea under its own weight. Oahu's Diamond Head is a product of its last gasp 300,000 years ago. Here, on Haleakala's southwestern flank, we see a volcano in its death throes. Its last eruption was around 1790 at the end of the road ahead. It was a "typical" surface flow; lava squeezed from a vent and flowed downhill. The eruption that created the large hill toward the sea, called Pu'u Ola'i, or Earthquake Hill, was not.

Hawaiian legend states that before the 1790 eruption, this was the last place on the island to erupt. Imagine how it must have looked if there were villagers living here at the time. Lava began quietly pooling beneath the surface in what was sup-

posed to be just another "typical" surface flow. But because it was so close to the shoreline, sea water seeped into the magma pool. This water immediately flashed into steam, building up the pressure in the lava pool. Earthquakes began rumbling as the earth struggled to contain the pressure. Villagers may have begun to notice small amounts of steam coming from the ground. As more lava and sea water combined, something had to give. Suddenly, the ground ripped open with a tremendous explosion as fountains of bright orange and red lava shot into the sky. It must have been spectacularly large, because the entire hill you see before you was created as the gas-frothed lava fell to earth and piled up to form the 360-foot Pu'u Ola'i, perhaps in as little as a week. (Looks taller, doesn't it?)

Hiking up Pu'u Ola'i is more difficult than it looks. The trail to the top marches through the cinders (called *tephra* by geologists, in case you just *had* to know) that make up this mass. So, as you take a step up, the tendency is to fall back a few inches, making the climb more tiring. But the view from the top is magnificent. You can see Big Beach below on one side and much of Wailea on the other. At press time the state had the trail closed for safety evaluation.

You may see signs in the area warning of deer crossing. These aren't a joke. Nine axis deer from India were brought here in 1959. They were supposed to have a low reproductive potential, but Maui's romantic atmosphere apparently affects deer as well, because in the brief time they've been here, they've multiplied to around 10,000 and are considered a nuisance. Many of them live in this area and are occasionally whacked by passing cars. Golfers at Wailea's courses may find additional hazards on the greens as the deer come down from the mountains during times of drought Upcountry and leave souvenirs on the greens. They're most plentiful on Pu'u Ola'i.

There might be a few food stands on the side of the road in Makena. The best is Makena Grill after Big Beach across from the lava rock wall at Secret Cove. Awesome fish tacos.

MOLOKINI

To residents and visitors in the know, the name Molokini conjures up images of crystal clear water and bright, vivid coral. If nature hadn't made this offshore island, the Hawai'i Visitors **A REAL GEM** Bureau would have done it. This aquatic wonder was created when an undersea vent, held under pressure by the ocean's weight, busted loose with lava and ash, building up what is called a tuff cone. The northern half has been eroded away by wave action, creating a semi-circular reef far enough offshore to be clear of runoff or sand. So underwater visibility is nearly always 100 feet, sometimes 180.

Visiting Molokini means taking a boat from either Ma'alaea (10 miles away) or Kihei Boat Ramp (6 miles). Though it seems close to Maui, don't try to take a

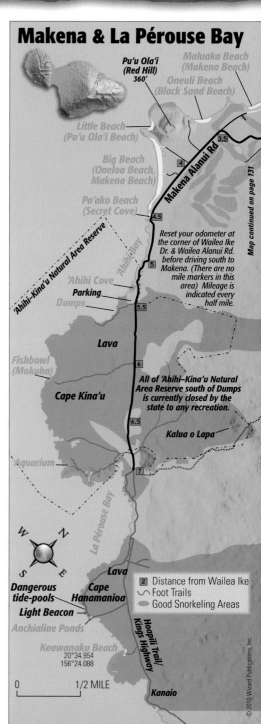

Makena & La Pérouse Bay

Pu'u Ola'i
(Red Hill)
360'

Maluaka Beach
(Makena Beach)

Oneuli Beach
(Black Sand Beach)

Little Beach
(Pu'u Ola'i Beach)

Big Beach
(Oneloa Beach,
Makena Beach)

Pa'ako Beach
(Secret Cove)

Makena Alanui Rd

Map continued on page 131

'Ahihi–Kina'u Natural Area Reserve

'Ahihi Bay

'Ahihi Cove
Parking
Dumps

Reset your odometer at the corner of Wailea Ike Dr. & Wailea Alanui Rd. before driving south to Makena. (There are no mile markers in this area) Mileage is indicated every half mile.

Lava

Fishbowl
(Mokuha)

Cape Kina'u

All of 'Ahihi–Kina'u Natural Area Reserve south of Dumps is currently closed by the state to any recreation.

Kalua o Lapa

Aquarium

La Pérouse Bay

Lava

Dangerous
tide-pools
Light Beacon

Cape
Hanamanioa

Anchialine Ponds

Keawanaku Beach
20°34.954
156°24.088

0   1/2 MILE

Hoapili Trail/
Kings Highway

Kanaio

2 Distance from Wailea Ike
Foot Trails
Good Snorkeling Areas

© 2010 Wizard Publications, Inc.

Perfect days end with a perfect sunset.

kayak there. Currents and winds between Molokini and Maui are too strong for most kayakers.

The crater is a marine and bird sanctuary. You're not allowed to walk on the island. Once inside the crescent, you'll find the water inviting. See page 209 for more on snorkeling and diving Molokini. In the past, the crater was visited often by a lonely monk seal who was famous for swimming right up to divers. Boat captains nicknamed him Humpy because of his...*unusually* friendly gestures toward swimmers. The seal was apparently unaware of the law prohibiting human contact with monk seals. If any monk seals visit Molokini while you're there, just remember that *they* have to initiate any contact.

The horizontal notch on the back of the crater is caused by wave cuts. If you were to SCUBA dive down 250 feet, you'd find a similar wave cut, evidence that the ocean was *much* lower during a past ice age.

According to lore, the 19th-century King Kalakaua wagered Molokini in a hand of poker with a local rancher. When the king lost the hand, he reneged, proclaiming that he hadn't wagered Molokini, but rather *omole kini,* which is a bottle of gin.

LA PÉROUSE BAY

As you approach the end of the road, look on both sides of you. It appears to be a lumpy, tilled field, just waiting to be planted. That's a field of a'a lava rock, and it looks just the way it did when it erupted two centuries ago. Turn your attention to the split lava mound uphill just before the road's end. This is where the last eruption took place on Maui. Local legend states that there was a family living there at the time. An old woman came one day and asked for a chicken to eat. The family refused, saying that they first had to sacrifice some to the volcano goddess, Pele. The old woman raged, saying that *she* was Pele, and how dare they refuse her? She sent lava flowing their way. The mother and daughter fled toward the mountain, but Pele seized the two and turned them into stone. The hill you see, split in two, is made up of the mother and daughter, forever separated by a vengeful Pele.

La Pérouse Bay is as far as you can go by car in South Maui. It's renowned for two things: dolphins and wind. Dolphins are relatively common early in the morning. A pod patrols the area, and we often see them here around 7 a.m. and at Big Beach by around 10 a.m. But we often go months without seeing them at all. (Maybe dolphins take vacations, too.) Scientists think that, while resting, dolphins are able to turn off much of their brain (including the part that runs their echolocation abilities). They do a sort of snooze-and-cruise at La Pérouse in the early hours, counting on the fact that the shallow water and a light bottom will alert them to predators in the absence of their sonars. This means that, in the morning, dolphins are *literally* operating on half a brain. (Come to think of it, so am I before my coffee.)

When was the Last Eruption of Haleakala? 1790... Or is it 1490?

Ask most people on Maui, "When was the last time there was an eruption here?" and you'll be told 1790. It's said so often it's considered an unchallenged fact. The truth is, no one knows when it happened. The 1790 date is based on the fact that when George Vancouver visited here in 1794, he drew a map showing the lava flow at Cape Kina'u (at the end of the road in South Maui). But when the French explorer La Pérouse visited earlier in 1786, his map didn't show the cape. This, coupled with the fact that the flow looks very young, allowed people to divide the time and conclude that the eruption occurred "around 1790."

The problem is this: As a mapmaker, La Pérouse was terrible. He didn't get anything right. And his map of the shoreline was so crude and inaccurate, you can't use it to determine anything—other than the fact that La Pérouse probably flunked out of cartography school. You'd never recognize these islands from his map. Recent carbon-14 dating puts the eruption closer to 500 years ago, give or take a century. And by analyzing crystals in the lava, they can check the direction of the earth's ever-changing magnetic field. The crystals don't match the flows that we know happened on the Big Island in 1801.

What about historical accounts? There were people living here and, after all, two centuries isn't that long. Didn't they witness it? Sure, they did, but nobody wrote it down. The Hawaiians didn't have a written language until western man invented one in the 1800s. The only known historical accounts come from two sources. One is an American missionary who came to Maui in 1841. He said the native Hawaiians had told him their "grandparents witnessed it." Hmm, pretty slim. The only other account is from a Hawaiian cowboy named Charlie Ako. In 1906 he told a reporter that his father-in-law told him that his grandfather had seen the flow when he was "old enough to carry two coconuts from the sea to the upper road," which was 4–5 miles. The reporter plugged in the various ages and dates, assuming 33 years per generation, and came up with around 1750.

So we have map readers saying 1790, historical accounts saying 1750, and some scientific tests saying around 1490. Since we had to use some date, we mention the 1790 date in this book. But now you know the full story.

So now if someone tells you that the last eruption took place in 1790, you can look them directly in the eye and tell them with smug certainty...mmmaybe.

It is illegal to chase or harass dolphins or do anything that disrupts their natural behavior. It may be hard to imagine slow, clumsy swimmers harassing sleek, fast dolphins, like a lowly crop duster harassing an F–16 fighter. If you're swimming near them, dolphins can distance themselves from you almost instantly and with very little effort. But when they're resting, they're not in a very fast mood. They don't *want* to work to distance themselves. So if you swim in the same water near them, don't shoot like a shotgun in their direction. You can slowly meander toward their general vicinity, but you shouldn't try to box them in or head them off at the pass. They may initiate the contact, if they are interested. Many times we've been in the water and had dolphins come over to check us out. Most of the time, however, they keep themselves at a cautious distance. If they don't stay away, you can only interpret their actions as curiosity. In short, don't harass or chase them or try to grab them if they come close. If people continually bug them, they'll simply stop coming to La Pérouse, and we'll all lose.

Wind is also a La Pérouse trademark. If you look at the RAINFALL MAP on page 27, you can see that wind coming from the northeast (our usual trade direction) will build up along the bottom of Haleakala and get ejected where the flank ends here at La Pérouse Bay, shooting out toward Kaho'olawe island. The wind-caused chop on the water will usually start at the south end of the bay and work its way north throughout the day. The dividing line between choppy and calm water is often sharp, often around 100 feet wide.

La Pérouse Bay was well known in ancient times as a place where night marchers could be found. Called Huaka'i po, it refers to spirits who are still trapped on earth and generally cause mischief at night. To this day, there are places Hawaiians avoid at night because of night marchers. On Kaua'i there was a night marcher area that had an unusual string of bad car wrecks, which many believed were due to these spirits. (Police, however, blamed the wrecks on the other type of spirits—the kind in a bottle.)

Past La Pérouse there is a hike to a usually deserted black, white and green sand beach called Keawanaku. The setting is incredible and the snorkeling can be great there, but the hiking trail has some obnoxious footing. See ADVENTURES on page 244.

Looking at the map you'll see the upper highway less than 3 miles uphill from Wailea. Access to Haleakala, Upcountry and the Hana Highway is so near and yet so far. There's a very handy dirt road connecting the upper highway to Wailea, but the company that owns it won't let anyone use it. (They blame that old demon—*liability*.) The county is *discussing* the *concept* of *planning* to *talk* about *considering* a bypass, but in the meantime, it's a 30-mile detour through Kahului to get up the hill.

SOUTH MAUI SHOPPING

The Ma'alaea Harbor Village is near the Maui Ocean Center, a good stop after your boat trip from the harbor. Just make sure you tie down your kids, or you'll watch them career off the island from the wind here. Moonbow Tropics has a good selection of island-style clothing, as does 808 Clothing Company whose stuff reflects locally-designed and silk-screened patterns and sayings like, *No Worries*. Da Beach House is worth a stop for surf gear for teens. The Original Red Dirt Shirt has dirt-stained T-shirts. (Be sure to wash *separately*.)

Kihei Gateway Plaza off Piilani Highway behind the Tesoro Gas Station is where you'll find a Water Wear Outlet for swimsuits. Maui Clothing Co. has a huge store with items for the whole family.

Up Piikea Avenue is Piilani Village Shopping Center, featuring Hilo Hattie, which is a great place for aloha wear. They also have tons of souvenir gifts. If golf is your passion, stop in at Roger Dunn Golf. There's a large Safeway supermarket here, too.

Back on South Kihei Road you'll find Longs Drugs Kihei Center that has Longs Drugs, a good stop for souvenirs, mac nut candies and coffee, and they're open until midnight. They also have water shoes and tabis. Next door in Azeka Mauka. Who Cut The Cheese (besides having a daring name) has a gourmet selection of cheese and wines. Shoe lovers will feel right at home at Paradise Sandal Co. Don't miss Birken & Bailey's Too where Birken (or Bailey) can help you sniff out the right souvenir for your pet back home. Across the street in Azeka Makai, White Pebbles has a blinding selection of beads—finished strings or loose. For the quilter, check out Maui Quilt Shop.

If you're short of time and have a long list of souvenirs to purchase, try the Kihei Kalama Village across from Kalama Park. There's parking in the back. This covered arcade has lots of small stall-type shops that carry wide varieties of Hawaiian-style items from art glass to coconut carvings to local foodstuffs.

Farther south, Kama'ole Beach Center has Honolua Surf Co., a good place for excellent surf wear. Their long-sleeved T-shirts are wonderful to don after snorkeling or diving. Hawaiian Moons has health foods and snacks.

South Maui's upscale shopping venue is The Shops at Wailea at Wailea Iki and Wailea Alanui. Here you can find Gucci, Tiffany, Fendi, etc., not to mention a hot pink, feather boa and rhinestone-trimmed Princess phone for $450. For the rest of us, there is a great selection of sunglasses at Shades of Hawai'i. Martin & MacArthur has well-crafted koa items. Consider Blue Ginger for adorable cotton kids' clothes (and moms', too), and Sand People has nice items with a beach theme for the home. If you've run short of cash after your shopping spree, consider picking up a salad, drink and a bag of chips at Whaler's General Store. Take it to the beach in the new swimsuit you just bought at Maui Water Wear.

In Wailea Town Center, stop at Wailea Wine if you have a condo in the area or want a picnic for the beach. They have gourmet foodstuffs, cheeses, a large selection of wines, cigars; and they'll *deliver*.

SOUTH MAUI BEST BETS

Best Place for a Stroll—Shoreline Path from Mokapu Beach to Polo Beach

Best Snorkeling—Between Po'olenalena and Palauea

Best Cold Treat—Homemade Ice Cream Sandwich at Hula Cookies

Best Place to Toast Your Da Kines— Little Beach

Best Example of What Should Be a Misplaced Decimal Point...But Isn't— $350 to Use a Cabana *for One Day* at the Grand Wailea

Best Long Beach Stroll—Ma'alaea Bay

Best Boogie Boarding—Kama'ole III

Best Place to See Richie Valens Roll in his Grave—Hearing *La Bamba* at Kahale

Best Night Life—The Triangle Across from Kalama Beach Park

The desolation of uninhabited Kahoʻolawe, its hardpan exposed by unchecked erosion, is a vivid reminder of what both indigenous and modern man can do to the land. West Maui is in the background.

One of things that adds to the exotic nature of Maui is the abundance of offshore islands. Somehow, seeing multiple islands across the water adds mystery to the scene. Islands are never more intriguing than when they are tantalizingly out of reach. Because of the way they are sprinkled about, no other Hawaiian island has such great views of offshore islands. For instance, when you awaken for your first day at Kaʻanapali, you are confronted by islands dominating your view. Is that Kahoʻolawe? No wait… that's the other part of Maui; the land bridge is below the horizon. Is that Lanaʻi? No, Molokaʻi is where Lanaʻi should be. Take a look at the fold-out front cover map and the graphic above to orient yourself. Molokaʻi dominates the view from Kapalua, Lanaʻi is offshore of Lahaina, and Kahoʻolawe is the closest to South Maui.

We haven't attempted to make this a complete guide to other nearby islands, but you may want to know a little about your neighbors. Some can even be visited by boat trips listed on page 207 or by helicopter trips listed on page 186. Since Maui is the gateway to the resorts of Lanaʻi, we're including some information on them here.

KAHOʻOLAWE

If you're staying in Kihei, Kahoʻolawe is the impressive island offshore behind the tiny crescent islet of Molokini. Though it looks enticing from afar, Kahoʻolawe is an ecological mess.

History revisionists (most of whom have almost certainly never visited Kahoʻolawe) attribute Kahoʻolawe's ecological woes to either the military or western man in general. The truth can be a little more embarrassing. When the ancient Hawaiians discovered these islands, they found on Kahoʻolawe a fragile dryland forest. It was a marginal environment to live in due to its location in the rain shadow of Maui. Dry, thin soil populated by hearty but water-starved trees and shrubs marked the windswept island. In the course of their settlement, the Hawaiians cut down most of the trees on the island to make canoes, for firewood and other purposes. Without roots to hold the soil together, erosion became the thief that stole the essence of Kahoʻolawe.

In fact, by the time Captain Cook first encountered the islands in the 1770s, Kahoʻolawe was no longer inhabited and was instead used only as a campsite for visiting fishermen. When the king of the Big Island invaded Maui in the 1780s, he made a separate trip over to Kahoʻolawe and was furious when he discovered there was nothing to steal or plunder there and only a few fishermen to terrorize. When Maui children of that era asked their parents why nobody lived on the island across the waters, they were told it was because the island was sacred. Perhaps, but it was also used up.

In the mid-1800s the Hawaiian government used Kahoʻolawe and Lanaʻi as penal colonies. Crimes that got you banished to Kahoʻolawe included rebellion, theft, divorce, breaking marriage vows and murder. Starvation was rampant there and desperate escape attempts were common.

Later, western man introduced feral animals: goats, pigs and cattle. Their destructive hooves and grazing quickly completed the ecological rampage.

During WWII the military took control of Kahoʻolawe and used it for target practice. It was later seized by direct presidential order for exclusive use by the military. But the damage from their target practice was minimal compared to what the island had already experienced and was mostly limited to a smaller area. (Hitting a stationary island of 44½ square miles is, after all, a pretty poor demonstration of marksmanship. Their goal was to hit a certain *part* of the island.) Often, the military would put an old jeep in an open area and fire at it. Residents of Kihei grew up to the booming sound coming from 7 miles across the water. After a half-century of live fire, President Bush (Sr.) signed an executive order in 1990 halting all target practice on the island. Even after an expensive multi-year "cleanup," there are a large number of unexploded small ordnance scattered about the entire island; enough to make it a dangerous place to wander around.

The result today is an island robbed of her topsoil in many places, leaving nothing but an unforgiving hardpan layer. The areas that still harbor plants feature mostly gray shrubs and grasses. There is no permanent source of water other than wells. But despite that, there is a stark beauty to the place. It looks nothing like the rest of Hawaiʻi. But don't count on booking your Kahoʻolawe vacation anytime soon. The island was transferred to native Hawaiian control in 1994. They are trying to replant the island with native plants and increase the amount of soil. It's a hot, tiring job, but it's hoped that future generations will find a Kahoʻolawe that is much like what the initial Hawaiians found. Going back in time is a rare event in this world, and islands don't often get a second chance.

Maybe this time Kahoʻolawe will benefit from our hindsight and our diligence.

LANAʻI

For most of the 20th century Lanaʻi was known as the pineapple island. Almost 98% of the island was owned by Dole Pineapple, and pineapple dominated this 140½-square-mile island. In the late '80s the owners (the island is now privately owned by a mainland family named Murdock) decided that owning a secluded Hawaiian island was more valuable than owning pineapple fields. So they got out of pineapple and began marketing Lanaʻi as the "private island," complete with two high-end resorts and excellent golfing.

The population is around 3,200 and most work for the landowner, often paying cheap, subsidized rent. More than once we've seen residents taking the ferry to Lahaina to pick up stacks of pizzas for delivery back to Lanaʻi City. (Lanaʻi is a tad out of Domino's delivery range.)

Lying in the rain shadow of West Maui, Lanaʻi is arid, receiving only 10–20 inches of rain annually in most locations, and it's certainly not the most attractive island you'll visit. Some of its beaches, however, are excellent (though occasional heavy storms from the south can muck up the water for as long as six months at a time). Taking the Expeditions Maui–Lanaʻi Ferry (661–3756) for $30 each way is the most popular way to get there. (Sit on the right/starboard side.) There are also flights into the airport.

Lanaʻi is an amazingly relaxing place to stay. The second day into our first visit, we were tempted to call the front desk and complain that someone had broken into our room and surgically removed our bones. You can actually *feel* motivation and ambition draining from your body. The downside to the relaxing nature is the lack of options available to you here. The island is dominated by a few players who have more control over you than you may realize. For instance, the company that does most of the boat activities, Trilogy, also owns the island's Dollar Rent A Car (800–533–7808) and the only gas station, and you may find yourself wondering if they prefer that you take a profitable tour rather than rent a car. Because renting a car can be difficult—there are fewer than 3 dozen vehicles to accommodate all 362 rooms. (Molokaʻi has *10 times* that number of cars for a similar visitor count.) And rental car prices will shock you. In fact, *everything* is expensive on Lanaʻi. (You'll be forgiven if you start to wonder if Lanaʻi is the Hawaiian word for, "It costs *how* much?") It's easy to let expenses get away from you since nearly every place on the island lets you charge things to your room. (It's called check-out shock, and it can be fatal for those with weak hearts.)

Though resort personnel "aren't supposed to tell you this," there is another company renting JEEPs on the island with prices better than Dollar's. Adventure Lanaʻi Ecocentre (565–7373) also gives coolers, etc., with the JEEP, has fewer restrictions on where you can drive (*that's important*), and their mud tires are better than Dollar's. Sure, their JEEPs are a bit more banged up. But that's because they allow *you* to bang 'em. They also have ATV and bicycle rentals and tours.

If you rent a JEEP, use it! Although Lanaʻi's not the prettiest island, if you don't mind eating some dust and getting your hands dirty, it's a JEEP-lover's dream. Especially recommended is the 4WD Munro Trail that skirts the island's misty upper ridge. (Parts might be inaccessible if it's been raining a lot.) The views of Maui and Molokaʻi are awesome up here, and the pine trees, ferns, wild turkeys and pheasant transport you to another world.

If you drive your JEEP west of town you come to the Garden of the Gods, a very dramatic collection of weathered boulders eroded over eons in a serene setting best seen in the early morning. Past here a dirt road leads down to Polihua Beach, over a mile long and super wide. Take a tip from us and *don't* drive on the sand at the north end of the beach. Beneath that sand lurks a swampy goo that will snag your vehicle. And you'll spend hours and hours trying in vain to get it free, then someone else will get stuck trying to help and…Sorry, had a flashback.

At the north end of the island you'll find miles of empty beaches and a shipwreck off to the left. (There's another wreck to the west but it's hard to access.)

And for expanding your knowledge and appreciation for the island, you want to stop at the Lana'i Culture and Heritage Center in town. They are a wealth of good information on all things Lana'i.

The main beach at the hotel is probably among the top 10 beaches in the state. Called Hulopo'e Beach, it has a huge sand deposit and good swimming coupled with unreal snorkeling on the left (southeast) end of the beach. Venture along the rocky shoreline away from the beach, and you're treated to some very dramatic underwater scenery. Not because of the coral (which is sparse) or the fish (which are abundant) or visibility (often a bit cloudy), but because of the canyon-like lattice structure of the lava and dead coral. Chasms, holes, stacks and arches create a miniature Bryce Canyon with exciting possibilities. Avoid during moderate to high surf, however, or it may get *too* exciting due to surginess. Occasionally, large Kona storm runoff causes severe water cloudiness that can last for many months. You can easily walk to the beach from the ferry landing.

Staying on Lana'i

The island has only three places to stay, and two are Four Seasons Resorts.

Renting a JEEP on Lana'i allows you to discover the mouth-watering views of Moloka'i and Maui during your drive down to the north coast.

Go to our website for more detailed reviews and aerial photos.

Manele Bay (800–819–5053), which is actually on harder-to-pronounce Hulopo'e Bay, has the more Hawaiian feel. At check-in your credit card is momentarily whisked away to be run through their special NASA-designed hydraulic credit card press, capable of pumping more money out of your credit card than you ever imagined. The resort is very pretty and tropical, and the restaurants are good, though pricey. (There's a dress code at one of the two restaurants.) Rates are from $395–$6,500 per night.

The Lodge at Ko'ele (800–819–5053) is the most expensive lodge you ever saw and certainly the ritziest. Located 1,700 feet up in the misty, cool center of the island, the lodge is for those who want a formal, less Hawaiian experience. (Some Hawai'i residents like it for this very reason. They consider it a getaway.) The place looks more like an English manor than a Hawaiian hotel. Tea time is from 3–5 p.m. We're partial to the black currant tea with scones while sitting next to the fireplace reading Tennyson or Shelley. (OK, so we don't *really* read those dudes, but *dang,* the tea sure is good.) Food is the weak spot here. It's worth nowhere near the $45–$65 you'll spend in the formal dining room. Even the bar charges *$7* for pineapple juice (which ironically is *imported* to this former "pineapple island"). Room rates are $310–$1,575.

As an aside, you can always tell when the owner of the island is flying in on his private jet. Lawns around the island get mowed; trash is swept up.

Hotel Lana'i (866–971–2782) is a 10-room hotel that predates the large resorts. It's for the "budget traveler" to Lana'i. (If there is such an animal.) There are no TVs (except in their cottage), air conditioning, phones or radios in the rooms, but they have mini fridges and ceiling fans. The single-wall construction means the sound carries easily from room to room. The rooms are very clean. Rates include continental breakfast. The rooms are $99–$169, and their cottage is $199. Their Lana'i City Grille restaurant isn't much cheaper than the other resorts, but the food is good. Prices are $35–$50. Other Lana'i restaurants, such as Blue Ginger Café, are cheap but unremarkable. Consider the good sandwiches and pretty decent pizza at Pele's Other Garden.

MOLOKA'I

Moloka'i is a long, skinny island of immense beauty and unimaginable sea cliffs. It's 260 square miles, though it was once much larger. The island owes its shape to the type of cataclysmic event that sometimes occurs with Hawaiian volcanoes. Much of the volcano from east Moloka'i broke off and fell into the sea hundreds of thousands of years ago, where *half-mile-sized* chunks of rock rolled to a stop 100 miles away. The landslide created awesome sea cliffs that are up to 3,000 feet high—the highest in the world—which are continually undercut by the ocean's waves. Think about the mind-boggling forces involved in that event. The entire Pacific rim was affected as tidal waves of skyscraper heights ravaged shorelines thousands of miles away. Moloka'i is not alone in experiencing this kind of apocalyptic event. The Big Island had a slide 120,000 years ago, and the resulting wave swept over Kaho'olawe and tossed chunks of coral up to the 1,000 foot elevation level on Lana'i. Kaho'olawe and probably Lana'i and Ni'ihau also experienced monster landslides.

The population of Moloka'i is around 8,000, and there is not a single traffic

3,000 foot sea cliffs are the tallest on the planet, and the offshore scenery they provide is the essence of exotic.

light on the whole island. Not all is rosy on Moloka'i, however. The island has a perpetually dismal economy. Most of the residents are on some kind of government assistance. Though the island's nickname is "the friendly island," you may find just the opposite. Though they are very friendly with each other (the only repetitive motion injury residents are likely to suffer is from drivers constantly waving at each other), many (though by no means all) tend to be pretty reserved with visitors. In fact, more stink eye greets visitors to this island than any other. (It's a favorite of many visitors due to its undeveloped nature, but many complain of feeling unwelcome.) NO TRESPASSING signs are conspicuously few. You either belong somewhere or you don't, and residents don't need signs to tell them that.

Local residents, many of whom are adamantly opposed to more visitors, had a nasty little war going on with the island's largest landowner, Moloka'i Ranch, which owns over *a third* of the island (mostly on the drier western half). When the ranch built a pipeline to carry

water to another part of the island, vandals destroyed it. While the ranch suffered tens of millions of dollars in losses from their operations, residents stopped them from doing any development. As a last ditch effort to save the business, Moloka'i Ranch threw a Hail Mary. They proposed developing a 500-acre strip of land at La'au Point on the extreme southwestern tip. They agreed to use proceeds from the sale of luxury lots at the otherwise inaccessible land to rebuild the long-closed Sheraton resort and to set aside 50,000 acres (over ¾ of all their land holdings) for conservation. But residents wouldn't hear of it. Handmade SAVE LA'AU signs went up all over the island and local activists influenced the land use commission to turn down Moloka'i Ranch's plans.

So in 2008 the company essentially quit the island. They closed their two remaining resorts, got rid of their cattle operations, shut down the gas station and movie complex in Maunaloa and closed off access to their third of the island indefinitely. The foreign owners say they will sit on the land until the business environment warms up on Moloka'i, but locals think they'll ultimately sell it.

Visiting Moloka'i

The two best ways to visit from Maui are either a boat/car trip, or fly over for the mule ride to Kalaupapa.

Moloka'i Princess (667–6165) will take you over several days a week (call for the changing schedule) and give you a car for five hours of exploring; it's $236 for the driver, $109 for others. They also have van tours, but you'll probably prefer your own car. Once on island, your biggest decision is which way to go. Either turn right (east) if the weather's good, or left if it's not. East wanders along the dry, southern part of the island. Private fishponds line almost the entire shoreline. With no one in front and no one in your rear-view mirror, Moloka'i feels like it's all yours. Once twenty miles out of Kaunakakai, the scenery turns dramatic (and the road narrows). The sweet payoff 30 miles from Kaunakakai is the end of the road, and the vista alone is almost worth the trip. Hala-wa Valley is isolated, quaint and strikingly beautiful. Backed by tall waterfalls, the descent into the valley is marvelous. Once inside, Moloka'i's "friendly" nickname be-comes laughable. There's a good dirt road and path leading back to the falls, but makeshift signs tell you not to go. (Unless you pay someone for a guided tour, of course.) Just revel in the bayside scenery. It's as good as the waterfall anyway.

Toward the middle of the island, a 6-mile detour from the highway leads to Moloka'i's biggest must-see, the Kalaupapa Overlook. Moloka'i was notorious in the 1800s as the site of the state's leprosy settlement. Leprosy may have been brought back to Hawai'i by a chief who had visited abroad in 1840 or by Chinese laborers a bit later. Located on an isolated peninsula called Kalaupapa, stricken patients were banished there when their condition was discovered. They didn't come here to live with the disease; they came to die. It was a hideous and vile place in those days, completely neglected by a government that

A crowd of one gathers on a Moloka'i beach.

only wanted to forget it existed. A 33-year-old priest from Belgium named Father Damien arrived in 1873 and tended to the unfortunates, living closely with them. Giving no thought to his own safety, he eventually contracted the disease and died there in 1889. The method of transmission was baffling to 19th-century doctors. They had no way of knowing that over 95% of the human population is naturally immune to the disease, which means that 19 out of 20 priests sent to Kalaupapa could never have contracted it. Damien was genetically unfortunate to be among the 5% who could.

Though his last 16 years of life were a selfless dedication to the most reviled and abused people among us, Damien was tormented on his deathbed with the fear that he was unworthy of heaven. The Catholic Church felt otherwise, and in 2009 he was officially declared a saint.

Though the disease has a cure now, there are still about a dozen elderly former leprosy patients living at Kalaupapa, which is now a national park. (Some Kalaupapa residents prefer the more modern term, Hansen's Disease; others prefer to leave it as *leprosy*. All hate the term *leper*.) Mule rides down into the area are the most popular activity on Moloka'i. (See ADVENTURES on page 240.) If you get a chance, rent the 1999 movie, *Moloka'i: The Story of Father Damien*.

From the unbelievably beautiful overlook, you realize why 19th-century Hawaiian officials chose this place. After the volcano collapsed and created the sea cliffs, the apparently cold magma chamber came back to life for one last creation. It erupted at the base of the cliff and created land that is adjacent to, but utterly apart from, the rest of the island. Only a manmade trail, gouged in the side of the cliffs, allows land access.

As you stand at the overlook, with the wind whistling through the trees, the ghosts of misery and pain that were banished there a century ago can seem all too real. It's ironic that a place once so despised is today a visitor attraction. Perhaps that's the only way to completely clear away the haze of despair that once filled the air.

Most of the workers at Kalaupapa live there, but there are a half dozen workers who hike in every day. *Big deal,* you say! Well, yeah, it is. The hike includes going down and then up a 1,700-foot-high mountain—*every day*. They say the biggest hazards are the mules on the trail that don't like to be passed and have a nasty habit of kicking them when they try. Now *that's* a commute!

The other attraction near the overlook is Ka-ule-o-Nanahoa or Phallic Rock. It's a 5-minute uphill walk. To the ancient Hawaiians, the 6-foot-tall stone in the shape of a gigantic…well, *you* know…represents fertility. It's really quite a remarkable…uh, formation. (It may have had some human help.) Even today, some Hawaiians believe that if you sit or sleep on it, it will make you conceive. Legend states that it's what remains of a husband who should have kept his eye on his work.

The west side of Moloka'i is drier and flatter. Vast beaches line much of the shoreline. You'll have the opportunity to create the only footprints in long stretches of sand though some of the west side beaches can get pretty windy. If you're returning your car from either the west or Kalaupapa, don't bother driving back to Kaunakakai to gas up. Save the 20 minutes and eat the extra few bucks to have the rental car company gas up.

While in Kaunakakai, the best food is Moloka'i Pizza Café. The pizza is definitely as good as any you'd find on Maui. Very good sauce and fresh, light crust. They also have sandwiches and pasta.

Ideally shaped to provide calm swimming much of the time, Kapalua Beach is a West Maui winner.

Of all the Hawaiian islands, Maui probably has the most user-friendly beaches. Nearly all of the sand beaches on the island are concentrated in the more protected leeward areas of West and South Maui. If you were designing your own island, that's *exactly* where you'd put them, because the other side of the island is exposed to more surf and runoff. The few beaches in Hana are good, but the remaining windward beaches near Kahului won't ring your chimes.

Because of this topographic blessing, Maui is considered by many to be the *Ocean Island.* In fact, so much of the Maui experience is centered around beaches (to a greater degree than any of the other Hawaiian islands) that we've had to endure countless hours assessing the characteristics of each individual beach. Which ones worked best for snorkeling, boogie boarding, swimming or just plain frolicking? Sometimes this research was as simple as determining if a sunset mai tai worked better at one beach than another. (See, and you thought that writing guidebooks was all fun and games. There's a *serious* work ethic involved.)

Here you can snorkel exceptional reefs, boogie board till you're raw, take a 3-mile beach walk, dig your fingers into genuine volcanic black sand, catch rays on a red sand beach, and sip a cocktail under a palm tree on a golden sand beach. Maui's beaches have earned their legendary status.

BEACH SAFETY

The biggest danger you will face at the beach is the surf. Though most beaches are on the calmer part of the island, that's a relative term. Most mainlanders are unprepared for the strength of Hawai'i's surf. We're out in the middle of the biggest ocean in the world, and the surf has lots of room to build up. We have our calm days when the water is like glass. We often have days where the surf is moderate, calling for respect and diligence on the part of the swimmer. And we have the high surf days, perfect for sitting on the beach, watching the experienced and the audacious tempt the ocean's patience. To get current weather forecasts, call (866) 944–5025. For a surf forecast, call 572–7873 or see page 2 of the *Maui News*. Don't make the mistake of underestimating the ocean's power here. Hawai'i is the undisputed drowning capital of the United States, and we don't want you to join the statistics.

Other hazards include rip currents, which can form, cease and form again with no warning. Large "rogue waves" can come ashore with no warning. These usually occur when two or more waves fuse at sea, becoming a larger wave. Even calm seas are no guarantee of safety. Many people have been caught unaware by large waves during ostensibly "calm seas." We have swum and snorkeled the beaches described in this book on at least two occasions (usually more than two). But beaches change. The underwater topography changes throughout the year. Storms can take a very safe beach and rearrange the sand, turning it into a dangerous beach. Just because we describe a beach as being in a certain condition does not mean it will be in that same condition when you visit it.

Consequently, you should take the beach descriptions as a snapshot in calm times. If seas aren't calm, you probably shouldn't go in the water. If you observe a rip current, you probably shouldn't go in the water. If you aren't a comfortable swimmer, you should probably never go in the water, except at those beaches that have lifeguards. There is no way we can tell you that a certain beach will be swimmable on a certain day, and we claim no such prescience. For instance, a strong storm and accompanying swells one year swept lots of sand from South Maui beaches and mucked up the water so badly, it took months to recover making beachgoing a different experience. There is no substitution for your own observations and judgment.

A few standard safety tips: Never turn your back on the ocean. Never swim alone. Never swim in the mouth of a river. Never swim in murky water. Never swim when the seas are not calm. Don't walk too close to the shorebreak; a large wave can come and knock you over and pull you in. Observe ocean conditions carefully. Don't let small children play in the water unsupervised. Fins give you far more power and speed and are a good safety device in addition to being more fun. If you're comfortable in a mask and snorkel, they provide considerable peace of mind in addition to opening up the underwater world. Lastly, don't let Hawai'i's idyllic environment cloud your judgment. Recognize the ocean for what it is—a powerful force that needs to be respected.

This is a good time to repeat that water shoes make entering and exiting beaches that aren't 100% sandy *much* easier. Kmart in Kahului, Longs Drugs and lots of other stores sell them. Even if you *think* a beach has a completely sandy bottom, toes have well-known magnetic properties and will often attract that lone jagged rock, ruining an otherwise perfect beach day. While snorkeling, we like to use water shoes and fins that fit over them. See SNORKELING on page 224 for more.

Theft can be a problem when visiting beaches. Visitors like to lock their cars at all beaches, but piles of glass on the ground usually dissuade island residents from doing that at secluded beaches. We usually remove anything we can't bear to have stolen and leave the car with the windows rolled up but unlocked. That way, we're less likely to get our windows broken by a curious thief. Regardless, don't leave anything of value in your car. (Well...maybe the seats can stay.) You might want to find a place to discretely stash your keys and other valuables. We don't take a camera (except disposables) to the beach unless we are willing to stay there on the sand and baby-sit it. This way, when we swim, snorkel or just walk, we don't have to constantly watch our things.

Use **sunblock** early and often. Don't pay any attention to the claims from sunblock makers that their product is waterproof, rubproof, sandblast proof, powerwash proof, etc. Reapply it *every couple* of hours and after you get out of the ocean. The ocean water will hide sunburn symptoms until after you're toast. Then you can look forward to agony for the rest of your trip. (And yes, you *can* get burned while in the water; that's where most people here get cooked.)

Water quality around most of Maui can be amazingly clear. (Just look at the photo on pages 2–3.) The Pacific Ocean is kind enough to provide a roughly east-to-west current that constantly replaces our water with clean, clear, open ocean water. There are, however, several spots where geography and human action conspire to mess up the water, and we don't recommend swimming there.

They are: north Kihei, off Lahaina (especially the north part of town), Kahana (sometimes), Kahului Harbor and around Pa'ia. Waters in these areas can be unpleasant, so avoid them.

Consider using one of those disposable underwater cameras. Even if you don't go in the water, they will withstand the elements. Their quality is better than most people think. The close-up dolphin shot on page 219 was taken with one.

Always remember that in Hawai'i, all beaches are public beaches. This means that you can park yourself on any stretch of sand you like. The trick, sometimes, is finding the legal public access and finding a parking spot. We'll try to point out a way to all of the island's beaches.

In general, **surf** is higher and stronger during the winter, calmer in the summer, but there are exceptions during all seasons. Compared to the rest of the island, South Maui waters *tend* to be calmer year round. When we mention that a beach has facilities, it usually includes restrooms, showers, picnic tables and drinking water.

Mornings are almost always best. Wind in South Maui and north of Lahaina in West Maui picks up in the late morning and early afternoon.

Beaches that are *supposed* to have **lifeguards** are highlighted with this ➕ symbol. They are **D.T. Fleming** and **Hanaka'o'o** in West Maui, the three **Kama'oles** in Kihei, **Big Beach** in Makena, and **H.A. Baldwin**, **Ho'okipa** and **Kanaha** near Kahului. Also **Hana Bay** in the summer.

Lastly, remember that just because *you* may be on vacation doesn't mean that residents are. Consequently, beaches are more crowded on weekends.

We're starting our BEACHES section at the upper left side of the island and working our way down the coast in a counter-clockwise direction.

WEST MAUI BEACHES

West Maui doesn't have *as many* good beaches or good snorkeling areas as South Maui, but the best ones here really shine.

❖ Punalau Beach

How appropriate that we start the beaches section with a beach that almost nobody's heard of. Also called **Keonehelele'i Beach** and sometimes Windmill Beach, it's ⅓ mile long and backed by abundant shade trees. During high surf (usually in the winter), large, well-formed waves break on a lava bench particularly close to shore, making it a perfect place to watch the surf. During calm seas, the beach is fronted by a bouldery tide-pool and clean water, making the snorkeling interesting, though shallow. Swimming and snorkeling are only advisable during very calm seas since unusually strong currents can form during higher seas. Access is from a *rough* 4WD dirt road ⁷⁄₁₀ mile past (east of) the 34 mile marker. You'll have to walk a few minutes down to the beach. During the week few visit this beach compared to other beaches in the area. Public access has historically been tolerated by the large private landowner. Popular with local kite surfers.

❖ Honolua Bay

A REAL GEM

This is one of the more awkward areas to describe. That's because water conditions are more variable than most, and there's no sand beach here. It's a popular snorkeling and diving destination. At times Honolua has breathtaking underwater scenery—tons of fish, turtles and coral—and great visibility. (See photo on pages 2–3.) Other times, for a variety of reasons, you can't see diddly here. If there's been a lot of rain lately, a stream on the left (west) side of the bay will generally muck up the water. Snorkelers are usually steered to the left side of the bay, but the right side has better coral and visibility, though it's deeper and used often by SCUBA divers.

Honolua Bay is a reserve, making fishing and spearing illegal, so fish counts *can* be high here. Water is colder due to

OK, OK. So the name Slaughterhouse Beach doesn't exactly look good on a postcard. But the beach sure does.

freshwater springs percolating up from the ground. Unlike most island beaches, mornings aren't *necessarily* best here. Summer is better than winter. If you see lots of surfers out around the point to the right, it means snorkeling conditions aren't at their best.

Parking may be a problem here. You probably won't see the 32 mile marker on Hwy 30, but past it are the stairs down to Slaughterhouse Beach (described below). Then ½ mile past Slaughterhouse are several small turnouts where you'll find well worn paths leading about 4 minutes through vine-covered trees to the water. Enter the water at an old boat ramp. Water is always cloudy at the shoreline, but usually improves as you go farther out.

If those turnouts are full, you'll have to drive past them and park where you can. Portable toilets on the highway.

Honolua is occasionally canvassed by car break-in maggots, so don't leave anything valuable in your car.

Maui Land and Pineapple owns nearly all the land at Honolua and has always allowed free access, yet you may see nasty, homemade signs saying KEEP OUT. Long story involving lawsuits and accusations of squatting, but the bottom line is that MLP has historically been totally cool with you using the bay.

❖ Slaughterhouse Beach

Ooh, doesn't *that* sound inviting? The Hawaiian name is **Mokule'ia Bay** (which itself is often misspelled as **Makuleia**). This beach gets its commonly used name from a long-gone slaughterhouse that used to be above the cliffs. This relatively small pocket beach has lots of sand in the summer, which can almost disappear during winter surf. The snorkeling to the right *can* be good, but the beach is subject to water-clouding runoff from an intermittent stream to the left (south-

west). There's some shade in the mornings, but none in the afternoon, and the beach is *partially* protected from afternoon winds. The morning views of Moloka'i are stunning; you won't see more detail from anywhere else on Maui. Located ⁷/₁₀ mile north of the 31 mile marker on Hwy 30 (you probably won't see the incorrectly placed 32 mile marker). Access to the beach, 100 feet below the road, is via a concrete stairway.

⊕ D.T. Fleming Beach Park

Swimming is similar to Oneloa below: good during calm seas, but vulnerable to rip currents when the surf picks up. In fact, these two beaches used to be one, until the West Maui volcano, in its dying days, sent lava to the coast to form Makalua-puna Point, splitting the bay in two. D.T. Fleming is long and wide. There's lots of shade, courtesy of ironwood trees. Picnic tables, BBQs, lifeguards, showers and restrooms all make the beach very popular with locals who come to relax and talk story (shoot the breeze), so weekends can be very crowded. The right side gets occasional runoff, so the ocean isn't as clear as nearby Oneloa. Boogie boarding can be good. Afternoons can bring an irritating wind, so be sure to bring that old BBQ grill you've been meaning to have sandblasted. (Mornings are calmest.)

❖ Oneloa Beach

A REAL GEM

Not to be confused with the other beach of the same name in South Maui. Despite the huge number of resort dwellings behind this long, luxurious beach, it is surprisingly uncrowded most of the time. It's a deceptive beach. The public access deposits you on the eastern (right) third of the beach, and you quickly conclude

The left side of often-forgotten Oneloa Beach in West Maui is usually deserted.

that this ¼-mile long, wide sandy beach has bad swimming and snorkeling because of a lava bench in the near-shore waters seemingly extending the whole length. Visitors often turn around and leave at this point. What they can't see is that the left third of the beach usually has a padded sandy bottom, making the swimming delightful when calm. (Occasionally, the winter surf can temporarily erase some of the sandy bottom.) The snorkeling around the left end can also be very good with lots of fish and some wild rock formations, but don't do it when the surf's up, or a washing machine effect will bounce you around. Plus a rip current forms. Take time to climb up the rocks on the left side to poke around the tide-pools and cove. Boogie boarding on the left side can be good for the intermediate *sponger* (local slang). This beach is susceptible to wind. (The GEM designation only applies when the wind and surf are low.) Early mornings are best. The extreme right side is somewhat protect-ed from the wind, but, of course, the swimming and snorkeling aren't very good there. (But we do like hunting for lost golf balls there, from the nearby golf course. If you find a club, you know the guy was having an off day.) No shade or facilities except for a shower and *powerful* faucet and sometimes a hose near the parking lot. From the highway, take Office Road till it dead ends, turn left, then right on Ironwood Lane. If it's too windy for a day here, consider the more protected Napili Bay or perhaps Kapalua Beach.

❖ Kapalua Beach

A REAL GEM Well known as one of the best swimming beaches on Maui, the bay is usually very protected, making timid swimmers happy. The water isn't necessarily the clearest, so snorkeling is not that hot, and the offshore waters can be rocky. You'll do well to bring your water shoes so you can walk about in the ocean without fear of stubbing your toe.

But Kapalua is a great place to wade into the ocean without worrying about getting beaten up by the surf most of the time, and the palm trees behind the beach are very picturesque (helping to disguise the surprisingly ugly ultra-expensive condos there). There are two access paths—one at the north end (which was closed at press time due to construction) and the other near the Sea House Restaurant at Napili Kai condos. The sign says NAPILI LANI, and there's a yellow fire hydrant nearby. Drive down and look for a blue beach access sign.

❖ Napili Beach

A REAL GEM

An excellent beach that seems to generate more fun per square foot than any other beach in the area. It's very recessed into the shoreline, which blocks much of the after-noon wind along here. The sand is steep, so the waves slap the shoreline then recede quickly, creating an impressive undertow during high surf. The offshore waters are quite sandy. This combination creates the best beach on the island for an activity called Monastery Tag (named after a beach in California where we invented it one day after a SCUBA dive). Now bear with me here, it's going to sound strange, but we've shown others how to do this and they *love* it. The three ingredients you need are a steep beach, unchecked (unprotected) waves and a padded, sandy bottom. Basically you lie in the water at the surf's edge and zip up and down the beach up to 40 feet each way on a thin cushion of water, digging feet or hands into the sand to control your ascent and descent. Like a low-to-the-ground sports car, the sensation of speed is greater.

Grain for grain, Napili Bay seems to invite more fun than any other beach in the area.

Here, you're only inches above the sand, and the trick is to go as far up the shore as possible without getting beached. To people on the beach it looks like you're scraping along the sand, but actually you're unscathed as you orient the shape of your body for maximum efficiency. As with all worthwhile and important endeavors, it takes years of practice and dedication. (You see, and you thought we spent all our time doing only *frivolous* stuff.) A mask and snorkel make it easier. On your back, front, head first or feet first, it's important to master them all. You really feel the power of the ocean this way. Best conditions are usually at the center/right portion of the beach.

The beach can get fairly crowded. Two accesses to the middle and south end are from Hui Drive (cutting through Napili Sunset) and Napili Place (limited parking and the public access sign is sometimes *conveniently* missing), both off Lower Honoapiilani Road. See map on page 53.

❖ Keonenui Beach

Usually a respectably wide white pocket of sand and fairly attractive. Sometimes natural sand migration strips away much of the beach, making it narrow. Slightly cloudy water, sandy bottom, steep shorebreak. On occasion, seaweed blooms create marginal water quality. Fronting the Kahana Sunset on Lower Honoapiilani Road. Only public access is from the north along the shoreline path.

❖ Ka'opala Beach

Nasty, uninviting piece of shoreline beach that gets its water from a foul creek ½ mile south of here. (Current runs north.) How appropriate that Ka'opala translates to *trash*. We see uninformed visitors swimming here and can't help wonder if they bring something exotic back from the islands that they didn't count on. Occasionally, the creek runs dry, and the ocean cleans out a bit here.

❖ Kahana Beach

Not a bad beach, not a great one. In the past they've had problems with seaweed washing ashore here, but the seaweed blooms have been minimal lately.

❖ Pohaku Park

Pretty little park for picnics or sunsets, but the water is another must-miss. Yucky. Also called **S-Turns Park**. Located just north of the Noelani condos.

❖ Honokowai Beach Park

The swimming and snorkeling are poor, but it's a good place to come with your lunch (Honokowai Okazuya Deli is nearby) and eat to the sound of the surf. On the southern end of Lower Honoapiilani Road.

❖ Keka'a / North Beach / Airport Beach

This stretch of sand fronts what used to be the old Ka'anapali Airport and runs to Honokowai Beach Park. In general, it's a somewhat narrow, sandy beach and the nearshore waters are rocky, so swimming is only marginal. Water shoes will help protect your feet. The (preferred) southern section is accessible from Halawai Drive between the 25 and 26 mile markers. The northern stretch has an access next to the Ka'anapali Beach Club. (See map on page 51.) Snorkeling is fairly good at the southern section once you get 100 or so feet offshore. The northern stretch of the beach sometimes has small amounts of the seaweed that is so common (and heavier) farther north.

The south end of Kahekili Beach Park has the sandiest bottom—and the dreamiest water.

That seaweed is common until you get to Napili Bay, which is clean.

❖ Kahekili Beach Park

A REAL GEM

A superb park, glorious beach and excellent facilities, including covered tables, a large parking area, restrooms, showers and lawn area. A windbreak running north of here *partially* protects you from afternoon winds. Kahekili is a popular place for SCUBA diving. Several companies do introductory shore dives here.

Conveniently, the best snorkeling is directly offshore of the pavilion, about 75 feet or so where a nice variety of coral and some fish await. Just plain ol' swimming offshore of the park facilities is not so good, suffering from hidden rocks at the water's edge that you can't see without polarized sunglasses. But if you walk down the concrete path south (left) toward Black Rock, you'll find that when the sidewalk ends, so do the hidden rocks in the water (for the most part), and from there all the way to the end of the beach (¼ mile) is a sandy, frolicker's delight. (Winter surf sometimes temporarily erases some of the sand, exposing rocks not normally present.) A stream near Black Rock brings colder, fresh water onto the surface a few dozen feet from shore but doesn't affect things *near* the shore. There's a rumor that an airplane went into the water between the pavilion and Black Rock. (Ka'anapali Airport used to be to your right.) We've spent many hours looking for it and have been unsuccessful. Let us know if you find it. When surf's up, there's a current that runs from Black Rock along the shore heading north. Bigger surf can make the water cloudy and difficult to enter. If it's not calm and you choose to swim anyway, better to walk down and let the current aid you coming back to the pavilion.

Kahekili is a magnificent place for an early morning swim, or just bring your cup of coffee and set the day's tone here. Lana'i and Moloka'i are usually bathed in bright light, and the often-tranquil waters create an unusually serene atmosphere.

Access is off Hwy 30 between 25 & 26 mile markers. Take Kai Ala Drive. (Puukoli Street is across the street.)

❖ Black Rock

A REAL GEM

This is the large, black lava rock (called **Pu'u Keka'a**) that separates the two halves of Ka'anapali Beach. (It's also where Hawaiian spirits went to meet their ancestors. See page 50 for more.) The snorkeling around the rock is legendary and mostly lives up to the hype. Lots of fish and a decent amount of coral. Start from the Sheraton side and work your way around the rock; it's mostly a wall of coral-encrusted lava. The part nearest the beach is the *least* interesting. Only one area around the corner has a lava shelf. Be careful there of surges. Watch for turtles that come to the area as customers of cleaner wrasse fish stations. When returning back to the Sheraton Maui Resort side, if you notice a current around the corner, swim away from the rock along the beach about 75 feet. The current should end, and you can swim back to the beach. (That current is from the weak longshore current that bumps up against Black Rock and slithers around it.)

❖ Ka'anapali Beach

This beach has a dozen different, often conflicting names. Pick a handful of free magazines around the island and each may have a different name. Some

A REAL GEM

names were apparently invented out of the blue. Technically, Ka'anapali Beach is everything from Keka'a (North Beach) to Hanake'o'o (Canoe) Beach, but we'll bow to the more common usage and designate it as the sandy beach from Black Rock south to Canoe Beach, including a section known as Dig Me Beach. (See map on page 51.) Ka'anapali is one of the finest beaches you'll find on Maui. This portion fronts most of the Ka'anapali resorts and Whalers Village. There's a concrete path running the entire length of Ka'anapali Beach, from the Sheraton to the Hyatt. It's a *great* place to be at sunset. This beach turns into a kickin', hoppin', happenin' place as all eyes are cast toward the sunset. Dinner cruises ply the waters, beachside restaurants hum, and couples walk the glorious beachside path holding hands and wait-

It might not be a hidden, untrampled beach, but Ka'anapali never disappoints.

Hanaka'o'o/Canoe Beach is the resting place for many of the island's competition canoes.

the north end is good. The middle offers a nice sandy bottom and good **bodysurfing** when the waves are right. When the surf's up, waves break on the somewhat steep beach with greater force, and swimming is not advised.

The north end of the beach is the best, from Ka'anapali Ali'i Resort to Black Rock. It's a lovely plain of sand and clean water. The southern end in front of the Hyatt and Marriott has a foot-gouging reef near the shore and sometimes seaweed in the water.

ing to greet the night. It's busy but not offensively loud. If you're staying in West Maui, you should strongly consider spending one evening doing a stroll along this path, then dining at one of the restaurants along here. There are five free parking lots along the beach. Since the north end of the beach is best, check for vacancies from north to south. The last one, at the Hyatt, usually has empty spots and, since we often see employees parking there (which they're not *supposed* to do), I'm sure they won't mind if you take one of *their* regular spots. You can also park at the Whalers Village Shopping Center. Any shop will validate if you spend around $20 (which is *easy* to do).

The waters at Ka'anapali are great when calm. Snorkeling at Black Rock on

⊕ Hanaka'o'o / Canoe Beach

A major hub of West Maui activity, you have your choice of jet skiing, boogie boarding, body surfing, watching canoe races and...oh, yeah, swimming. Snorkeling is poor due to bad visibility. There are covered picnic tables and facilities, and the beach is popular with locals, especially on weekends. Access is from the parking lot between the 23 and 24 mile marker. Wander north from the lot.

❖ Wahikuli Wayside Park

South of Ka'anapali, this long sliver of shoreline is wedged between the highway and the sea. Often nearly empty during the week, there are restrooms and showers, but the restrooms can be pretty scary. (County parks are notorious for their bad restroom maintenance.) The northern end is best, but fairly yucky water and little sand make it a forgettable beach park unless you're just looking for a place to eat your picnic lunch. Between Lahaina and Ka'anapali. Wahikuli means *noisy place,* an appropriate name given how close the beach is to the highway.

❖ Lahaina

Lahaina is good for a lot of things, but beach-going ain't one of 'em. The waters off this busy town are usually murky and not suitable for swimming. **Pu'unoa Beach** at the north end is also known as **Baby Beach**, but you probably won't want to spend time there. **Kamehameha Iki Park** (formerly Armory Park) near 505 Front St. is also a place where you could slip into the water, but why would you want to? West Maui has better beaches elsewhere.

Just south of Lahaina town near the 18 mile marker is **Launiupoko Park,** a popular place for beginner surf lessons, though water quality makes it unsuitable for snorkeling. Nearshore waters slope gently, so even small waves last a while. Picnic tables and BBQs make it a good place to bring cookables.

❖ 14 Mile Marker

Many dive shops and free magazines steer snorkelers to a spot on Hwy 30 called Mile 14 (referring to the mile marker). To put it bluntly, the snorkeling there usually bites. In fact, we wonder if they have even snorkeled there in the last 10 years, because its reputation is based on something that doesn't exist anymore: namely, clear water and live coral. Visibility *may* be 20 feet *on a great day*; it's 5 feet on more days than we'd care to admit. And though there is coral, more than 90% of it is dead, perhaps choked to death by runoff from a now-defunct sugar company.

From the highway, it *looks* like it will be wonderful. Driving along, you see lots of reef and contrast, giving the *illusion* of good snorkeling, but it's usually cloudy. It varies with the tides and seasons and is sometimes better, but odds are you're likely to be disappointed. However, if you're absolutely terrified of the ocean, this site has two things going for it: It's usually calm and protected, and it's often shallow enough to stand up. You will see some fish up close, but *compared to other island snorkel sites,* it's only suitable for the ultra timid. The best snorkeling is 200 yards out to sea *west* of the 14 mile marker; snorkel boats take paying passengers here to a place called **Coral Gardens**. But it's too far away from shore, and the visibility, though improved, can still be topped elsewhere.

❖ Ukumehame & Papalaua Parks

These are stretches of beach lining Hwy 30 between the 11 and 13 mile markers. Access is easy: Just drive up, open your door and fall out. The only good snorkeling is where the road leaves the shoreline, ascending toward the tunnel heading southeast. The reef and visibility improve markedly. But you'll have to swim from the last stretch of sand at Papalaua, and that can be tiring. Best just to enjoy the beach for what it is—a good place to pull over and revel in the view.

❖ Scenic Lookout

Though not a beach, the snorkeling below the scenic lookout between the 8 and 9 mile markers 2 miles southwest of Ma'alaea on Hwy 30 is fantastic. Extraordinary fish counts often bless the area. The problem is getting in and especially *out.* The trail from the railings is the easy part. At the bottom, entry and especially exit from the water are difficult. Do so only when calm, wear water shoes into the water, and pick your spot carefully. While exiting, remember the difficult-exit rule: Work with the ocean and let it do the work for you. You can use a surge to bring you up onto a rock if you do it right, or you may get badly scraped up. While in the water, snorkeling to the right is best. Be careful of surginess. Divers will find deeper waters fairly quickly.

SOUTH MAUI BEACHES

When it comes to good beaches, South Maui has an embarrassment of riches. This is where the tropical beach dream comes true. Perfect stretches of thickly padded sand usually kissed by gentle surf, clear water and palm trees create an instantly pleasing atmosphere. The surf is usually flat in the winter and very small in the summer. The only downside to South Maui beaches is afternoon wind. Shielded by Haleakala during the morning, winds tend to start slithering around the mountain at north Kihei in the late morning and work their way south throughout the afternoon. At the other end, La Pérouse Bay is where the morning wind starts and works its way northward as the day progresses. This means that *morning* almost always offers the best conditions, both for swimming and snorkeling. The last area to get windy and choppy is usually around Wailea, and that's also where the best beaches are, so we're in luck.

❖ Ma'alaea Bay
If you're looking for a long beach stroll, have we got a beach for you. Stretching from the end of Hauoli St. at Haycraft Park for 2½ miles down to north Kihei, this beach is a walker's delight with no buildings on the beach. The waters off the Ma'alaea end aren't the friendliest, and winds and *sometimes* seaweed can be irritating, but beach strolls are great

here. As you near Kihei, a portion of the shore is known as Sugar Beach. Here you can sometimes rent windsurfing boards and other beach paraphernalia. Be careful on the soft sand beyond the tide line as occasional kiawe trees (an odd choice to plant behind a beach) sprinkle painful thorn-filled twigs on the sand.

❖ Maipoina 'Oe Ia'u Beach Park to Kalama Beach & Cove Park
One of the dirty little secrets (literally) about Kihei is that you can't—or at least in our opinion often wouldn't *want* to—swim along the coastline anywhere from the northern part of Kihei town to Cove Park. We've shown it on the map as a SEAWEED area. We've caught *a lot* of flack from politicians, the media and local bigwigs for printing this, but none of them has disputed it. We've learned that much of the criticism we've received from locals about *Maui Revealed* is really misdirected fury at this disclosure. People in power here simply don't want us to tell you about it. But here's the skinny, anyway. The water in much of that area is nasty. This problem has been going on for over 30 years, and anyone who tells you it's a thing of the past should be looked at skeptically since they probably have an agenda. A discharge ditch running through the center of Kalama Park sometimes drains nasty water into the area. Slow but ever-present northward currents take the nutrient-rich water north until it dissipates. Algae flourishes in this water, making the ocean here a bit smelly, murky, full of seaweed and generally unpleasant. (From Kama'ole I all the way south, the water is *completely* unaffected.) Even when the ditch is dry, nutrients may be seeping into the ground and out to sea,

and the non-native seaweed in the area flourishes. We hate to tell you this, especially if you're renting a wonderful-sounding beachfront place in this area, but it's something you need to know. There are times when the water clears up, such as when storms flush the area or light winds affect the currents. The problem is certainly not as bad as it was in the early 2000s. Some years it's worse than others. But it can still be a recurring issue. When it's bad, avoid Kalama Beach and everything up to and including Kalepolepo Park (and *sometimes* Maipoina ʻOe Iaʻu Beach Park). Some of the beaches, such as the one in front of Koa Lagoon, have the dead seaweed scraped off each day. Others don't. Surfing lessons are common at Cove Park, which is not quite as bad in the morning since the ocean current has cleaned the water that has been driven south by after-noon winds. (I find it one of the more relaxing places to do stand-up paddle-boarding and have spent many a morning here.)

Kamaʻole Beach

A REAL GEM

Kamaʻole Beach is broken into three parts, cleverly named Kamaʻole Beach I, II and III. Kamaʻole I is the biggest and best of the three—a long and pretty stretch of fine sand with good swim-ming much of the time, restrooms, show-ers and a lifeguard. Access is a snap, and your car is very close to the water. Across the street is a convenience store, in case you get hungry or thirsty, and there's a lawn area at the south end of the park. You'll find very good snorkeling around the rocks bracketing each end, especially the north (right) end. (That end is also called Charley Young Beach.) Kamaʻole II is also a good beach, though not quite as long or as nice as Kamaʻole I. Here, too, good snorkeling exists around the rocky points defining the beach. Of the three Kamaʻoles, Kamaʻole III is the

The three Kamaʻoles: Not a Mexican rock group, just a nice trio of beaches.

most popular with locals. There is a small spot here where waves focus, even during calm seas, which makes the boogie boarding as reliable as you're gonna get in South Maui. There's some decent snorkeling at the north end near the rocks, but beware of a particularly bad surge there if the sea's not calm. There is a *huge* lawn at the south end of Kama'ole III, which makes a great place to fly a kite or toss a Frisbee or football, and there's a limited playground for the keiki. Unfortunately, Kama'ole III is also the messiest of the three beaches due to its usage, and the sand beach area is relatively small. All three Kama-'oles are easily identified from South Kihei Road between Alanui Ke Alii and Keonekai roads. All have showers and restrooms. On S. Kihei Road. See map on page 129.

❖ Keawakapu Beach

A REAL GEM

One of the most criminally underrated beaches in South Maui. Very long with gobs of fine sand on and offshore. The only resorts on the beach are at the north end. The rest is lined with *very* expensive houses. The area in front of the main public access has a huge, well-padded sandy bottom, perfect for frolicking with minimal fear of stubbing your toe on a rock. (You've never *really* cursed until you've cursed a beach rock that has attacked your foot.) If you walk to the south (left), the beach widens, and you'll find another large sandy bottom area. This part of the beach is amazingly underused. Farther south is the third Keawakapu entrance. (The first two have parking lots at the intersection of South Kihei Road and Kilohana and near the Mana Kai Resort.) Few people other than locals even know about this third entrance (which has a shower) at the unnoticed end of South Kihei Road, and the water off-

shore is very well sanded. (This is probably a good time to tell you that sunglasses that are *polarized* are amazing at detecting dark rocks on the sandy bottom.) Mornings are best; afternoons can be windy. One caveat about Keawakapu: Some plants on the backshore attract bees, which usually aren't a problem, but it's sometimes possible to step on an errant bee blown onto the sandy shoreline, especially in the windy afternoon. At the south end of S. Kihei Road. See maps on pages 129 and 131.

❖ Mokapu & Ulua Beach

These two beaches are usually spoken of in the same sentence since they share the same parking lot north of the Shops at Wailea. When you take the short path down, the beach on your left is Ulua, on the right is Mokapu. The sand at Ulua doesn't extend as far offshore as most of the other beaches in the area. We prefer Mokapu; it's more picturesque, is used a bit less and has slightly clearer water. Ulua is a popular dive spot. Though a tad overdived, it's nice with a lot of coral, albeit crowded, and the visibility is often poor. Night dives have pretty easy access—a big plus. The 51 parking stalls fill up *early* since most slots are snagged by dive companies taking students here for introductory SCUBA lessons. Access to Mokapu isn't dependent on the parking lot, however. You can park at the southern Keawakapu lot and stroll around the corner along the beach to the left to get to Mokapu. You're at Mokapu when you see a wooden walkway inland.

❖ Wailea Beach

A REAL GEM

An outstanding beach! Over ⅓ mile long, this classic crescent of sand has been ranked by several beach rankings (yes, there *are* people who do

Sigh! Lovely Wailea, just another amazing South Maui beach.

that) as the best beach in America. Terrific clear water, fine-grained sand, picturesque setting, calm waters most of the time, excellent swimming; Wailea should be on your short list of beaches to visit while here. The biggest problem at Wailea is parking. The resort has provided a parking lot, accessed just past the Grand Wailea, but it may fill up if you don't get there early. (However, the Wailea parking lot usually fills up *after* the Ulua/Mokapu Beach parking lot.) Showers and restrooms are provided. As with all South Maui beaches, morning is better than afternoon, though Wailea won't get windy as early as beaches farther north. Snorkeling can be decent at each end when calm. Boogie boarding can be very good for novices at the far south (left) side when there's a little surf. (But remember, small surf is often a South Maui hallmark, so boogie boarding is not always possible.) Waves at Wailea are short, close to shore and easy to catch without fins. Just stand there and jump with them. Stay just far enough away from the rocks at the end of the beach to avoid them. The tiny cove just past the rocks at the south end has a rocky bottom. Good for sunbathing, but not for swimming.

❖ Polo Beach

Easy access and more parking than other Wailea beaches, Polo has restrooms, a shower, picnic tables and BBQ grills on the lawn above the beach. The beach isn't as deep as some other Wailea beaches, and there are a few more hidden rocks in the sand, but it's a fine beach, nonetheless, and the water is usually clear. Parking is ample and rarely fills up. There are beach chairs lining the beach, though they're *presumably* for guests of the Fairmont Kea Lani, which backs the beach. Located 2 miles from the Wailea Ike intersection; see map on page 131.

❖ Palauea Beach

A REAL GEM Used primarily by local residents who take the short path through the trees to this lesser-known beach, it's not usually crowded during the week. Also called **White Rock**, the snorkeling around the rocky point on the left is *very* good. It's also good on the right side, though the water isn't as clear as the left side. The gently sloping shoreline is loaded with sand in the middle and provides excellent swimming much of the time. The bay is recessed, so it doesn't get as windy in the afternoon as other beaches. No facilities except maybe a Porta-Potty, but the easy access and quality of the beach make it a winner. Off Makena Road; see map on page 131.

❖ Po'olenalena Beach

A REAL GEM

Probably the least known and certainly least used large beach in the Wailua/ Makena area. It's also known locally as **Paipu Beach, Pepeiaolepo Beach, Love Beach, Keauhou Beach** and sometimes **Makena Surf Beach.** *(How can something so little known have so many names?)* Nearly ½ mile long, there have been times when we've found other Wailea beaches crowded and found this beach nearly empty during the week. (Weekends are busy here, as all beaches can be.) The water offshore is mostly a broad, flat, gentle, sandy bottom with only occasional outcroppings of rock. The beach is gently sloping, making the water especially good for swimming during the normally calm seas. When there's a little surf, the left (south) side can offer good boogie boarding. The beach is interrupted toward the right (north) side by lava. Scramble over the lava rocks or take a shoreline trail, and you may have the northern third of the beach to yourself.

The beach is bracketed by lava points on each side, and the snorkeling around them is exceptional and little used compared to other snorkel sites. Tons of fish and a very healthy coral community,

Palauea Beach is one of the lesser known South Maui beaches.

especially as you venture away from shore along the points, make it a worthy snorkel destination. Usually *lots* of **turtles** at the left and right sides and even the occasional lobster. (By the way, lobsters are sometimes known locally as *bugs.* When you hear someone say, *Hey, brah, we go catch bugs,* it means he's going lobster diving.) The right end of the beach is rarely snorkeled and is one of our favorite snorkel sites on the island. So let's see... We have great swimming, great snorkeling, easy access, good boogie boarding when there's some surf and a general lack of crowds. *What's not to love?* The two accesses are on either side of our "imaginary" 2 mile marker on the map on page 131. The second one is a bit farther south at the Makena Surf and, though limited to nine stalls, is often unused. It's better since it has showers nearby. Go through the unlocked gate and along the walkway. If they're full, use the first access.

One quick nag: The coral and fish in this area haven't been exposed to lots of people. The coral isn't trampled and broken, and the fish haven't been fed much. Please don't start the tradition. Fish feeding completely messes up the balance, leaving only a few aggressive species while driving away the meeker fish. And while snorkeling, be *real* careful not to bump into the coral with your fins, and don't stand on it or grab it. This will keep the reef here pristine and beautiful. (OK, end of nag.)

Just south of Po'olenalena is a public access (with only six parking stalls) that leads to **Chang's Beach**. Cut off from Po'olenalena, it's a wonderful little cove with fantastic snorkeling offshore and a sandy beach to lie on. When there's some surf, the boogie boarding here can be awesome.

❖ 5 Graves / 5 Caves

A good SCUBA site and fairly good snorkeling. Turtles are common, and there are several caves. Once in the water, divers should head straight out, slightly to the right and look for the caves along the wall. Entry is from a small, semi-protected rocky cove off Makena Road. See map on page 131. You'll walk by a small graveyard (with *seven* graves that we counted, and probably more in the faint lava rock outlines). Sometimes referred to as 5 Caves, sometimes 5 Graves, but neither seems to be accurate. On Makena Road; see map on page 131. If you're lucky on a SCUBA dive, you'll find the elusive bubble cave near the shoreline. The air pocket inside is sealed and the ocean's surge constantly changes the pressure, causing your ears to continuously flux and a cloud of pressure-induced haze to form and dissolve instantly with every surge. *Real* cool.

❖ Makena Landing Beach Park

A marginal place for snorkeling, but it's usually calm with easy entry, making it a popular place to launch kayaks and do intro or night SCUBA dives. The visibility is best on the north side, which also has good coral.

❖ Maluaka Beach / Makena

A REAL GEM

You'll be forgiven if you get confused as to where Makena Beach is. So is everyone else. Ask a local for directions, and you could end up in one of *four* places. Oneloa Beach, also called Big Beach, is often called Makena Beach or sometimes Big Makena Beach. (It's also called Makena State Park.) Makena Bay, just north of here, which also contains Makena Landing, is sometimes called Makena Beach. Sometimes Po'olenalena Beach is called Makena Surf Beach. And lastly this beach is sometimes called Makena Beach. It's usually called Maluaka Beach, as the signs often say. Hey, don't blame us—we're just the messengers. For clarification *(ha!)* we'll call this beach Maluaka Beach.

Fronting the Makena Beach Resort, this wide, pretty beach slopes gently, providing good swimming during calm seas, especially toward the center of the beach where a thick padding of sand awaits. During calm seas keiki (kids) splash about with abandon. There is shade at the south (left) end, as well as restrooms, showers and picnic tables. Parking is past the Makena Beach Resort, where Makena Road back-tracks, 3⁶⁄10 miles south of the Wailea Alanui/Wailea Ike intersection. (See map on page 131.) If the lot's full, try using Makena Road just south of Honoiki. You can drop off people and beach gear at the sand, then park your car about 100 yards from the drop-off area, near the Keawala'i Church. Don't walk through the church cemetery.

The snorkeling off to the left (south) is very good with good coral and fish, and usually *lots* of turtles. In fact, this area is one of the famed ***turtle towns*** that some snorkel boats take people to see. Off to the right also offers good snorkeling.

❖ Oneuli Beach / Black Sand Beach

A REAL GEM Less known than other beaches in the area since it's not well marked and can't be seen from the road. Those who do know about it usually call it simply *Black Sand Beach.* It's on the north (right) side of that large hill in Makena called Pu'u Ola'i, and you access it from the short, bumpy, but usually passable dirt road shown on the map on page 133. (Keep an eye out for deer on this road.) Once you're at the salt and pepper

Why aren't you wet yet? Maluaka Beach in front of the Makena Beach Resort has good swimming and great snorkeling.

Oneuli Beach/Black Sand Beach is often lost in the shuffle of world-class South Maui beaches.

beach, it's easy to see how it formed. Pu'u Ola'i is essentially a large mound of lava cinders created from an enormous lava fountain. Wave action has bitten into the cinder cone, causing the loose black cinders to fall into the ocean where they are ground into black sand. Over the years shells have been pulverized into sand and coral has been…well, *processed* by parrotfish, adding salt to the pepper.

The water at Black Sand Beach is usually calm, but the sand gives way to a lava shelf at the water's edge, making the swimming marginal. However, the snorkeling can be great, and turtles are very common on the left side near the hill. Visibility is usually cloudy near the shore, so head out and to the left for lots of coral, turtles and fish. If it's calm, you can snorkel all the way around Pu'u Ola'i, and it gets even better. Beware of any currents by occasionally stopping to see if you are drifting. Kayakers sometimes visit the beach, but it's rarely crowded.

➕ Big Beach / Oneloa / Makena

Big Beach is what many people think of when they think of a Hawaiian beach. It is considered by many to be *the* beach

on Maui. (Not to be confused with another beach in West Maui also called Oneloa Beach.)

A REAL GEM

Almost ⅔ mile long and over 100 feet wide, this beautiful crescent of golden sand is a dream for swimmers, snorkelers, frolickers and sometimes boogie boarders. When seas are calm, the water is very inviting. You won't find it empty; it's one of the more popular beaches. But you *will* find it enchanting.

During the '60s hippies from the mainland came to Maui looking to get back to nature, and they found their nirvana at what was then an isolated beach. Unable to remember its Hawaiian name, Oneloa (meaning *long sands*), they referred to it as simply Big Beach, a name that has stuck. (They also called it Makena Beach, which is incorrect. Makena Beach is farther north, but that name, too, has stuck.) After several years of hippie occupation, disease outbreaks from a lack of hygiene, lack of proper waste disposal, and contaminated water supplies along with rampant drug use, authorities raided and evicted the illegal "campers" in 1972. Today Big Beach is a state park. Porta-Potties and picnic tables are available. Parking fees were in flux at press time.

The large hill on the north (right) end of the beach is called Pu'u Ola'i, or Earthquake Hill. It was the site of the huge eruption described on page 132.

From the right side of the beach, you can take a short trail to a promontory. (Walk up a little, then turn left rather than continuing up the steeper gravel portion.) On the lava promontory, 20 feet above the water, there are several short trails leading shoreward that end at nice places to watch the sunset. The views of Big Beach from up here are delicious. On the other side of the promontory is a smaller beach. Let's see. The big beach is known as Big Beach, so what do you think the hippies called the little beach? Hmm, that's a toughie. How about **Little Beach**? (Darned clever, they were.) This ideal pocket of sand tucked away in a nook of Pu'u Ola'i offers great swimming, snorkel-

ing, boogie boarding and bodysurfing. As it's not visible from the road, it is often used by nudists, which, by the way, is illegal in Hawai'i. (We tell you this so that if nudity bothers you, you may want to pass on Little Beach. Hmm. I wonder if there's another reason they call it Little Beach...) Another thing you need to know is that Little Beach is occasionally (but not too often) occupied by squatters in makeshift tents, creating an unfriendly atmosphere. Aside from these caveats, you may want to take a peek at Little Beach from the trail on the promontory overlooking the sand to see if it's right for you that day. If it is, head on down and stake a claim to some sand. Weekends at Little Beach can be packed. The ocean has a sandy shoreline bottom, excellent for swimming, and the snorkeling around the points at both ends of the beach is good during calm seas. If you swim to Little Beach from Big Beach, the current can make swimming back annoying. Consider walking back if it's a problem that day.

There are two parking lots for Big Beach that you'll see from the road.

Jewel-like waters and endless sand—Big Beach lives up to its name.

Actually, if you're not going to Little Beach, consider driving past the second lot and park on the road at the south (left) end of the beach where there's shade on the beach and less crowds.

You have several food options via road stands nearby. Your best bet is Makena Grill, closer to Secret Cove (below), or the plate lunch stands. Avoid Jawz Tacos.

❖ Pa'ako Beach / Secret Cove

A REAL GEM

This beach is *literally* a hole in the wall, or at least access to it is. That impressive rock wall you see just past (south of) Big Beach hides some impressive beachfront homes. But across from telephone pole #E2–3 (the first pole you encounter past Big Beach, in case someone steals the marking) is an opening in the wall, a legal public access. Walk through and you find a beautiful little pocket of sand. This is a popular place to get married, and for good reason. In the morning the views of Kaho'olawe and Molokini from this pocket are outstanding, and the little beach simply looks charming. Since it's small, it doesn't take much to fill it up; mornings are best. Off to the left, in front of a beach house, is a smaller pocket of sand. The beach doesn't really have a name other than Secret Cove. But the point on your right is called Pa'ako, so we'll call it that.

❖ 'Ahihi Cove

Located just inside the 'Ahihi–Kina'u Natural Area Reserve (where it's illegal to capture or spear fish), the fish life here can be excellent, though visibility tends to be cloudy. No sand beach, but the cove is usually protected from wind and surf and access and water entry are fairly easy. Dumps (below) offers better snorkeling for those who are experienced. South of Wailea; see map on page 133.

❖ Dumps

Yeah, I went snorkeling on Maui at a place called Dumps. Makes you want to brag to all your buddies back home, huh? Well, the state actually *wants* you to snorkel here, because they closed off access to the shoreline south of here, including the snorkel sites Fishbowl and Aquarium. Located just past impossible-to-miss 'Ahihi Cove, Dumps (named after a now-vanished rubbish dump) has pretty mature coral and reasonable fish counts. Visibility usually isn't great. The winds can blow you out to sea, and the surge can get rough near the shore. Though you'll see lots of life, we suggest this spot only for intermediate snorkelers and even then only on light wind and surf days. After your 5-minute walk to the shore (and the only spit of sand near the center of the cove), kick out past the exposed rock, 25 yards out, and go right. The best area is near the low black cliffs.

❖ La Pérouse Bay

In South Maui, this is as far as you can go by car. There's no sand beach here, except for some small pockets at the south end of the bay, but the fish life is rich. La Pérouse Bay is a great example of incomplete information. We won't even guess how many times we've been there and seen visitors carrying their snorkel bag to the shore, only to come out several minutes later dejected, saying they couldn't see anything. All they were told, either in the snorkel shop or from one of the free magazines, is that there is good snorkeling "at La Pérouse Bay." But the visitors saw diddly. That's because the visibility there at the end of the road is *terrible.* The private estate, situated on the bay to the right, is where visibility is the worst. But if you go *past* their little cove, staying along the shoreline on the right, each successive cove gets clearer (though never crystal clear), and the fish life gets better and better. About four coves down, the fish life is some of the best you'll find *anywhere on the island*. The variety is incomparable. At press time, however, the state had "temporarily" closed that part of the shoreline to snorkeling.

La Pérouse is a common place to see dolphins in the early morning. A large pod seems to cruise this area, heading northward as the morning progresses. We often see them here around 7 a.m., then at Big Beach around 10 a.m. Turtles are also relatively common, though more so just north in 'Ahihi Cove.

❖ Keawanaku

Any local reading this will say, *where?* That's because this beach really has no name and has been virtually unknown until now. It's past the end of the road in South Maui. You need to hike to it. See ADVENTURES on page 244 for more. At times the ocean reclaims the sand here.

THE BOTTOM OF MAUI

Past Keawanaku the shoreline is rocky and windy, and the seas are usually harsh. Other than one inaccessible pocket at the base of a cliff and a tiny seasonal sand patch, you could explore the entire 30 miles of shoreline (which we've done), and you won't find *one* sand beach until you get to Hana. The only area frequently accessed (mostly by locals) is Nu'u Bay, described on page 112 and the unnamed black sand patch between the 29 and 30 mile markers.

HANA BEACHES

Hana has only a few beaches. *Ahh, but what beaches!* A red sand beach, a black sand beach and the best body surfing beach on the island. Since there's no way you'd ever drive all the way to Hana just for a day at the beach, we've deviated from our usual format and listed them in HANA HIGHWAY SIGHTS.

THE NORTH SHORE OF HALEAKALA– FROM HANA TO CENTRAL MAUI

Hana is on the eastern tip of the island, and once you're west of Hana, the shoreline turns rocky. There are a few bays that you can visit (listed in the driving tours), but they don't have sand and are exposed to the higher surf normally present all along this windward coast. Not until the towns of Pa'ia and Kahului will you find beaches, and they are *not* in the same league as South and West Maui's beaches.

➊ Ho'okipa Beach Park

This is the only beach on this coast that visitors will probably be interested in. Near the 9 mile marker on Hwy 36, it's upcurrent of most of the runoff that plagues other area beaches. It's widely recognized as perhaps the best place in the world to windsurf, and boarders from everywhere make their pilgrimage to this spot. If you're not an expert, don't try. If the ocean doesn't get you, the surprisingly snobbish windsurfers will. (Novices use Kanaha Beach.) But this is a *great* place to watch the hordes of windsurfers as well as the pounding surf that often racks the shore. (Windsurfing is not allowed until 11 a.m.) It's uncommon *not* to have wind here. Car break-ins are a problem, so don't leave any valuables in your car.

➊ H.A. Baldwin Park

At the 6 mile marker on Hwy 36, it has a huge lawn, a long crescent of sand, good body surfing (though it's easy to get pounded into the sand here), lifeguard, full facilities, pavilion and nice views of West Maui. The downside is cloudy water from nearby runoff and very crowded conditions on the weekend. During the week it's good for a beach stroll, though you *may* find this one of the smellier beaches due to the seaweed thriving from the runoff. Farther east, Lower Pa'ia is simply a disgusting beach access 2/10 mile west of the 7 mile marker. 'Nuff said.

❖ Spreckelsville Beach

A mixed bag. On the plus side, it's a long, attractive beach with unusually firm sand, deserted most of the time during the week with nice views of the north coast. Several areas have a bench of lithified sand (sandstone) near the water's edge that provides some protection for keiki (kids) and nervous swimmers after you check for safety. On the negative side, current and wind are pretty dependable companions all day long, the water is cloudy, and (the clincher) jets departing the island fly over part of the beach, which can rattle your jaw. The best part of the beach (farthest from the airport) is at the 5 mile marker on Hwy 36. Take Nonohe to Kealakai. The other part, off the unmarked road between the 4 and 5 mile marker, is more avoidable.

❖ Kanaha Beach

This is where most visitors take their windsurfing and kitesurfing lessons. (See page 231 for more on these.) As a beach destination it won't twirl your tassels, but it's perfect for these wind-related activities. In front of Kahului Airport off Amala Street. See map on page 66.

❖ Waiehu Beach

This beach and nearby Waihe'e Beach are the last beaches on the windward side. Kind of anti-climactic to end it this way after so many great beaches, but these beaches are mostly used by shoreline fishermen and local residents and don't offer much for visitors. The water's a bit murky, the shoreline rocky, and currents can be a problem.

Hana doesn't have many beaches, but the few it does have, like Red Sand Beach, are exceptional.

*Boat trips are wildly popular on Maui, but we were nervous about publishing this photo.
The water is so clean, clear and calm, it makes the photo look like it was retouched. We promise,
we don't use tricky photographic filters or computers. This is really how it looks on a good morning.*

Pick your fantasy; name your dream. If you had to pick the one thing that keeps people coming back to Maui year after year, this would probably be it. Just about everything you dream of doing in the tropics is available here. This is where it all comes true. But where should you go, and with whom should you go?

Most sources of visitor information, free and not free, tend to steer visitors to the same group of large activity providers, such as boat tours and helicopter companies. Some of these are good companies, but we've found some to be large, arrogant visitor-processing machines that seem to take their status for granted. We've spent countless hours *anonymously* reviewing smaller companies in addition to the larger ones to give you options you won't find elsewhere.

Be *skeptical* when looking at advertisements from different companies. Everyone claims to be the "best." Everyone is "world famous." Everyone claims to have been "voted number one." You could drown in their sea of hype.

Activity providers in Hawai'i are also notorious for using computers to place leaping whales on their ocean tour brochures or showing kayakers paddling up to waterfalls where it's not possible. Or how about the tour company that advertises that with their jungle tour they'll show you "hidden waterfalls" in Hana? Wow, sounds intriguing. Too bad the "hidden waterfall" photo on their brochure is actually the artificial falls in front of the Grand Wailea Hotel in South Maui. There are shameless attempts to capture your business, and you need to be vigilant in picking who you go with.

The activity industry on Maui is *massive.* Be suspicious of recommendations from activity desks and activity booths that often only "recommend" companies that give them the biggest commissions. (Those commissions are *30–50%* of the total cost of the activity.) Some are contractually bound to certain companies. Even many hotel concierges work this way. Our reviews reflect our personal observations, opinions and experiences. We actually see and *do* this stuff (always anonymously), and this section reflects what we saw. We don't get any money for steering you in a certain direction, a claim that very few can make. While it's true you can *sometimes* get good deals booking though activity companies (or get good deals if you trade some of your precious Maui time for a timeshare presentation), we *strongly* suggest you decide which company you want to go with *before* you see them, and don't let them steer you elsewhere. Also, some companies will give you a discount if you book directly, cutting out the activity brokers.

July, August and Christmas are busy times on Maui, and it may be difficult getting what you want on short notice. If you have your heart set on a particular activity, consider reserving it from the mainland (by phone or Internet; the latter often has discounts), just to make sure there's room for you. For all local phone numbers, the area code is 808.

These are those four-wheeled things that look like Tonka Toys on steroids with knobby tires. They are often used by ranchers these days to chase cows. And they're quite a bit of fun to ride. At press time only one company was doing tours on a regular basis.

Kahoma Ranch ATV (667–1978) is the local company. On the plus side, the scenery is pretty good. You climb 1,700 feet in 30 minutes along a dusty road. (If you're looking for a Maui souvenir, you'll end up with several pounds of Maui dirt embedded in every part of your body.) There are reservoirs (with simple waterslides), views of Moloka'i and Lana'i and the awesome Kahoma Valley. (It's to the left of the giant *L* above Lahaina.) The ATVs are large, 2-seater, side-by-side models that drive more like a car. The downside is the way they're run. Guides are quiet and not overly personable. Snacks are composed of water, granola and pineapple. Groups can get large and unwieldy. (Ask to be in a smaller group, if possible.) Their 2½-hour tour (2 hours is what we got) is $129 per person, if you're a couple. Singles pay $199.

You *will* get dirty on these tours, so dress accordingly with closed-toe shoes and long pants. And if you're prone to hay fever, remember these are cattle ranches, which are essentially grass farms with living, edible lawn mowers.

The biking scene on Maui is certainly more varied than on the other Hawaiian islands. In addition to simply peddling around the neighborhood, there's the famous Haleakala downhill ride and the less-famous Skyline downhill mountain bike ride.

From Haleakala Downhill

This is probably the one you've heard about since more than 70,000 people per year were doing this at its peak, and you need to know how dramatically it has changed since what are affectionately known as "the old days." Back then you started near the summit of 10,000-foot-high Haleakala and cruised downhill virtually the whole way down to the ocean. If you opted for the sunrise tour, you'd get to see sunrise from the mountain the Hawaiians called *house of the sun,* which can be glorious. (Unless you don't dress warmly enough.)

Well, in 2007 the park service banned commercial bike riding from within the park boundaries, citing "safety concerns." (Oddly, those safety concerns don't extend to those doing the downhill ride on their own, which is still legal.) Today, the biking companies are forced to start their tour from the 6,500-foot level. You'll still see the sunrise if you opt to do so, but afterward you'll drive down a third of the mountain's elevation and start your tour lower. Most of the companies were not as up front as we'd like about the tours as they are currently done. Some, such as Maui Downhill, still promote the tour with apparently older photos taken from much higher up the mountain than they ride now. And Maui Mountain Cruisers shamelessly touted the whole 10,000-foot downhill ride on their website years after the ban. When we pointed it out to them on the phone, they said, "Yeah, we gotta fix our website."

Most people are picked up at their hotels or condos between 2 and 3 a.m. A quiet or surly stupor fills the van during the 2-hour or so drive up the moun-

tain, as thoughts such as, "Whose stupid idea was this?" or "There better not be any darned sing-alongs on the van" dominate the morning.

Once at the top, most people soon learn that they are seriously underdressed. Temperatures from the low 30s to the upper 40s, coupled with 30 mph winds at times, can turn the rarefied air to a symphony of groans and brrrs. See page 119 for more on the sunrise and how to prepare for it. When you get cold, you can sit in the van and drink coffee to keep warm.

There are three large companies that do this tour. The big guys are: **Mountain Riders** (242–9739) which rides 28 miles to the ocean; **Maui Downhill** (871–2155), which only rides 15 miles to Pukalani and **Maui Mountain Cruisers** (871–6014), which rides almost to the ocean. They take 13 people per trip, with a guide in front setting the pace and a van (called a sag wagon) pulling up the rear. Anyone who gets uncomfortable can climb in the van at any time. All three companies use comparable bikes whose wide seats are appreciated if you haven't been on a bike in a while. It's $150–$190 for the sunrise trip, cheaper if you want to sleep in a few hours later. **Cruiser Phil** (893–2332) is smaller and a bit more personalized. **Bike It Maui** (878–3364) is $130 and includes breakfast at Café O'Lei in Kahului at the end.

A Word of Warning

Because so many people do this, it's tempting to think that the danger must be minimal. It's not. From road rash to broken bones to deaths, this activity has taken its toll on visitors. The first time we did it, we invited visiting relatives to go. Back then you went from the summit, and we brought our 15-year-old niece. With only 2 miles left on the ride, a bee landed on her (not an uncommon occurrence) and, distracted, she failed to negotiate a turn and took a vicious tumble end-over-end right in front of us, landing on boulders 15 to 20 feet from the road. Even with a motorcycle helmet, she had head injuries (a deep gash all the way to the skull) and was hospitalized. It literally took over a year before her head injury symptoms abated.

Part of the problem is that riders in groups are strongly prodded to ride at least 20 mph, or the tour companies claim they'll be ticketed. And 20 mph (often faster) is pretty fast on some stretches, especially when you're still stiff from the cold or haven't ridden a bike in several years. Though the age limit is 12 years old, we don't recommend it to anyone under 16. (Incidentally, those generous souls at Mountain Riders refused to refund her parents' money even though they spent much of the day at the hospital. Also, in case they're reading this, our niece is still waiting for your promised complimentary *I Survived the Haleakala Downhill Ride* T-shirt, which seemed particularly appropriate considering how it ended.)

A Few Thoughts

A small flashlight can be handy at the nearly lightless pre-sunrise summit; many people hurt themselves stumbling around. Sunglasses are recommended on the ride because most helmets don't have eye protection. Contact lens wearers should bring drops. The colder you allow yourself to get before the ride, the stiffer you'll be during the ride. Lastly, if you're going to do the sunrise trip, do it early in your trip, when your body clock is still on mainland time.

An alternative to the massive downhill companies is to bike it on your own. Companies will take you to the edge of the park (at the 6,500-foot level) and let you ride down on your own after perhaps first visiting the summit for a sunrise. And if you can arrange your own transporta-

The view of clouds, ocean and Central Maui below are tempting, but don't take your eyes off the road.

tion (commercial companies can't do this), you're allowed to ride all the way from the summit in the park, if you like, just like the good old days. The increased risk of not having a guide in front of you blocking tackle is balanced by the fact that you get to go *at your own pace*. Also, you can choose a different route if you want. For instance, **Haleakala Bike Company** (575–9575) is located in Haʻiku. So instead of stopping at the 2,000-foot level or taking uninteresting Baldwin Avenue at the end, you can take the more scenic Kokomo Road (first stop sign outside of Makawao) into Haʻiku with just a little uphill riding past Makawao. It's $70 for the drop-off at the park boundary; for $115 add a sunrise at the summit. A pretty decent outfit, and they have some of the better bikes on the summit complete with disc brakes and front suspension.

Mountain Bike Haleakala's Spine

One of the most interesting bike rides in Hawaiʻi is down the lesser-known spiny side of Haleakala. See ADVENTURES on page 238 for more.

Renting a Bike

Of all the Hawaiian islands, Maui has the best biking opportunities. If you want to rent a bike, in West Maui try **West Maui Cycles** (661–9005) and in South Maui call **South Maui Bicycles** (874–0068). It's around $30–$60 for road bikes, $60 for mountain bikes, $15–$35 for city bikes. Both companies offer impressive high-end bikes. Consider renting in advance and leaving yours at home.

Sponger shreddin' 'em. (Surfer lingo translation: Boogie boarder riding waves.)

BOAT TOURS

See OCEAN TOURS, page 207.

Boogie boarding (riders are derisively referred to as *spongers* by surfers) is where you ride a wave on what is essentially a sawed-off surfboard. It can be a real blast. You need short, stubby fins to catch bigger waves (which break in deeper water), but you can snare small waves by simply standing in shallow water and lurching forward as the wave is breaking. If you've never done it before, stay away from big waves; they can drill you. Smooth-bottom boards work best. If you're not going to boogie board with shorty fins (which some consider difficult to learn), then you should boogie board with water shoes or some other kind of water footwear. It allows you to scramble around in the water without fear of tearing your feet up on a rock or urchin. Shirts are very important, especially for men. (Women already have this problem covered.) Sand and the board itself can rub you so raw your *da kines* will glow in the dark.

In **South Maui**, if the surf is low (as is often the case), your best chance to catch waves is at Kama'ole Beach III. You also stand a good chance at the far south end of Wailea Beach. If there are moderate waves, Kama'ole III is probably too strong. Consider the middle of the beach at Kama'ole I, midway along Wailea Beach, Mokapu Beach, Keawakapu Beach (especially in the middle just south of the two-story house with the blue tile roof) and Big Beach. A great spot when the swells are right is at Chang's Beach next to Po'olenalena Beach. (See page 163.)

In **West Maui**, consider Hanake'o'o/ Canoe Beach, Ka'anapali Beach, left side of Oneloa Beach, and Slaughterhouse Beach in the summer. Some shoreline stretches south of Lahaina can be great. Just drive along and look for conditions.

Boards are easy to rent anywhere. It should cost about $5–$10 per day, $15–$20 per week.

CAMPING

Ah, camping in the tropics. The ultimate in low-cost housing. Although Maui isn't loaded with camping opportunities, there are several places worth noting.

Haleakala National Park has some of the best camping on the island. Drive-up campgrounds are at the seashore at Kipahulu (near the pools at 'Ohe'o, but there's no water) and at Hosmer Grove near the crater. Three-night maximum. *Inside* the crater, overnight tent camping at Holua and Paliku requires free permits. Apply in person at the park the day of your trip; no advance reservations. If they're booked up, tough toenails. Same 3-night max (2 nights at a site).

There are three *highly* coveted cabins inside Haleakala Crater, with free wood (limited) for the wood-burning stove, and *everybody* wants them. We know people who schedule a trip to Maui simply because they were able to get reservations at a cabin. The cabins hold up to 12, but it's only one party per cabin. The application process is complicated and involves a lottery. You may also have to entertain park officials with juggling or magic tricks and perhaps wash their cars. Call the number below to find out how to apply up to three months in advance, or better yet, go to their website calendar. (We have a link to the giant URL off our website.) You can call between 1 and 3 p.m. to check on cancellations, if you're not too choosy about which cabin you end up with. Your whole party is required to watch a leave-no-trace video (the purpose of which is to discourage you from pooping on the trail) before descending into the crater. Cabins cost $75 per night ($60 if you get a cancellation).

Haleakala National Park
Attention: Cabins
P.O. Box 369
Makawao, HI 96768
(808) 572–4400

State campgrounds are near Wai'anapanapa Black Sand Beach and at Polipoli Park (high in the mountain). Call **State Parks** at (808) 984–8109 for permits. $18 per night per party. Five-night max. Wai'anapanapa has 12 overpriced cabins available for $90 (they're *real* basic—don't expect linens or even toilet paper!), and there's one at Polipoli also for $90.

There are only two **county campgrounds:** Kanaha Beach Park (near Kahului Airport) and Papalaua (near Lahaina. Call 270–7389 for $5–$8 per person permits.

The **YMCA** in Ke'anae is one of the best deals on the island. For $18 per person you can share a cabin (tent camping is $35 *per family*). They also have two more modern ocean-view cottages for $150 per night. BBQ grill available (bring food, charcoal and linens). Spring and summer are the busiest; book in advance by calling 248–8355.

Camp Olowalu (661–4303) on the way to Lahaina in Olowalu has tent camping for $10 per person per night and 6-person cabins for $20 per person per night. (Cots, not beds, there.) The grounds can feel crowded if just half of the 36 sites are taken. Basic amenities and cold water showers.

Camp stove gas can usually be found at **Airgas/Gaspro** (877–0056) in Kahului, **Sports Authority** (871–2558) in Kahului, and **Walmart** (871–7820).

Deep sea fishing is synonymous with Hawai'i. Reeling in a massive marlin, tuna or tough-fighting ono is a dream of many fishermen. When there's a strike, the adrenaline level of everyone on board shoots through the roof. Most talked about are the marlin (very hard fighters known for multiple runs). These goliaths can tip the scales at over 1,000 pounds. Also in abundance are ono, also called wahoo (one of the fastest fish in the ocean and indescribably delicious), mahimahi (vigorous fighters—excellent on light tackle), ahi (delicious yellowfin tuna) and billfish.

Most big fish like to cruise through deeper waters than those found off the leeward side of Maui. (The Big Island is blessed with deep water right off the Kona shore.) The shallow water here that the whales love tends to be shunned by large pelagics. On Maui you'll have to take a 30- to 60-minute boat trip to areas where the undersea topography drops off steeply. But fear not. Once there, large game fish await.

Most boats troll nonstop since the lure darting out of the water simulates a panicky bait fish—the favored meal for large game fish. On some boats, each person is assigned a certain reel. Experienced anglers usually vie for the corner poles with the assumption that strikes coming from the sides are more likely to hit corners first.

Hawai'i, the fish belongs to the boat. What happens to the fish is entirely up to the captain, and he usually keeps it. You could catch a 1,000-pound marlin and be told that you can't have as much as a steak from it. If this bothers you, you're out of luck. If the ono or other small fish are striking a lot and there is a glut of them, you might be allowed to keep it—or half of it. You *may* be able to make arrangements in advance to the contrary.

Charters leave from Lahaina and Ma'alaea. Though there are 4-, 6- and 8-hour charters, many won't do 4 hours since half the time is eaten traveling to and from the fishing grounds. We recommend the 6-hour trips. Mornings offer best conditions. Prices are $100 and up per person for a 4-hour shared charter. You can do a private 6-hour charter for $800–$1,100. 8-hour private charters go for $1,000–$1,300 or more for the big boats. Usually, the bigger the boat, the higher the price since nearly all are licensed to take only six passengers. Individual boat rates can change often depending on the season, fishing conditions and whims of the owners. Consequently, we'll forgo listing individual boat rates since this information is so perishable and instead list a few companies that we recommend. Call them directly to get current rates. If you have four or more people, make it a private charter so you can exercise more control.

If you're easy-queasy, take an antiseasickness medication. There are people who never get sick, regardless of conditions, and those who turn green just watching *A Perfect Storm* on DVD. Nothing can ruin an ocean outing quicker than being hunched over the stern feeding the fish. Scopolamine patches prescribed by doctors can have side effects, including (occasionally) blurred vision that can last a week. Dramamine or Bonine taken the night before and the morning of a trip also seems to work well for many, though some drowsiness may occur. Ginger is a mild preventative. Try powdered ginger, ginger pills or even *real* ginger ale—can't hurt, right?

Tipping: 10–15% split between the captain and deck hand is customary, if you are pleased with their performance. If the captain is a jerk and the deck hand throws up on you, you're not obligated to give 'em diddly.

Boats to consider in West Maui are **Absolute Sportfishing** (669–1449), **Start Me Up** (667–2774), **Finest Kind** (214–8510) and **Luckey Strike** (661–4606). The latter takes more than a dozen anglers.

In Ma'alaea there's **Makoa Kai** (661–0336), **Piper Sportfishing** (242–8350), and **Rascal** (874–8633). The latter is a typical 6-pack. Their fighting chair looks more like an electric chair, but at least they let you keep some of the fish. Expensive at $250 per person or $1,050 for the boat for 6 hours. They'll also tag and release.

Gliders are engine-less aircraft that are towed into the sky by another airplane, cut loose, then soar using either thermal updrafts or mechanical updrafts (caused when wind is deflected upward by mountains). Unfortunately, East Maui doesn't have either of those conditions, making soaring nearly impossible. Despite their name, **Skyview Soaring** (248–7070) in Hana gets around this by using a motorglider. During the one-hour flight you spend half the time slowly motoring your way up to the top of Haleakala (clouds permitting). Then they cut the motor, and the second half is spent gliding your way back to Hana. It's quiet and peaceful in the hot, cramped, two-person cockpit, and the pilot is good about letting you fly the airplane as much as you want on the way down. (Or you can take photos out the tiny window.) If you want a genuine glider experience, complete with updrafts, you gotta go to O'ahu. If you want the freedom that an engine brings to see the sights, try Hang Gliding Maui in Hana or one of the helicopter companies. But if you want a relaxed and quiet ride down the slopes of Haleakala, these are the guys to go with. $250 for the one-hour ride, $150 for 30 minutes. At the Hana Airport. They tend to be a bit disorganized, so make sure your reservation is solid.

OK, OK, let's be honest. A place that's known as the *windsurfing* capital of the world surely can't have world-class golf, right? So you'd think. But the truth is the golfing on Maui can be outrageous. Granted, it's probably not *quite* as good as some on the Big Island, but some courses are pretty close and will blow away most of the courses you've ever played on the mainland. The trick here is to play *early*. Wind can be the instrument of your doom here, and the later you play, the greater the doom.

Overall, South Maui courses offer the best golf and are usually calm in the mornings with winds picking up around 11 a.m. or later. Sunshine is almost guaranteed. West Maui courses at Ka'anapali

can offer similar weather with more wind. West Maui's Kapalua courses are *very* windy nearly *all* the time, but best in the morning. Passing showers are common.

At both South and West Maui courses, *greens break toward the ocean*, no matter what your eye tells you. They may even break uphill if it's toward the sea. Also, dress codes (collared shirts) are enforced more here. **Carts** are included and mandatory, unless otherwise noted.

SOUTH MAUI COURSES

If you only get a chance to golf once on Maui, we'd recommend South Maui. The exceptional morning weather, views of Kaho'olawe and Molokini, and three of the best courses on Maui make the golfing incredible. If you're a great golfer, you'll prefer Makena North. If you're a decent golfer, you'll probably prefer Wailea's Gold or Emerald courses. We'll start at the extreme south and work our way up.

Makena Resort (891–4000)

Although Makena has two courses, the South Course was in flux at press time. That's OK, because the North Course is among the best on the island, though a definite ego bruiser.

The **North Course** is where really good golfers come for a challenge. The narrowness and adjoining fairways keep it tight. Hole 6 is an odd split fairway. Stay on the left side during your drive to give you a better shot at the green, but not so far left you roll into the gorge. Be sure to look behind you at the view of Molokini. Some of the greens are as fast as pool tables, so be careful. The back nine is much nicer on this course. At 13 you have a splendid elevated vantage from the blues to the fairway below with scattered bunkers and a nice wide spot to shoot for. Number 14 is an incredible 611-yard romp downhill. Just blast away on your drive, and pat yourself on the back for your distance. 15 is pretty narrow and likely to bite you on the butt.

The course is excellent (though it could use better marked paths) and views are stellar. No metal spikes.

Rates are $185. It's $125 after noon, $99 for twilight. This represents a deep price cut, making it one of the better deals on the island at press time. Kama'aina is $75. Located just south of Makena Beach and Golf Resort; see map on page 131.

Wailea Golf Club
Gold and Emerald (875–7450)
Old Blue (875–5155)

The Wailea courses are among the most beautifully maintained courses on the island, with fewer hazards and more forgiving play than the Makena course (though they're still very challenging). The first two are Robert Trent Jones, Jr. layouts, whereas the older Blue Course is an Arthur Jack Snyder affair. All have GPS-equipped carts.

The most popular is the **Emerald Course.** It's wider than the Gold and starts things off nicely with a gently tapering 354-yard fairway march toward the ocean. Number 4 is another very picturesque hole. Kaho'olawe beckons from offshore. You may see other players on the 10th green, as it's shared with hole 17. Hole 15 is a tough 395 yard uphill par 4. Count yourself among the few who par this bugga. Too soon you come to the 18th. What a way to polish off a game! Smack toward the 360-foot-high Pu'u Ola'i. You're eventually rewarded with a half dozen bunkers surrounding the green. This course has been named the most "woman-friendly" in golf rankings in the past.

Wailea Gold also makes a good first impression as the fairway wanders down 400 yards with striking views of offshore islands. *Oh,* this is going to be a good day. There's only one small water body on the whole course, so live it up. Hole 7 is a long 567 yards with a nicely placed dogleg. Hole 8 is proba-

Course	Par	Yards	Rating	Fees
Dunes at Maui Lani	69	5,861	69.9	$112*
Elleair Maui	71	6,404	71.5	$120
Ka'anapali Royal	71	6,700	74.2	$235
Ka'anapali Kai	71	6,388	70.7	$195
Kahili	72	6,554	72.3	$99
Kapalua Bay	72	6,600	71.7	$208
Kapalua Plantation	73	7,263	75.2	$268
Makena Resort North	72	6,567	72.0	$185*
Pukalani Country Club	72	6,882	72.9	$87
Waiehu Municipal	72	6,330	70.5	$55
Wailea Golf Club Old Blue	72	6,797	72.2	$190*
Wailea Golf Club Emerald	72	6,407	70.4	$225*
Wailea Golf Club Gold	72	6,653	71.6	$225*

Carts are included and mandatory at all courses except Waiehu.
Metal spikes aren't allowed in South Maui.
Yards and ratings are from the blue tees.
* Lower fees may be available in summer months at these courses.

bly the most picturesque—a tough 188-yard par 3 lined up perfectly with offshore Molokini. This hole always reminds you that it's wonderful to be alive. Hole 9 has a pretty intimidating lava embankment in front of you, but it's not as far as it looks. Just give it your usual swing and don't try to kill the ball, and you'll make it. It's the well-defended green that you should worry about. At #11 you might as well get your sand wedge ready. More sand around the par 3 green than many South Maui beaches. Both courses are off Wailea Golf Club Dr. See map page 131.

The **Old Blue Course**, set among luxury homes off Kaukahi, is (as the name implies) older and noticeably duller. Don't get us wrong. If it were the only course on Maui, you'd tell everyone back home how great the golfing is here. But everything is relative, and compared to the Gold and Emerald courses, it's an also-ran. Individual holes don't stand out much, good or bad. They're all nice, but none great. Hole 4 at 562 yards offers a blind par 5, and the second shot may also be blind as well. At 14, slicers will need to drive carefully, lest you hit another driver on Wailea Alanui Road. The Old Blue is easier on the ego and may lack pizazz, but it's still a fun, relaxing course.

Rates for the Gold and Emerald courses are $190 if you're staying at a Wailea resort or $225 if you are staying outside of Wailea. Old Blue course is $190 for everyone. But they may offer lower "special" rates. No metal spikes. If you want **lessons**, Wailea has the best facilities and instructors in South Maui for $150 per hour.

Elleair Maui
(874–0777)
This is a hard course to get excited about. The fairways aren't in the same league as the Wailea or Makena courses, and the views are marginal at best. And, unfortunately, the rates aren't cheap enough to justify the trade-offs. The layout is wide open and not very

Tasty views and tasty fairways—golfing on Maui can be a feast.

imaginative. Here's the Tee box, there's the green. Smack the ball and keep it moving. Hole 6 is probably the prettiest with a water hazard on the right, but it wouldn't rate a second look at other island courses. The back nine seem to receive less love and winds seem stronger. Afternoon winds make it mandatory to keep the ball low on holes like #10, lest the headwind bring your foward progress to a disappointing halt.

We're not trying to beat up on Elleair. It's just that you won't get the mouth-watering, grin-inducing Maui golf experience you might be looking for. If it's the price that got your attention, try the Dunes at Maui Lani instead. Rates are $120, or $70 after 11 a.m. Mauka of Piilani Hwy off Lipoa in Kihei.

WEST MAUI COURSES

West Maui offers nice courses in *extremely* windy Kapalua, or lesser courses in somewhat calmer Ka'anapali. We'll describe them from the farthest north heading south. At both Kapalua courses you can place food orders from your GPS cart and pick it up at the restaurants.

Kapalua (669–8044)

Wind, wind, wind. It's important to keep the ball low here, as 30–40 MPH winds *are common.* Kapalua courses are difficult and require concentration and strategy. At Kapalua, seriously consider keeping your scorecard in your pocket or bag because it's easy to lose it to the wind here. (Of course, if you're playing for a few bucks a hole and losing, here's your chance to get out of it.)

Kapalua Plantation Course has traditionally maintained their fairways and greens beautifully, but they haven't been quite as pristine on recent visits. Of the two Kapalua courses, the wind seems strongest here. For what it's worth, it's been our observation that although some tough courses are still fun for higher handicap golfers, this one will eat them up and spit them out. Plantation is a serious course for serious golfers who seem to universally wear serious expressions. None of the dreamy glow of other courses; this is golfing to the death.

Hole 3 is your first crack into the wind, and it's here where most learn the need to shoot those line drives. Pop it up, and it'll come right back at ya. At 4, your drive is uphill, into the wind and blind. Hey, nobody said this course would be easy. Hole 5 is 532 yards with a head/cross wind and a deep ravine to your right. At 6, they made wicked use of hills. Lose control near the green, and God knows where it will roll. Hole 8 requires a wonderful lob over a gorge onto the green littered with bunkers. One hazard not on the scorecard is the profusion of pineapple bugs that fly into your face while you are driving your cart. Don't open your mouth while cruising, or you'll see what I mean. Hole 10 is another blind, uphill, into-the-teeth-of-the-wind hole, with a cleverly located bunker near the green. Par 5 hole 15 has a healthy dogleg ending in a hungry dip well shy of the green. But if you pop it up too high coming out of the dip, no telling where the wind will take the ball. The course ends nicely with an endless 663-yard trek with the wind and elevation helping you. **Rates** are $268 *(hurt me!),* $218 for Kapalua guests, $158 for twilight. Past 31 mile marker on Hwy 30.

Kapalua Bay Course is closer to the ocean than the Plantation and the easier to play. There's not an overabundance of sand on this course. The fairways meander among several golf course communities. Hole 4 marches right toward the ocean, and glorious #5 actually shoots over the ocean. This 205-yard par 3 is one of our favorites on Maui. You have to hit over the strikingly blue ocean onto the green. Hole 9 shoots over a gentle hill toward the ocean—very picturesque. Note the unseen creek bisecting the fairway on hole 11. It's a ball-stopper. Hole 16 is most unusual. It's a 371-yard par 4 with a pond bisecting it and a creek running *down the center* of the fairway, right where you want to be. Add the wind and an undulating fairway, and you have a very interesting hole. On Kapalua Ave. **Rates** are $208, $183 for Kapalua guests, $138 for twilight.

Kapalua Golf Academy (662–7740) is armed with state-of-the-art teaching equipment. From private lessons to multi-day schools, this is the best place on Maui to earn your spikes.

Ka'anapali Golf Course (661–3691)

Golf in Ka'anapali goes back to the '60s, comparatively ancient by Hawai'i golf standards. And while the course is fun, it ain't cheap. The course is flatter than the Kapalua courses, and it's also a more relaxing play. In recent visits the fairways were in the best shape we've seen them in years, and the greens are fast and very consistent. Wind is far less of a factor (in the morning especially), and rain is uncommon. The Royal (North) Course is the most popular and difficult, with the Kai (South) Course having the reputation of being "woman-friendly." Cars and homes are always close by on the north. Ka'anapali's best asset is its location, so close and convenient to Ka'anapali resorts. Though not as nice as Kapalua (even with the latter's slight dip in quality), the diminished wind and rains are refreshing. Both courses have fewer hazards than Kapalua.

The **Royal Course** hole 5 is a pleasant 473 yards, with the second half straddling the beach (a large, but unlikely sand trap). Instead of Kapalua's ironwood and Cook Island pine trees, coconut trees are your floral companions here. (And they're a lot less intrusive, too.) Overall, the holes aren't as distinctive as other courses around the island. **Rates** are $235, it's $189 for Ka'anapali guests, $130 for twilight.

The **Kai Course** is certainly easier. The hardest thing is crossing Ka'anapali Parkway in your cart. Things start out with a wide open 490-yard trot to the green. Greens are huge and only slightly undulating. Fewer people make more leisurely play, especially in the afternoon (though that may bring winds). The 4th green is right near the train trestle of the Lahaina Ka'anapali Railroad. The 8th fairway is one of the prettier ones on this course. It's 537 yards with short coconut trees most of the way. The South Course seems to receive a bit less maintenance than the north, but it's nice to have fewer houses and cars around. **Rates** are $195, $149 for Ka'anapali guests, $109 for twilight.

CENTRAL & UPCOUNTRY COURSES

There's one really good reason to consider golf outside the resort areas—*price!* No $200 greens fees here. Though the quality of the courses may be better elsewhere, if you can't stomach the price, consider some of these courses.

Dunes at Maui Lani (873–0422)

Maybe the most underrated course on the island. You get a lot of golfing for your $125. Granted, it's not close to the ocean and winds can be fierce here, but it's not as bad as at Kapalua. Opened in 1999, the course has a delightful layout and lots of character. The designer, Robin Nelson, made splendid use of the natural rolling terrain of this natural sand dune area. With a name like Dunes, you shouldn't be surprised to find lots of sand, and you may end up wearing out your sand wedge. Well-placed, numerous and very deep bunkers, along with the wind, create a formidable challenge. Mornings are calmest.

This is an out-and-back design with the wind usually blowing to your left on the first 10 holes (except #6). Hole 4 has smashing views of the West Maui Mountains spiced with its steep, deep, vicious bunkers. Hole 6 is a nice 178-yard over-water par 3. The small but bottomless sand trap in front of the hole is unseen, and if you shoot too far, you may soar past the hill behind the green. At 10, you need to listen for the bell from the previous golfers telling you it's clear to shoot. It's a blind, downhill volley par 4, one of the best holes on the course. You end the game with a hideously difficult 558-yard par 5, probably into the wind as the angles have shifted a bit with a narrow strip of land between the lake and the bunkers. You par this one during afternoon winds, and you're my hero.

Rates are $112, $79 for twilight and $49 for kama'aina. No metal spikes. On 380 1⁴⁄₁₀ miles south of Puunene Road.

Kahili (242–4653)

Located in Central Maui on the windy slope of the West Maui Mountains, the layout, views and price make this a compelling course. The fairways are often undulating and they make good use of sand traps and a few water hazards. The greens are very fast, and we were impressed with the fairway conditions. Winds can really pick up in the afternoons. Views of the West Maui Mountains are bracketed on occasion by some nice distant ocean views from your vantage point 500 feet above sea level.

The narrow gorge in the middle of hole #6 is hungrier than it looks, so even if you don't feel threatened, it (or the trap on the right) will likely bite you in the

'okole. On hole #7, be mindful of the strong crosswind. Overall, this is an underrated and underappreciated course.

Rates are $99, $79 for twilight and $54 for kama'aina. GPS carts included. On Hwy 330. See the right side of the West Maui map on page 45.

Waiehu Municipal (270–7400)

For a municipal course it's in pretty decent shape. The front 9 are at the ocean. Holes 5–8 are a delight as you hug the shoreline. The course was unmarked at press time, and visitors constantly ask, "Is this hole such and such?" The course is pretty light on hazards; bunkers are mainly around the greens, so the play is relatively easy and relaxing. In fact, the biggest hazard is its popularity. Weekends are a zoo, but weekdays aren't *too* bad, though certainly busier than resort courses. Winds are steadier here, not as gusty, and usually kick in around 11 a.m. The back nine was built several decades after the first and are up the mountain. Hole 13 is a beautiful elevated drive to the ocean with a dogleg right. Utterly spectacular. This is the only course on Maui where you can always walk; you don't have to use the $20 carts. (Pull carts are $5.)

Rates are $55. Residents can play for nearly half that, hence the popularity. North of Kahului on Hwy 340 1¼ miles north of Waiehu Beach Road. No credit cards.

Pukalani (572–1314)

You realize right off the bat how utterly straight this course is. The designers must have had an unusual fear of curves, but it's great for beginners. No fairway sand at all. Holes are mostly long but pretty straightforward. Even the greens read fairly true. None of this breaking-uphill-if-toward-the-ocean stuff, and most are pool-table flat. This is a great course to cut loose on. Accuracy and strategy aren't a big deal. Just hit the ball and have fun. Hole 3 is certainly the most interesting. Par 3 over a gulch onto the green. Don't like that option? Fine. Then hit to the *other* green below the hill. (It's nice to have choices.) If no one's behind you, play both and take the better score. (Did I say that?) Bring something warm as it gets chilly up here. **Rates** are $88; $61 for twilight, $43 for kama'aina. At the end of Pukalani Street off Old Haleakala Highway in Pukalani. (See map on page 115.)

This section actually encompasses two activities. Powered hang gliding (you and your instructor sit in a seat in an microlight aircraft using a specially designed hang glider wing pushed by a motor) and paragliding (similar to a parachute and is unpowered). I'm a little uncomfortable lumping them together because they are so radically different, but it seems more logical to organize it this way.

Powered Hang Gliding

First, I need to get something out of the way. Flying a powered hang glider (known as a trike) is different than any other type of aircraft. When I was growing up, I used to have a recurring dream that I could flap my arms and fly like a bird. My father flew little Cessnas, which, though fun, felt more to me like a car in the air than flying like a bird. I had forgotten my flying dreams until I reviewed a company on Kaua'i that gave lessons in this odd little craft called

a trike. As soon as my instructor and I took off, I realized that a person *really could* fly like a bird. *This* was what the flying bug felt like! I was so smitten with the craft that I eventually hired the instructor on Kaua'i to teach me, and now I fly trikes myself. So although I have no personal interest in any company teaching trikes in Hawai'i, my perspective isn't as remote as it is for most activities. After all, it's not possible to anonymously review some companies, like Hang Gliding Maui, because I know the pilot. (We're both members of the small lightsport community.)

With that explanation, powered hang gliding is the activity I recommend, for several reasons. One, it's the safest of the two flying methods, *by far.* You have an engine, the craft is bigger and more stable, and it even has a powered parachute attached to the craft...just in case. (Even my dad's Cessna can't make that claim.) Trikes take off and land on regular runways (in this case in Hana), and the ease and grace of the craft is glorious. (Rent the movie *Fly Away Home* if you want to see what they're like.) It's as close to flying like a bird as any form of flight I know. Trikes are what I have come to love so much and, in my opinion, are the safest form of lightsport flight available. (I'm not a daredevil and wouldn't fly them myself if I felt unsafe in them, though any time you're in the air you're potentially at risk, even on the airlines.) I grin like a fool every time I fly and have never reviewed an activity that generates more enthusiastic responses from other participants. It seems that whenever I see people coming off a trike (since I use the same airports that the trike companies do), passengers are frothing at the mouth with excitement, proclaiming that it's the best thing they've ever done on vacation.

*Taking a lesson in a powered hang glider
surrounded by the waterfalls of Hana—
what could be cooler?*

The local company is **Hang Gliding Maui** (572–6557). Located out in lovely Hana, the pilot, Armin Engert, is certified as a Certified Flight Instructor and is well known and respected in the ultralight and hang gliding communities. I can't review him *anonymously*, but I can tell you that his skill as a pilot is something I aspire to. Armin has a still camera mounted on the wing to take photos of you during your lesson for $40, or a DVD for $80—just in case no one back home believes you. There is a 240-pound weight limit. The cost of a half-hour, in-air lesson is $170. It's $280 for an hour. Reserve in advance. Expensive? Perhaps. But it's so unspeakably cool that the memories will stay with you for a lifetime.

Paragliding

Paragliding is, in my opinion, a much less safe method of flying. You are very susceptible to gusts of wind and to landing where you *don't* want to land. **Proflyght** (874–5433) jumps off Haleakala, hanging below what is essentially a gliding parachute. This company has been doing this here on Maui for years, and I'm sure they take safety very seriously. We've stopped and spoken with them many times (anonymously), and they seem professional and knowledgeable. That said, as someone who has piloted many types of craft, I'll tell you that personally, I am too uncomfortable to fly with them. Not because of this particular company, but because of my skepticism regarding this type of flying as a whole. The chutes are prone to collapsing (unlike rigid or flex-wing flyers), and I know too many long-time pilots who've only received injuries while flying this particular type of wing. If you choose to fly, it's $185 for a 15-minute 3,000-foot descent or $95 for a 1,000-foot descent. Have fun.

HELICOPTERS

To see Maui from the sky is to explore areas you can't reach by land. Paradise in the tropics is a breathtaking experience from the air. There are radically different reasons on each of the Hawaiian islands to take a helicopter tour. We've never been shy in our strong advocacy for helicopter tours of Kaua'i and even the Big Island. Kaua'i, aside from being astoundingly beautiful, has three jaw-droppingly compelling reasons to take a helicopter tour: the Na Pali coast, Waimea Canyon and Wai'ale'ale Crater. The Big Island, too, has an aerial objective worth flying to: the active Kilauea volcano, which is awesome from the air. Maui has...some *very* pretty scenery. But is it worth the big bucks you'll have to shell out for a helicopter flight? It depends. As a pilot myself with over a thousand hours in the skies over Hawai'i, I can tell you that flying along the Hana coast and through the West Maui Mountains is fantastic, especially when it's been wet. It's incredible, but I don't get the same lump in my throat as when I fly over Kaua'i or the Big Island's Kilauea volcano. If a flight over Kaua'i doesn't move someone, then they can't be moved by anything. If a flight over the Big Island's volcano doesn't excite, then check your pulse. But a flight over Maui isn't like that. It's very nice, very pretty, but it's probably not as much of an emotional event. It's simply cool. Maui has much to experience, but helicopters aren't as vital here as they are elsewhere.

Then there's the fact that helicopter flights are more expensive on Maui than the other islands. Even companies with outlets on the Big Island or Kaua'i often charge more for air time on Maui. It might be because of the confiscatory commissions (up to 50%) paid to activity booths on Maui, and maybe it's also because that's what the market will bear here.

Choosing a company depends on what you want. They fly similar routes and charge similar prices. At one end, Blue Hawaiian is probably the tightest operation and flies 6-passenger A-Stars and the more cush Eco-Stars. Alexair, on the other hand, in addition to their A-Star has a sporty Hughes 500, and they'll take the doors off if you like.

Companies have four main flights, listed with the best ones first.

#1 West Maui/Moloka'i Sea Cliffs

This is the best of the flights to take. After seeing West Maui and the beautiful and inaccessible Honokohau Falls, you fly across the channel and look at the stunning 3,000-foot sea cliffs of Moloka'i—an awesome sight, never to be forgotten. Then slip through the middle of Moloka'i, along the fringing reefs, then back to Maui. After going up Olowalu Valley, into the center of West Maui, you'll come out 'Iao Valley to end the hour-long flight for about $330.

#2 Circle Maui

You won't actually circle the island, and some companies see more of West Maui than others. For our Air Maui "com-plete island" flight, the West Maui portion only went into one valley before reversing back to the airport. The benefit over the Moloka'i flight is that you get to see East Maui, which, hopefully, includes a peek into Haleakala Crater (clouds permitting—they aren't allowed to fly *into* it but instead look over the rim) and the Hana coastline. An hour for about $330.

#3 West Maui

You'll see West Maui's 'Iao Valley, another valley with beautiful waterfalls called the Wall of Tears, and the pretty northeast coastline. It's 30 minutes of flight for $170 or more.

#4 East Maui

Similar to the circle island without West Maui. 45 minutes for about $260.

A Few Tips

These prices are list prices. Many companies will give some kind of discount if you ask them. Ask them about coupons, Internet discounts, or tell them you'll book through an activity booth if they don't discount it some. Sometimes they'll deeply discount if you book at the last minute, especially single passengers. In the late afternoon, call around and ask if they have room the next morning, and you may get a better rate.

If you decide to take a flight, consider doing it early in your trip. It'll help orient you to the island.

Company	Phone #	Tours	Aircraft Type	2-Way*
Air Maui	877–7005	1, 2, 3 & 4	6-Pass. A-Star	No
Alexair Helicopters	877–4354	1, 2, 3 & 4	A-Star & Hughes	Yes
Blue Hawaiian	871–8844	1, 2, 3 & 4	A-Star & Eco-Star	Yes
Pacific Wings	873–0877	Maui & Big Island	High Wing Plane	No
Sunshine	871–0722	1, 2, 3 & 4	A-Star & Eco-Star	No
Volcano Air Tours	877–5500	E. Maui, Big Island Kilauea	Low Wing Plane	No

* *Indicates whether craft contains a microphone for you to talk to the pilot.*

Morning is almost always best. Be done by 10:30 a.m. for best viewing conditions. Wind and clouds increase as the morning and afternoon progress, and conditions get bumpier.

For photos, use a fast shutter speed. Don't let the camera touch the vibrating window. Glare from the window can be a problem while filming. A circular polarizer can cut through almost all of it. Few point-and-shoot cameras will accommodate polarizers, but all SLR cameras will. Dark clothing also reduces glare.

Only two companies (see table) have a microphone so you can talk to the pilot. This is very nice because often you'll have a question about something you see. Others may say they don't have mikes for safety reasons, but that's laughable. For instance, one company has you hand notes to the pilot if you have questions. Which do *you* think is safer—the pilot *hearing* your questions, or *reading* your note while flying? Most probably don't have mikes for money reasons and because they don't want to be "annoyed" by your questions.

For some reason, helicopter pilots are notoriously bad with their facts during narrations. Our Air Maui and Sunshine Helicopter flights had such bad "facts" that we bought the movies of the flights to see how much conveyed was correct. The results were pretty poor, especially Air Maui's.

The state charges extra to park at the Kahului heliport, and the lot often fills up.

Don't wear earrings; they interfere with the headsets.

Here's the deal on seating: The best seats are up front—period. They may tell you otherwise in order to console you with your backseat position, but the front seat offers better visibility and allows the island to rush at you. Seating is *supposed* to be dictated by weight, and lighter peo-

Early morning helicopter flights sometimes show the summit of West Maui—before the clouds roll in.

ple usually go up front. (Though some companies, like Sunshine, will sell you the front seat for extra, somehow getting around the whole weight and balance thing.) Also, single riders often get placed up there since companies don't like to break up couples.

If you are sitting in the back, you want to be on the side where all the action is. On the West Maui/Moloka'i trip, the left seats are the best because of the route. On the Circle, East or West Maui trips, it depends on the direction they go. If they visit the south part of Haleakala and the crater first, then head up and then along the Hana coast, the left side is best. If they head straight for the Hana coastline, the right side is best. Talk to them on the phone and ask which route they're taking, then request a seat where the main action will be on *your* side. They may not *guarantee* seats, but make sure they know that you'll consider them weasels if you don't get the seat you're looking for. Most of the time you'll be accommodated, even while they claim that "the computer assigns seats" or "the weather dictates our route." If they don't sound accommodating, go elsewhere.

Many companies now video the trip and will sell you the DVD afterward. That's kind of cool, and you can hear your pilot on the movie, but the quality of these recordings won't match what you can buy from a pre-recorded DVD, where sights were captured in their best light. It's your call as to which, if any, you want.

Most companies use 6-passenger A-Stars. **Blue Hawaiian** and **Sunshine** have some flights on their cush and roomy Eco-Stars (or Whisper-Stars). They're larger inside and the windows are bigger, but it's 20%–30% more than an A-Star. Think of it as the difference between business class and first class. If you've got the extra cash, it's a heck of a ride.

AIRPLANE TOURS

Without as many narrow valleys as Kaua'i or the Big Island's Hamakua Coast, hovering isn't as important here, so airplane tours are a good alternative to more expensive helicopter flights.

Volcano Air Tours (877–5500) can leave from either Kahului or West Maui Airport and tours East Maui before heading to the Big Island to show you the active volcano. It's 2 hours in the air for $385–$425. (Depends on which airport you leave from, what time of day, what your hair style is, and if you can name all the state capitals.) The only ding is it's a low-wing 9-passenger aircraft, so the view is partially blocked, but the windows are very large and everyone gets a window seat.

Pacific Wings (873–0877) does private charters and will go wherever you want to go, even interisland.

IMPORTANT NOTE

If this section seems shorter than you would expect, it's because we put *lots* of shorter hikes in the HANA HIGHWAY SIGHTS chapter and elsewhere. There are many 10–30 minute hikes sprinkled in those sections since we felt that you were more likely to hike them on a driving tour than head out there for that purpose alone. Also, one of the tastiest trails on the island, at **'Ohe'o Gulch** (AKA **Seven Sacred Pools**) is in the SOUTHEAST MAUI SIGHTS chapter. See page 200 for more on HIKES DESCRIBED ELSEWHERE.

If you're going to do much stream hiking or wet rock hopping, pick up tabis (fuzzy mittens for your feet), which cling well. You'll find them at the various Longs Drugs or at Kmart in Kahului.

The clean, clear waters of Namalu Bay along the Kapalua Coast Trail.

WEST MAUI HIKES
Kapalua Coastal Trail

Let's start this section off with an easy hike that has surprises even the trail builders didn't realize. It is owned by the Kapalua Resort, and they request that you stop by Kapalua Adventures on Office Road to sign a waiver. They even have free shuttles if you want to do the trip one way. Although it's less than 2 miles from end to end, you can get 3+ miles of hiking out of it if you take other opportunities.

The trailhead starts at D. T. Flemming Beach near the Ritz-Carlton. (The other end is at Kapalua Beach, but it's tough to park there.) The first section is not along the coast and fairly boring, so we suggest you park near the corner of Office and Lower Honoapi'ilani roads. You can start with a diversion to Dragon's Teeth (described on page 54) before walking down the road to the beach access at Oneloa Beach. Head to the beach from there, turn left and you're along the shoreline.

Cruise the boardwalk here with beautiful Oneloa on one side, and insanely expensive condos on the other. As the trail ascends slightly, our map (and Kapalua's, for that matter) shows a trail down to the point, but it's hard to spot. We suggest you stay on the main trial until the other half of the loop spur trail becomes obvious at an intersection where you either turn left (to stay on the main trail) or right, toward the ocean. Head right, heeding signs telling you to stay on the trail since birds nest in burrows in the ground here. Keep going toward the ocean and the point that extends into the sea.

This is Hawea Point and it contains some absolutely *beautiful* tide-pools with clean, clear water. You'll have to boulder-scramble down to them if you want a closer look. One of the pools to the left makes a great place to take a dip on calm days because it's deep enough, and the large, rounded boulders don't have any fragile features that might be damaged by your feet. (Watch for the occasional sea urchin.) Next to that is a small pool shaped like a Japanese soaking tub that gets warmer thanks to the surrounding rock absorbing more solar heat. Though partially protected by the ocean, stay away from the pools if the ocean is raging or threatening, or you could get in trouble fast. Winter can bring particularly big waves and big dangers.

From here, you have the option to explore further. There are lots of cool things along the shoreline and it's an old public access, so you're allowed to poke around. There's a cove littered with coral rubble, more tide-pools and there's a trail that ends at Namalu Bay with protected waters.

Ultimately, you work your way back to that intersection and continue on the Kapalua Coastal Trail, which cuts through some condos and end at Kapalua Beach. Either retrace it back to your car at Oneloa, or see if you can get a shuttle (665–9110), if you are a resort guest.

Two-Tiered Tide-Pools of Honolua

Most of the island is composed of a porous lava shoreline, making deep tide-pools a rarity. On page 60 we point out the Olivine Pools, which we discovered for our first edition. More recently, we found the heretofore unknown two-tiered tide-pools of Honolua.

The shoreline along these stretches looks somewhat artistic and exotic. It's made from a fine-grain, light-colored rock and sandstone. At one area the ocean smashes against the shoreline, bathing an upper pool in a clean shower of seawater. As it fills, it overflows into the lower pool by way of a small but lovely waterfall, which is usually constant at high tide. This lower pool is attached to the ocean, and the cycle is repeated. The results make for a great place to take a dip and a wild, raw shoreline to explore.

These pools are best at high tide with the upper pool over 6 feet deep in places. This is not a good place to be when the ocean's raging. When 10-, 20-

Though it looks too sculpted to be real, the upper tide-pool feeding the lower tide-pool creates a lovely setting for a cool, ocean dip.

and even 30-foot waves tear up the shoreline, the pools become a dangerous washing machine and you'd become a limp rag if you got near them. Use your good judgment when assessing the safety here. When smaller but still active surf prevails, it's fun to be in the lower pool as waves come charging into the cove next to (but separated by lava from) the lower pool. Wear water shoes or, better yet, tabis so you can walk around the pools more easily. It's usually windy out here, but the lower pool is *partially* protected by some lava.

To get here, after the 34 mile marker, pull over to the turnout on the ocean side. Underneath the ironwood pine trees you'll see a path leading down the hill that turns into an old washed-out road. Shortly, on the right hand side, you'll notice three thick posts along a side road. This leads you down a long hill with old broken glass to a point overlooking the sea. From this windy point you get great views of Punalau Beach to your right; the two-tiered pools are to your left. Take the path behind you that leads up the hill to the dirt road. You'll pass through the remains of an old cattle gate, and another 300 feet ahead the road splits three ways. Take the road heading straight toward the tide-pools. When you're heading out, you can bypass the hike down to the windy lookout by just following the dirt road back to your car. The landowner, MLP, has been pretty cool about allowing access to areas under their domain, but at press time

Remember, there are lots of short hikes listed in Hana Highway Sights, like this one at Pua'a Ka'a, and a longer, delightful hike listed in the Southeast Maui Sights chapter.

they had stopped growing pineapple here, so we're not sure if access will continue to be allowed.

Acid War Zone to the Blowhole

There's a quicker way to reach the Nakalele Blowhole shown on page 57, but hiking to it along this route is definitely more fascinating. There is a small parking lot near the 38 mile marker past Kapalua near the northernmost

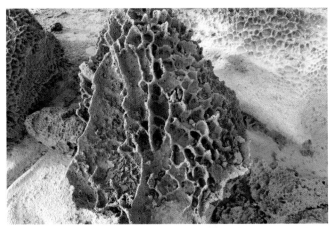

The land is literally being dissolved along the acid war zone hike.

point on the island on Hwy 30. You are allowed to hike on the old jeep road and past the light beacon that leads to the blowhole. This is not a long hike—at most 30 minutes each way without side trips—but the terrain is excellent.

See map on page 58. From the parking lot, make your way toward, then along, the sea cliffs. In recent years people have been stacking stones at the grassy field, creating a quirky atmosphere. Please don't stack any in the acid war zone. The trail is vague and spotty, but you shouldn't have trouble making your way as you first walk through a gulch toward your right before reaching the cliff. (Other paths are more inland but less interesting.) Keep going right. The cliffs are pockmarked with crags and caves, and the bouldery landscape around you is awesome. About 10–15 minutes into the walk, just before a light beacon, you'll notice some small pools below the cliffs. From down there you can see how big the sea arch you saw from the cliffs really is. Down at the pools there's decent swimming and a crack in the rock toward the sea that snorts air during high surf. The scenery is pretty down there, but

access is tricky. You need to hop along boulders, then scale a questionable ladder with a questionable rope tied to a questionable rock. These pools might not be worth it. Infinitely better pools might be available at the Olivine Pools on page 60.

Back on the trail, you descend past the lighthouse, and here the trail snags the uninformed. A small blowhole shooting from the notch of a lava shelf and wall fools most hikers. Probably 90% turn around here. But wait: This *ain't* the blowhole! Continue along the shoreline, and soon you come to an alien landscape. It looks like a war zone fought with acid. Billions of tons of sea spray, blown by the wind, have carved up the soft rock here. The land is literally being eaten in front of you. Take your time to examine some of the lava formations up close. This part of the island is like no other. The surroundings are so surreal that we're amazed no one has used this area in a movie yet.

About 20–30 minutes into the hike you come to the **Nakalele Blowhole**. There's a nice vantage point above and slightly upwind of the hole. (But you can still get wet when the ocean behind you occasionally explodes sea spray.) You can make your way around the lava to the bottom. Stay upwind to remain dry. See page 58 for more on the blowhole itself. Return the way you came.

Though not overly strenuous, this hike can be a windy affair, sometimes too windy. (Nakalele means *the leaning* because the wind is sometimes strong enough, especially during the summer, to lean into it.) If the wind is blowing you away and you still want to see the blowhole, see page 58 for a more direct (though less interesting) route. Wear good shoes; flip-flops are a bit too casual for this terrain.

Ohai Trail

In a previous edition we called this trail remarkably dull. That's because when presented with a 50–50 choice, we did it the wrong way. We rehiked it again and discovered that this 1²/₁₀ mile loop trail is infinitely better if you go *to the right* at the sign, counter-clockwise.

Located ⁷/₁₀ past the 40 mile marker on Hwy 30, pull into the parking lot and you'll see the trailhead. You'll be walking through native plants ranging from 2 feet to head high. You're inland at first and there's very little to see…just be patient. Halfway into the path you'll turn to the ocean and see a small side trail on your right side heading out on a point. Walk out here and look to the east. This is your first view of the coastline leading up to the pointed Kahakuloa Head. Now as you continue the trail you'll find yourself walking along a windswept area with small rocky hills dotting the view. There is even a bench to sit and contemplate the ocean. The last quarter of the hike rewards you with great views of the coastline and the Nakalele Blowhole in the distance. The highest hill you pass has a side trail to the top that affords the best views.

An easy hike, yes. But you get plenty of bang for your buck on the last half.

Mushroom Rock Shore Hike

This is one of those *you're-on-your-own* hikes. Explore a wild, gorgeous shoreline, go as long as your desire takes you, then take the easy way back. The hiking is makeshift much of the way. Not much trail, just make your way, and be careful of the wind and crumbly soil and rock. It's not strenuous unless you want it to be. Like the blowhole hike, wind can sometimes be a problem here.

In West Maui after the 41 mile marker on Hwy 30 (and just after the END OF STATE HWY sign) there's a turnout on the ocean side. (See map on page 62.) From here, walk toward the ocean, then toward your left to a bluff overlooking the shoreline. The cliffs in front of you are striking, even for Maui. After overlooking a small islet, you'll see several discontiguous cow paths (and sometimes no paths) to your right. If you amble the right way, you'll quickly come to a cove with a shallow reef and a rusty old pole holder driven into the rock. The little rock sticking out is an enviable place to ponder the shoreline if you're not too afraid of heights. All is presided over by a mushroom-shaped rock to your right. By the way, the snorkeling on the downwind side of the reef below is exciting, but only when calm (which is not too often). Experts only. From here, either make your way back the way you came or trudge up a gully-looking feature in the crumbly soil. Then make your way back to the shoreline to your right. Perhaps you'll stop at the mushroom-shaped rock before making your way around and then along the shoreline.

From here there's no real trail most of the time. You're exploring. Sometimes you're along the shore, sometimes you'll have to make your way inland around the large lava hills. The scenery is wild, raw, striking and, quite often, it's all yours. You can't really get lost since you're following the ocean, and the highway is not too far inland. You can spend from 30 minutes to several hours, depending on how far along the shore you want to go and how fast you go. But you won't soon forget this piece of shoreline. This is a delicious, secluded Maui ocean hike. The wind and spray have carved and chewed the landscape with unequaled artistry, and, with no crowds or trails, sometimes you feel like you're the only person in the world.

If you hike a mile along the shoreline (less as the crow flies), you'll come to the **Olivine Pools** described on page 60. Keep an eye out for yellow/orange stripes in the lava. These are deposits of ash from when the island was young and restless. Gigantic volcanic explosions caused the ash layers that were covered with later lava flows. Erosion now reveals what a violent volcano this was in its youth. Not far past here you'll have to ascend from the ocean and walk along the sea cliffs. Southeast of here there are areas where residents of Kahakuloa have dumped some of their garbage, the only mood spoiler. Continue as long as you want, then make your way inland to the highway and walk back to your car.

Waihe'e Ridge Trail

A very pretty trail with smashing valley views and a vigorous forest to gawk at. You'll gain about 1,500 feet over the 2½ miles to the end (then return).

You'll want to do this hike early since clouds moving in later in the morning diminish the view. We like to be hiking this trail by 8 a.m. to maximize our weather chances.

From Kahului, get on Hwy 340 heading north. (See map below.) At $\frac{9}{10}$ past the 6 mile marker is the road to Maluhia Boy Scout Camp. Another $\frac{9}{10}$ mile up that road is the trailhead.

The trail gets your heart pumping right away, as a cement road climbs 200 feet in short order. Then the dirt path to the left ascends through a forest of guava, kukui, swamp mahogany and Cook Island pines. In ½ mile you've gained 400 feet. Shortly after, a switchback corner reveals a pretty gulch and a bench facing **Makamaka'ole Falls**. Ahead is a peak and the trail switchbacking up. Clouds often come up the gulch and down from the ridge, colliding right in front of you. (And sometimes *into* you.)

Soon you get your first incredible view of Waihe'e Valley. It's beautiful! Some paths through the grass afford closer looks. Look down and you may see the Waihe'e Valley Trail. Now the trail is along the ridge, and you're blessed with numerous commanding views (clouds permitting).

Several switchbacks and flat areas later, you'll eventually reach the end of

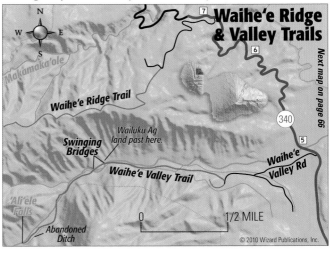

Waihe'e Ridge & Valley Trails

Makamaka'ole

Waihe'e Ridge Trail

Swinging Bridges

Wailuku Ag land past here.

Waihe'e Valley Trail

Waihe'e Valley Rd

340

'Ali'ele Falls

Abandoned Ditch

0   1/2 MILE

© 2010 Wizard Publications, Inc.

Next map on page 66

the line—a hill called **Lani-lili** at 2,563 feet. If the clouds haven't moved in yet, the views are grand. If you've got your head in the clouds, enjoy the aural and visual silence.

Waihe'e Valley Trail

This one's a 2-mile (each way) pretty valley hike that wanders along a dirt road, then a trail through forest, ending at a pleasing man-modified waterfall. It takes about 1½ hours each way. It's moderately strenuous since you're only climbing at the beginning. Then it's fairly flat for the rest of the hike. Along the way you'll need to cross the stream twice on old swinging bridges, then cross twice without them.

To get there, you head north of Kahului on Hwy 340. Before the 5 mile marker is Waihe'e Valley Road. (See map on page 195.) Turn mauka. After ½ mile veer right at the Y and follow signs for Waihe'e Valley Plantation. At a booth you'll be charged $6 per person to enter. The plantation land stops at the first bridge. Past that the land is owned by Wailuku Ag. and, though you'll be tempted to continue, a NO TRESPASSING sign is at the bridge. They used to grant access to *all* hikers, but after a dispute with the plantation, they only extend their aloha to Maui Eco-Adventures tours. If you happened to go on their tours, this is what you can expect.

After your initial climb (around 300 feet), the road levels and becomes prettier. This trail parallels two ditches built in the 1880s and 1905. Some of the tunnels bore through *blue rock*, a hard lava that requires enormous effort. Mostly Chinese immigrants worked on these ditches and tunnels, and they did it with dynamite, picks, compressed air and percussion drills. The

The Waihe'e Valley hike crosses the stream on two swinging bridges.

various barricades along the way are there to prevent *vehicular* access, not hikers. Always stay on the main trail, not the sidetracks.

The trail soon becomes notched deep in the mountain, and the river's below you. Then you come to your first swinging bridge. (You may have to cross a small stream first if the water diverter is overflowing.) Use the guide wires, and walk with your knees bent to absorb your footfalls to minimize the swinging. If you're uncomfortable, the stream's probably dry here, and you can cross on its bed if you want. In a few minutes, the next bridge crosses the stream before it's diverted. A trail bypasses the bridge, but you'd have to boulder-hop.

Two more crossings (without bridges) require boulder-hopping for a short distance. The beauty of the valley here is incredible and the trails smells of flowers and fruit. Mosquitoes are more numerous—did you bring your bug juice?

Just before the trail ends, an opening in the vegetation exposes the back of the valley with the gorgeous 2,000-foot **Mana-nole Falls** a mile away. (It looks farther.) An abandoned portion of the ditch leads you to the 'Ali'ele Falls, modified as an abandoned diverter. (Also labeled as 'Ele'ele on some maps.) The roar of the falls can be delightfully loud. Local kids often come here on weekends or during the week in the summer. According to Hawaiian legend, you were supposed to throw a ti leaf in the water here. If it swirled around and around, you were permitted to jump. If it made a circle, then went under, that meant you shouldn't jump because a lizard god (called a mo'o) would seize and kill you.

Lahaina Pali

This is a trail that slips up over part of the West Maui Mountain, peaking at almost 1,600 feet. Along the way you get excellent elevated views. Unfortunately, this is a shuttle hike, with trailheads 6 miles apart (by car), a bit less by foot. Either hike to the top and return, or go one way if you've arranged transportation at the other end.

The biggest tip is to start from the Ma'alaea side in the morning. See map on page 45. You're already 200 feet up, and the sun will be at your back. The bumpy dirt road (usually passable in a regular car) to the trailhead starts at the 5 mile marker on Hwy 30 and goes toward the mountain. Drive for five minutes and park in a dirt lot. The incline starts out gentle, which gives your body a chance to start revving up. Once at the slopes of the West Maui Mountains the grade is steeper but unwavering. This was a road for people and horses built in the 1800s, and like all good road builders, they wanted the grade constant. (But it's steep enough that they probably had to keep their horses in first gear.)

There's virtually no shade, but the near-constant winds cool you enough to give you more stamina than you'd typically have. There's not much indication of how close you are to the top, and the ceaseless climbing can lull into a thousand-yard stare-type stupor. Don't forget to stop and turn around often. The grand views of central and south Maui are fantastic.

Without warning, the giant windmills from **Kaheawa Wind Farm** burst into view, signaling your proximity to the 1,600-foot level. They're still too far away to hear the whirring of the blades, but they're impressive nonetheless from this distance. *Each* of the 20 windmills generates 1½ million watts.

After climbing to the top, your vantage point changes as you descend to the other trailhead at Hwy 30's 11 mile marker. The ocean and offshore island views create an exotic landscape. You'll overlap two roads on the way down. Bring lots of water 'cause you'll sweat it out.

UPCOUNTRY & HALEAKALA HIKES
Haleakala Crater

There are more than 41 miles of trails inside Haleakala Crater (if you include the Kaupo Gap Trail), and the views from inside are incredible. The catch is that you need to descend 2,400 feet (and, of course, *ascend* on your return) down **Sliding Sands Trail** over a 3⁸⁄10 mile span (each way) to get to the bottom. You can get to the bottom via **Hale-mau'u Trail** (which is only 1,400 feet down and 4 miles each way), but that trail, though beautiful and less steep, is more vulnerable to bad weather. If you want to hike many of the trails at the bottom, you'll need to camp inside. (See CAMPING.) Sliding Sands itself is incredibly scenic, even if you choose not to go all the way to the bottom. Consider just wandering down until just before you start to worry about the ascent. If you want a longer Haleakala hike, one of the best hikes on the island, see ADVENTURES on page 243.

At the far end of the crater is the **Kaupo Trail**, which descends all the way down the mountain. You'll only access it if you're camping. Though it's easy to look at a map and think that an all-downhill trail might be easy, don't be fooled. The footing in many places is slippery with soft dirt and fist-sized loose rocks, and it can be steep. The constant downhill can put enormous strain on knees and other things you didn't think of—like your toenails. If your shoes don't fit right, you may find that the unrelenting tapping will cause you to lose them. (Trust me. Been there. Done that.)

Polipoli State Park

An example of the varied nature of the island, this is a hike through a redwood forest. Here? On Maui? Yup. Back in the 1920s and '30s the state and the Civilian Conservation Corps undertook a reforestation program in this area that had been destroyed by cattle. They planted redwood, sugi, cedar and many other types of trees (though these are not native to Hawai'i). The trees have since flourished.

Getting there is part of the fun—if you like narrow, winding roads. See map on page 115. From Kahului on Hwy 36, take 37 to the *second* 37/377 intersection (near the 14 mile marker on 37), and take 377 north for 1⁄3 mile or so, then turn right on Waipoli Road. From here you'll have 6 miles of a winding paved road that offers smashing views of all of West Maui and the valley between the two great volcanoes. Believe the signs that tell you to watch for mindless cattle on the road. You'll even pass through an open gate with a cattle guard. After 6 miles (it'll seem longer), the road becomes unpaved. This last 4 miles is bumpy but *usually* driveable in regular cars despite the sign that says 4WD ONLY. You'll see lots of dead trees from a fire in 2007 that burned 1,700 acres but spared the redwoods.

Once at the parking lot (you took the right fork near the end) you'll want to walk back up the road for 300 feet. Walk past the yellow gate and you'll find the start of the **Redwood Trail** to the right of a cabin. Now you begin your descent into the forest. The area looks much more like Northern California than Hawai'i, and the coolness of the air at 6,000 feet is a refreshing change. The descent is fairly gentle and constant. Be aware of tree roots in the trail that may try to trip you. About 25 minutes into the hike you come to the large redwoods. Some of the red-

A forest of redwoods reaching for the clouds is the last thing you expect to find in the tropics, but Upcountry's Polipoli State Park is one of Maui's surprises.

wood trees are around 100 feet tall and dead-on straight with trunks up to 6 feet in diameter. Pretty impressive growth in so short a time. When the Redwood Trail ends at 1⁷⁄₁₀ mile, either retrace your steps or take the **Plum Trail** and make it a 5-mile loop hike. (This is preferred.) A trail map to Polipoli is on page 239.

Assuming you make it a loop, the Plum Trail somewhat gently regains most of the 1,000 feet you lost on the Redwood Trail. When Plum Trail meets **Haleakala Ridge Trail**, take the left turn. Haleakala Ridge Trail ends at Waipoli Road. (You had to pass by the Polipoli Trail.) Here you'll have a smashing and very expansive view all the way down the mountain to the shoreline. Weather permitting, you'll see three of the Big Island's volca-

noes—Mauna Kea (nearly 14,000 feet high), Kohala in front of it and Mauna Loa to the right. Up till now you probably haven't had any wind on this hike, protected by the ridge from the normal trade winds. But here on the ridge the wind can be howling.

To get back to your car you'll have to head back down Haleakala Ridge Trail and hang a right on Polipoli Trail.

These trails are very nice when the weather is good, but dark when it gets really cloudy. Go early in the morning for the best conditions. It takes most people 3–4 hours to complete the loop, and it's moderately strenuous. Despite what you might hear, this trail is not open to mountain bikes.

Weather can be cold and rainy at this altitude. Other trails, such as the Boundary

Trail, make nice, if long alternatives. Avoid the wreched Upper Waiakoa and Upper Waiohuli Trails unless you want to get lost and angry.

HIKES DESCRIBED ELSEWHERE

Short and not-so-short trails are described in other parts of the book for several reasons, either because of their remoteness, adventurousness or shortness. They include **Punalau Falls** on page 82, the marvelous **Wailua Iki** on page 86 and **Upper Pua'a Ka'a Falls** on page 87, the **Red Sand Beach** on page 94, **Venus Pool** on page 101, the **Pipiwai Trail** with the waterfalls, including the **Infinity Pool** on page 106, and **Alelele Falls** on page 108. The ADVENTURES chapter starting on page 235 has the **Four Falls of Na'ili'ili-haele**, **Mountain Bike Haleakala's Spine** (which you can also hike), a **hike in a lava tube**, and the **Haleakala Crater Grand Loop**. And West Maui has the **Olivine Pools** on page 60 and **'Iao Valley** on page 65. There's also the short trail around **Kealia Pond** on page 128.

OTHER EAST MAUI HIKES

In addition to the hikes mentioned above, there are a few other East Maui hikes worth noting.

Wai'anapanapa Coast Hike

One of the nicer coastal lava hikes you'll find. It displays the raw coastline, backed first by palm and hala trees, then showcases the most recent lava flow in the Hana area that created the black sand beach. Though there's no big climbing, the second portion of the trail is somewhat undulating, so you have lots of little climbs, and the footing is awkward. This hike can last anywhere from 30 minutes to 4 hours, depending on your thirst for scenery.

You start at Wai'anapanapa State Park near Hana (see page 91 for directions). Park to the right of the main beach, walk to the shoreline, and head right along the shore. Soon a low-hanging sea arch and a blowhole (that only blows during monster surf) indicate the kind of scenery you'll see. (Don't get too close to the tapered blowhole; it's a one-way trip down.)

About 10 minutes into the hike, at an area marked by some offshore rocks and a couple of arches, stop and listen for a hissing sound. The ocean's waves are undercutting

Lava arches are common along the coast of the Wai'anapanapa hike.

Some hikes require luscious treks through bamboo forests.

the lava here in some places, and when the tide is right, waves will force air up through a tiny hole and you can actually hear and feel the ocean breathing. (Get too close and you'll feel it spitting, too.)

The colors are very vivid as you walk along. The raw black coastline smashed by white frothing water next to impossibly blue ocean all backed by lush, green palm trees makes a delicious meal for your camera. Soon you'll pass an enormous grove of hala trees, noted for their cage-like roots. Some locals call them tourist pineapples, as their fruit does look similar. (Real pineapples grow on bushes, not trees.)

Angry seas can make this hike even more dramatic. The water is so clean and clear, and it's exhilarating to see large waves punish the shoreline here. At one point, the trail passes a natural split in the land. The lava bridge keeps you from falling in. A little farther along the trail has a big step down; it's preferable to a vague trail going around.

In about 30 or so minutes you come to meager remains of a small heiau (temple). Nobody knows what it was used for. The trail gets vague for a minute, but should become clearer shortly after. Ahus (small piles of rock) help mark the trail. The footing has been pretty good up till now, but from here it becomes harsher and clumsier. Hiking shoes or boots can be helpful, as can a walking stick. You'll be walking on young (500-year-old) lava that created the black sand beach as lava shattered on contact with the sea and the new sand drifted into the bay.

Watch for columnar lava. These (usually) six-sided lava columns are at the shoreline in several places. They form when unusually thick lava ponds, cools more slowly, shrinks and cracks. The cracks work their way deeper and deeper as the rock cools, so the lava literally pulls itself apart. When you pass an old fishing shack, it's 2 miles to Hana Bay. The prettiest part of the trail is behind you. Large red ants seem to be making a good living off the stark lava here. Keep walking until you're halfway to being tired, or you get to Hana Bay, whichever comes first, then turn around. It's about 7 miles (round trip) to Hana Bay, if you go that far. Make sure you bring water; lava fields make you thirsty.

Waikamoi Nature Trail

Between the 9 and 10 mile markers on the Hana Highway. Two nature loops, one about 10 minutes, the other about 30 minutes make a pleasant diversion on the Hana Highway drive if you need to stretch your legs a bit, but it's not worth driving out there just for this. This hike is good for families, and you gain, at most, 200 feet.

If you start from the left-most trail and work your way up the gradual incline, there are a few concrete benches scattered along the way. Sometimes there are nice views of the highway beneath you and the valley beyond. Patches of bamboo interrupt the hala, strawberry guava and huge, towering eucalyptus forest. At the intersection, either take a right (back to your car for the 10-minute hike) or left for the longer one. The latter eventually leads to a picnic area with BBQ. The sign there says END OF TRAIL, though, in fact, the path continues. When it forks, take a left and walk a few minutes, and it leads down to a stream and dam. The view is nice there despite the lack of water flowing over the cliff.

If you're feeling adventurous, you could hike ⅓ mile up the stream itself from here. It's relatively flat, your feet will get wet, and it can get slick on the rocks. If you persevere, you come to a pretty 45-foot waterfall and pool in a natural amphitheater. Give yourself an extra hour or two for this side trip.

Back at the picnic area, on your way down to your car on a 4WD road, if you veer to the left, it leads to a small reservoir. Otherwise, continue back to your car.

Wahinepe'e

This hike takes you up a hunters' road, through a bamboo forest and then links up with a road paralleling one of EMI's diversion ditches. During the first part you'll be climbing constantly, gaining about 250 feet. Note the density of the bamboo around you.

You start at the dirt road ²⁄₁₀ mile past the 10 mile marker on Hwy 360 (Hana Hwy). Once at the top (about ¼ mile), take a left, and the road will pass 2 small waterfalls. The payoff for this hike isn't a single tongue-wagging view or falls, but rather a nice trek through a healthy forest of eucalyptus, koa and several other species, many draped with vines. About ½ mile into the ditch road, you come to an intersection. If you go right at this and every other intersection, it will bring you to the upper road. Straddling the upper road, the forest is even healthier and prettier up here at 1,200 feet. Take the road as long as your interest holds out, then retrace your steps by taking lefts at the intersections. Make mental notes where the intersections were; there are more than the map shows. We had a tough time mapping this area, even from the air. This hike takes anywhere from 20 minutes to 6 hours, depending on how far you go. If you go all the way to the upper road, you gain 1,000 feet. It's a nice forest trek. As for access, this is a reserve, but EMI has the water rights. See page 75 for more on that.

SOUTH MAUI HIKES

The state of Hawai'i has shut down most of the hiking in South Maui by closing the trail to the top of Pu'u Ola'i and all hiking at the 'Ahihi-Kina'u Natural Area Reserve. But we have a more adventurous hike across a lava desert on page 244.

HORSEBACK RIDING

If you want to see the countryside but don't want to walk it yourself, you need your very own beast of burden. (I always loved that phrase.) Maui has lots of horseback rides, from forest to plains to lava fields to the inside of a crater. Some are awesome; some are a snore. Picking one depends on what you want to see.

Pony Express (667–2200) is our hands-down favorite. They go down Sliding Sands Trail to the bottom of Haleakala Crater. The views are unlike anything you've ever seen and positively drop-dead gorgeous. This is a *great* trip. They only take 8 people per day, so it's a good idea to book as far in advance as possible—3 weeks during busy times, 2 weeks during slow times. Call even earlier from the mainland to ensure your spot.

Since they want you near the summit of Haleakala at 9:15 a.m. (though they leave later), you might want to come up for the sunrise, then check out some of the short trails and overlooks before meeting them.

The ride is a single file, nose-to-tail affair, and you'll probably only trot a little coming up. But the way the unspeakably beautiful crater changes and unfolds effortlessly as you descend the trail will stay with you for a lifetime. Distances look huge as you descend the 3$\frac{8}{10}$ miles to the floor 2,400 feet below. The air is usually crystal clear inside, almost like there's no air at all. Once at the bottom, you have lunch at a trail junction. Croissant sandwiches never tasted so delicious than when you've had them in the crater. There are some bees around, attracted to the horse droppings, but few people seemed to mind. On the way back up, you see the

The first time we ever climbed 2,400 feet back up out of Haleakala Crater, we didn't even break a sweat. Of course, we had help.

crater from the other direction. How is it that it can still enrapture someone after several hours?

The trail can be pretty dusty, and the sun is strong up here. Expect to pass envious hikers on the way back up. Wear a long-sleeved shirt, a jacket and a hat. Cheap gloves are also advisable since you can burn the back of your hands while holding the reins. Weather is usually good in the crater and winds far less than up above. Most of the rain here comes in the winter. There's no restroom at the bottom. At $182 for the 4-hour trip, it may sound pricey, but the quality of the trip is unmatched. We've reviewed lots of horseback rides throughout the state, and we'd be hardpressed to think of one we enjoyed more. They also have cheaper rides at their ranch, but the views can't compare. The biggest negative? We've found (and reader e-mail confirms) that guide attitude has slipped lately, and a snotty guide can bring the experience down.

Other Buckaroos

Mendes Ranch (871–5222) has a pretty nice ride on their beautiful ranch in West Maui. It's about 2 hours of riding followed by a BBQ lunch (for an extra $20) back at the stables. They ride up to a spectacular overlook of Waihe'e Valley, then head to the ocean for more good views. It's a nose-to-tail ride (on sad and tiredlooking horses) with only two *very* short runs allowed. (But hey, running is hard to come by on Maui rides.) Guides range from helpful and friendly to aloof. In all, a good trip for $110. Our only complaint is that they make outrageous and false claims to get you in, and it's really not necessary. For instance, their brochure says (and has for *years*) that you'll "gaze down into Eki Crater to view some of Maui's largest waterfalls." Well, *Eke* Crater is at 4,400 feet elevation, near the center of

West Maui. Wow, what a view that would be! On the phone they say you'll ride up to 3,000 feet. Hmm, still pretty awesome. The guide says you'll make it to 2,000 feet. The reality? You go to *1,000* feet. C'mon, guys, just be accurate. The ride is good enough without the inflated claims. On Hwy 340 at 7 mile marker.

Makena Stables (879–0244) is in South Maui on the expansive Ulupalakua Ranch. The small scale of this stable translates into very well cared for horses, good equipment and personalized attention. They seem proud and protective of their horses. The opposite of lush, this ride goes through kiawe (mesquite) groves and lava fields up to Kalua o Lapa Crater. Enjoy the nice views of the island of Kaho'olawe, La Pérouse Bay, 'Ahihi-Kinau and the lava flow from this intensely windy 500-foot elevation. Ride back down through shaded stretches of the King's Highway to the bay. The 2½-hour morning ride is $145; the sunset trip, which goes a little longer, is $170. Sincere, dedicated guides, but on our ride they were short on snacks and long on local politics. As far as sunset rides go, this one has great views.

Lahaina Stables (667–2222) in West Maui is our least favorite due to the drab trailside scenery and destination. A thatched picnic hut beside a manmade reservoir provides the only shade you'll find on this ride, and views of the offshore islands are their best asset. The guides do their best to make up for the unwelcoming trailside scenery. 2-hour morning ride for $115; $140 for the 2½-hour late morning ride gets you a modest deli lunch. The $125 sunset ride includes a snack. Higher maximum weight limit than many others.

Also in West Maui, **Ironwood Ranch** (669–4991) is a tidy stable and, although the greeter may be short on social graces, they are long on safety and use the info you give in a survey about your skills to match you up with one of their celebrity-named horses. The trail goes through some boring fields but is punctuated by ironwood groves and the Maile Pai Valley where you'll find ferns, dry creek beds and some nice rock outcroppings. You emerge from the valley onto the upper reaches of the plantation, providing grand views of offshore islands and the West Maui Mountains to your back. The contrasts are particularly nice at sunset. 1½-hour morning ride is $90; 2-hour morning or sunset rides are $120.

Upcountry there's **Pi'iholo Ranch** (357-5544) in Makawao. You drive up and away from the coastal plains into a cool eucalyptus forest, then arrive at their posh ranch center. Although this spread has a showy rodeo air, trail rides don't hold second-class status here. Their work shows in nicely laid trails and eager horses. On the trail, meander through forested valleys and wind-swept pasture lands. The climax of the ride (hold your hat) is the ascent to windy Pi'iholo Hill with 360-degree views. The elevation allows you to escape the extreme weather conditions that can accompany rides at lower and higher elevations, making it a particularly good choice for a midday ride. 2-hour morning and afternoon rides are $120. A 3-hour picnic ride is $180.

And in Hana you have **Maui Stables** (248-7799). They have a fairly unremarkable ride up and down a path but it leads to a commanding view overlooking Waimoku Falls. There you sit for an hour in the dirt under the sun and listen to their...cultural presentation, which is fairly unique. It's where you'll learn a history of humanity that is probably not in any book that you've read. Their narration is sincere and passionate though many may find it a bit off the chart at times. This 3-hour trip is $150. (Less if you book direct.)

Jet Skiing

Call them Jet Skis, Wave Runners (which are brand names) or personal watercraft—whatever your name for them, these motorcycles of the sea can be rented near Lahaina from **Maui Water Sports** (667-2066) from mid-May to mid-December. (They have to close during whale season.) Their attitude is kind of snotty, but you don't care much while you're riding. They use fairly powerful Yamahas and pretty much give you free rein in their circular course. That's good because it gives you more freedom...but it also leaves you free to hurt yourself. If you've never ridden before, these animals are a scream (literally, for many riders).

Early morning is usually very smooth, late afternoon choppy. Late morning seems a good balance giving the water some texture. They offer ½ hour for $70, full hour $98. The half hour will tucker out most people, especially if you're like me and you drive it like it's stolen. Spend the extra few bucks for the goggles, and experiment with different ways to hold your feet while you sit. Despite their brochure's claims, you're actually given little instruction, so be careful. If you go fast enough during bumpy seas, turns will be like a controlled crash, so don't turn too fast unless you know what you're doing. Extra riders are allowed for $19, but we recommend one person per craft. Doubling up seems to increase the risk of the passenger falling off, from what we observed. Some people seem to feel that these craft are hazardous to the ocean; others say modern jet skis are no different than regular boats. We honestly don't know which is the case; we're just saying what it's like to rent one. They meet off Canoe (Hanaka'o'o) Beach.

KAYAKING

Kayaks are a fun way to see the coastline. None of Maui's rivers is fit for kayaking, but the shoreline offers lots to explore.

Areas to kayak are south of Olowalu in West Maui starting at Papalaua Wayside Park between the 11 and 12 mile markers. Paddle southeast along the pretty shoreline below the highway, staying close to land to keep winds from making your life more difficult. Most put in near the 14 mile marker, but it's much less interesting there.

If you can arrange it, in the afternoon it's nice to put in at Kihei and let the wind help you go down the coast, then come out at Makena Landing. Kihei winds tend to blow from north to south along the coast; West Maui winds tend to go from nothing to blowing offshore, which is more dangerous.

Also consider the coastline south of Big Beach at 'Ahihi Cove heading south. You can go around Cape Kina'u to Fishbowl, Aquarium and on into La Pérouse Bay, but be watchful of winds, especially in the afternoon.

Some companies put in at Makena Landing because it's so easy to launch. The kayaking from there is fairly good, though not great.

Winds will be your biggest factor. Don't let a breeze help you down a shoreline if you have to paddle back against it. Unless you've arranged for pickup, better to paddle in less breezy areas. The ocean can go from calm and light winds to wavy with strong winds over a span of about 100 feet. Whitecaps on the water are caused by wind, and it's easy to drift from a protected area to an exposed area. Stay alert.

Many of the big resorts rent kayaks by the hour for confiscatory amounts. At press time the state was in the middle of a permit crackdown, and many of the companies that rent kayaks had been driven out of business. We weren't able to find any reliable non-resort sources for renting kayaks in West Maui. In South Maui **South Pacific Kayaks** (875–4848) has singles for $40 and doubles for $60 at Makena Landing. **Big Kahuna Adventures** (875–6395) in Kihei has singles for $40, doubles for $60.

For guided tours, consider **Maui Eco Tours** (891–2223), **Maui Kayaks** (874–4000) and **South Pacific**.

In Hana, **Hana-Maui Kayak & Snorkel Reef Watch** (248–7711 or 264–9566) has short, kayak/snorkel trips at Hana Bay for $89.

KITEBOARDING

See Windsurfing, page 231.

LAND TOURS

There are several companies that provide various types of land tours. Some are better than others. **Temptation Tours** (877–8888) does van tours of the Hana Coast for around $200. Though we recommend that you drive this yourself, if the winding road bothers you, this tour is better than not seeing the Hana Highway at all. Don't

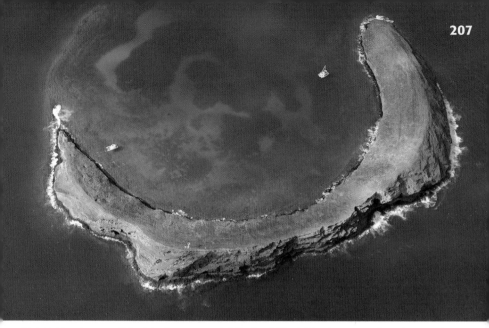

Molokini is where you'll find the best water visibility in all Maui. Dive boats use the submerged corner and snorkel boats explore the inside.

believe everything you hear, however. We've heard some fairly bad information from them. We once had one of their drivers (not knowing who we were, of course) upon seeing a copy of this book tell us that "the authors of *Maui Revealed* have had their houses burned and their cars torched for revealing too many secret places on the island" and that the state of Hawai'i was "banning the book." Obviously, none of that's true, and we could only conclude that they simply make this stuff up as they go along.

Valley Isle Excursions (661–8687) provides guided van tours.

Lahaina Ka'anapali Railroad (661–0080) is listed as one of the "must-dos" in much of the free literature strewn about the island, but we can't help wonder if they've actually done it. Picture a slow-moving train that chugs through abandoned sugar cane fields, along a golf course and through a residential area. Dull, pointless and overpriced. Some kids may like it, but adults should blow their money elsewhere. In Lahaina. $23 for adults, $16 for kids.

Ocean Tours

This is probably the single biggest activity that people pay to do on Maui, and for good reason. The calm, clear waters make it a boater's heaven. Maui's boating conditions are superb due to the shape of its coastline, and it has close island neighbors to visit.

In some ways, this is one of the most difficult sections to write about. The section's length is a testament to your varied options. *So* many choices and fleeting characteristics make it dizzying. We may take a boat tour and rave about it, but the day after we go to press, the boating company may sell their 50-foot sailing yacht and begin taking passengers out on an inflatable raft from Walmart. It's hard to keep up.

Most of the boats leave from Lahaina or Maʻalaea (close to Kihei). A few boats leave from the Kihei Boat Ramp and Kaʻanapali Beach.

Boating trips can generally be broken down into four types:

Snorkel Trips
Pure Sailing Trips
Whale Watching *mid-Dec.–mid-May*
Dinner Cruises

Many of the snorkel trips *claim* they also whale watch, but that usually means they'll simply make a beeline to their snorkeling spot, hoping to spot one of the buggers. It's like calling them fishing boats because they drag a lure behind them on their way to Molokini.

We need to clarify something up front. Taking a boat trip on Maui is like making a dessert with chocolate, ice cream and peanut butter. No matter how you combine the ingredients, you're gonna end up with something sweet and tasty. (See, *that's* what I get for writing while hungry.) The boater's ingredients are the boat, sun, water and fish. Unless the weather is horrible, even if you're boating with complete idiots, odds are you're still going to have a fun, relaxing time, because boating Maui's often-placid waters can't be beat. Since not all boating companies are created equal, our job is to steer you to the ones who seem to do the best job (and away from the idiots). We've anonymously ridden scads of boats off Maui, and the difference is striking. But remember as you read these critiques: Even bad boat trips are usually fun.

We've noticed that there seem to be two types of crews: Those composed of cocky guys and gals who spend all their

Boat	Phone	Max. Passengers	Type of Boat	Departs	Wet Suits	Snorkel Stops	Rest Rooms	Food
Alii Nui	875-0333	60	65' Sailing Cat	Maʻalaea	Yes	1	Yes	Buffe
America II	667-2195	24	65' Racing Yacht	Lahaina Sailing Trip				Snack
Blue Water Rafting	879-7238	24	27' & 30' Raft-like	Kihei	No	1–4	No	Del
Cinderella	244-0009	6	50' Sailing Sloop	Maʻalaea Sailing Trip				Del
Four Winds II	879-8188	130	55' Sailing Cat	Maʻalaea	Yes	1	Yes	BBC
Gemini	669-0508	49	64' Sailing Cat	Kaʻanapali	Yes	1	Yes	Buffe
Hawaiian Sail Canoe	281-9301	6	Sailing Canoe	Wailea	No	1	No	None
Hula Girl	667-5980	49	65' Sailing Cat	Kaʻanapali	Yes	1	Yes	Menu
Island Princess	667-6165	149	65' Power Boat	Lahaina	Yes	2	Yes	Del
Kai Kanani II	879-7218	80	65' Sailing Cat	Makena Bch	No	2	Yes	Del
Lani Kai	244-1979	70	53' Power Cat	Maʻalaea	Yes	2	Yes	Del
Mahana Naiʻa	871-8636	68	58' Sailing Cat	Maʻalaea	Yes	2	Yes	Del
Ocean Riders	661-3586	18	30' Rigid Hull Raft	Lahaina	No	3	No	Del
Pacific Whale	249-8811	49–149	Power Cats	Maʻ & Lah	Some	2	Yes	BBC
Paragon	244-2087	38/24	47' Sailing Cat	Maʻ & Lah	Yes	1	Yes	Del
Pride of Maui	242-0955	149	65' Power Cat	Maʻalaea	Yes	2	Yes	BBC
Prince Kuhio	242-8777	149	92' Power Boat	Maʻalaea	Yes	2	Yes	Del
Quicksilver	661-3333	125	55' Power Cat	Maʻalaea	Yes	2	Yes	BBC
Scotch Mist	661-0386	25	50' Sailing Sloop	Lahaina Sailing Trip			No	Bev
Seafire	879-2201	22	39' Raft-like	Kihei	Yes	2	No	Barel
Trilogy I–VI	874-5649	49–96	Sailing Cats	Everywhere	Yes	2	Yes	Deli/BBC

time and energy showing their crewmates and you how impossibly cool they are. (The old *don't you wish you were as cool as me* syndrome.) Then there are crews who channel more of their effort to help ensure *you* have a good time. We obviously lean toward the latter.

SNORKEL TRIPS
Where They Go

Most boats go to two locations. Ma'alaea departures usually do their first stop at Molokini and the second at **Turtle Town**. *Where is Turtle Town?* you may ask. The answer seems to be, *Wherever they say it is.* Different companies take people to different "Turtle Towns," and it seems to be more of a marketing gimmick. (After all, doesn't the name *sound* intriguing?) For instance, a boat might call the area off Keawakapu "Turtle Town." Well, the snorkeling there is pretty boring, and you're not likely to see many turtles. Another "Turtle Town" (one of the better ones) is off the Maui Prince. One is near Ma'alaea. There are two near Po'olenalena, etc. Despite the picture the salesmen paint of waters swarming with turtles, the odds are probably 50–50 that you'll actually see one. Don't go with the *expectation* that you'll swim with turtles. If you do, great. Otherwise, just enjoy the water, coral and fish. Visibility will seem merely fair, but that's only because you probably just got spoiled for life at Molokini on the first stop. People who would have been *thrilled* with 80-foot visibility before, suddenly sniff indignantly because it's not 180 feet like Molokini on a good day. By the way, some are now using the name *Turtle Arches*, which sounds even better, doesn't it?

Molokini is 3 miles off Maui's coast and 10 miles from Ma'alaea Harbor. It's one of the most widely known snorkel and diving spots in Hawai'i. (See photo on page 207.) It's a sunken crater that is now a marine sanctuary. The floor is well coated with colorful coral. It's illegal to feed the fish here, though you'll quickly realize by their behavior that these little beggars *are* hand fed. (We've even seen boat personnel feeding them after telling passengers not to do it.) There's no need for you to do it; fish *assume* you will. The fish count inside isn't as great as other places on Maui, but it's still high, and with the incredibly clear visibility (usually 120–180 feet), it's a good place to snorkel. The bottom topography isn't overly interesting, just a gently sloping floor. We've repeatedly snorkeled the entire crater, and the best snorkeling is usually on the inside left (from the outside looking in—the side closest to Maui). Boats that park elsewhere usually tell you *they* park in the best spot, but they're wrong. (SCUBA diving is a different matter.) The inside right is second best, with the center the least interesting. (That's relative; the center still has lots of coral and fish.) Don't stay in one place; swim over near the shore for more coral, then to deeper water for more fish. During normal trade winds, the center/left (between the Prince Kuhio and Pacific Whale Foundation boats) is where winds may deposit any fine floating debris and sometimes cloudy water, so it's best to avoid that part. It's *usually,* though not always, reasonably calm inside.

Molokini's biggest problem is its popularity. On a given day over 1,000 snorkelers may visit the crater—sometimes twice that many. Each boat moors in a certain spot, and you are asked to stay close to your boat. If you're in a less interesting part of the crater, you may need to swim through a sea of other snorkelers and violate the boat rules to get to a better part.

But stay inside the crater and away from the far edges, especially the far right side (as you're looking inside) where the crater wall is submerged. Currents there can be bad.

Probably the best advice we can give about Molokini is to discard any pre-conceptions. So much has been written and said, so many exaggerated paintings exist, so many doctored photos, that people get a certain picture in their mind of what to expect. Best to go in with a blank slate, and you'll probably leave full of wonder.

If you take a boat from Lahaina, you usually stop at **Coral Gardens**. There's more than one, but one is offshore of the 14 mile marker. It offers lots of beautiful coral and decent, though not stellar, visibility. (But better visibility than shore-bound snorkelers will find.) Another Coral Gardens is below the Hwy 30 tunnel.

Lana'i is also a popular day destination. It can offer good snorkeling, but boats often go to a comparatively dull area called Shark Fin Cove, sometimes called Lighthouse Cove, instead of more exciting areas elsewhere. (This cove is a convenient place to park big boats.) Also, though the cause is debated, it's undeniable that the water quality around Lana'i has suffered in the past few years. We've seen heavy rainstorms muck up the water all around the island, and the effects can last well over six months. So, while Lana'i can be good, it's not guaranteed.

A Few Tips

Some companies can be real stingy with the food. After your first snorkel you're apt to be pretty hungry and may not be offered any food. Consider bringing your own stash of snacks with you. You may be able to sell them to other hungry customers at prices confiscatory enough to pay for your trip. *I have a bid of $8 for a chocolate chip cookie. Do I hear $9?*

Another consideration is warmth. Though the water temps range from 75° to 80°, you may want to consider renting a thin wetsuit from a dive shop to keep you snug. The second snorkel site tends to chill people, especially in the winter. (February has the coldest water.) Of course, boats that rent wetsuits tend to *under*-report the temperature about 5°–10° to convince you to rent.

Catamarans are twin-hulled and slice through the water much more cleanly than single-hull boats and, if wide enough, are more stable (less rocking) on the water.

If you're uncomfortable using the boat's snorkel gear (either for sanitary or fitting reasons), consider renting it elsewhere and bringing it along. Most boats have only one size mask. Also, when you defog your mask (using either dedicated goo or your own spit), rub it hard into the inside glass then rinse quickly.

If you want a towel, you'll probably have to bring your own.

Small, white tip reef sharks, which are essentially harmless, are sometimes seen at Molokini. *Don't worry* about them. Worry about getting sunburned.

Below deck is a bad place to be if you're worried about getting seasick. Without a reference point, you're much more likely to let 'er rip down there. If you *tied one on* the night before, do yourself a favor and take Dramamine, Bonine or apply Scopolamine patches *before* you go. Ginger is also a very good preventative and treatment for seasickness.

People come off these trips *toasted,* especially in the summer. Make *sure* you slather on the sunscreen, or you'll be sorry for the rest of your trip.

Morning snorkel trips nearly always offer better snorkeling and calmer seas.

The only upside for **afternoon snorkel trips** is price. The only time we recommend windier afternoon trips is when you only want to sail.

Allow enough time to find a **parking** spot. At Ma'alaea they can fill up if your boat isn't one of the first to leave, and you'll have to park at the aquarium, where some boats use buses to drive you back to the harbor. In Lahaina, the Mala Ramp can also tax parkers' patience. For Lahaina Harbor, consider the lot near Prison Street.

Don't take any inflatable raft trips out of Ma'alaea. Too much bumpy travel time across windy Ma'alaea Bay. Only go from the Kihei Boat Ramp and Lahaina. Inflatables from Lahaina to Lana'i are bumpy, too.

SNUBA (page 227) is often available. Inside Molokini Crater it's harder to justify the extra $50 or so as you really won't see much more than the snorkelers see a few feet above, but it's kind of fun. (Other locations make more sense for SNUBA.)

BEST SNORKEL BOATS OF THE BUNCH

Probably the best of the *big* boats is **Four Winds II** (879–8188). This is a 55-foot power catamaran that makes morning treks to Molokini. Though they take up to 130 people, the boat is nicely designed to accommodate many without feeling as crowded as some of the others. There's a good mix of sun and shade, and the upper deck perimeter bench seats allow you to spin around and face the water while resting on the railing—a nice touch. Their usual mooring spot at Molokini normally has clear water, though fish counts might be better elsewhere. Their food setup is also the best of the lot. All the pulled-pork sandwiches, chicken, hot dogs and veggie burgers you want are waiting for you when you

Snorkeling, BBQ and thou. What else is there?

get out of the water. Open bar (beer and wine only) longer than any of the others. One negative aspect—they don't go to a second site—can be a positive in that they spend more time at the crater, making it feel more leisurely. (Their second "turtle town stop" is where they stop just outside the harbor on the way back and point out turtles. In fairness, it *is* a good place to spot them—you just won't swim with them.) Our only real gripe is their unrelenting sales pitches throughout your voyage. All boat operators want to sell you T-shirts and DVDs, but these guys carry it to a level that starts to get annoying. All in all, however, Four Winds is a winner. Morning Molokini trip is $89, afternoon trip to Coral Gardens or occasionally Molokini is $42. SNUBA, Rx masks, underwater camera and wetsuits available for extra. Their hefty see-through sea-boards are *very* nice for timid kids and adults. The "glass bottom" on the boat itself works well for kids, but adults might not be too impressed. Freshwater hose shower on board, and there's a slide into the water.

Their other boat, **Maui Magic** is a very different product, and we're not as fond of it as we are the Four Winds II. The boat's older, less comfortable and feels more crowded. It's essentially a barge of cramped benches with almost no shade. Though they head down the interesting Kanaio Coast first, they stay so far from shore that you won't appreciate much detail. The 54-foot power cat doesn't handle swells well, either. Their second stop is at Molokini. $112. In short, stick with the Four Winds II.

The best big boat in *West* Maui is **Hula Girl** (667–5980). The crew (including hands-on owners) is particularly laid back and friendly, and the boat is well-designed with a luxuriant, spacious feel, even when full. They leave from Ka'anapali Beach and go to either Olo-walu or Honolua Bay for snorkeling. (They usually *sail* back from the latter rather than *motor*.) The boat cuts nicely through the water, even in big seas. When they sail downwind the trampolines up front are fantastic places to be. SCUBA is available. One thing that is unusual is the food. It's extra. So instead of a free but limited menu, you get a larger selection and the quality is very good. But expect to spend an extra $10–$30 in addition to the $89 price.

Also consider **Gemini** (669–0508) which is a 64-foot cat that leaves from Ka'anapali Beach and usually heads to Honolua Bay. Hot buffet lunch and a pretty good crew for $99.

The best of the medium-sized boats is **Paragon** (244–2087). They use 47-foot sailing catamarans and have good snorkel gear and crew. These guys *really* like sailing and are much quicker to raise and maintain their sails than most companies, often sailing both ways, not part of one way. (Their piddly 90 HP outboard is probably also a good reason to keep the sails up.) The boats hold 38, and there's shade for ⅓ of the passengers, plus what the sails provide. Riding the net (lying on the front trampolines) is a hoot on the way back. Soothing and dry if it's calm, thrilling and wet if seas are up. The outsides of the trampolines are the wettest. At Molokini they moor at a pretty good spot, and they let you roam the crater—no short leashes. The deli lunch isn't as satisfying as others' BBQs, and their ladder into the water is poor, but overall, this is a very good product. Since it's smaller, expect a slightly bumpier ride than Four Winds II. Ma'alaea to Molokini trips are $100, no second snorkel spot. For their Lana'i trip they snorkel outside Manele Bay, and then give you a picnic lunch to take ashore. $159 for the Lana'i trip, which only takes 24.

Four Winds II and Paragon don't snorkel at two spots. If that's a priority, **Pacific Whale Foundation (PWF)** (249–8811) has eight boats and a variety of tours. Started as a whale conservation eco-tour, PWF takes more people on the water than any other tour on Maui. If all their boats ran at full capacity, they could carry almost 1,000 people per day. Not bad for a nonprofit organization. We've noticed that the destination of each boat changes with the seasons. (Scheduling must be a nightmare for these people.) Call or visit their website for the most current matching of boats and tours.

Besides whale watching, PWF has snorkeling tours around the island. Their best selling excursion visits Molokini and "Turtle Arches" from Maʻalaea for $80. They also snorkel Lanaʻi from Lahaina for the same price. A longer 6½-hour tour goes to both sites (weather permitting) for $95 (not recommended for small children). On these trips you can expect to be on one of PWF's big double decker boats, the **Ocean Voyager**, **Ocean Odyssey** or **Ocean Quest**. These sister ships offer easy water entry, continental breakfast, BBQ lunch and beer, wine and mai tais for you and 129 of your closest friends. The **Ocean Spirit**, **Ocean Intrigue** and **Ocean Discovery**, all 65-foot power cats, are mainly whale watching boats that go snorkeling in the off season. They're scrawnier than their big boats and tend to rock more than most catamarans. Our last choice is the **Ocean Explorer**, whose real narrow design doesn't encourage walking around. Avoid it.

Their mooring spot at Molokini is not very good. Coral is sparser than at other spots, and the floating debris that sometimes accumulates in the center might be present.

They've been *real* stingy in the past with food, but have been a bit more generous lately. (After that second snorkel,

you're ready to tackle a shark, and getting *one* small piece of chicken or *one* hot dog might not cut it.) We can't go out with them on all of their boats every week, so let us know if they slide back into the *miserly food* mode.

Also, sometimes their eco-approach can get heavy-handed to the point of being silly. On a past trip to Lanaʻi a pod of dolphins cruised through a sea of snorkelers, went beyond them a hundred yards, then came back to be with the swimmers again. Chance of a lifetime, right? But PWF yanked everyone out of the water! When we asked why, they piously responded, "We don't swim with dolphins; it's illegal." (Which is untrue. It *might* be illegal to jump in *after* you encounter them because it might alter their behavior, but it's perfectly legal and only common sense to *stay* in the water when the *dolphins* are clearly initiating the encounter.) We haven't seen any evidence that they've changed this policy.

Don't get us wrong: PWF does a good job for the most part. Their customers have fun, their bigger boats are inexpensively priced, they're *great* with kids, and their crew seem to be of a higher than normal caliber. Expect long, slow-moving lines when you check in at Maʻalaea.

The longest running operator on the island is **Trilogy** (874–5649). We were very critical of them in the past, and they have systematically fixed nearly all of their flaws over the years. Their six big catamarans (all creatively named) leave from Lahaina, Maʻalaea, Kaʻanapali and even Lanaʻi. They run with some of the friendliest crews we've encountered and offer services that no one else can. You can snorkel Molokini or cruise Kaʻanapali, but their main attraction is an all-day trip to Lanaʻi. At $189, it's pricier than most, but worth it.

Once there, you have the option to go on a high-speed rafting adventure to Shark's Fin Cove for an extra $49—

Newcomers to the sport need to realize that canoe paddling requires knowledge, experience—oh yeah, and a little water.

Saturdays only. (No snorkeling there.) It's much better than the free scenic ride into Lana'i City. Most of your time is spent relaxing and snorkeling at Hulopo'e Beach via a shuttle from the harbor. It's been reported that dolphins frequently mingle with guests here. The snorkeling isn't that great and the fact that they require you to wear a floatation device, even if you're a Navy Seal, doesn't help. This is the policy on all their tours and our only real gripe with them.

Before leaving Lana'i, you have a great BBQ lunch under their private pavilion. (The place is starting to look like Camp Trilogy.) Then they try to sail on the way home, depending on the winds. Usually they serve ice cream and you can get a beer or mai tai as you cruise back to the harbor. Some of their other boats don't have a liquor license, so check with them first, if that is a concern. You may be able to BYOB, but they don't call a lot of attention to this policy.

Trilogy is the sole company allowed to operate this kind of tour on Lana'i.

Their service is top-notch and makes others look pedestrian. (You have to walk to the beach from the harbor if you go with anyone else.) Their other trips to Molokini and Ka'anapali are $110. They also do whale watching trips and provide SNUBA on some boats. Call for complicated rates.

Blue Water Rafting (879–7238) is a rigid-hull inflatable (a V-shaped hull surrounded by a rubber pontoon). They do things different. From Kihei Boat Ramp you head down the coast, past La Pérouse Bay to a lava flow at Kanaio (which literally means *the bastard sandalwood tree*). After exploring the unusual lava formations, you head back, usually to La Pérouse Bay to a rather dull snorkeling area, then stop at another, better site for snorkeling and a deli lunch. The boat does a scorching 40 knots, and the ride is a blast (though less comfortable than a cushier boat and certainly wetter). Little shade. Consider a light, waterproof jacket for the morning trip out and wet riding later. $100 for 4 hours. They also have a 5½-hour trip for $125 that includes Molokini, but we recommend the shorter trip. Best seats are on the back, left side. Wind past La Pérouse can be fierce, hence their early start. No alcohol allowed.

The **Kai Kanani II** (879–7218) is a beautiful boat. It's spacious but can get crowded when full. Rated to hold 80 passengers, even with just 60 it feels packed. Luckily the staff is helpful, the food is good, and the open bar has beer and mai tais. Their sleek boat takes much less time to get to Molokini than Ma'alaea boats and powers through big waves as if it were the calmest of days. Easy to recommend considering its launching point from the Makena Beach Resort. $114 for Molokini and Turtle Town. It's about half that for the 6:30 a.m. 2-hour trip.

OTHER SNORKEL TRIPS FROM MA'ALAEA

Alii Nui (875–0333) has a very nice 65-foot sailing catamaran and a good crew. They feed you very well (3-drink max on the beer, wine and champagne) and take you to either Molokini or around the corner to "Turtle Town" (at Olowalu) for snorkeling. They have SCUBA available for an extra $75–$85, and the boat doesn't feel as crowded as some of the others. But you pay a hefty premium for all this at $145.

Mahana Nai'a (871–8636) has an older 58-foot sailing cat. $90 for Molokini and "turtle town." Kind of crowded for up to 68 passengers.

Pride Charters (242–0955) uses a 50-foot, single-hull, rather spartan and uninspiring boat called **Leilani** and a 65-foot catamaran called **Pride of Maui**. The latter has a *very* crowded feel with 136 people packed on board: the quintessential cattle boat. Even with smaller crowds it feels like a lifeboat on the *Titanic*. Un-

comfortable backless benches on top with no shade. On the plus side, they park in a good spot at Molokini. Their second spot, "Turtle Town," is at 5 Graves/5 Caves. They have a slide and SCUBA and SNUBA available, and a small number of wetsuit rentals for snorkeling. For their BBQ lunch they precook burgers, chicken, hot dogs and veggie burgers, wait till they're cold, then line you up and reheat them. Get in line early as it can take *forever*. Open bar after second stop. At $96, the trip is not a good deal.

Lani Kai through **Friendly Charters** (244–1979) has a 53-foot power cat that takes 69 people. Interior shade. $98 for Molokini and turtle town. You can do better.

Prince Kuhio (242–8777) is Maui's 92-foot, 149-passenger cattle boat (when full, which is not too often). They do Molokini and Turtle Town (at the Makena Beach Resort). Their mooring spot at Molokini is not very good. One positive is that the boat's real easy to get around on. $99. Also, they'll pick you up at your hotel for $15.

Quicksilver (661–3333) is a 55-foot power cat that carries up to 125 people. It's crowded when full, and the single stairway between decks is congested at almost all times. Most of the seats are in the shade. They have a good spot at Molokini but don't spend much time there. In the water their leash is so tight it's more like a choke chain. Don't even think about straying too far. And even though they advertise they go down to the Kanaio Coast to look for dolphins, we've only experienced them slowly cruising down the Makena Coast pointing out celebrity houses and making fun of other boat operators. Lastly their Turtle Town spot is too deep for snorkeling and had few turtles. In short, an easy trip to *not* recommend. $95.

OTHER SNORKEL TRIPS FROM LAHAINA

Island Princess (667–6165) is a 65-foot, single-hull boat that does morning trips to Molokini from Lahaina for $70. It's twice as far as a trip from Ma'alaea and their second stop is near Olowalu. Going to Molokini from Lahaina in this type of boat isn't a great way to go. Plus it really rocks when moored. Consider driving to Ma'alaea for your Molokini trips. Kids 6 and under ride for free, and there's a floating water trampoline. You can BYOB if you want.

Ocean Riders (661–3586) uses a 30-foot rigid hull inflatable to circumnavigate Lana'i for $139. These are rougher and wetter than more traditional craft, and shade is not too ample. But they snorkel three spots, and it's nice to see Lana'i's more interesting windward side. They even visit Lana'i's shipwrecks. Their most intriguing product is when they visit Moloka'i's north shore. Seeing the sea cliffs from the ocean is awesome. Unfortunately, they rarely do this because of winds. Even when calm, they seem reluctant to book the trip. Too bad. If you get lucky, you'll see quite a sight. Bring something to keep warm or dry.

OTHER SNORKEL TRIPS FROM KIHEI

If you just want to take a quick snorkel trip out to Molokini and don't want all the frills, **Maui Dive Shop** (879–3388) takes their 32-foot, single-hull boat from Kihei Boat Ramp to Molokini (only 4 miles) then "Turtle Town" for a 3-hour tour. (Just like Gilligan's Island.) Up to 24 people (which makes it *crowded*), continental breakfast and juices and sodas. No frills, but for $60 you ain't paying for frills. Snorkelers can accompany divers on their boat dive charter, but that costs $80 since you're taking up a diver's spot. By the

way if you find yourself on their boat, the Kai Anela, it's had a more *intimate* relationship with Molokini than any other boat. Seems it sank there after an embarrassing incident, and was later raised and is now used for tours.

Seafire (879–2201) is an unimpressive, raft-looking, rigid-hull craft with minimal shade that goes to Molokini and Turtle Town for $55. Cheap, no frills, 3 hours, 2 stops. Only if price is paramount.

PURE SAILING TRIPS

You're not really heading anywhere, and you aren't really interested in *doing* anything—you just want to sail. Most boats are sloops (single hull with little or no shade other than what the sail provides). If you're up front, sloops require you to move more often than the twin-hulled catamarans (cats). When it's too windy to go on a snorkel trip, it's probably great for sailing.

America II (667–2195) is the real deal—a genuine 12-meter racing yacht that participated in America's Cup. It's a fast, sleek sloop that takes 24 people (which is crowded). Price is cheap at $50 for 2-hour sails three times a day. Boat is usually full; reserve in advance. Snacks and soft drinks provided. By the way, if you take a $25 whale watching trip, they won't raise sails.

Scotch Mist (661–0386) is a 50-foot sailboat that accommodates 25 (which would be too crowded for comfort since it's not a wider catamaran), but they usually take about a dozen. They'll go out with as few as 2 passengers, which makes for a *very* relaxing time. Their 2-hour afternoon sail is just right to whet your nautical appetite. No shade except for the sail. Below deck is a bit dreary, but on top it's a nice, clean boat, and the experience is fun. Sodas, beer and wine provided. Add champagne and chocolates to the sunset trip. Out of

Lahaina; 2-hour afternoon or sunset sails are $50 and $60, 4-hour morning snorkel sail is $100.

Cinderella (244–0009) is a nice-looking sailing yacht. Comfortable in back, less so up front; it holds 6. Pricey at $250 per hour. Snorkeling available. They have a deli meal, but you can shave off some of the price if you want to bring your own food.

If you want something a little different, **Hawaiian Sailing Canoe Adventures** (281–9301) takes up to 6 people on a genuine Hawaiian sailing canoe. It's not the fastest boat on the water, but it's a thrill to glide just above the surface on the boat's trampoline. Leave from Polo Beach and sail up and down the coast, snorkeling off the Grand Wailea. The captain has been sailing and racing since he was 16 and fills the trip with history and legends. It's very personal, relaxing and easy to recommend. $99 ($79 for kids). They go out at 8 a.m. and 10 a.m.

WHALE WATCHING

Is seasonal and described on page 230.

DINNER CRUISES

Are listed under ISLAND NIGHTLIFE on page 287.

Parasailing is where you become a human kite, attached to a parachute and pulled by a boat via a long rope. It's a 7-10-minute ride, though that includes reeling in and reeling out. It's been our experience that parasailing *looks* more fun and thrilling than it really is and doesn't seem worth the money. Think of it as a $65+ amusement ride. (People afraid of heights, however, will no doubt be properly terrified.) Off Lahaina, at least the view of town is grand. At press time, the companies all left from West Maui and only from mid-May to mid-December. (They have to close during whale season.) **West Maui Parasail** (661–4887) has 800- and 1,200-foot lines for $65 & $75. Tandem rides available. **UFO Parasailing** (661–7836) has a 7-minute 600-foot ride for $65, a 10-minute 800-foot ride for $75 and a 1,200-foot ride for $85.

One tip (*especially* for guys): Don't wear any slippery shorts, or you may cinch forward in your harness resulting in…the longest 7 minutes of your life.

OK, here's where Maui's often placid waters pays off. The diving here can be incredible. The usually calm morning waters off South and West Maui make boat rides short and sweet. In addition to its nearshore dives, Maui has two great offshore dives. West Maui has the awesome **Lana'i Cathedrals II** to journey to, and South Maui has the humbling **back wall of Molokini**.

We've noticed that, overall, the dive operations on Maui seem to be of a slightly higher caliber than the other islands, perhaps because there's so much competition. Prices can be lower, too. (It's good to see that *some* things are actually cheaper on Maui!) They're usually more professional here with less of the *dive shop attitude*. You know the attitude— when you go into a shop, and the guy behind the counter never gets off his stool or takes off his sunglasses, doing everything he can to convey the impression: *I'm so cool—don't you wish you were just like me?*

However, many of the dive companies have provocative brochures showing divers cavorting with all sorts of critters, including the holy grail of SCUBA encounters, the whale shark. We're not saying it doesn't happen; just don't *expect* it. People have been known to experience spontaneous human combustion, but we've never seen *that* happen either. We only know one friend who claims to have swum with a whale shark here. (And he lies a lot.)

So you'll know our perspective when we review companies, we should tell you what we do and don't like when we go on a dive. On a bad dive, the dive master takes the group on a nonstop excursion that keeps you kicking the whole time. No time to stop and explore the nooks and crannies. Good outfits will give you a briefing, tell you about some of the endemic species here, what to look for, and will point out various things on the dives, keeping it moving but not too fast. Bad outfits kick a lot. Good outfits explain the unique qualities of Hawai'i's environment. Bad dive masters may tell you what *they* saw (but you missed). Good companies work around your needs, wishes and desires. Bad companies keep everyone on a short leash. Good dive masters know their stuff and share it with you. Bad dive masters don't know squat but imply they know it all in order to impress you. As divers, we like companies that wander toward the boat for the latter part of the dive and allow you to go up when you are near the end of your tank, as opposed to everyone going up when the heaviest breather has burned up his/her bottle.

During times when we feel the diving conditions are bad (poor vis or big swells), we like to call around and ask about conditions. We appreciate the companies who admit it's bad, and we hold it against those who tell us how wonderful conditions are.

THE TOPS ON MAUI

The best companies we've found have been in South Maui. Regardless of the profession, it seems that the cream sooner or later rises to the top. So it is with the dive industry on Maui. Without question, the best dive outfits on the island are **Prodiver Maui** (875–4004) and **Mike Severns** (879–6596).

Prodiver takes only 6 on their ample boat, so you never feel crowded. They have a good boat, good crew, good pace and a good attitude. They treat you well and handle the dives just right. The current owners have backed off a bit on snacks and beverages (feed me, feed me), but you can tell that the joy of diving hasn't left them. It's $139 per 2-tank, gear is $10.

If they're full, **Mike Severns** is also a quality outfit top to bottom. Everyone gets a computer, good gear and plenty of snacks. Their knowledge is so accurate it borders on wisdom and their briefings are the most precise we've found. With perfectly led dives, a good 13-passenger boat (2 groups, which can get a bit cramped and clumsy) and the right attitude, this is a great company to go with. With so many years of experience, they are very adept at finding critters and showing them to you, and their knowledge is phenomenal. Since they know the sites so well, they key in on what to brief you on before the dives. Many companies do this, but nobody does it as well. $130 for a 2-tank, $15 extra for gear. Book both in advance.

Ed Robinson (879–3584) is also a very well-run company and is a very acceptable alternative. Good ascent policy, good briefing, they go nice and slow during the dives, and their divemasters seem pretty knowledgeable, if a bit cocky. But most do a good job and have a good attitude. They have two 12-passenger boats (groups of 6). As opposed to Mike Severns' bent toward education, these guys tend to stress the fun of diving more and lean toward finding rare stuff to round out your dive sightings résumé. They also do the best in the food department. Their boats, like most single-hull boats, rock a lot in heavy swells, but that's usually only relevant when they go to Lana'i. The Wednesday Lana'i trip from South Maui is, however, wonderful, though the trip is long. An easy company to recommend. It's $130 for 2-tank plus $20 for gear, but they usually won't do the Molokini back wall except on the $170 3-tank, which is a very good excursion. (They only want experienced divers on that 3-tank dive.)

Maui Dreams (874–5332) does good shore dives along South Maui. Their enthusiasm is evident and welcome. It's like you're diving with friends.

They'll go out with only one person if necessary, even for a night dive. That's unusual for a dive company. (They could use a better briefing and maybe some food.) $69 for one tank, $99 for two, gear included.

Maui Dive Shop has several locations on the island, including a large shop in Kihei (879–3388) and a giant 5,500 square-foot shop in Lahaina (661–5388). Their shop personnel can be snotty and short with customers, especially at the Kihei location. Though you certainly won't find many steals, the Lahaina shop is pretty complete, including lots of surfing supplies.

As for diving, they do a pretty decent job, though it's a bit of a processing machine. Not bad, but not in the same league as the others mentioned above. They have boat, shore and night dives.

West Maui companies don't fare as well. The best boat dive company is probably **Extended Horizons** (667–0611). It's not their services that shine. Light snacks for food, and their shorties

Sometimes swimming in a crowd isn't so bad.

Hawaiian Reefs—*Why is it that...?*

What is that crackling sound, like bacon frying, I always hear while snorkeling or diving?
For years this baffled people. In the early days of submarines, the sound interfered with sonar operations. Finally we know the answer. It's hidden snapping shrimp defining their territory. One variety is even responsible for all the dark cracks and channels you see in smooth lobe coral. A pair creates the channels, then "farms" the algae inside.

Why are there so few shellfish in Hawai'i? It's too warm for some of the more familiar shellfish (which tend to be filter-feeders, and Hawaiian waters don't have as much stuff to filter). But Hawai'i has more shellfish than most people are aware of. They hide well under rocks and in sand. Also, people tend to collect shells (which is illegal), and that depletes the numbers.

Why do coral cuts take so long to heal? Coral contains a live animal. When you scrape coral, it leaves proteinaceous matter in your body, which takes much longer for your body to dispatch.

How did the early fish get here over the vast open ocean? Often in the form of larvae, which could travel in the ocean's current for long periods of time without the need to feed in the inhospitable open ocean.

What do turtles eat? Dolphins. (Just teasing.) They primarily eat plants growing on rocks, as well as jellyfish when they are lucky enough to encounter them. Unfortunately for turtles and lucky for us, jellyfish aren't numerous here.

Is it harmful when people play with an octopus? Yes, if the octopus gets harmed while trying to get it out of its hole. Best to leave them alone.

Why does the ocean rarely smell fishy here in Hawai'i? Two reasons. We have relatively small tide changes, so the ocean doesn't strand large amounts of smelly seaweed at low tide. Also, the water is fairly sterile compared to mainland water, which owes much of its smell to algae and seaweed that thrives in the bacteria-rich runoff from industrial sources. We don't have an upwelling of cold, nutrient-rich waters common on the mainland, which causes plankton there to thrive.

Why is the water so clear here? Because relatively little junk is poured into our water compared to the mainland. Also, natural currents tend to flush the water with a continuous supply of fresh, clean ocean water.

Why do my ears hurt when I dive deep, and how are scuba divers able to get over it? Because the increasing weight of the ocean is pressing on your ears the farther down you go. Divers alleviate this by equalizing their ears. Sounds high tech, but that simply means holding your nose while trying to blow out of it. This forces air into the eustachian tubes, creating equal pressures with the outside ocean. (It doesn't work if your sinuses are clogged.) Anything with air between it gets compressed. So if you know someone who gets a headache whenever they go under water...well, they must be an airhead.

are, frankly, insufficient for many people. And their sales pitch at the end of the dive is tacky and cheesy. They stop the boat, make speeches about how good the dive and crew were, then start their tip jar ceremony while they strongly push the T-shirts and photo CDs. What sets them apart, however, is their lust to go to more than the standard dive sites. 12 divers max, which is crowded. They often go to Lana'i. $149 for 2-tank plus only $30 for gear. Shore dives are $109 for 1-tank.

Lahaina Divers (667–7496) is a big company with fairly big boats that hold up to 24 people. If full, it's pretty crowded, but when there are fewer divers, it's a good trip. They have a loose policy on keeping divers together underwater. Good unless you're a novice or want things pointed out. Friendly crews. We liked their Carthaginian (a sunken ship) sunset dive with the second tank at Mala Wharf where nightlife sometimes abounds. $149 for the shipwreck, $129 for their Lana'i trip. They also have the training to handle divers with disabilities.

WHERE TO DIVE

Though most boat captains will poll their customers, asking where they want to go, they'll try to steer you to places they think are good that day. Three off-shore places stand out as some of the best diving in Hawai'i.

One of the coolest is **Cathedrals II** off Lana'i. Most boats leave from Lahaina, but some, like Ed Robinson, do some trips from South Maui. Not only is the large lava room with several entrances here dramatic, but the sea life can be great. On a 2-tank dive here we saw, among other things, four reef sharks, two *huge* octopuses, a frogfish *(very cool),* harlequin shrimp, ghost shrimp, pipefish, a titan scorpionfish, lots of black coral, slipper lobster and— oh, yes—*a pod of dolphins!* (This was one of the single greatest day dives we've ever done.) Obviously, Cathedrals won't always deliver dives like that, but it *can* be awesome. Not necessarily an ad-vanced dive. You need to specifically book this trip. Boats leaving from Lahaina offer shorter treks. Dive lights are helpful. **Cathedrals I** is also great, but not as good as II.

Another standout location is the **back wall of Molokini**. This is *outside* the crater. It's not necessarily the fish life that makes this a good dive, though the fish are numerous. Rather, it's the dramatic way the wall plunges into the abyss. Its presence is never far from your mind. And as you round the corner from Molokini's shadow to the sunlight (penetrating to an incredible depth), it forms an awesome spectacle. Later, you may look down and see a black tip reef shark cruising the neighborhood 90 feet below you—and another one 90 feet above you. This is an easy dive to go deep, and most companies will screen to make sure you're up to the task. Since there's nothing much to stop you from going all the way, it's important that you be comfortable regulating your buoyancy. We don't want you setting any new depth records in your state of rapture of the deep. Bring a light for the shadow side.

The *inside* of Molokini isn't nearly as dramatic to dive as the outside, but it's easier. Either way, trips to Molokini are very short. It's only 7 miles from the Kihei Boat Ramp.

A newer dive site is the Carthaginian. Scuttled here in 2005, it rests in 95 feet of water. The boat was painted and rigged to resemble an old whaling boat, and underwater the wreck appears older. The easily accessed interior is fairly wide open, and in time the fish count should increase.

Good Shore Dive Locations

From South Maui to West Maui, all are described in greater detail under BEACHES.

Black Sand Beach (Puʻu Olaʻi) has good coral, turtle and fish life, but you'll have to swim along the hill's shoreline over 800 feet to get to the areas deep enough to justify SCUBA. Around the point, before Little Beach, there are some excellent caves. Ocean entry is over a lava shelf; try only during calm seas. Visibility is poor until you leave the shoreline area. Just follow the hill around as far as your will takes you. Dive boat captains call this site *Red Hill*.

Ulua is where intros usually take place in South Maui. There's lots of good reef, though visibility tends to be poor.

Makena Landing is usually calm with easy entry, making it a popular place for intro or night dives. The visibility is best on the north side, which also has good coral.

5 Graves/5 Caves, described on page 163, can be excellent.

Scenic Lookout, described on page 157, can be exciting, though the gear-hauling and entry is a bit annoying.

Black Rock is fun, and there are dive companies at nearby resorts.

Kahekili Beach Park is a popular intro spot because of the easy entry. Kick straight out for best conditions.

Honolua Bay *can* be incredible. Though depths rarely exceed 40 feet, the right side of the bay has an extensive reef area and lots of fish. (The opening photo on pages 2–3 is Honolua Bay.) Eels are common. Head out 100–200 feet before dropping.

Mala Wharf is a twisted pile of rubble from a badly constructed wharf that makes a great artificial reef. Night dives are best. At no deeper than 30 feet we've seen conger eels, octopuses and even oval squid. From Mala Ramp, you can see the old broken wharf and how to get there.

IF YOU'VE NEVER DIVED BEFORE

Intro dives are how nearly all of us certified divers started. You'll get instruction, and a dive instructor will be nearby during the dive. Most do it as a shore dive. Though certified, we still do intros with companies to see how they do. Most intros take place at Ulua Beach in South Maui or Kahekili Beach in West Maui. If you have any asthma, heart disease, high blood pressure, ear problems or are on medication, call the dive company before you arrive. They may need a signoff from your doctor for some things.

Of the companies we've listed above, **Maui Dreams** (874–5332) in South Maui does the best job for intro dives, and they are very reasonably priced at $89 for a 1-tank, $109 for a 2-tank.

The two things that annoy us with companies doing intros are patronizing attitudes and the use of 63-cubic foot (or smaller) tanks. Most new divers suck a lot of air, and 80s, though heavier, are the way to go, not the smaller 63s. (Perhaps this is cynical, but maybe some use 63s so that they can get you in and out faster since your air won't last as long.)

OTHER DIVE COMPANIES

There are tons of them out there. We haven't been impressed with **Maui Dive Shop's** intros. There's absolutely nothing about **Boss Frog** that we like—pushy, rude and abrupt. **Makena Coast** is adequate. **Beach Activities** (662–8207) has painless shore dives at Black Rock for $79. **B&B SCUBA** (875–2861) has a pretty nice shop in Kihei. And their boat trip is…Did we mention that they have a pretty nice shop? And SCUBA **Shack** (879–3483) has a 700+ horsepower rocket that gets you out to Molokini in 7 minutes flat. It's one cool ride.

A FEW TIPS

Despite assurances that the gear has been checked out, if you rent gear to dive on your own, it's a good idea to hook the regulator to the tank before you drive away from the shop. Though we have our own gear, we often rent from shops and boats to evaluate the gear, and we've had problems with leaking regulators and tanks not filled completely with some shops. Anyone can have it happen once, but if it happens twice at a shop, we'll dump on them.

Dives, like snorkeling, are usually best in the morning. Afternoon winds can lower visibility and raise surf.

Some companies try to put you in 63-cubic foot tanks. If you don't want to be rushed, tell them you want 80s. Many will comply.

I'd like to pass on a tip that has helped my diving more than any other. I used to be a less-than-stellar breather, never the last one out. I tried skip breathing—holding your breath while not ascending, which, of course, you're *not* supposed to do—but only got marginally better results at the cost of headaches caused by a buildup of CO_2. Then I learned the secret to make a tank last a long time. Breathe *continuously*, never stop, but do it slowly. A long, slow, deep inhalation followed immediately by a drawn out exhalation keeps CO_2 from building up and keeps your body from thinking it's low on air. (I use my tongue at the top of my mouth to spray the air out slowly.) You never feel deprived, and the tank lasts *oh, so long*. The only downside is less silence during your dive. Now, I'm almost always the last

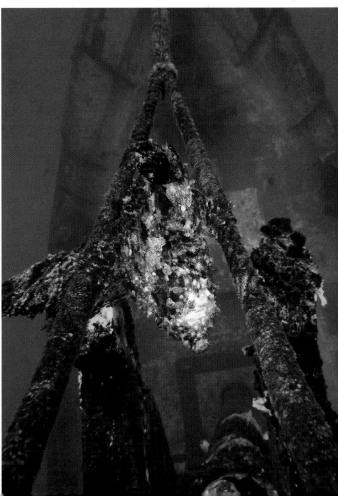

One of diving's holy grails—the elusive frogfish—straddles the forestays at the top of the sunken wreck, Carthaginian.

one out, and only the tables tell me when to come up, not my gauge. See your dive instructor. (That's the diving disclaimer equivalent of *see your doctor*.)

Here we go again, frothing at the mouth about the water. But give us the benefit of the doubt here. The truth is that snorkeling on Maui can be outrageous. Clean, clear water in many locations, calm surf much of the time, and gobs of fish and coral. The trick is knowing where to go. We've literally snorkeled miles and miles of coastline, from the top of West Maui to the bottom of South Maui, looking for good spots. If you look at our maps, the areas shaded in darker blue represent our best finds. In general, the best snorkeling is in South Maui, though West Maui does have a few gems.

We'll admit that we're snorkeling junkies and never tire of experiencing the water here. If you snorkel often, you can go right to our list below of recommended areas. But if you're completely or relatively inexperienced, you should read on.

For identifying ocean critters, the best books we've seen are *Shore Fishes of Hawai'i* by John Randall and *Hawaiian Reef Fish* by Casey Mahaney. They're what we use. You should see plenty of butterflyfish, wrasse, convict tang, achilles tang, parrotfish, angelfish, dam-

Here fishy, fishy, fishy...

selfish, Moorish idol, pufferfish, trumpet-fish, moray eel, and humuhumunuku-nukuapua'a or Picasso triggerfish—a beautiful but very skittish fish. (It's as if they somehow *know* how good they look in aquariums.)

We know people who have a fear of putting on a mask and snorkel. Gives 'em the willies. For them, we recommend boogie boards with clear windows to observe the life below.

A FEW TIPS

- Feeding the fish is generally not recommended because it introduces unnatural behavior to the reef.
- Use *Sea Drops* or another brand of anti-fog goop. Spread it *thinly* on the inside of a dry mask, then do a quick rinse.
- Most damage to coral comes when people grab it or stand on it. If your mask starts to leak or you get water in your snorkel, be careful not to stand on the coral to clear them. Find a spot where you won't damage coral or drift into it. Fish and future snorkelers (not to mention the coral) will thank you.
- Don't use your arms much, or you will spook the fish. Just gentle fin motion. Any rapid motion can cause the little critters to scatter.
- Water temps range from 75° in February to 80° in September. The lower end may seem chilly; consider renting a short, thin wetsuit.
- We prefer using divers' fins (the kind that slip over water shoes), so that we can walk easily into and out of the water without tearing up our feet. (If you wear socks or nylons under the shoes, it'll keep you from rubbing the tops of your toes raw.)
- If you have a mustache and have trouble with a leaking mask, try a little Vaseline. Don't get any on the glass—it can get *really* ugly.

THE BEST AREAS TO SNORKEL

See the writeups in the BEACHES chapter for info on each specific area. Some snorkeling sites have specifics you need to know.

South Maui Snorkeling

At press time our favorite spots—**Fishbowl**, **Aquarium** and the excellent coves along the north side of **La Pérouse Bay** were closed to snorkelers. You'll have to settle for nearby **Dumps**. Don't bother with the part of La Pérouse nearest your car. The entire point separating **Po'olenalena Beach** from **Palauea Beach** is great, especially from the Po'olenalena side. Also, the south end of Po'olenalena is good. Between **Maluaka** and **Black Sand Beach** there's some good snorkeling. The point separating **Kama'ole I** and **II** is pretty decent. North of **Keawakapu** works pretty well, as does south of **Wailea Beach**, though you'll have to go out farther there.

West Maui Snorkeling

The **scenic lookout** between the 8 and 9 mile marker is good if you can deal with the dicey entry and exit. **Honolua Bay** offers excellent snorkeling about ⅔ of the time. **Black Rock** at Ka'anapali Beach can be superb. The south end of **Oneloa** in Kapalua is good much of the time. The 14 Mile Marker on Hwy 30 is ridiculously overrated, but the area below the cliffs southeast of the 11 mile marker is good if you can deal with the long swim.

ODDS & ENDS

Renting gear is easy. Maui is littered with rental places, and you won't have any trouble finding them. We probably lean toward **Maui Dive Shop's** many locations (879–3388). They also have wetsuits and divers' fins available for extra that will fit over your water shoes.

Most places charge about $2–$8 per day, $10–$30 per week for gear. Many shops have low prices in hopes of luring you in and then selling you other activities or timeshares. Also keep in mind that at some shops, the employee gets a commission for selling you more expensive gear. Get what *you* want, not what *they* want you to get. Make sure the mask fits without having to suck in too hard through your nose. Snorkels with drain valves and dry snorkels work better than ordinary tubes.

The most common way that visitors get bad **sunburns** is while snorkeling. You don't feel it coming because of the cool water. Do yourself a favor and consider wearing a T-shirt.

Don't judge a snorkeling site by the first 20 feet. Shorelines are often cloudy. You'll usually have to venture farther out for good quality.

It's a good idea to check on the **snorkeling conditions** the day before you plan to snorkel. Call (866) 944–5025 for a weather forecast. For a surf forecast, call 877–3611, or check page 2 of the *Maui News* newspaper.

GUIDED SNORKEL TOURS

If you're intrigued but nervous about snorkeling, **Ann Fielding's Snorkel Maui** (572–8437) offers a very patient and methodical lesson/tour for $120 each (for two people). The price drops to $95 each for 3 or more people. She'll spend several hours with you, getting you used to the gear and water, then lead you along a South Maui tour. Snacks included. Ann is a real-life marine biologist with great knowledge, so you'll learn much about our marine environment. Be sure and book with her in advance.

SNUBA is sort of like SCUBA-lite. Good for those nervous about taking the plunge. This is at Molokini.

If you're a little hesitant about trying SCUBA, consider SNUBA. That's where you swim below a raft with tanks and a 20-foot hose, regulator in mouth and an instructor by your side. Anyone 8 and older can SNUBA. (You need to be age 12—or 10 through PADI—to SCUBA.) At press time we couldn't find anyone who was *reliably* doing SNUBA trips from the shore. But some of the boat trips listed under OCEAN TOURS have SNUBA available, usually for around $50. Specifically, read about **Four Winds II**, **Lani Kai** and **Pride of Maui**. Groups of 4–6 per trip; expect about 30–40 minutes underwater.

If you're looking to be pampered, there are lots of spas on the island. Some are definitely better than others.

The grandest by far is appropriately named **Spa Grande** at Grand Wailea (875–1234, ext. 4949). It's the largest (50,000 sq. ft.), most elaborately decorated, rich-feeling spa on the island. You name it, they've got it. They have a unique series of specialty baths, in addition to your treatment. Like most spas, you might feel a bit processed at the beginning, and the service isn't as grand as the surroundings. Also, try not to look too closely, or you'll notice that the infrastructure could use a bit of a facelift. But once you start, they'll transform you from a raving lunatic to a smiling idiot. And make sure you take advantage of the awesome facilities before or after your treatment. (Mornings are slowest.)

The **Four Seasons** (874–8000), also in Wailea, is smaller but has something called a cocoon treatment, which is the closest you'll ever get to having your bones liquefied. They also have oceanside massages. The locker rooms are beautiful and furnished with pretty much everything you'll need and then some. Nice treatment rooms. Outside guests have access to the fitness room for an extra $25.

In West Maui, the **Westin Maui's Heavenly Spa** (661–2525) rooms are dark, moody, quiet and relaxing. Services are good. Guests pay extra for use of the fitness room.

Nearby **Spa Moana** (667–4725) at the Hyatt Ka'anapali has great massages, but the rooms are bright and unacceptably noisy. Hearing toilets flush, lawn mowers and screaming beachgoers sort of kills the moment.

You won't *Run Silent, Run Deep.* You won't hear the sound of sonar pinging away in the background. And it's rare that anyone shoots torpedoes at you. But if you want to see the undersea world and *refuse* to get wet, *dis is da buggah*. **Atlantis Submarine** (667–2224) uses a 48-passenger sub out of Lahaina that ambles along over a reef, which is, to be honest, a bit plainer than the type you'd choose to snorkel or SCUBA, but it's still cool. They also visit a sunken wreck called the Carthaginian. This is the opposite of an aquarium—this world belongs to the fish, and *you* are the oddity. This

$109, 40-minute ride is a kick. Most kids like it if they are old enough to appreciate the sights. We took friends on this trip once, and a huge manta ray cruised by the window. Of course, their 2½-year-old son was *far* more impressed with the plastic fish card tied to the inside hull than the 14-foot ray just outside the window. But adults like it, and even certified divers like us get a kick out of it. Claustrophobics will probably be too busy staring through the windows to be nervous. Photographers will want to use a fast shutter speed and turn off the flash. Mornings are usually best. Wear a bright red shirt, and watch what happens to its color on the way down. Also, if you book the last trip of the day and it's whale season, you might get to spend extra time on the transport boat whale watching.

A cheaper substitute to a sub is the **Reefdancer** (667–2133). It's a semi-submersible—a boat with large windows below. After a 20-minute (each way) ride to the site, they glide over a shallow reef for 20 minutes as divers scavenge for critters to bring to the window. Kids under 8 will probably love it, as will those too skittish to try snorkeling. It's also roomier than the sub. Only $35, and kids under 6 are free. The 1½ hour ride is too long; stick with the hour.

ＳＵＲＦＩＮＧ

Ho, da shreddin's da kine, brah. (Just trying to get you in the mood.) Surfing is synonymous with Hawai'i. And why not? Hawaiians invented da buggah. Lessons aren't as difficult as you may think. They put you on a large, soft board the size of a garage door (well...almost), so it's fairly easy to master, at least at this level. Surf is usually very small in South Maui, often too small even for beginners, and the wind that arrives late morning and in the afternoon complicates the learning process. Lahaina is a *much* better place to learn. Plus, the South Maui area where they teach—Cove Park because of its fairly reliable surf—has yucky water. (See page 158 for more on that.)

In Lahaina, try **Goofy Foot Surf School** (244–9283). They're very good teachers and guarantee that you'll ride a wave or it's free. Two-hour lessons are $65 per person for groups of 5, $150 for a private lesson, $250 for a couple. By the way, a goofy footer is a person (in this case the owner) who surfs with his *right* foot forward instead of the usual left. Pretty goofy, huh? We also liked **Girls Gone Surfing** (280–0103).

If you're in Kihei and don't want to drive to Lahaina, try **Big Kahuna Adventures** (875–6395). $60 for two hours.

If you're experienced, West Maui has easily accessible water, so you may want to simply drive along and look for the kind of waves that work best for you since it's very swell-direction dependent. Launiupoko State Park south of the 18 mile marker often has a good break, though it's kind of far out there. The area south of the 19 mile marker can also be good.

Lahaina Harbor has a very dependable break, even in fairly low surf.

Honolua Bay is one of the best sites—if you know what you're doing.

One site that's received national attention is **Jaws**. An unusual formation below the surface kicks in when the surf gets bigger than 15 feet (which happens about a dozen times a year in the winter). Then the waves become magnified and form a curved shape. They have been known to reach 70 feet here. Only a handful of experts can surf Jaws (using

Jet Skis to tow them out and save their bacon when needed). Less than 15-foot surf means zippo is happening. (We're assuming you only want to *watch* at Jaws.) If the surf is pounding, the most direct route from Hwy 36 is Hahana Road (between the 13 and 14 mile markers). Go to the left on Hahana after the fork, and take the dirt road at the end of Hahana. It's along a gulch (there will be trees and such along your right). If it's real dry, a regular car *may* make it, but probably only 4WDs should try. If wet, consider one of the other roads among the fields. (See map on page 115.) It's private land, so ML&P may opt to close the road.

The best surf shops are in Kahului. They include **Second Wind** (877–7467) and **Hi-Tech** (877–2111). In Lahaina, try **Honolua Surf Co**. (661–8848) or their Kihei shop (874–0999).

By the way, a collection of surfboards is known in surfing lingo here as a *quiver*. A little kid surfer who doesn't have a job or car yet is called a *grommet*. Double *overhead* is when the waves are huge, and if you get good enough, you might get a chance to visit the *green room*. If someone says your girlfriend is *filthy*, it's a compliment. And a *landshark* is someone who says he surfs…but doesn't.

Lest you think of yourself as da best island surfer, consider this: Hawaiian legend states that Chief Kihapiilani once surfed a wave from Maui to Moloka'i. He was said to have been adorned with leis, and that no surf spray was found on the flowers. *Hey, we don't make up the legends, we just report them.*

Stand Up Paddling, or **SUP**, is the latest craze in the surfing world. The hardest part about learning to surf is standing up on the board while it's moving. This sport has made things easier by giving you a board big enough to dance on. SUP boards are wider, thicker and longer than the biggest long boards people commonly learn to surf on. SUP instruction focuses on keeping

Advice to boogie boarders—duck!

your balance while using a tall paddle to move you into the waves. (This provides an excellent central core workout, with your feet—of all things—hurting the worst.) The sight of people standing and dipping long paddles in the water has earned SUP surfers the subversive title "janitors" or "moppers" from traditional surfers. The size of the board, as well as the fact that you are already standing up, gives you an advantage in catching waves early. You don't have to drop in exactly where the wave is breaking. Moppers can catch waves behind the lineup, but all surfing rules apply once you've caught the wave. Traditional surfers will be more inclined to drop in on your wave since they'll feel that you didn't work as hard to get it as they did.

Because it's a relatively new sport, rates are unpredictable. Call the surfing guys listed above.

Maui is the undisputed whale watching capital of Hawai'i. The shallow water between islands here is the whales' preferred birthing area. Few industries in Hawai'i bring as much shameless phony advertising as whale watching. Computers allow fake scenes with relative ease. (For the record, we don't use computers to doctor our photos.) Some show whales leaping so close to boats you think they're going to get swamped. Just so you know, boats are forbidden by federal law from getting closer than 100 yards. The fine for violating a whale's personal space is obscene. Whales are allowed to initiate closer contact (and they're rarely fined), but in general, count on staying a football field away. That's OK, because these oversized buggahs are so big that at that distance they're still incredibly impressive.

Though they're not the only whales here, **humpbacks** are the stars of whale watching. They work in Alaska during the summer, building up fat, then vacation here from December to March or April where the females bear their young and the males sing the blues. More than 1,000 whales come to the islands each year, and the mothers and calves stay close to shore. Only the males sing, and they all sing the same song, usually with their heads pointed down. No air bubbles come out while singing, and scientists aren't sure how they do it. Humpbacks don't eat while they're here and may lose ⅓ of their body weight during their stay in Hawai'i. (I doubt that very many *human* visitors can make that claim.)

There's no question that whale watching varies from year to year. Some years the humpbacks are boisterous and raising hell, constantly breaching, blowing and generally having a good time. Other years they seem strangely subdued, as if hung over from their Alaska trip. What's really going on is that some years Maui's whales visit other Hawaiian islands. Perhaps whales, too, want to avoid getting into a rut.

See OCEAN TOURS on page 207 for a description of the different boats. The best whale watching company, not surprisingly, is **Pacific Whale Foundation** (249–8811). After all, this is their passion. It's around $30 for a 2-hour trip. Their knowledge is phenomenal, and the trips are fun. They even have hydrophones to listen to the beasts. Of their different crafts, the Ocean Spirit and Ocean Odyssey are their better boats. Avoid their Ocean Explorer. Narrow and tight.

Lots of other companies do whale watching trips. Most outings are 2 hours, and they charge around $40. Bring binoculars if you have them.

From land, good places to spot whales are from the Scenic Lookout between the 8 and 9 mile markers or the light station at McGregor Point between the 7 and 8 mile markers, both on Hwy 30 past Ma'alaea. Whales are *much* easier to see when there are no whitecaps.

Windsurfing

Windsurfing is the result of taking a surfboard and attaching a sail to it. When properly instructed, you can zip along faster than the wind. It's a first-class adrenaline charge.

No matter where you go in the world, if you ask people where to find the best windsurfing on the planet, Maui is nearly always rated as the best. That's because of an accident of geography. Our amazingly consistent trade winds from the northeast are speeded up near Kahului by the venturi effect between the two mountains, so it's always windier there than the general trade speed. The shoreline orientation means the wind is usually along the shore to slightly onshore and parallel to the wave direction. Perfect!

By common agreement, no windsports are allowed before 11 a.m. (Surfers get to use the waves up till then.) This is strictly enforced by local residents. Also, if you're interested in advanced lessons or simply renting your gear, local regs state that companies aren't allowed to deliver. You'll have to bring the gear yourself. (Beginners on longboards are exempt from the delivery rule and the 11 a.m.

Hard-core windsurfers, you have arrived. You've reached the promised land at Ho'okipa.

rule because winds after 11 are considered too difficult for learners.) Unless you're advanced, don't try to windsurf at Ho'okipa, the mecca of windsurf spots. Local users won't allow beginners at the sacred spot, and there is no shortage of young toughs there to enforce the ban on novices. Beginners, instead, will find Kanaha Beach near Kahului Airport the best place to learn.

A 2½ hour lesson is about $80 per person with 3 people per class. During that time you'll actually windsurf, though tacking and jibing (changing directions by heading into or away from the wind) may elude you. In general, it's a hard sport to master at the beginning, and you should expect to fall in the water 70 or so times during your lesson. So don't be discouraged if you're not streaking like the wind gods you see around the island. (Falling's not so bad; in fact, you'll probably get real good at it.) Shorter and slimmer people seem to learn board balance more quickly. During your lesson, don't be shy about asking your instructor to show you *exactly* what you're doing wrong.

The companies we've had good luck with are **HST** (871–5423) and **Action Sports** (871–5857). All meet at Kanaha at 9 a.m., but you'll have to go to their nearby offices to pay. (No exchanging money at the beach.)

Wear a T-shirt to keep the mandatory life jacket from rubbing you, and wear water shoes while boarding. (Most companies provide.)

KITEBOARDING

Also called kitesurfing, it's a bit less known than windsurfing, so we're putting it here. Imagine a modified surfboard, shorter and boxier than a normal board, with fins at both ends and straps for your feet. Then let a special, controllable four-line kite drag you along. As in windsurfing, you don't have to go the direction the wind takes you—you have control. Despite what some instructors tell you when they want to sign you up, it's harder to get up on the board than windsurfing. But *oh,* what fun it is! More fun than windsurfing once you're comfortable on the board. One way you can prepare before you get here is to buy a two-line kite and master it so that you can instinctively maneuver the kite. It's not that hard, but it helps if you can steer the kite without thinking.

Lessons are *expensive.* The best place to learn is either **Action Sports** (871–5857) or **Kiteboarding School of Maui** (873–0015), both in Kahului. Action Sports has a 3½-hour lesson for $280. This is a group lesson, but there's one instructor per student. KSM has 3-hour lessons for $270 and a 6-hour lesson (over 2 days) for $495. **Aqua Sports** (242–8015) has intro lessons for $280. We love how they use radio helmets to give you tips once you're soloing. Teaching methods differ. First you need to learn how to operate the kite (which is a hoot). Next comes body dragging. Though it sounds like something they do to you if your credit card is declined, it's actually when you let the kite drag you through the ocean while you manipulate it. Then comes the good part—*riding the board.*

Most companies claim you'll be riding the board after the first lesson, but don't be disappointed if that doesn't happen. It ain't easy, brah, and instructors privately concede that few are able to get on the board the first day.

If you want to *watch* kiteboarding, head over to Kanaha in Kahului. Kiteboarders use the west (left) end.

If you're already a kiteboarder, note that it's illegal to venture near the end of the runway at Kanaha in Kahului. See map on page 66.

Ever seen movies where military commandos don a harness, hook a pulley onto a steel cable and zip down into the action? This is similar—without the hostile fire at the end.

Ziplining has become big business on Maui, and an arms race of sorts was created as companies sought longer and longer lines. Claims of longest, biggest and fastest are common. We zipped every single line on the island, and the differences are big. Some companies offer sunset or full moon zipping; contact them if this is a priority. Don't wear too-short shorts or the harness will get under your skin (so to speak). Minimum age is 10.

Flyin' Hawaiian Zipline (463–5786) is our favorite. They took an area that was a reserve and built *8 ziplines* stretching well over 2 miles, with the last one a wild 3,250 feet across a valley where my GPS showed a top speed of 56 MPH. Instead of zipping back and forth across the same gulch, you make a continuous journey toward Ma'alaea Bay. The views are the best of the lot.

On the other hand, it'll take you five hours on the mountain to do this since you'll wait longer between zips (one person at a time) than with other companies. (The quality of your group will make a big difference since you'll get to know each other.) And the company has

Ziplining across the West Maui Mountains—the ultimate leave-no-footprint experience.

indicated that they won't take more than 40 people *per day* on this trip to minimize impact to the land, so you might want to book this far in advance. There are short, steep hikes between zips and winds are often *nukin'* in this area, especially in the afternoon. (It'll mostly be a quartering tailwind.) A *chicken skin* moment comes when your group plants an endangered flower somewhere along the course. (*Very* cool.) Wear sunblock and sunglasses. You gotta be between 75 and 250 pounds. Light snacks and juices served. $185.

Our next choice is **Kapalua Adventures** (665–3753). They are in a green, verdant area 1,900 feet above Kapalua with pretty scenery and views. Two people can zip beside each other. (Though with all due respect to Isaac Newton, while zipping, all objects *don't* fall at the same rate. The bigger they are, the faster they fall.) You'll be given jackets in case it rains, and snacks and juices are provided. Like Flyin' Hawaiian and Pi'iholo, your harness keeps you facing straight ahead, and you don't have to stop yourself at the end—braking blocks do the deed. Book the Upper Mountain Loop, *not* the Lower since the zipping is duller on the lower and you won't get the 2,300-foot line. It's $184 for 5 zips and will take 3½ hours. Minimal hiking. 60 to 250 pounds. Lunch is provided.

Pi'iholo Ranch (572–1717) has a similar tour to Kapalua, but the scenery is different. Less tropical-feeling, more gulch-filled eucalyptus forest above Makawao at 2,800 feet. It's pretty, but not *as pretty* as Kapalua. They have side-by-side zipping with one easily-fixed flaw. At the end of the zip a dangling rope threatens to flog your face as you come crashing in. It's unnerving. The tour is otherwise well run, and there's little hiking—just steep scrambles up wiggly ramps to the tops of the towers. Rain is not uncommon, and stinky jackets are available. The $140 4-line zip's farthest line is only 1,065 feet. Opt for the 5-line zip for $190 if you can afford it since you'll have one ride that's 1,400 feet and a final one that's a magnificent 2,800 feet long. 75 to 275 pounds.

Skyline Eco-Adventures (878–8400) started it all here with a tour upcountry in Haleakala and one above Lahaina (which they call Ka'anapali). In those days Skyline was pretty cool, and you had to book *way* in advance. Our review was pretty enthusiastic, and the product hasn't changed. But our job is to review companies *relative to each other*, and as early builders, they've lost the arms race of length and speed, seem quaint and under-achieving by comparison, and you often zip back and forth on short hops across the same terrain. Their harness system means landings are less structured—you have to stop yourself on a ramp (or one of the guides will help), though that may add to the adventure for some. You'll have more flexibility in your zipping position. No side-by-side zipping here.

The longest zip at the Haleakala location is 710 feet. But it's cheap at $95. At Ka'anapali most zips are 500–700 feet, and the longest of the 8 zips is 1,000 feet. I got up to 33 MPH on that one. Ka'anapali is dusty and often hot when the breeze isn't blowing. But they feed you sandwiches and juices, and views are pleasing. Their marketing department deserves a medal because the photos are far more compelling than reality, and the zips are so short you won't have time to look around. Ka'anapali is $150 for four hours, one of which is trucking up the mountain. 80 to 260 pounds. The hiking is nearly all downhill.

Having adventurous fun and perhaps helping the environment—yeah, works for us.

Some of the activities described below are for the serious adventurer. They can be experiences of a lifetime. We are assuming that if you consider any of them that you are a person of sound judgment, capable of assessing risks. All adventures carry risks of one kind or another. Our descriptions below do not attempt to convey all risks associated with an activity. These *adventures* are not for everyone. Good preparation is essential. In the end, it comes down to your own good judgment. Also, please read our note on personal responsibility on page 42. It's particularly relevant to this chapter.

SPEAR AN INVASIVE FISH

This is one of those adventures that can also be good for the environment. In the 1950s some short-sighted government officials decided it would be a *great* idea to introduce a beautiful fish from French Polynesia to Hawaiian waters in an attempt to create new fisheries. So they brought in 2,000 peacock groupers (now known locally as roi.) It was a disaster. The fish thrived, consuming and pushing out native species. And to add insult to injury, the fish isn't even edible, because individual fish have an extremely high incidence of ciguatera (reef fish poisoning) in their flesh, which is toxic to humans. So now Hawai'i is stuck with a fish that doesn't belong here and is harmful to our environment. What to do? *Spear 'em, brah.*

Spearfish Maui (205–8585) takes snorkelers out and teaches them how to free dive and spear fish. To be honest, they will harvest more than just roi, but they are very knowledgeable about which fish are appropriate to take and the volume of fish you actually hit will be small. (In fact, no one caught anything when we reviewed them, but we had a blast, nonetheless.)

This hiker (pictured at the bottom of the falls) reached the fourth, and best, falls at Na'ili'ili-haele. It's not too far, but it does include overcoming a hurdle. (Literally.)

It costs $149 for the four-hour experience and about half of that is the logistics of getting you to the water, and land instruction. You need to be a reasonably good snorkeler and comfortable in the water...And you need to know your own limitations. We found that the company's weak point was evaluating their potential customers as to whether they were up for the job. Having spent many years in Hawai'i's ocean, I'm very comfortable in somewhat rough seas (which we had the day we went out with them, launching from a lava platform), but Spearfish Maui had no way of knowing that and didn't ask. You'll probably be kicking a fair amount, and the fish aren't usually at the surface—you need to dive down to them. They'll teach you proper breathing techniques and show you how to work the spear gun. You'll be with them the whole time.

In the end you'll walk away with a greater appreciation of how to harvest fish face-to-face. And maybe you'll help rid the islands of an introduced pest.

THE FOUR FALLS OF NA'ILI'ILI-HAELE

Quite a mouthful. But imagine *four* waterfalls, one right after another, in a beautiful setting, and all relatively near the highway. It's the kind of scene most people dream of.

First things first. The trail is on EMI land. (See page 75 for more on that.) Unlike most land EMI uses, they actually own this parcel. (Most of the rest is leased from the state.) Locals have simply used the trail for years without a problem, but we'll leave it up to you to secure permission from them. The trailhead is 6/10 mile past the 6 mile marker (it's misplaced on the *left* side of the road instead of the right) on Hwy 360 across from some tall Cook Island pines. There's a dirt turnout on the right with a trail through a wire fence.

At first the trail can be slippery, awkward and steep as it goes down through bamboo to a ditch, which you may have to hop over if there's no board there. (If you fall in, you'll have a very bad day.) Once across, don't take the narrow trail to the right; stay on one of the two main trails in front of you (they converge). This will take you to a stream. After you boulder-hop across—IMPORTANT!—follow the trail as it parallels the bank upstream to the left. Don't take one of the false trails heading up the hill. Soon after, you *might* see an intermittent waterfall coming from a reservoir, but it's not one of the four falls.

Several minutes later the trail peters out, and a spur trail to the left takes you to the first waterfall (which you'll hear). The 15-foot falls are nice but a bit too small. (Oh, my, we're getting spoiled.) Cross the stream (boulder-hop again), and the trail continues on the other (east) side (with a slippery and dicey incline

at the beginning). Up through the bamboo (with a few awkward spots), and you'll soon come to waterfall #2. This is as far as many will go. Falls #2 has most of the ingredients people want. Very pretty with a nice swimming pool, rounded pebble shore with sun and shade. You may find yourself falling asleep to the sound of the water.

One of the things that separates a hike from an adventure is uncertainty of outcome. So it is here. On the left side of the falls, a trail leads up to...a dilemma. A fairly sheer 12-foot rock face is in your way. There are two more falls ahead. There may be a rope or a ladder or whatever (which we don't vouch for) to assist your climb, but it's not easy. And coming back down isn't much fun either. Most will probably settle for the first two falls. If you don't, here's what to expect.

It has probably taken you 30 minutes to get to falls #2. After overcoming the rockface, head up-stream for 10–15 minutes, and you'll come to a long pool. A trail on the right side through the wild ginger helps, but eventually you'll have to get in the water and swim 100 or so feet up the pool. (Have I lost you yet?) Don't try to go up and over; you *gotta* get in the water. Then you'll scale a man-high waterfall (#3), walk around the bend, and claim your prize: a gorgeous waterfall, at least 35 feet high (maybe more) in a drop-dead gorgeous scene. It's official. You have now arrived at paradise.

Na'ili'ili-haele Falls

360
6

Vague Ditch

Falls?

Main Trail

N
W E
S

0   1,000 Ft.

Falls

20°52.706
156°12.635

Now, that's a lot to go through to get to a waterfall, even a beautiful one. Why do it? Because it's a lot to go through, and it rewards you with a beautiful waterfall. That's it. Nothing deeper than that. Just an adventure you never would have had back home.

In case you're wondering, *yes,* there are more waterfalls past #4. And *no,* you'll never see them. It would be crazy to scale falls #4. Don't even think about it.

Water shoes or tabis are a big help for the last part of the journey. If you want to take a photo of falls #4, either get a waterproof bag, waterproof camera, or hold your camera high while swimming the length of the natural pool. (Hard to

do.) We've noticed that stream flow has been lighter than previous years, and we're speculating that EMI is snagging more water from their ditches upstream. Hard to say what you'll find.

MOUNTAIN BIKE HALEAKALA'S SPINE

OK, so everyone's heard of the Haleakala Downhill bike ride mentioned on page 172. But few are aware of this—there's a road called Skyline that meanders down the *other* side of the volcano, and it makes an incredible downhill *mountain bike* ride. After Skyline's downhill trek you have 2 miles of relatively flat dirt road, then almost 6 miles of paved, downhill, *yee-haw* riding. Best of all, there are no commercial operators clogging the roads. (Some might tell you you're not allowed to mountain bike it, but the truth is *they're* not allowed to do it *commercially.*)

Here's the deal. To do this you'll probably need two cars—one to leave at the end of Waipoli Road, the other to take you and your bikes to the summit of Haleakala. You'll probably find that renting a cheap-o car for a day is less expensive than renting a mountain bike (which is kind of odd when you think about it). Leave the car and a bike rack (which you get when you rent the mountain bikes) at Waipoli and Hwy 377 (the upper highway—see map on page 115), then head to the summit (not the upper visitor center).

Once at the top, ride your bikes down the short road, hang a right (the 21 mile marker is there), and at the next intersec-

The spine of Haleakala with its chain of craters makes a glorious mountain bike ride. All downhill without the crowds.

tion stay to the left to get to Skyline Road. (If the nasty government sign bothers you, see page 125 for an explanation.) Skyline is just over a mile downhill from the summit.

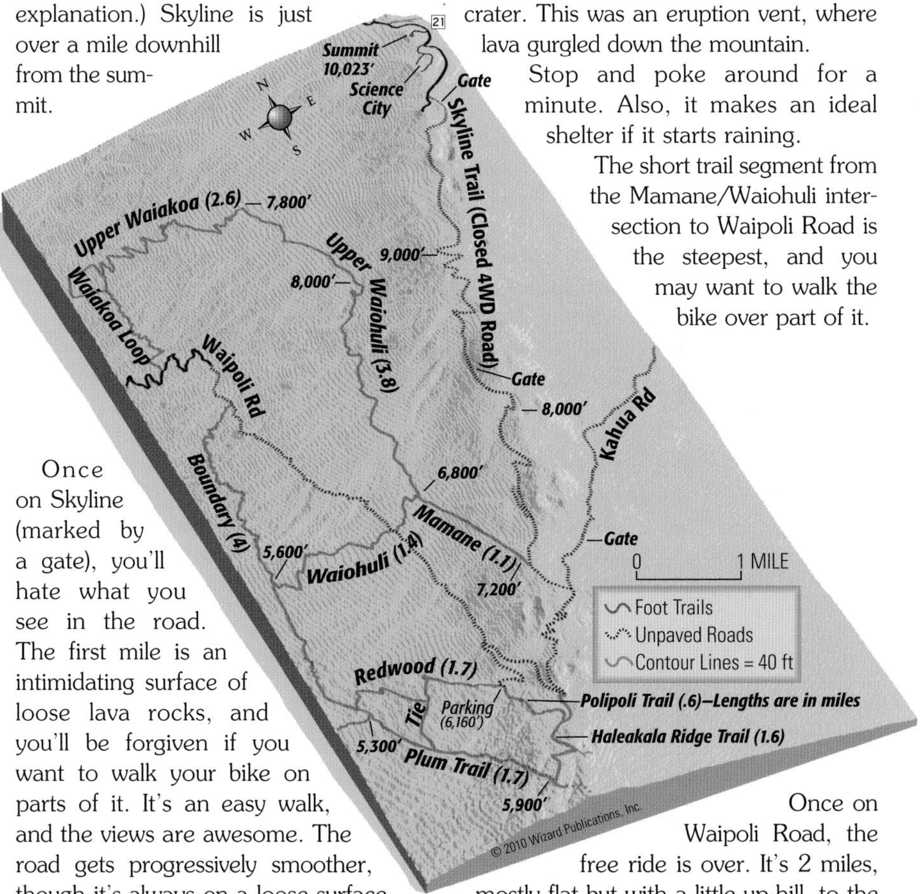

Once on Skyline (marked by a gate), you'll hate what you see in the road. The first mile is an intimidating surface of loose lava rocks, and you'll be forgiven if you want to walk your bike on parts of it. It's an easy walk, and the views are awesome. The road gets progressively smoother, though it's always on a loose surface, so don't get too crazy. Avoid locking your front tire, or it will wash out. The road continues to improve the lower you get, and the riding gets more fun since you're a bit less worried about your traction. A gate at 3½ miles into the trail is easy to walk around.

Watch for the Mamane Trailhead at almost 5½ miles into Skyline; it's on the right and easy to miss. This is perhaps the best part of the ride. It's just over a mile on a smooth, but narrow trail with killer views, and it seems tailor-made for mountain biking. The intersection of Mamane and Waiohuli is marked by a large lava pit crater. This was an eruption vent, where lava gurgled down the mountain. Stop and poke around for a minute. Also, it makes an ideal shelter if it starts raining.

The short trail segment from the Mamane/Waiohuli intersection to Waipoli Road is the steepest, and you may want to walk the bike over part of it.

Map labels:
Summit 10,023'
Science City
Gate
Skyline Trail (Closed 4WD Road)
Upper Waiakoa (2.6) — 7,800'
Upper Waiohuli (3.8)
9,000'
8,000'
Waiakoa Loop
Waipoli Rd
Boundary (4)
5,600'
Waiohuli (1.4)
6,800'
Mamane (1.1)
7,200'
Gate — 8,000'
Kahua Rd
Gate
0   1 MILE
Redwood (1.7)
Parking (6,160')
Tie
5,300'
Plum Trail (1.7)
5,900'
Polipoli Trail (.6)–Lengths are in miles
Haleakala Ridge Trail (1.6)

⌢ Foot Trails
⋯ Unpaved Roads
⌢ Contour Lines = 40 ft

© 2010 Wizard Publications, Inc.

Once on Waipoli Road, the free ride is over. It's 2 miles, mostly flat but with a little up-hill, to the paved part of Waipoli Road. Raise the seat and take it slow. Once on the pavement, the 1½-lane road is a delightful, extremely winding, downhill joyride. Keep the speed down, and watch for cars on this sparsely driven road. All told, you rode almost 16 miles and lost nearly 7,000 feet!

Some Tips

You'll probably want to lower your seat *a lot* for the downhill part, bringing more comfort, stability and a lower center of gravity. This also allows you to use the legs more to keep some weight off your 'okole on the bumpy parts. Rent a bike with front and rear shocks (for about $85) to keep your tush from getting tender.

It's good to cover your limbs and use a full face helmet (in case of a fall). Lava-induced road rash is a tad more severe.

Some may not like the narrow Mamane section. They (and those who miss it) can continue on Skyline where it will wrap around to Waipoli. Add 2 miles of pedaling if you do it this way.

This adventure will take most of the day, if you include the shuttling. A good time frame is to pick up the car in Kahului and pick up the bikes at around 9 a.m. (We use **Haleakala Bike** 575–9575 in Ha'iku because they are a good shop and conveniently located for this.) Then head to Waipoli to leave the car.

If you've never mountain biked before, yes, you can probably do this. We've taken a novice and she loved it, but she rode *nice and slow* and walked when she felt uncomfortable. Sure, the riding surface is more challenging than the traditional downhill ride, but you go at your own pace, which is a big deal for safety. Oh, and bring a tire patch kit.

DAY TRIP TO MOLOKA'I'S KALAUPAPA

Moloka'i's formerly notorious Kalaupapa leprosy settlement (see page 144 for more) is an isolated peninsula on the island's spectacular north side. Surrounded by sea cliffs thousands of feet high, the views from here, not to mention the incredible history, are available as day trips from Maui. The most popular way is **Moloka'i Mule Rides** (567–6088), which takes you down a 1,700-foot cliff to the settlement below. Book in advance. It's $199, which includes lunch and the tour below. If you're already on Moloka'i, you can walk the trail yourself.

Once at the bottom, **Damien Tours** (567–6171) takes you on a historical 4-hour tour of the settlement. It's $50, but *excludes* your transportation to Kalaupapa and *doesn't* include lunch. (Supplies here are hard to come by and they only get barge service *once a year*.)

TAKE YOUR OWN BOAT TO MOLOKINI

There are lots of charter boats you can take to Molokini. But what if you want to do things your own way? Only one company, located in South Maui, rents power boats, **Sea Escape** (879–3721), at 1979 South Kihei Rd. They'll meet you at the Kihei Boat Ramp and set you adrift. Take it virtually any place you want. And with speeds of up to 35 MPH, you can go to a lot of places. The catch? Price. They charge $110 per hour (3 hour min.) on the 17-foot rigid hull inflatable, and $145 per hour (5 hour min.) for their power cats. Fuel is extra. Now, that's a *big* chunk of money. But if you have 4 to 6 people, it's not quite as painful when you split it. Seeing the area this way is a real hoot, but nobody ever said hoots were cheap. For liability reasons they prefer that you've at least driven a power boat before. On calm days we like to explore the bottom of the island. They have water skis, fishing poles, Porta-Potties, etc., available for extra. We've even taken SCUBA tanks down south and dived absolutely pristine areas. Whatever you do, make sure that when you're captain, you practice giving meaningless orders with an arrogant snarl. *Swab the decks, batten down the hatches, bring me a flagon of grog, matey, or ye'll walk the plank for sure. Arrrgh.*

HIKE IN A LAVA TUBE

Maui Cave Adventures (248–7308) has an interesting tour. Their land has access to Ka'eleku Cave, a lava tube from Hana's past. The cave has some nice formations. This isn't like mainland mineral caves. Lava tubes aren't as colorful. But it's a fascinating journey through a volcanic pipeline.

They have $12 self-guided tours with signs discussing various *-ologies* and now have much better flashlights than in the past. They've marked various formations with signs explaining what you're seeing.

By the way, if you ever wanted to see what utter blackness looks like, the kind where you can't tell whether your eyes are open or closed, have everyone turn off their lights. That's darkness like you've never seen.

TRY A NIGHT OR SCOOTER DIVE

Some people say SCUBA diving is no longer considered an adventure *in and of itself.* Too mainstream, too common. Hmm, fair enough. But these dives are another matter entirely. Night dives are inherently exciting and unpredictable, as your eye follows the powerful light, wondering what it will reveal. You don't see anything that's beyond your beam, and that adds to the fun. You may come across parrotfish wrapped in their natural transparent sleeping bags, moray eels out free swimming, lobsters (known here as bugs) trying to avoid being tomorrow night's special, needlefish strangely attracted to your light, Spanish dancers

A skylight interrupts the pitch-black darkness of Ka'eleku Cave.

shaking their maracas, perhaps even a manta ray. You never know what a night dive will bring. Maybe little, maybe the motherload, but a whole different crew works the reef's night shift. The same reef you may have seen yesterday suddenly seems so much more mysterious and thrilling in your night light.

See the SCUBA section for recommended dive companies. Most (though not all) do night dives. Examples are **Maui Dreams** (874–5332), which does 1-tank shore dives for $79. **Ed Robinson** (879–3584) has 2-tank boat night dives for $150. **Maui Dive Shop** (879–3388), does 2-tank night dives to Molokini, a South Maui spot or a night *shipwreck* dive in South Maui for $140.

Scooter Dives aren't your usual cerebral exploration. These dives are an unabashed thrill ride, like an underwater roller coaster. Forget finding exotic fish or colorful reefs. Here, the object is to cruise like you belong here. It wasn't until my first scooter dive that I realized that humans can be incredibly graceful in the water. Usually we look clumsy and awkward. But scooters allow you to maneuver like a sea lion. They are amazingly precise and easy to learn. After just a few minutes' practice, it's easy to skim the bottom, do loops and corkscrews, and soar like an underwater eagle. In short, they're a blast!

Keep in mind that having a scooter doesn't eliminate the laws of biology. You're still not supposed to rise faster than a foot a second. And the scooter makes depth changes so effortless and subtle, you'll often find yourself with some pretty ferocious mask squeeze if you're not careful. Here's where the breathing

Cruising in style.

This is one long and winding trail (Sliding Sands) that you don't have to go back up. At least, not this way.

tip mentioned on page 223 really pays off. Because you're almost always exhaling, it provides a safety cushion for the depth changes. But be cautious and aware of what you're doing. If you're doing a loop, don't do it too shallow where the relative differences in depth are more pronounced. Also, you don't burn much air, but should still ask for an 80 tank. And make sure your BC is nice and snug. Things tend to come loose more easily with the increased speed.

Prodiver Maui (875–4004) at the Fairmont Kea Lani uses scooters that allow up to an hour-long dive. They will also take you to 5 Caves/5 Graves, a cool spot. Maui Dreams (874–5332) also does scooter dives for $99. Island Scuba (667–4608) in South Maui at the Wailea Marriott and Beach Activities of Maui (662–8207) at the Sheraton also do this. 5-Star has several resort locations. They like to stop often and explore the reef by fin, which isn't as much fun as a nonstop ride. Tell them if you don't want

to stop. They also have a shore dive package that includes a day, night and a scooter dive for $249. Otherwise, expect to pay around $100.

HALEAKALA CRATER GRAND LOOP

One of most incredible hikes on the island. It takes you down into glorious Haleakala Crater, across the floor, then back up via another trail. The views are unspeakably good, and the colors are amazingly varied. All told, it's a 13-mile hike. Though you start at 9,800 feet and eventually drop to 6,600 feet, you'll only climb back up 1,400 feet to the 8,000 foot level. Granted, climbing 1,400 feet isn't a picnic, but it's much easier than recapturing the 3,200 feet of gravelly footing you lost coming down. See map on page 120.

Doing this hike necessitates leaving a vehicle at the Halemau'u Trailhead between the 14 and 15 mile marker and then starting at the Sliding Sands Trailhead past the 20 mile marker. You can either leave your car at Halemau'u and try to get a ride up, or rent an extra cheap-o car for the day. The latter is a sure thing, whereas getting a ride isn't.

Park at the Visitor Center and start at the Sliding Sands Trailhead around the corner. It's downhill virtually the entire way—and hard on the knees—then you'll pay the piper during the last 2½ miles. More on that later. On the way down, you may want to take the side trip to Ka Ku'u o ka 'O'o. The crater reveals its character only as you continue changing elevations and angles.

After the trail levels, descends, then levels out again, you'll take the spur trail (there's a horse hitch at the intersection) to the left, heading north. Looking at the map, you'll want to veer right, then left at the next intersections to visit Kawilinau, formerly the Bottomless Pit. (The map makes this simpler.) See page 123 for more on this pit. Turn left and about 100 yards past the pit is an area called Pele's Paint Pot. Minerals in the rock created this colorful rock canvas.

If you have a few extra calories you need to burn, you can take a side (un-maintained) trail up a ridge near here that overlooks the Dinosaur spine and the grandness of the crater itself. This is one of the most expansive views on the island and a real treat. Only go up as far as time permits; you *don't* want to be hiking out in the dark.

After the Silversword Loop, our old friend green will start to return as the vegetation increases while you get closer to the mountain and the Ko'olau Gap. Stop and rest at Holua Cabin if you wish, envying the lucky buggas who literally won the lottery for the right to stay there.

In another mile, it will be time to pay your dues. In terms of elevation, you've had it pretty easy for these last 10 miles.

Now it's time to sweat. Fortunately, the trail switchbacks are only moderately steep. One of the seemingly endless switchbacks wanders over to the other side of the mountain, giving you a magnificent view (clouds permitting) of the Ko'olau Gap. Make sure to stop many times on the way up to enjoy the incredible views.

A Few Basics

Bring *gobs* of water with you. You lose water at a ferocious clip at this altitude. Since the only real climbing is at the end, it's no big a deal to drag more water than you *think* you'll need, *suck 'em up* all day, and pour out the excess before starting the climb. Also, bring a hat and sunblock. You fry fast up here. Rain is possible, especially at the end as you're climbing back up. A light rain jacket is a good idea, especially in the winter. Dress warm for the top and cool for the bottom. You never know what kind of weather you'll encounter on this hike. I was up on Dinosaur Spine once GPSing the trail for our iPhone app and exploring past the point where the trail was obvious, looking (unsuccessfully, it turned out) for more trail. Thick clouds moved in so fast that, if I hadn't had my GPS breadcrumb trail to follow back, I would have been lost and stranded in the clouds.

HIKE THE LAVA FIELDS TO AN UNNAMED BEACH

How about a hike along a lava trail that leads to a black and white sand beach that is usually deserted and was unnamed until this publication? From the end of the road in south Maui, where most cars park at La Pérouse Bay, a lava trail (not the gated road mauka of the shoreline) begins your journey along a shoreline that is young and raw and where surf claws at the jagged lava. For the first half mile kiawe trees provide intermittent shade. Watch for wild goats that seem less skittish than other goat-filled areas we've hiked around the state. See map on page 133.

Once the trees are gone, the sun becomes unrelenting. Good thing you brought *lots* of water, because there's none along the way. You'll pass spur trails that lead to local fishing spots. After 2 miles you come to a light beacon. (Stay out of the calm-looking but dangerous tide-pools just north of the beacon.) A rough path along the shoreline goes down to an unexpectedly pretty point dominated by black and red lava, some green vegetation, cobalt blue ocean, bleached white coral litter and green pools. These are brackish anchialine ponds, caused by spring water seeping into lava depres-

sions. They may look inviting to cool off, but they are way too fragile to accommodate recreational swimming. The area is hot and harsh, beautiful and lonely. But your destination is still a mile away. Take a vague trail (hopefully marked by some white coral) to the right of the most vegetated pond *away* from the ocean till you come to a wide main lava trail where you'll turn right.

The trail (now called the Hoapili Trail or Kings Highway) cuts across Cape Hanamanioa. This 6-foot-wide path was made in the early 1800s and was probably used to transport cattle across the harsh lava. As you walk this part of the trail, keep this in mind: The ancient Hawaiians crossed trails worse than this *barefoot*. In fact, they often had to run through the sharp lava where there were no trails at all during battle. But for the rest of us tenderfoots, we recommend hiking boots to pro-

Keawanaku, a hidden oasis in a sea of harsh lava, is only available to those willing to hike to it.

tect the ankles. The footing on the Hoapili Trail is made of mostly fist-sized chunks of lava and is obnoxious.

An ancient phrase associated with this area is "the cloudless rain of Honuaula." Many a time we've hiked in this area and felt rain, though no cloud was even remotely nearby (due to the strong winds along the flank and the rain clouds up the mountain).

Just over 2 miles into the lava field trail you'll see lots of vegetation at the shoreline (700 feet away). A spur trail leading there starts at a small lava rock wall just to the right of the main trail. The main part of the spur trail leads to Keawanaku Beach. (Other vague trails leading off the spur trail are avoidable.) This area has several structures, including the remains of a Hawaiian heiau (religious site).

Normal trade winds build up along the southern flank of Haleakala and often howl along this part of the island. The beach itself is normally protected from these trade winds. We've hiked to this beach during unusually strong trade winds, when gusts exceeded 50 mph and the ocean was an ugly mess of whitecaps, only to find the bay at Keawanaku calm, windless and protected. (During less common Kona winds from the south, it would be a different story.) The snorkeling off to the left (east) of the bay is exceptional along the 10–20 foot lava wall, covered with coral and loaded with fish. The bay is usually (but not always) protected from much of the surf, and the water can be beautiful and clear. The natural protective wall extends farther than it looks from the shore, bending around to the left and extending farther. The right side has several caves that you can explore if there's no surge or surf. (Surge would bounce you around in there.)

This beach is a jewel set amid the unforgiving lava, mostly black sand with white and a touch of green sand. (The latter comes from a semiprecious gem called olivine.) There are some beach boulders near the shoreline, but a generous repository of sand offshore *usually* keeps the shoreline relatively sandy, except after severe storms, which can temporarily move the sand offshore, usually during the summer. The area (and a nearby point) was called Keawanaku, and some old-time Hawaiians used the name for the beach, but it is not listed in any of the old literature as having that name. (Perhaps because the flow is relatively recent and the beach so new, the Hawaiians never named it.) Nonetheless, we have deferred to the old-timers and called it Keawanaku Beach. Sit on the beach under a kiawe tree and watch the waves striking the columnar lava. Piles of rocks attest to those hardy souls who have tried camping out here. (If only they'd known *before* that at night, the beach becomes *alive* with cockroaches.)

It was 3 miles getting to Keawanaku but only 2 going back since you'll stay on the Kings Highway all the way.

SWIMMING WITH SHARKS

Have you ever visited a large aquarium and wished you could observe the fish and sharks from the *other* side of the glass? Here's your chance and the experience is ridiculously cool.

Three times a week the Maui Ocean Center in Ma'alaea allows two pairs of divers to spend around 40 minutes swimming with sharks, stingrays, puffer fish and all the other species in their three-quarter million gallon exhibit. And while the draw might be the 20 or so sharks in the tank, it's surprising that after a short amount of time many people start to forget that they're supposed to be afraid of sharks and find themselves oddly at home. Actually, we found it one of the most relaxing dives we've ever done, and during our dive the spotted eagle ray was the star. She loved to be touched and fed clams in their shells. We never realized how incredibly *loud* rays are when they crunch clam shells. In fact, you might not realize just how noisy the open ocean is until you've dived in this quiet tank. And with no current, surge or long swimming, you may be amazed at how little air you draw from your 50-cubic foot tank.

There's nothing about this dive we didn't like—except the price. It's almost **$200** per person and *doesn't* include SCUBA gear, which you'll have to rent elsewhere. (They say the price is steep because their insurance rates are so high.)

Don't think of this as a death-defying shark encounter. The sharks don't seem very interested in feeding on divers. Think of this as the best chance you'll ever have to spend quality bonding time with sea creatures. In the open ocean these animals avoid you. But in this tank, you're one of the gang. The adventure here is to discover just how wondrous these animals really are when you're given the chance to observe them close up for so long.

You need to be a certified SCUBA diver and since they take so few people, call the Maui Ocean Center (270–7075) well in advance.

It's hard to believe that swimming with sharks can be so relaxing. But on this dive, it is.

Yes, this table will do just fine, thank you.

By their very nature, restaurant reviews are the most subjective part of any guidebook. Nothing strains the credibility of a guidebook more. No matter what we say, if you eat at enough restaurants here, you will eventually have a dining experience directly in conflict with what this book leads you to believe. All it takes is one person to wreck what is usually a good meal. Many of us have had the experience when a friend referred us to a restaurant using reverent terms indicating that they were about to experience dining ecstasy. And, of course, when you go there, the food is awful and the waiter is a jerk. There are many variables involved in getting a good or bad meal. Is the chef new? Was the place sold last month? Was the waitress just released from prison for mauling a customer? We truly hope that our reviews match your experience. If they don't, *please* let us know. (It alerts us to both problems *and* jewels to check.)

This ISLAND DINING chapter was pretty overwhelming for us. A huge number of choices made it difficult to select which ones to include. (And hey, we can only *eat* so much!) Restaurants come and go, but if there's a place that you *really* loved (and don't forget the ones you *really* hated), please drop us a line at the address or e-mail on page 4.

Unlike some travel writers who announce themselves to restaurants (to cop a free meal, if the truth be told), we always review *anonymously* and only expose ourselves after a meal (not literally, of course) *by phone* if we need additional information. By their reviews, many guidebooks lead you to believe that every meal you eat in Hawai'i will be a feast, the best food in the free world. Frankly, that's not our style. Like anywhere else, there's ample opportunity to have lousy food served with a rotten ambiance by uncaring waiters. In the interest of space, we've left out *some* of the dives. We did, however, leave in enough of these turkeys just to demonstrate that we know we live in the real world. Restaurants that stand out from the others in some way are highlighted with our ONO symbol.

For each restaurant, we list the price *per person* you can expect to pay. It ranges from the least expensive entrées alone to the most expensive plus a beverage and usually appetizers. You can spend more if you try, but this is a good guideline. *The price excludes alcoholic beverages since this component of a meal can be so variable.* Obviously, everyone's ordering pattern is different, but we thought that it would be easier to compare various restaurants using dollar amounts than if we used different numbers of dollar signs or drawings of forks or whatever to differentiate prices between various restaurants. All restaurants take credit cards unless otherwise noted. When we mention that prices are reasonable, please take it in context. We mean reasonable *for Maui*. (We *know* you pay less back home.) Food in Hawai'i is expensive, even if it's grown here. (You probably pay less for our fruit on the mainland than *we* do here.)

When we give directions to a restaurant, *mauka side* of highway means "toward the mountain" (or away from the ocean). The shopping centers we mention are on the maps to that area.

And remember when making reservations that the area code is 808.

The definition of **local food** is tricky. Basically, local food combines Hawaiian, American, Japanese, Chinese, Filipino and several other types and is (not surprisingly) eaten mainly by locals.

Pacific Rim is sort of a fusion of American and various countries' cuisines around the Pacific, including Asian and Hawaiian. It's a fine (and subjective) line between American and Pacific Rim. We don't have a separate **Seafood** section because nearly every restaurant on Maui serves fish.

Lu'au, those giant outdoor Hawaiian parties, are described at the end.

When a restaurant requires **resort wear**, that means collared shirts for men (though nice shorts are *usually* OK) and dressy sportswear or dresses for women.

Some restaurants have the annoying and presumptuous habit of including the tip in the bill automatically. Be on the alert for it or you may double-tip. And what if you get horrible service and don't *want* to tip? Then you're left in the awkward position of making them remove it.

Dining at the resorts is expensive, but you probably aren't being gouged as much as you think because their costs are exorbitant. One resort GM we know confided that they had over $7 million in revenue for their food and beverage department one year, but only made $100,000 in profit. (And this was the first year they had ever made *any* profit on food.)

Below are descriptions of various island foods. Not all are Hawaiian, but this might be of assistance if you encounter unfamiliar dishes.

ISLAND FISH & SEAFOOD

Ahi–Tuna; raw in sashimi or poke, also seared, blackened, baked or grilled; good in fish sandwiches. Try painting ahi steaks with mayonnaise, which *completely* burns off when BBQ'd but seals in the moisture. You end up tasting only the moist ocean steak. Most plentiful April through September.

Lobster–Hawaiian spiny lobster is quite good; also called "bugs" by lobster hunters. Keahole Lobster is simply Maine lobster flown to the Big Island where it's revived in cold water.

Mahimahi–Deep ocean fish also known as a dolphinfish; served at a lu'au; very common in restaurants. Sometimes tastes fishy (especially if frozen), which can be offset in the preparation.

Marlin–Tasty when smoked, otherwise can be tough; the Pacific Blue Marlin is available almost year round.

Monchong–Excellent tasting deepwater fish, available year round. Usually served marinated and grilled.

Onaga–Also known as a ruby snapper; excellent eating in many preparations.

Ono–(Wahoo) *Awesome* eating fish and can be prepared many ways; most plentiful May through October. Ono is also the Hawaiian word for delicious.

Opah–(Moonfish) Excellent eating in many different preparations; generally available April through August.

'Opakapaka–(Crimson snapper) Great tasting fish generally cooked several ways. Common Oct.–Feb.

'Opihi–Limpets found on ocean rocks. Eaten raw mixed with salt. Texture is similar to clams or mussels.

Poke–Fresh raw fish or octopus (tako) mixed with seaweed (limu), sesame seed and other seasonings and oil.

Shutome–Swordfish; dense meat that can be cooked several ways. Most plentiful March through July.

LU'AU FOODS

Chicken lu'au–Chicken cooked in coconut milk and taro leaves.

Haupia–Coconut custard.

Kalua pig–Pig cooked in an underground oven called an imu (hot rocks go *inside* the beast), shredded and mixed with Hawaiian sea salt. Outstanding!

Laulau–Pork, beef or fish wrapped in taro and ti leaves and steamed. (You don't eat the ti leaf wrapping.)

Lomi salmon–Chilled salad consisting of raw salted salmon, tomatoes and two kinds of onions.

Poi–Steamed taro root pounded into a paste. It's a starch that will take on the taste of other foods mixed with it. Best eaten with kalua pig or fish. Visitors are encouraged to try it so they can badmouth it with authority.

OTHER ISLAND FOODS

Apple bananas–A smaller, denser, smoother texture than regular (Cavendish) bananas. Most people mistakenly eat them unripe. You need to wait until the skin turns predominantly brown.

Barbecue sticks–Teriyaki-marinated pork, chicken or beef pieces barbecued and served on bamboo sticks.

Bento–Japanese box lunch.

Breadfruit–Melon-sized starchy fruit; served baked, deep fried, steamed, or boiled. Definitely an acquired taste.

Crackseed–Chinese-style, spicy preserved fruits and seeds. Li Hing Mui is one of the most popular flavors.

Guava–Tart fruit whose inside is full of seeds, so it is rarely eaten raw. Usually prepared with lots of sugar, so it's used primarily for juice, jelly or jam.

Hawaiian supersweet corn–The finest corn you ever had, even raw. We'll lie, cheat, steal or maim to get it fresh.

Huli huli chicken–Hawaiian BBQ style.

Ka'u oranges–Grown on the Big Island. Usually, the uglier the orange, the better it tastes.

Kim chee–A Korean relish consisting of pickled cabbage, onions, radishes, garlic and chilies.

Kulolo–Steamed taro pudding.

Liliko'i–Passion fruit.

Loco moco–Rice, meat patty, egg and gravy. *Never* served as health food.

Lychee–A reddish, woody peel that is discarded for the sweet, white fruit inside. Be careful of the pit. Small seed (or chicken-tongue) lychees are so good, they should be illegal.

Macadamia nut–A large, round nut grown primarily on the Big Island.

Malasada–Portuguese doughnut that is dipped in sugar.

Manapua–Steamed or baked bun filled with meat.

Mango–Bright orange fruit with yellow pink skin. Distinct, tasty flavor.

Manju–Cookie filled with a sweet center.

Maui onions–Grown in Kula; sweet. Some people eat them like apples.

Musubi–Cold steamed rice, often with sliced Spam rolled in black seaweed.

Papaya–Melon-like, pear-shaped fruit with yellow skin best eaten chilled. Good at breakfast.

Pipi Kaula–Hawaiian-style beef jerky. Excellent when dipped in poi. (Even if you don't like poi, this combo works.)

Plate lunch–An island favorite as an inexpensive, filling lunch. Consists of "two-scoop rice," a scoop of macaroni salad and some type of meat, either beef, chicken or fish. Also called a Box Lunch. Great for take-out.

Portuguese sausage–Pork sausage, highly seasoned with red pepper.

Pupu–Appetizer, finger foods or snack.

Saimin–Thin Chinese noodles cooked in a Japanese-style chicken, pork or fish broth. Word is peculiar to Hawai'i. Local Japanese say the dish comes from China. Local Chinese say it comes from Japan.

Shave ice–A block of ice is "shaved" into a ball with flavored syrup poured over the top. Best served with ice cream on the bottom. Very delicious.

Smoothie–Usually papaya, mango, frozen passion fruit and frozen banana, but almost any fruit can be used to make this milkshake-like drink. Add milk for creaminess.

Taro chips–Sliced and deep-fried taro; resembles potato chips.

WEST MAUI AMERICAN

Beachwalk Market & Pantry
100 Nohea Kai Dr. • 667–1200

ONO Ka'anapali—Why would we give an ONO to a place that serves $11 burgers and Pizza Hut pizza? Because it's on Ka'anapali Beach, and you can take your food and plop down in the sand (or use their tables off the beach). Selection is pretty good with packaged salads, sandwiches and fruits, plus some grilled items. Pizza Hut never tasted so good until you've eaten it on the beach. At the pool next to the beachside path at the Marriott Ka'anapali. The Hyatt also has a similar set-up called **Umalu**, but it's not as conveniently located, and the Westin's version, **Sea Dogs**, is terrible. Beachwalk is $7–$12 for breakfast, $9–$17 for lunch and dinner.

Bubba Gump Shrimp Co.
889 Front St. • 661–3111

ONO Lahaina—Remember the movie *Forrest Gump,* when Bubba describes all the ways you can fix shrimp? Well, the owners of this small chain apparently didn't see it because most of the recipes mentioned in the movie aren't on the menu. But that's OK because this is a fairly easy place to like. The whole restaurant is based on the movie, and the dishes are named after its characters. Very friendly service (so friendly the waiter may come and sit at your table as he takes your order)—fun, loud and over the water. Waves actually splash under the window tables, if you're lucky enough to get one. The food is mostly fairly good (certainly not great) with lots of shrimp dishes (obviously!), fish, some steak, burgers and salads. The peel-and-eat shrimpers' net catch makes a good appetizer, and they have some very good fresh fish. Their Medal Margarita is smokin' good, and the portion is hefty. We only have two complaints: They won't take reservations (and long waits are common), and they obviously want to turn tables over fast. When we eat here, *we* set the pace by finding a nice way to tell them we're not in a hurry. Overall, a fun atmosphere and acceptable food make a good experience. We've certainly seen them drop the ball, but they're good about fixing things. Between Lahainaluna and Papalaua. **$13–$25** for lunch and dinner. If you've been to the Bubba Gump in Kona, note that this one is better.

Cheeseburger in Paradise
811 Front St. • 661–4855

Lahaina—A legendary place, it's fun to try at least once. Sharing a name with a song by Jimmy Buffet (who promptly sued them when he discovered the restaurant), the decor has plenty of eye candy to keep your eyes busy during your stay. Only *some* of the food is reasonably good. (Ironically, the cheeseburgers are their weakest offering, and the fries are an appalling $5 extra.) The Polynesian coconut shrimp are tasty but come with only six shrimp along with a large mound of fries. Their cocktails tend to be fruity and tasty. We've

gotten quite a few e-mails from readers about this place, and they're oddly split between those who love it and go back repeatedly and those who balk at the rather ordinary burgers and the busy atmosphere, and, as wishy-washy as it sounds, we agree with both views. (This location serves over $7 million worth of food per year.) Often packed, with lines as long as *1½ hours* (which is ridiculous), service and the overall experience, surprisingly, seem *better* when they are busy (they get into a rhythm) and diminish with the crowds. **$9–$13** for breakfast, **$10–$20** for lunch and dinner. Vegetarian burgers available. Right on the water on Front Street and Lahainaluna. No reservations. If you're wondering where the ONO is, well, we moved it to **Cool Cat**. *Certainly* not as good an atmosphere, but way better burgers. They also have a location at Shops at Wailea in South Maui called **Cheeseburger Island Style** (874–8990), but it lacks the energy of the Lahaina location. This Wailea location, however, is good for breakfast. Big portions and tasty food.

Coffee Store
5095 Napilihau St. • 669–4170

Napili—An acceptable, though not compelling, place to go for your morning coffee. Decent (though too-often old) baked goods and an agreeable coffee selection. Not the most compelling coffee joint. In Napili Plaza near 29 mile marker on Hwy 30. **$3–$6**.

Cool Cat Café
658 Front St. • 667–0908

ⓄⓃⓄ Lahaina—As a consumer, it doesn't seem like it should be that hard to serve a good burger, but so many places fail. Not here, and for that we are grateful. Fresh fixin's, toasted buns and tasty variations. Try their onion rings for a side. Your food takes awhile, but it's worth the wait, so chill out, Daddy-o. (Oh yeah, the atmosphere is a half-hearted attempt at a '50s beatnik theme.) They also have lots of sandwiches to choose from. Desserts include malts, shakes (made the old-fashioned way, thick and tasty), root beer floats and brownie sundaes. **$11–$19** for lunch and dinner. (More if you move to pricier items such as the steak or ribs.) On the top floor of the Wharf Cinema overlooking Banyan Tree Park. Bartending is their weak point—stick with beer.

Dollie's Pub & Café
4310 Lwr. Honoapiilani • 669–0266
Kahana—A bar with food. Average pizza and beer with sandwiches and some pasta. They're often too generous with the vast amount of pizza cheese; consider asking them to tone it down. Service is a bit scant. Wish we could say more, but the price isn't too bad. (Well, I guess their bottled beer selection is pretty good.) **$13–$20** for lunch and dinner. In Kahana Manor Shops just south of Hoohui Street. (See bottom of map on page 53.)

Fish Market Maui
3600 Lwr. Honoapiilani • 665–9895
Honokowai—After hearing good things we stopped in to give it a whirl. After a few trips we can say that it's important that you avoid the crab melt at all costs. Consider the ahi because…it's not the crab melt. **$9–$15** for lunch and dinner.

Foodland Deli
878 Front St. • 661–0975
Lahaina—OK, so it's merely a grocery store deli. But you can grab some fairly tasty sandwiches for relatively little money. **$4–$7** and you're on your way. In Old Lahaina Center off Front Street and Papalaua.

Gazebo
5315 Lwr. Honoapiilani • 669–5621
 Napili—Gazebo benefits a lot from its location. Eating near the shore with wicked ocean, Napili Bay and Moloka'i views for…*relatively* little money (for this area, at least) makes the food and service seem better. They've got a good selection of omelettes, and their signature mac nut pancakes are pretty good. Lunch is burgers, sandwiches and salads. Both are served simultaneously from 7:30 a.m. to 2 p.m., though breakfast items are better than lunch. Birds can be a problem. They only have 14 tables and fill up quick (they don't take reservations), so either arrive well before they open or you'll have to wait, perhaps a *long* time. **$9–$14** for breakfast, **$11–$15** for lunch. South of Kapalua. Park at Napili Shores toward the back and walk through the resort.

Hard Rock Café
900 Front St. • 667–7400
Lahaina—Similar to the Hard Rock Cafés on the mainland but with tasty views of the ocean and Lana'i. Rock 'n' roll memorabilia (especially guitars) line the walls as music fills the air and music videos provide the eye candy. (The music is sometimes too loud—outdoor tables are quieter but have less ambiance.) Burgers, salads, sandwiches, steak and some pastas and fajitas. Most portions are large. Desserts are large and delicious. Frankly, it's not the kind of place we like to go to for dinner, but we'll go there for pupus and a beer. **$15–$30** for lunch and dinner. In Lahaina Center on Front and Papalaua streets.

Honolua Store
502 Office Rd. • 665–9105
 Kapalua—Do you ever wonder where employees in an

ultra-expensive resort area eat? Well, for many, it's right here. They get an ONO because it's cheaper than most of your other options in Kapalua. Inexpensive food is as scarce in Kapalua as RV parks. Simple breakfasts. Lunch is burgers, fish and chips, pizzas and sandwiches. Some of the specials on the board can be compelling. And the food's not bad at all. Order at the counter (or coffee bar) and take it away. It's the only place in the area where two can easily eat for under $20, especially at breakfast. On Office Rd. near the Ritz. (Quite a contrast.) $6–$10 for breakfast, $8–$15 for lunch and dinner.

Hula Grill
2435 Kaʻanapali Pkwy. • 667–6636

ONO Kaʻanapali—We're always nervous giving Hula Grill an ONO. Food can be good. It can also be awful. They have good appetizers, but some of the staff seem unusually inept. Their desserts are outrageous, and they make some great fish. The ambiance is *very* nice—next to Kaʻanapali Beach with great water views and killer sunsets. Sandwiches, burgers and lots of salads for lunch; steak, seafood and pasta for dinner. In Whalers Village. $10–$15 for lunch, $25–$35 for dinner.

Kimo's
845 Front St. • 661–4811

ONO Lahaina—Dreamy location along the water's edge for lunch. Dinner is upstairs and slightly away from the water. (Some of the otherwise excellent dinner views are cut off by the roof-line.) Lunch items are hit or miss, but mostly pretty good. Good burgers (need better fries, though). Their Hula Pie for dessert is worth the accolades. At dinner you can eat downstairs (which at night is designated as the bar) where some cheaper items are available.

Otherwise, dinner is steak and seafood, usually with good results. Kimo's has a good atmosphere and usually good food. $11–$15 for lunch. $20–$40 for dinner (except the cheaper burgers). Good place for a sunset cocktail. Between Lahainaluna and Papalaua. Reservations recommended for dinner.

Lahaina Coolers
180 Dickenson St. • 661–7082
Lahaina—An acceptable place for a meal and a cocktail. (They have some nicely concocted tropical drinks.) Food's not bad. Burgers, sandwiches, fish tacos, pasta and salad for lunch. Mostly steak with some chicken and fish and pizza for dinner. None of the entrées has us fantasizing about coming back, and the ingredients taste a bit cheap. But we won't steer you away, either. $10–$15 for breakfast, $11–$18 for lunch, $15–$30 for dinner. On Dickenson near Wainee Street.

Lahaina Grill
127 Lahainaluna Rd. • 667–5117

ONO Lahaina—One of the nicest restaurants in West Maui. Food, service and setting are all rock solid. There's no view here, but the tasteful decor is complemented by outstanding food. This chef *really* knows flavors, such as the tequila shrimp and firecracker rice. Unbelievable flavor combinations. Duck, steak, lamb, fresh fish. We haven't had a bad meal here yet. Prices are *very* high, but if you're looking to splurge, you'll be pleased with the results. It's the kind of place that doesn't seem to change over the years. $30–$55 for dinner. Reservations recommended. Near Front Street.

Lahaina Mai Tai
839 Front St. • 661–5288

ONO Lahaina—A great location right on the water just north of Lahainaluna. At dinner they open up the rooftop, which offers coveted airy tables. The menu is an assortment of kalua pork sandwich, portobello sandwich (awesome), fish tacos, fish and chips, then add fresh fish, unusual seafood enchiladas, a little steak and more at dinner. Results are good, although portions are a tad small on some items. The appetizer menu is tempting but pricey. While it's true you're paying a premium for the waterfront location, the food and service justify it all. By the way, their mai tais match their boast—absolutely the best we've had on the island. You'll get misty-eyed when the glass is empty. **$17–$40** for lunch, **$30–$40** for dinner.

Leilani's on the Beach
2435 Ka'anapali Pkwy. • 661–4495

ONO Ka'anapali—Two totally different menus and two totally different experiences. Downstairs, the **Beachside Grill** menu is a bargain, considering the location and setting vs. the price. Stir fry chicken cashew or BBQ ribs are **$17** or less at the beachside setting. (Killer Hula Pie dessert.) You can order this menu at lunch or dinner. For the regular dinner menu upstairs, it's mostly steak, seafood and ribs for **$18–$28**. *Usually* good service and fairly good food, but with a *tasty* view, hence the ONO. At Whalers Village. Often busy, reservations recommended, though they *do* reserve some space for walk-ins.

Mama's Ribs 'n Rotisserie
5095 Napilihau St. • 665–6262

Napili—Ribs and rotisserie chicken are their thing, and it's mostly take-out. (Just a few outdoor tables.) Solidly average best describes it, except for tastier whole chicken (which, at $16, tastes curiously similar to Costco's $5 chickens). Plate combo meals with so-so sides of beans, slaw, etc. also available. Despite the name, you're *not* treated like family here (unless blank indifference is the usual atmosphere at home). In Napili Plaza off Hwy 30's 29 mile marker. **$7–$24** for lunch and dinner. Credit cards accepted over $25.

Maui Brewing Co.
4405 Honoapiilani Hwy. • 669–3474

Kahana—Here's the deal: In our last edition we said the beer can leave an unsavory aftertaste because…it left an unsavory aftertaste. A number of readers (not to mention the restaurant owner) took issue. (Some readers said, "You folks must be *Bud* drinkers.") We love good beer and have taken others here. Further research/reviewing and a consensus opinion has caused us to make the following conclusion: The beer *still* leaves an unsavory aftertaste. Sorry, that's how we call it. But maybe we're off our rocker, and you'll love the place. (The *Bud* comment hurt, though.) The food consists of pizzas, sandwiches, some pastas, fish and chips, and brats. (We almost mentioned that we didn't like the pizza either, but we didn't want to pile on.) **$13–$30** for lunch and dinner. In the Kahana Gateway Center.

Maui Swiss Café
640 Front St. • 661–6776

Lahaina—The only thing Swiss about this place is the name and the owner. It's basically an Internet café/sandwich shop (so we put them under American). And if you don't see anyone working there when you walk in, your server is most likely one of the people on the Internet. The sandwiches, such as roast beef or turkey, BLTs, tuna, and ham and cheese are pretty good. Breakfast is mostly bagels, donuts or a simple egg combo plate. **$7–$12** for lunch and early dinner. **$3–$7** for breakfast. Between Dickenson and Prison streets, across from Banyan Tree Park.

Melting Pot
325 Keawe St., #A202. • 661–6181

Lahaina—Part of a chain with over 150 locations, it's all about the fondue. You sit at a table with warmers and order various stuff to dip into your molten cheese, sauce or chocolate. Bread, steak, seafood (including lobster), veggies, strawberries…Dip to your heart's content. They also have salads and non-dipping entrées. Very nice atmosphere, and we like the food, but the prices scare us and there's no view. The menu structure makes it hard to predict—figure **$30–$60** per person for dinner. In the Lahaina Gateway Shopping Center, 2nd floor, next to Barnes & Noble.

Moose McGillycuddy's
844 Front St. • 667–7758
2511 S. Kihei Rd. • 891–8600

Lahaina—This is a hopping place at night. Dinner is mostly steak (cow, not moose) and some seafood. It's popular with singles looking for…well, what singles are *always* looking for. Entertainment and dancing at night. Lunch consists mostly of burgers. However, avoid having breakfast here unless you have *a lot* of time. Because if it takes 10 minutes for them to acknowledge your existence, 20 minutes to get a table and 25 minutes to get your food, you've donated almost an hour of your morning to the Moose before you even get a chance to eat. And for some reason, people are less willing to wait for breakfast than lunch or dinner. As for the food…we're talking biscuits and gravy even a starving moose wouldn't touch. **$7–$12** for breakfast, **$10–$20** for lunch, **$15–$35** for dinner. On Front Street. Also in Kihei.

Pineapple Grill
200 Kapalua Dr. • 669–9600

Kapalua—An unexpectedly good find at a golf course restaurant. The atmosphere is sort of upscale Hawaiian and the large selection of steak and seafood is coupled with a pretty vast and well-chosen wine selection. (Though their sommelier might not be as helpful as you'd like.) Torches outside make up for the lack of view at night. Items have an Asian twist, such as the excellent Asian braised short rib or the sake-soy grilled mahi mahi. Good porterhouse steak. Presentation is flawless, though service might be a tad lacking. **$12–$20** for lunch, **$30–$55** for dinner. Reservations recommended. At the Bay Golf Course.

Pioneer Inn Grill & Bar
658 Wharf St. • 661–3636

Lahaina—A good place to go for breakfast, especially if you're taking a boat trip from adjacent Lahaina Harbor, and they open at 7 a.m. Service is fast and efficient. The big kahuna pancakes are giant, plate-covering items that are pretty impossible to finish off. (And hard to syrup without making a mess.) Lunch and dinner (same menu) are steak, salads, seafood scampi, fish, burgers and sandwiches. At the Pioneer Inn. **$9–$18** for breakfast, **$14–$26** for lunch and dinner.

Plantation House
2000 Plantation Club Dr. • 669–6299

Kapalua—Tongue-wagging views all the way down the golf course to the ocean and Moloka'i, along with a rich, spacious feel, create an effective and relaxing ambiance. Breakfast has several types of benedict and a few other choices. The small lunch menu has some sandwiches and lots of great salads (including one that's $18!). Dinner is mostly steak and seafood with a little bit of duck and a little bit of lamb. Quality has slipped enough to cost them their ONO, and service is also down. They'll often seat you and forget you. (You know, begging for your first cup of coffee in the morning at an expensive restaurant is surprisingly enraging.) We've also noticed, or at least perceive, that repeat residents seem to get much better service than visitors. **$10–$20** for breakfast (served until 3 p.m.), **$15–$22** for lunch, **$25–$45** for dinner. Hard to find. Take Hwy 30 north, 1 mile past the Kapalua exit, turn right at the Plantation Golf Course, then left at the clubhouse. Reservations required for dinner; collared shirt and no flip-flops.

Ruth's Chris Steak House
900 Front St. • 661–8815

ⓞⓝⓞ Lahaina—Part of a chain, they are unabashed red meat pushers, and they do it very well. Steak and lobster with an emphasis on steak. Yes, it's expensive. Even an optional baked potato is $9. Is any potato worth $9? Probably not. But if you get one, it'll probably be the best darned potato you've ever had. (Lest you think this is just another overpriced Maui eatery, we called some Ruth's Chris restaurants on the mainland, and the prices were the same.) They cook the steaks at 1,800°, and the results are tender and juicy and served on a *500°* plate to *keep* it hot. If you want lobster, get only that. The surf and turf entrée has a really small tail. Their chocolate sin cake is as dense as lead and just as deadly. Wine list feels particularly overpriced. Across the street from the ocean on Front Street in Lahaina Center, and in South Maui in Wailea at the Shops of Wailea. Dinner is **$25–$50** or more, if you get the steak and lobster.

Son'z Maui at Swan Court
200 Nohea Kai Dr. • 667–4506

ⓞⓝⓞ Ka'anapali—They call it a fusion of European and Hawaiian cuisine, so what the heck, we put them under American. Although owned by the same folks who run Sarento's and Nick's in Wailea, the service is much more toned down. Instead of stellar, it's merely very good. Atmosphere and food are also great. You're overlooking a beautiful pond and waterfall with resident swans at the Hyatt. The steak and seafood are good, but believe it or not, their best item is a Kobe beef *meatloaf*. (Strange, but impossibly delicious. If Mama had made it like that, I'd have eaten it more often.) The wait staff has some autonomy, so ask them if you want to deviate from the menu. **$35–$60** for dinner. Reservations recommended.

Soup Nutz & Java Jazz
3350 Lwr. Honoapiilani • 667–0787

ⓞⓝⓞ Honokowai—The ambiance is really hard to describe. Call it assorted kookiness. Nearly all the artwork was created by the owner, who occasionally plays guitar during dinner. But the food is good. Small menus for all meals, but the taste works. Sandwiches, salads and burgers (which are marinated and unusual) for lunch. Steak, pasta, fish and lobster for dinner. Sounds like a bigger menu than it is. But Hawaiian lobster (when available) for $28 is a good deal. **$8–$12** for breakfast, **$10–$13** for lunch, **$20–$30** for dinner (with a cheaper pasta). In Honokowai Marketplace, south part of Lower Honoapiilani Road. They open at 6 a.m. and have lots of coffee drinks.

Sunrise Café
693 Front St. • 661–8558

Lahaina—A tiny hole in the wall with just a few table in front (more in back), a scruffy no-frills decor and inexpensive food. If you're looking for cheap grinds, this place will do. Breakfast and lunch served all day, nothing over $10. Limited typical breakfast choices, local-style sandwiches for lunch. Food's not real flavorful, but it's not real bad. (Well...the pancakes are real bad.) At Market and Front Streets. Cash only. **$7–$10**.

Whalers Village Food Court
2435 Ka'anapali Pkwy.

(ONO) Ka'anapali—We certainly didn't give them an ONO because of the food. Five stalls with average food court options. Our happiness stems from the fact that the court offers some of the few cheap meals in Ka'anapali, and food always tastes better when you've just walked in off the beach. Even McDonald's tastes good when there's sand stuck to your feet. In Whalers Village Shopping Center.

WEST MAUI CHINESE

China Boat
4474 Honoapiilani Rd. • 669–5089

(ONO) Kahana—The food quality is good enough to merit an ONO, and the service has improved since our last edition. Tell them to spice up your food, and they will *fully* comply. **$8–$15** for lunch, **$12–$25** for dinner. Full bar. Instead of Chinese music, you're more likely to hear Pavarotti. From Honoapiilani Hwy (30), turn onto the road at Kahana Gateway Shopping Center, then turn right on Lower Honoapiilani Road. Across from Kahana Reef. See map on page 53.

China Bowl
2580 Kekaa Dr. • 661–0660

Ka'anapali—Chinese food is surprisingly rare in West Maui. This place is one of the few, and it's run by the same family that runs China Boat. We could tell by the decidedly unChinese music (usually jazz) playing inside. Lunch is a good bet here with nicely priced specials and big portions. We like the orange chicken. Items are fresh but sometimes drowning in sauce. Staff is warm and inviting, which makes this an easy place to recommend if you're craving Chinese comfort food. **$8–$13** for lunch, **$9–$20** for dinner. In the Fairway Shops.

WEST MAUI FRENCH

Gerard's
174 Lahainaluna Rd. • 661–8939

Lahaina—People are going to be shocked and angry that we didn't give Gerard's an ONO. We admit, the food's good. But it's just too overpriced. This section has lots of expensive restaurants, many providing an atmosphere you can't get back home. Gerard's, on the other hand, doesn't have anything you probably can't find in a reasonably sized city on the mainland, and it's *very* expensive. Lamb, pork, beef, veal, fish and chicken. There is no view, and the atmosphere at the courtyard and lanai tables is accompanied by traffic noise. Service is attentive, but we're appalled by the prices. Even dessert. I mean, $9.50 for two scoops of ice cream and chocolate sauce or for a *tiny* crème brûlée is ridiculous. If you're overlooking a gorgeous beach, *maybe*. But here? Only your wallet pain threshold can decide. We feel it's about a third overpriced, but maybe we're just savages. **$35–$60** for dinner. At the Plantation Inn.

WEST MAUI ITALIAN

Lahaina Pizza Company
730 Front St. • 661–0700

(ONO) Lahaina—This is probably the best pizza in West Maui at this time. Good views overlooking the ou get a table on the ocean ago-style, deep-dish pizzas have super-thick crusts that are surprisingly light. They also have some pastas and sandwiches. Pizzas take a while, and when they come, your first comment to the waiter is, "I didn't order it with tomatoes." They know. All pizzas come with very light sauce and stewed tomatoes. (They don't usually tell you.) They'll serve it without the tomatoes and with more substantial sauce (which is better), if you request it. Nice selection of beers and some wines. Service is sometimes snippy. **$12–$25** for lunch and dinner. On Front Street.

Longhi's
888 Front St. • 667–2288

ONO Lahaina—Longhi's is an institution in this town. Opened in 1976, the upscale Italian/seafood menu has historically been excellent and can be a favorite with many locals and visitors. They do wonderful things with lobster, shrimp and fresh fish. One tip to save money is to inquire about the portion size. They are often generous enough to split. Parking is via the free valet. Extensive wine list. Dinner is expensive (and everything is à la carte) at **$25–$120** per person (the latter price if you order the massive 3-pound lobster), **$15–$25** for lunch, **$10–$20** for breakfast. On Front Street at Papalaua. Reservations recommended. They usually don't open up the (preferred) upstairs tables until 6 p.m. We could have put them in either the American or Italian category (they call it Mediterranean).

Penne Pasta Café
180 Dickenson St. • 661–6633

Lahaina—Ah, so you *can* eat in Lahaina without paying a fortune. The food quality/price ratio is fairly good here, but they've slipped a notch; enough that we grudgingly removed their ONO. Pasta, sandwiches and salads with a little flatbread pizza. (The latter has an ultra-thin crust and makes a good appetizer for two.) Portions are more than fair, and the flavors work. It's not great. But you're not paying for great. Order at the counter, and they'll bring it to you. On Dickenson near Wainee. **$9–$15** for lunch and dinner.

Pizza Paradiso
3500 Lwr. Honoapiilani • 667–2929

Honokowai—The hype is pretty big at Pizza Paradiso. Signs and ads proclaim they were voted "best pizza on Maui," and reviews from a guidebook saying theirs was the "best pizza I ever had." After repeatedly eating here, we can't help but wonder—were they eating in the same place? In fairness, the crust is fairly good and unusual: spongy but effective. But the pizza is lifeless and tasteless, as well as overpriced. It's on par with a really good frozen pizza, but does that impress you? Even if two people order by the slice, four slices and two sodas for $22 is *steep*. They have a pretty good Greek salad here. Desserts are either the delicious but expensive homemade tiramisu or something less remarkable. **$5–$15** for lunch and dinner. At Honokowai Marketplace (between 25 and 26 mile marker on Hwy 30).

WEST MAUI JAPANESE

Kobe Steak House
136 Dickenson St. • 667–5555

ONO Lahaina—This is a teppanyaki restaurant. That is where you and seven other people gather around a grill as a talented, knife-wielding chef prepares your food in front of you. This restaurant seems to encourage the chefs to exuberantly engage the guests.

The results can be fun. The food is mostly steak, seafood and veggies. Although the food isn't great, it's fairly good and, combined with the lively atmosphere and joking style of some of the chefs, it's a place we like to return to on occasion. Sushi bar also available. Prices are **$15–$45** for dinner. Big spread, we know. But it depends on what you want. Reservations required. Between Luakini and Wainee.

WEST MAUI LOCAL

Aloha Mixed Plate
1285 Front St. • 661-3322

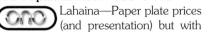 Lahaina—This is a particularly great place for lunch. Good and varied local style food, meaning it may be a bit fattier than mainland tastes, but most visitors seem to like it. Items like kalua pig sandwich, lomi lomi salmon and chow fun noodles. If these sound a little too alien, don't worry. There's something for pretty much everyone. Prices are reasonable for what you get, and portions are large for most (though not all) items. Service is usually friendly but understaffed. They have an outdoor deck and beachside tables. (No alcohol allowed at the beachside tables due to Maui's goofy liquor laws.) They sometimes let the hedge grow high enough to block the surf, and flies can be a problem at times. Reader e-mails are unusually passionate about this place. Two thirds love them; one third hates them. We side with the lovers. **$9–$15** for lunch and dinner. North of downtown Lahaina near the Mala Ramp.

Honokowai Okazuya Deli
3600 Lwr. Honoapiilani • 665-0512

Honokowai—How refreshing! A place in northern West Maui that serves good food but doesn't feel the need to soak you. Ambiance is…well, none, actually. Best to get it to go. The original owner was a former executive chef at Mama's Fish House and the Kea Lani, so they knew how to cook here. But instead of opening another highbrow (and high-cost) restaurant, they channeled their energies toward the lower-end market. The menu is diverse enough to eat here repeatedly. Teriyaki steak, spaghetti and sausage, fresh fish, kung pao chicken, steamed tofu—the menu is all over the place, and we weren't sure how to classify them. We like to take food over to nearby Honokowai Beach Park if it's not too windy. (There are a few stools inside, but it's hot.) This place doesn't change much from year to year, and we're glad. **$8–$15** for lunch and dinner. North of Ka'anapali on Lower Honoapiilani Road just north of Honokowai Beach in the AAAAA Rent-A-Space Mall. No credit cards. Closed Sundays.

No Ka Oi Deli
222 Papalaua St. • 667-2244

Lahaina—Huge sandwiches and salads served with a big smile at a great price. What more can you ask for? The prices are a welcome relief from the sticker shock that goes on just a block away on Front St. Sandwiches are basic but built on a grand scale, and the ingredients are fresh. Eat at the outdoor tables or take it away to a beach. On Wainee St. and Papalaua in Anchor Square. Only open 10 a.m. to 2 p.m. Open Monday through Friday. **$5–$8**. Cash only.

WEST MAUI MEXICAN

Cilantro
170 Papalaua Ave. • 667-5444

Lahaina—Paper plate prices (and presentation) but with

flavors. In addition to tasty standard Mexican items, they have rotisserie chicken, sandwiches and some seafood items. The food's excellent. Consider the taco al pastor—slow-cooked adobo pork with grilled pineapple salsa. And the nachos del sol are a great appetizer. Don't overlook the salsa bar to the right. Prices are not bad for the quality. Atmosphere is basic and simple. **$9–$15** for lunch and dinner. In the Old Lahaina Center. BYOB.

WEST MAUI PACIFIC RIM

Mala
1307 Front St. • 667–9394

Lahaina—Dine right next to the water in an uncrowded part of Lahaina. Boat-lovers will enjoy the close proximity to the moored boats offshore backed by Lana'i and the nearby Mala Pier. They seem to really know how to tie entreés with sauces and are adept at picking side items. The core menu includes wok-fried moi (a local fish), gourmet mac and cheese, and even a Kobe beef cheeseburger. Even the chips and salsa have a twist. That's not guacamole on the side, it's mashed edamame (boiled soy beans). Evening specials get more exotic and more expensive. **$10–$20** for lunch, **$15–$50** for dinner. On the north end of Front Street behind Lahaina Cannery Mall.

Pacific 'O
505 Front St. • 667–4341
I'O
505 Front St. • 661–8422

Lahaina—Lots of hype about this restaurant. Presided over by the acclaimed chef *James McDonald* (don't ask about the black sheep member of his chef family, *Ronald)*, Pacific 'O is considered the "in" place to eat. So does it live up to the hype? For the most part, yes. Great food, awesome beachside location and good service. That's what it's all about, right? Mostly fish with some steak sounds pretty typical. What's unusual is the way things are cooked. Lots of imaginative creations, often with an Asian twist. Coconut mac nut-crusted mahi mahi with a Thai peanut sauce, or pork chops and scallops in oyster garlic sauce with arugula pesto. Even the few beef selections are marked with their distinctive 'O touch. The outdoor tables can be a heavenly place to watch the sunset. Great wine and spirits list. For dessert, we like the lumpia. Though we're not big on dessert cocktails, consider heeding their suggestion to try a chocolate martini with it. Wow! Lunch brings simpler but well-chosen items including fancy salads. It's **$14–$18** for lunch, **$35–$45** or more for dinner. Reservations recommended. At the 505 Front Street Shopping Center.

Next door is their sister restaurant, **I'O**. Same executive chef, though the flavors lean more toward European. Not quite as good a location or ambiance as Pacific 'O, and it's not as popular, but the food's great here, too. **$30–$45**.

Roy's Kahana Bar & Grill
4405 Honoapiilani Hwy. • 669–6999

Kahana—Roy's is a local chain, and they serve wonderful and often smartly conceived food. The menu changes nightly and runs from fish to pastas to steak, all served with an Asian/island twist. Their fish is *always* a winner. We've never had a bad meal here, though it can get a little loud and rushed. Their baked chocolate soufflé is deadly but takes a while, so order it while you're still eating dinner. **$30–$45** for dinner. In Kahana Gateway on Hwy 30. Reservations recommended.

Sea House ✕
5900 Lwr. Honoapiilani • 669–1500

(ono) Napili—Spectacular location right next to the beach at Napili Bay. Try to reserve a window table. They thoughtfully leave sun screens down during the brightest part of the late afternoon, then raise them for sunsets, which are awesome from here. *Yeah, but what about the food?* Well, it's good, too. Dinner is fresh fish (which they *occasionally* overcook), lobster, filet mignon or chicken. Quality is usually very good and service is fair. Lunch is sandwiches (such as crab on Hawaiian sweetbread) and some sushi and salads. **$10–$15** for breakfast, **$12–$18** for lunch, **$25–$45** for dinner. On Lower Honoapiilani Road at Napili Kai Beach Resort. The south parking lot is small and fills up, so consider the northern lot. Both require you to grope your way through the resort to the restaurant.

Tropica at the Westin
2365 Ka'anapali Pkwy. • 667–2525

(ono) Ka'anapali—The restaurants at Whalers Village on Ka'anapali Beach tend to get crowded fast. This one, just down the beach path at the Westin Maui, fills up later. And with a great beachside location and good food, it's easy to recommend. It ain't cheap, but they're comparable to their neighbors. For dinner, it's mostly seafood and steak, and they really do the seafood well. (Absolutely *deadly* seafood bouillabaisse.) They also make a good lamb. Most of the tables are excellent (except for the back ones), and there's live music most nights. This is a great place for a sunset cocktail. The wine list, however, is small and embarrassing. The chocolate heaven dessert is a cake with a soft center and pomegranate syrup. **$30–$50** for dinner. Reservations recommended.

WEST MAUI THAI

Thai Chef
880 Front St. #A12 • 667–2814

(ono) Lahaina—A friendly, family-owned Thai restaurant that has eluded us in the past. Tucked away in the Old Lahaina Center near Front Street, the menu is similar to Maui Thai in Kihei, only cheaper. The service is warm and the curries warmer, just as we like them. Seating is limited, and large tables are often shared, making it a social occasion. Drinking is BYOB with no corkage fee. **$8–$20** for lunch and dinner. Dinner only on weekends. Closed Sun.

WEST MAUI TREATS

The Bakery
991-D Limahana Pl. • 667–9062

Lahaina—Hidden away in an industrial area, their baked goods are pretty good, reasonably priced (for Lahaina) and popular with locals. Strudel, croissants, bagels, macaroons, fresh bread, etc. Most items are quite tasty, though sometimes they seem old. They also have deli sandwiches, pizza and stuffed croissants. From Hwy 30 between Papalaua and Kenui, take Hinau mauka (toward the mountain) and turn right at the end. It'll be on the right side and isn't much to look at. **$2–$6**.

Cold Stone Creamery
900 Front St. • 667–2744

(ono) Lahaina—See review on page 274. Just as yummy ice cream. Near Papalaua. **$5–$7**.

Local Boys West
624 Front St. • 344–9779

(ono) Lahaina—Shave ice is so abundant on Maui, it's sometimes hard to call out which ones shine the most. This place has nailed it. Snow-like consistency, great flavors and huge sizes. And they chill the syrups to avoid the dreaded icing on the bottom. Every time we're near Lahaina we re-review them, just to be sure. **$4–$6.** Across from Banyan Tree Park.

WEST MAUI VIETNAMESE

Pho Saigon 808
658 Front St. #145C • 661–6628

ONO Lahaina—A quiet place in the Wharf Cinema Center. Their specialty is—drum roll, please—pho. This beef and noodle soup is the national dish of Vietnam. And this place has the absolute best on the island. Also try the summer rolls which are cool and light. **$9–$15** for lunch and dinner.

Saigon Seafood
888 Wainee St. • 661–9955

ONO Lahaina—A great place to grab a good, inexpensive meal. The place has a generic Asian am-biance including the noisy TV in the corner, so make sure you grab an outdoor seat. Ignore the food photos under the glass on the tables. (Trust us your food will look and taste much better.) The crispy noodles with beef is fantastic. Extensive menu; you really can't go wrong here. **$13–$20** for lunch and dinner.

SOUTH MAUI AMERICAN

Alexander's Fish, Chicken & Ribs
1913 S. Kihei Rd. • 874–0788

ONO Kihei—Fairly reasonable prices, but the portions are on the small side. For some items you get a choice of fried or broiled. Otherwise, everything else (including the mixed veggies) is fried. Their com-bos of two (fish, chicken, shrimp, ribs or veggies) are probably their best deal.

The food is tasty but a bit greasy. Service is green and confused. (Hey, everyone needs a first job.) Order at the counter, then wait for your num-ber and eat at the outside tables. On the mauka side of South Kihei Road across the street from the fake whale at Kalama Park. **$9–$15** for lunch and dinner.

Beach Bums Bar & Grill
300 Ma'alaea Rd. • 243–2286

Ma'alaea—Well, they ain't on a beach—they're across the street from Ma'alaea Harbor overlooking boats and the froth-ing ocean here. And service is real basic. (They'll watch you stir your coffee with a knife and never offer a spoon.) The food is adequate, nothing more, and flies can be a problem. **$7–$15** for breakfast (more if you order the *12-egg* omelette), **$11–$15** for lunch (burgers and sandwiches), **$11–$27** for dinner (add BBQ items and a fish entrée). In the Ma'alaea Harbor Village. Live music most nights.

Big Wave Café
1215 S. Kihei Rd. • 891–8688

Kihei—Better for dinner than breakfast and lunch. A well-chosen dinner menu of banana-crusted chicken with Thai curry (which is great) and crab-stuffed snapper as well as pasta, fresh fish and steak. Lunch is less impressive sandwiches, burgers and salads. Good root beer floats, though. **$10–$15** for breakfast and lunch, **$23–$30** for dinner. In Longs Center.

Blue Moon Café
362 Huku Lii Pl. #101 • 874–8600

Kihei—A large menu of sandwiches, sal-ads, some fish and local-style entrées, including kalua pork and teriyaki chicken. The potential is there, but they seem to cut too many corners. And even if they refer to "fresh fish" on the menu, ask anyway. It might be frozen. In the end the food is oddly unsatisfying. It can be fairly loud inside. At Kihei Gateway Plaza on Ohukai near Hwy 31. **$8–$15** for breakfast, **$9–$15** for lunch, **$13–$30** for dinner.

Buzz's Wharf
50 Hauoli St. • 244–5426

Ma'alaea—Great views of the boats coming in and out of Ma'alaea Harbor. Food is usually fairly good with definite exceptions. The prawns are great—they seem to use an excellent grade and prepare them in the shell with tasty results. Other items are hit or miss. Burgers, fish and teri chicken for lunch, steak and seafood for dinner. Overall, it's a good place to try after your boat trip, though it's pricey. At Ma'alaea Harbor off Hwy 30 south of the 6 mile marker. **$10–$25** for lunch, **$20–$40** for dinner.

Café O'Lei
2439 S. Kihei Rd. • 891–1368

Kihei—Enthusiastic readers first tipped us off to this place before we even knew they were there. Although not impressive on the outside, it's a reliably easy place to like with good food and reasonable prices at lunch, and pricier but dependable food at dinner. Lunch is a random selection of fish, chicken, pasta and sandwiches. Most items are great (though the tempura mahi mahi is too greasy). Love the mac nut-crusted chicken sandwich, and you gotta try the Manoa lettuce wraps for an appetizer or the onion soup. Dinner features mostly steak, seafood, some pastas and sushi. They'll serve you some lunch items at dinner if you ask. Our only complaint is the noise—it's often pretty loud inside. **$8–$14** for lunch, **$20–$35** for dinner with some pricier sushi. In the Rainbow Mall. Closed Mondays.

Carl's Jr.
15 Kapoli St. • 249–0787

Ma'alaea—Look, we don't normally review fast food restaurants, but we wanted to tell you that you can avoid this one without fear. A must-miss.

Dina's Sand Witch
145 N. Kihei Rd. • 879–3262

Kihei—Part sandwich shop, part pub popular with local regulars. A good selection of sandwiches, ¼-pound hot dogs, and saimin (which is good). Healthy portions and good ingredients. (Avoid the burrito, though.) The walls are literally wallpapered with money. Over the past 20+ years customers have given them currency, mostly ones, with their signatures and comments. Thousands of them cover the walls, creating a unique ambiance. **$9–$15** for lunch and dinner. Just north of Kihei town on the ocean side of Hwy 310 at the Sugar Beach Resort.

808 Deli
2511 S. Kihei Rd. • 879–1111

Kihei—Prices are super reasonable for the quality of the food. *Love* the chicken pesto panini, and the pasta salad really works. Between the hot and cold sandwiches, paninis and the salads, odds are they have something you'll want. They also have a few egg sandwiches and bagels at breakfast. Grab it and head to Kam II Beach since the seating is limited, and it gets hot. Across the street from Kam II Beach. **$5–$7** for breakfast, **$8–$11** for lunch.

Fat Daddy's
1913 South Kihei Rd. • 879–8711

Kihei—A BBQ joint with pulled pork, brisket, ribs, chili and brats. Atmosphere is a cross between a Maui lounge and a southern BBQ. The brisket is sliced in thickish slabs.

We much prefer the pulled pork which goes well with their excellent and savory BBQ beans. Service can be a bit scant but it is still a good place fill your BBQ craving. $10–$20 for lunch and dinner; more if you go for the full rack. In the Kihei Kalama Village.

Ferraro's at the Four Seasons
3900 Wailea Alanui Dr. • 874–8000
Wailea—Not a bad place to overpay if you're looking for a good view, and service and price are less of a consideration. While it's true that $12 gelato can *never* be justified, the dreamy location overlooking Wailea Beach at lunch is simply wonderful. Food is pretty good *$20* burgers (though a bit greasy), Thai beef rice noodle salad (avoid), sandwiches, sashimi, salads and panini. Dinner is upscale Italian-style steak, seafood and pasta. Tables are outdoors, and those closest to the beach are most recommended. $17–$28 at lunch, $40–$55 for dinner. Reservations required.

Hawaiian Moons
2411 S. Kihei Rd. • 875–4356
Kihei—A health food store with some so-so wraps, hot bar and smoothies. Pretty good baked goods. Across from Kama'ole Beach I. $5–$8.

Kihei Caffe
1945 S. Kihei Rd. • 879–2230
ONO Kihei—Breakfast is best (they open at 5 a.m.) with good omelettes, hearty breakfast burritos, huge loco mocos, biscuits and gravy (though they're a little salty), some truly kickin' raspberry twisties and the best turn-overs in South Maui, plus coffee drinks. Some of the outdoor tables are almost penned in, making it popular with parents trying to corral their keiki. (Kids seem to like the teddy bear or whale pancakes.) Lunch is mostly sandwiches, burgers and salads. Kihei Caffe makes mostly good food, and the breakfast selection is fantastic. The price certainly is reasonable. Long waits are not uncommon, and you order from the counter. Across from Kalama Park on the corner of Alahele. $7–$13 for breakfast and lunch. Cash only.

Life's a Beach
1913-E S. Kihei Rd. • 891–8010
Kihei—Burgers, Mexican items, some fried seafood and salads. A local watering hole. The atmosphere is funky, trashy and loud. They take cheap-tasting ingredients and combine them fairly well, and overall, it's priced about right. Good 3–7 p.m. happy hour with cheap mai tais and beer. $11–$18 for lunch and dinner. Across from Kalama Park.

Ma'alaea Waterfront
50 Hauoli St. • 244–9028
ONO Ma'alaea—The food here is superb and the flavor combinations well-conceived. They have many different kinds of fish prepared nine different ways: Cajun spice, broiled with Hawaiian salsa, baked in parchment paper, stuffed with Alaskan king crab, etc. Great cioppino (fish stew). Service is polished with a relaxed pacing. The parking situation is terrible with just a few spots. You'll probably have to park out on the street and walk to the place. But the food (when they don't overcook the fish) makes it worth it. The outdoor tables have beautiful views (and are often positioned to avoid the brunt of Ma'alaea's winds), but the indoor tables don't take much advantage of the location. Extraordinary wine list that changes constantly with over 150 wines. Reader e-mail hasn't been as enthusiastic as in the past, but our experiences have been consistently good here. Take Hwy 30 to Ma'alaea,

then turn on Hau'oli Road. **$30–$55** for dinner. Reservations strongly recommended in advance.

Outback Steakhouse
281 Piikea Ave. • 879–8400
Kihei—Steak, seafood and pasta. This is part of a national chain that is usually reliable. But at press time they were skimping on so many things in order to survive slow times that it made for some comical events. (The blueberry martini came with a *single* blueberry that was so small, we were literally unsure if it was fruit or simply an unwashed toothpick.) **$18–$35** for lunch and dinner. In the Pi'ilani Village Shopping Center at the corner of Hwy 31 and Piikea.

Peggy Sue's
1279 S. Kihei Rd. • 875–8944
ONO Kihei—Small but effective 1950s-style diner serving generous-sized burgers (a second 6-oz patty is $4 extra), ribs, salads, hot dogs and some sandwiches, such as steak, chicken and fish. Their burgers are fairly good. Portions are fairly generous for the price, and they have a good keiki (kid) selection with PB&J and grilled cheese sandwiches. Service can be slow because they are often busy, especially at lunch, and the servers seem overworked. (This has been going on for years.) Getting a table can be hard at peak eating times. Real milkshakes are tasty (love the peanut butter), and the jukebox (with quarter-fed players at each table) playing old 45s adds to the flavor. The food by itself wouldn't get them an ONO, but when added to the atmosphere, the place works. One problem: It can get *real* smoky inside if both doors are closed. Just remind them to open the back door; the kitchen hood will be able to keep up, and the smoke clears out fast. In Azeka Mauka

Shopping Center. **$11–$18** for lunch and dinner.

Pupu Lounge Seafood & Grill
1945 S. Kihei Rd. • 875–4111
ONO Kihei—This is a good place to go when you're looking for heavy appetizers (pupus) and a cocktail. They have regular entrées, too, that lean more toward seafood. But if you grab the pupu platter for two and maybe some coconut shrimp (which is pretty good) and top it off with a tropical drink, you'll probably leave with a smile. (Your waiter is also your bartender here. Usually a recipe for disaster, but they are often able to pull it off.) Their South Seas bamboo atmosphere helps keep things calming. Reader feedback is a bit less enthusiastic on this place, so maybe our experiences are off the mark. Across from Kalama Park. **$10–$15** for lunch, **$15–$30** for dinner.

South Shore Tiki Lounge
1913 S. Kihei Rd. • 874–6444
Kihei—Sandwiches, burgers and pizza. The atmosphere is a bit more effective than the food. The outdoor tables are a bamboo tiki decor with water sports videos playing against a backdrop of eclectic music. Pizza is average. Their best offering is their sausage sandwiches, if you take advantage of the condiments bar. All served on paper plates. Avoid the pathetic salads. Open till 2 a.m. **$8–$20** for lunch and dinner. In Kihei Kalama Village.

Sports Page
2411 S. Kihei Rd. • 879–0602
Kihei—A smokeless (indoor public smoking is banned on Hawai'i) sports bar with decent ½-pound burgers and sandwiches for $9 or $10 (but pitiful salads). Good pupu (appetizer) selection and (not surprisingly) a big

beer selection. **$9–$15** for lunch and dinner. Located in the Kama'ole Beach Center.

Stella Blues
1279 S. Kihei Rd. • 874–3779
Kihei—Readers have told us for years that Stella's is excellent, and it's a definite local favorite, but we found that it depends on when you eat. The food at breakfast looks and sounds good, but too often flavors are muted to the point of being bland. Take the delicious-sounding French toast as an example. How are they able to combine vanilla, cinnamon, eggs and bread to produce something so utterly tasteless? (Years of practice?) The smothered breakfast burrito is fairly good and hearty. Lunch is better with a large selection of sandwiches and several vegetarian items. All sandwiches (pretty good Reuben) come with chips, and it's an extra $1.50 for fries or pasta with feta and tomatoes (which is good). Dinner probably works best for us with food ranging from fresh fish to pasta to meatloaf, jambalaya and steak. Good veggie lasagna. **$8–$16** for breakfast, **$11–$17** for lunch, **$22–$35** for dinner. In Azeka Mauka Shopping Center.

Tommy Bahama's Tropical Café
3750 Wailea Alanui Dr. • 875–9983
Wailea—If you've ever shopped at a Tommy Bahama clothing store, this is the same concept. If you don't mind overpaying for good quality in an islandy, tropical, tasteful atmosphere, this is the place. How else can you describe tasty ribs that cost almost $40? Or $20 lunch appetizers or salads? Lunch is lots of expensive salads, sandwiches and tropical drinks that taste good but leave you miffed over the price. Desserts are scrumptious. Dinner adds steak, fish and chicken. It's **$16–$25** for lunch, **$35–$55** for dinner. In the Shops at Wailea.

Volcano Bar
3850 Wailea Alanui Dr. • 875–1234
Wailea—At the pool at the Grand Wailea, it's a good place to enjoy a cocktail and light food for a sunset in the winter. (Their 5 p.m. closing is too early most of the year.) Yeah, they have the usual resort $12.50 hot dogs (all beef, but at that price it should be ground up filet mignon) and $15 sandwiches, but you can grab something to drink and head to the beach for a relaxing late afternoon.

Waterfront Deli
3750 Wailea Alanui Dr. • 891–2039
Wailea—Finding cheap food in Wailea is about as easy as finding Mongolian food in El Paso. While it ain't exactly cheap, they got $7 sandwiches, $3 pizza slices and $6 Caesar salads. In the Shops at Wailea. **$6–$12** for lunch.

SOUTH MAUI GREEK

Pita Paradise
1913-M S. Kihei Rd. • 875–7679
(ONO) Kihei—We've never seen people who can do so much with pitas. Here they're freshly made and topped (not actually filled—it's more like a wrap) with all manner of ingredients. Chicken, veggies, fish, lamb and greens in clever combinations. Kebabs, too. Their ziziki bread makes a good appetizer. Dinner here can be interrupted by noise from the two nearby bars. Try the baklava ice cream cake for dessert. **$10–$15** for lunch and dinner. In Kihei Kalama Village.

SOUTH MAUI INDIAN

Monsoon India
760 S. Kihei Rd. • 875–6666
(ONO) Kihei—Fantastic Indian food with a great ocean proximity. They have an admirable selection of curries, tandori kababs, naan and vegetar-

ian dishes, and the results are dependably delicious. Try the monsoon kabab for an appetizer. And the lamb biriyani is awesome. Flavors are dazzling here. Service is deferential but sometimes a bit thin. **$16–$25** for lunch or dinner. BYOB. At the Menehune Shores, North Kihei.

SOUTH MAUI IRISH

Mulligan's on the Blue
100 Kaukahi St. • 874–1131

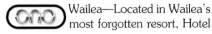 Wailea—Irish food such as Gaelic steak, fish and chips, corned beef and shepherd's pie (but no Irish stew) served in a campy, Irish pub atmosphere sometimes accompanied by Irish or other local live music most nights. Sunday is Celtic night. When he's in town, Willie K. knocks 'em dead on Wednesdays and some Thursdays. Most of the food items are pretty good. (Awesome apple pie.) Indoor and outdoor tables. Service can be slow. **$10–$15** for lunch, **$10–$25** for dinner. At the Wailea Blue Golf Course.

SOUTH MAUI ITALIAN

Antonio's
1215 S. Kihei Rd. • 875–8800

Kihei—Southern (Sicilian) style Italian, nice ambiance, spotlessly clean. The food is great for the money (except the calamari). Many varieties of pasta, some seafood, good lasagna, and the veal osso buco is delicious, as are the raviolis. The flavor combinations here are wonderful, and the service is super friendly. The home-made tiramisu is a good way to end it. Decent wine list. In Longs Center. **$12–$20** for dinner.

Capische?
555 Kaukahi St. • 879–2224

Wailea—Located in Wailea's most forgotten resort, Hotel Wailea Maui, they have a romantic atmosphere at the upstairs tables with elevated distant views of West Maui (and rooftops). Flavors are well-conceived with items such as cioppino (a seafood stew that is absolutely epic here), Italian herb-crusted opakapaka and shrimp Carbonara. Appetizers are very expensive and can really jack up the price of the meal. Wine list is excellent. Dessert features a 5-liquor tiramisu that's unusual and pretty boozy but a nice way to top off a meal. **$35–$60** for dinner.

Matteo's Pizzeria
100 Wailea Ike Dr. • 874–1234

Wailea—Their motto is "Italian Soul in the Heart of Wailea." Well, if Don Corleone ate here, he'd make them an offer they couldn't refuse. Like a cafeteria, you order and pay before you sit, and only the busboy visits your table unless you tell them you're ordering drinks. Salty and over-pureed artichoke dip, average pizza and a Bolognese sauce that took us back to junior high all point to a cheap experience. But the angel hair pasta is good. The open-air seating is nice and prices aren't high for Wailea, but you still don't get what you pay for. **$11–$20** for lunch and dinner. Across the street from the Shops of Wailea at the golf course.

Pizza Madness
1455 S. Kihei Rd. • 270–9888

Kihei—Pizza, hot and cold sandwiches, spaghetti and salads in a loud *rec hall meets sports bar* atmosphere. They are real proud of their pizza-making abilities, and it's justified. The sauce, crust and toppings play nicely together. Pizza is Maui's weak area, and this is probably the best pizza in Kihei. (The sandwiches are pretty good, too.) South of Lipoa St. **$10–$15** for lunch and dinner.

Shaka Pizza
1770 S. Kihei Rd. • 874–0331

Kihei—OK, here's the deal. It's **deliver** or eat in. The hot sandwiches are actually *better* when they're delivered. (Being wrapped up improves the bread.) Pizza, on the other hand, is actually best if ordered by the slice. (The reheating helps the crust.) We know these are weird observations, but that's how it is. Their regular pizza has extremely thin and fairly tasty crust, but unremarkable sauce and toppings. It's so thin that you'll be surprised at how much pizza surface area you can dispose of, so don't worry that their only size is the 18-inch. They also have thicker Sicilian-style pizza and gourmet pizzas, such as spinach, clam and garlic, and white pies that are fine, but not great. Cheese-steaks and other sandwiches also available, and overall, the sandwiches are their best asset, though pricey. A 14-inch sandwich is around $14! **$5–$20** for lunch and dinner. By-the-slice pizza reasonably priced. South of Welakahao Street.

SOUTH MAUI JAPANESE

Koiso Sushi Bar
2395 S. Kihei Rd. • 875–8258

ONO Kihei—This small-time operation gets no small claim: Best Sushi on Maui in our opinion. Make reservations to sit at one of the 12 seats at the sushi bar where the smiling owner/chef will serve up amazing traditional sushi. No fancy rolls or tricks here, just a small menu (written on the wall) and a single four-person table away from the bar. The fish is always melt-in-your-mouth fresh with clean flavors. Make sure to try the amazing creamy uni (sea urchin), and the hamachi sashimi competes with the best we've had anywhere. Don't take anyone here who is looking for a way to move wasabi to their mouth, it would be a waste of good fish. There are two sittings a night at 6 p.m. and around 8:30 p.m. Plan on spending **$30+** per person, which is worth every penny. In Dolphin Plaza. Closed Sunday.

Sansei Seafood & Sushi
1881 S. Kihei Rd. • 879–0004

ONO Kihei—Sushi, as well as non-Japanese food, such as seafood pasta, lobster, beef and duck served in a soothing atmosphere. Rolls are what they do best here. Consider starting with the fresh Hawaiian ahi carpaccio, and then dig in with the dragonfly roll (which is huge) and the panko-crusted seared ahi roll. Some items are pretty darned pricey, but you'll like the taste. **$25–$50** or more for dinner. Thur.–Sat. they have karaoke and half-priced sushi after 10 p.m. In Kihei Town Center near Foodland across from Kalama Park.

SOUTH MAUI KOREAN

Isana
515 S. Kihei Rd. • 874–5700

Kihei—A traditional Korean restaurant complete with tabletop grills. If you order off the BBQ menu, plates of raw, seasoned meat are served along with small portions of spicy vegetables. (Because of this, you'll want to get appetizers unless you're hankering for mostly protein.) They set up the grill, and you do the cooking. Don't be afraid to crank up the heat, or you'll be there a while. Portions are huge and may feed two, but they require two BBQ entrées to justify the grill. The sushi is pretty good, if a bit pricey. Try it for half price after 10 p.m. Wed.–Sat. Lunch and dinner are **$20–$35**. Between Ohukai and Kaonoulu.

SOUTH MAUI LOCAL

Da Kitchen Express
2439 S. Kihei Rd. #A107 • 875–7782

 Kihei—Good selection of local items, such as loco moco, teriyaki chicken, chicken katsu. The saimin could use a little work—you're better off with the won fat guy's chow fun. The teri chicken sandwich is good as is the kalua pork. The more adventurous will want to try the poke. If you're presently wanted by the CHOLESTEROL POLICE, don't come here—they may raid the place. But if you're looking for generous portions of not-so-healthy local food at cheap prices, you could do a lot worse than Da Kitchen. Don't order dessert; you won't have room for it. **$10–$15** for lunch and dinner. In Rainbow Mall under Café O'Lei.

Eskimo Candy Seafood Market & Café
2665 Wai Wai Pl. • 879–5686

 Kihei—Hard to find but worth the effort, this place is popular with local repeats. They have a great selection of inexpensive seafood items like fresh fish and chips (go for the ono over the marlin), shrimp tacos, seafood pasta, local items like the excellent wasabi poke, burgers and ribs. Keep looking around at the signs, and you'll see something you like. Nearly every item is very reasonably priced, and service seems genuinely friendly. Limited seating; consider taking out. From S. Kihei Road take Hale Kuai St. Across from Napa Auto. **$9–$18** for lunch and dinner. Lunch and dinner till 7 p.m. Closed Weekends.

SOUTH MAUI MEXICAN

Fred's Mexican Café
2511 S. Kihei Rd. • 891–8600

 Kihei—I know. With a name like *Fred's*, you're expecting *scrupulous* authenticity. Actually Fred was a regular at Moose McGillycuddy's on the mainland and suggested they name a chain after him. Whaddyano, they did. The food is good for the money, but we've noticed that you're best off sticking with red meat items. Decor is a mixture of crystal chandeliers and car hoods studded with light bulbs. Most items are under $13. Fajitas, tacos and massive burritos. (Too much lettuce, though.) The house margaritas aren't very good, but you'll like the top shelf. (Ask them not to load it up with too much ice.) The bar gets crazy on Taco Tuesdays, and the wait can be over 2 hours. All in all, it's a good value for the money. **$7–$12** for breakfast, **$11–$17** for lunch and dinner. Across from Kama'ole II Beach.

Jawz Fish Tacos
1279 S. Kihei Rd. • 874–8226

Kihei—Seems like they tried to be like Maui Tacos…and failed. The food's too pricey and not very good. Unlike Maui Taco, however, they *do* serve alcohol. **$8–$15** for lunch and dinner. In Azeka Mauka Shopping Center.

Maui Tacos
2411 S. Kihei Rd. • 879–5005
Kahului: Q. Ka'ahumanu Ctr. • 871–7726
Napili: 5095 Napilihau St. • 665–0222
Lahaina: 840 Wainee St. • 661–8883

 Kihei—This small, local chain is a good place to go for tacos and burritos. Nothing fancy, but it's not overly expensive. They have a good selection, and the portions are large. Their various locations are pretty different. The Kihei location (Kama'ole Beach Center) is their best, followed by Kahului (Queen Ka'ahumanu Center), then Napili (Napili Plaza), followed by the disappointing Lahaina location (Lahaina Square). Sometimes their food is warm instead of hot, and don't forget the condiments bar if you find you need more seasoning. $6–$11 for lunch and dinner. BYOB.

Taqueria Cruz
2395 S. Kihei Rd. • 875–2910

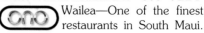 Kihei—Good food at extremely reasonable prices. Read the paper (not the posted) menu to get an idea how the meats are prepared. Then order at the counter and grab a table. Try the excellent blackened fish tacos or the hefty shredded beef burrito. Most items come with fresh cilantro inside. Tacos are only $2 on Tuesdays. Bottom line; it's the kind of place you'll return to for the quality and the value. BYOB. $6–$10 for lunch and dinner. Tucked at the back of the Dolphin Plaza across from Kamaʻole I Beach. Closed Sundays.

SOUTH MAUI PACIFIC RIM

Five Palms
2960 S. Kihei Rd. • 879–2607

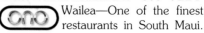 Kihei—They have one of the tastiest views of any restaurant. As soon as we walked in the first time, we knew we wanted to use their view for our dining section photo (page 249). It's right on the water and looks down Keawakapu Beach. They close off the upwind windows and open the downwind windows, allowing it to feel open-air without the normal afternoon winds messing things up. They also have outdoor tables. There are few bad tables in this place. The food is steak, seafood and lobster for dinner. In all the years we've been reviewing them, they *still* have the same problem far too often: food being served warm rather than hot. And spending $42 for fish and scant vegetables, then receiving it at nearly room temperature is hard to swallow. But the food is tasty. The crab cakes are an awesome appe-

tizer, and we also recommend the crab-crusted fish or the lamb. Sure, it's overpriced. But the setting is so good we're crossing our fingers and are trying to forgive some of their shortcomings like the *slooow* bar service. $10–$20 for breakfast (which features $11 pancakes), $14–$22 for lunch, $30–$55 for dinner. In the Mana Kai Resort.

Humuhumunukunukuapua'a
3850 Wailea Alanui Dr. • 875–1234

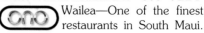 Wailea—Often called simply Humu (for reasons that should be obvious to anyone who sprains their tongue trying to pronounce it the other way), this is a truly memorable place to eat and *is sometimes* one of our favorites on the island. We say *sometimes* because they get good, then they lose their steam in a cycle almost as regular as sunspot activity. (They were in a good phase at press time, so we returned their ONO.) You're surrounded by and actually *over* a huge fishpond. Some of the fish and lobster swimming around are actually the main course (but don't tell them). Waterfalls and thatched roofs along with killer sunset views add to the exotic Polynesian feel. It's very expensive steak, lobster and seafood. The food tends to be very good, but sometimes service is too thin for these prices. If you catch them in the right phase (during their circular journey between awesome and complacent) you'll love the results. In the Grand Wailea Resort; allow an extra 10 minutes to walk through the fabulous grounds, or save time (and valet fees) by parking at the Wailea Beach access lot. $35–$60 for dinner.

Nick's Fishmarket
4100 Wailea Alanui Dr. • 879–7224

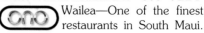 Wailea—One of the finest restaurants in South Maui.

Exceptional seafood in an elegant setting. The menu changes often, but we've never had a bad meal here. (We've had a few e-mails from readers who've had bad service, but we've yet to experience it.) Their Hawaiian lobster is fantastic. So is everything else. Consider the chocolate "decadense" for dessert. World-class wine list. The service is unbelievable. Order a drink and see if it takes more than a minute. (And their drinks are *well*-concocted.) It's the closest thing we've seen to saying, "Tea—Earl Grey—hot." (You either get that one or you don't.) It's like a contest to see how excellent they can make the service, but the tag team approach seems to confuse some diners. Though attentive, they *don't* come around every five minutes, when your mouth is full, asking, "How is everything?" They just keep a watchful eye on you. We've never seen a water glass go empty. So what's the catch? *Exactly what you think.* Nick's isn't cheap. But if you want steak and seafood and need a good pampering, Nick's is the place to go. **$35–$60** for dinner. In the Fairmont Kea Lani. Reservations recommended. Resort wear required.

Sarento's on the Beach
2980 S. Kihei Rd. • 875–7555

ONO Kihei—Over the years we get spurts of bad e-mails about Sarento's. It's not the food that bothers people; it's the service that irritates some. Personally, we like it, but the tag team approach confuses some diners. You get lots of attention from various staff, so if you want to be left alone, you might not like it here. The location is right on Keawakapu Beach, one of the most intimate beach locations on the island. Fresh fish, steak, osso bucco (veal shank) and pasta. It's hard to classify the style, sort of a Pacific Rim/Italian/local. **$35–$60** for dinner. But the food is usually awesome, and personally, we like the extra fawning they give customers here. The wine list is vast with a number of bottles costing more than $1,000. (Sorry, but that's just insane to spend $25 *per sip* of wine.) At the Maui Oceanfront Inn. Reservations recommended. Valet-only parking.

Spago
3900 Wailea Alanui Dr. • 879–2999

ONO Wailea—Lots of hype about this place, but guess what? They live up to it. This is Wolfgang Puck's Maui restaurant. (And old Wolfgang himself actually does cook here on occasion.) The dishes are simply unbelievable. The spicy ahi tuna poke in sesame-miso cones is unlike any appetizer we've ever had. Ginger mac nut-crusted mahi mahi is *ohhh* so good. Actually, everything we've had is good. Portions are pretty small, and you can drop a lot of money quick here. Appetizer prices are crazy high and can destroy your wallet. But their fantastic ocean view and world-class cooking make it a treat. Dinner is **$45–$70** and up. (The menu changes slightly each night and sometimes has items for $100.) In Four Seasons, Wailea. Reservations recommended.

SOUTH MAUI THAI

Maui Thai
2439 S. Kihei Rd. • 874–5605

ONO Kihei—Although ambiance is unremarkable, they unquestionably have some of the best curry in South Maui, especially the red. Lots of vegetarian items. If you ask for it hot, they won't save you from yourself. The pad Thai is not as recommended, however. And the Thai tea is way too sweet. No separate lunch menu, so it'll be pricey at lunch. **$13–$25** for lunch and dinner. In the Rainbow Mall.

Thailand Cuisine
1819 S. Kihei Rd. • 875–0839
Also in:
Kahului: 70 E. Ka'ahumanu • 873–0225

(ono) Kihei—Over 100 items to choose from (including *lots* of vegetarian items), and the entrées we've tried are quite good. The atmosphere is relaxing with Thai music filling the air. Their curries are flavorful, and they'll make them fatally hot if you desire. Prices are hard to predict. Dishes are $11 and up, and it depends on how many you order if you share. Figure **$12–$28** for lunch and dinner. In Kukui Mall. Their Kahului location isn't as nice an atmosphere, but the food's still good.

SOUTH MAUI TREATS

Cinnamon Roll Fair
2453 S. Kihei Rd. • 879–5177

Kihei—Perfectly named. Cinnamon rolls that are merely…fair. They are warm and gooey (they're good about putting more goo on top if you want) for about **$3**, but tend to be dry, as are the muffins. They also have cookies and coffee drinks, as well as deli sandwiches at lunch, for about **$8**. At Kama'ole Shopping Center, downstairs. Cash only; opens at 6 a.m.

Cold Stone Creamery
225 Piikea Ave. • 875–8811

(ono) Kihei—Part of a national chain. The name refers to the frozen slab of granite they use to mix whatever your little heart desires into their homemade ice cream—mixes like candy bars, berries, brownies, etc. Outrageous dipped waffle cup liners. Price is steep. You can easily spend **$6** for a medium cup, but that's for a *ton* of ice cream. In Pi'ilani Village Shopping Center off Hwy 31.

Hula Cookies & Ice Cream
300 Ma'alaea Rd. • 243–2271

(ono) Ma'alaea—Fresh-baked cookies are the specialty, and they do them pretty well. Occasionally, they're not fresh, despite the claims. But most of the time, they're wonderful. They also have so-so ice cream, which is magically transformed when it's in their killer homemade ice cream sandwich. **$2–$5**. In Ma'alaea Harbor Village.

SOUTH MAUI VIETNAMESE

Vietnamese Cuisine
1280 S. Kihei Rd. • 875–2088

(ono) Kihei—We really like the food here. Flavors will appeal to most people. The build-your-own Vietnamese burritos are great. And you *have* to try the rice-in-a-clay-pot. Stir it up first and look for the slightly burned parts. They're the best! Noodle dishes, rice dishes, stir fry dishes, plus steak. Lots of vegetarian items, too. Flavors may not be authentic, but most items are tasty. **$12–$22** for lunch and dinner. In the Azeka Makai Shopping Center.

CENTRAL MAUI AMERICAN

Anthony's
90 Hana Hwy. • 579–8340

(ono) Pa'ia—An excellent place for a morning stop on your way to Hana. (They open at 5:30 a.m. but don't serve breakfast until 6 a.m.) A nice coffee selection, and a *phenomenal* choice of teas coupled with baked goods (like the coffee cake) and eggs and such means there's something for almost everyone. And the price is pretty reasonable. They also have free Wi-Fi. Most meals are around $5. The place is a bit disheveled inside, but it's nice to have good food on Maui without getting hammered. **$3–$7** for breakfast and lunch.

(The latter is mostly sandwiches.) On mauka side of the road.

Café Mambo
30 Baldwin Ave. • 579–8021

ONO Pa'ia—A cool menu with unexpected items such as duck burgers and fajitas, kalua pig salad, organic tofu burger, spinach nut falafel, etc for lunch. The food is good, and they're friendly and quirky—exactly what you want in Pa'ia. Popular with locals, it can get loud inside. They play a movie on Thursdays during dinner. Hope you like onions, 'cause they sure do. $7–$10 for breakfast, $12–$20 for lunch, add a touch of fish and steak and a couple bucks at the top end for dinner.

Charley's
142 Hana Hwy. • 579–9453

Pa'ia—Good breakfast menu with the usual items, plus breakfast burritos, tacos and veggie entrées. Their highly touted eggs Benedict is pretty mediocre as are the biscuits and gravy, but the pancakes are great. Lunch is good burgers, sandwiches, some fish and stir fry. Dinner is mostly Italian. Pasta, pizza and ribs. Prices are high, but portions are generous. Overall, good food, lousy service, which cost them their ONO. It's known locally as an occasional hangout for celebrities who have homes on the north shore of Haleakala. So does Charley himself do the cooking? Hope not. Charley was a dog. He lives on as the restaurant's logo. $9–$14 for breakfast, $11–$18 for lunch, $12–$25 for dinner. By the way, ignore the carved wood sign that says, LAST FOOD STOP BEFORE HANA. Not even close to the truth.

Mama's Fish House
799 Poho Pl. • 579–8488

ONO East of Pa'ia—This is where we come when we want to treat ourselves, so let's cut to the chase: diabolically satisfying food and an extremely pleasing ambiance. They are right next to a beach and tide-pool; the only things between you and the sand are picturesque palm trees. If you opt for lunch or an early dinner, you may see windsurfers plying the waters off-shore. We like early dinners best. It's usually less crowded, and the views are as tasty as the food. Ask for a covered outdoor table—much preferred to the more crowded indoor tables. You know as soon as you walk up the gecko walkway and through the banyan tree root archway (which got that shape when it crushed a building) that this will be special. The mostly seafood recipes are very imaginative and change daily, so it doesn't make much sense to mention specific ones. But we've never had a bad meal here. They even give credit on the menu to the fishing boat or fisherman who caught each fish. Polish it off with a Polynesian Black Pearl dessert and a chocolate martini. The only negatives are that it is a poorly kept secret (so expect company and maybe a difficult time getting a reservation), service sometimes drops down to *merely good* (from the occasional stellar), and the price is *darned* expensive. (Avoid the $16 mai tais.) $40–$65 *or more* for dinner; you can shave $10 for lunch. But you won't mind paying top dollar if you get a top-quality experience, and you probably will. Northeast of Pa'ia on Hwy 36 just past the 8 mile marker. Reservations strongly recommended, and you may have to call later to *confirm* them.

Mana Foods
49 Baldwin Ave. • 579–8078

ONO Pa'ia—Why a grocery store for dining? Well, the unassuming building hides one of the best grocery stores in the state, and once you walk in the store seems to continuously expand in little nooks and corners. The reasonable prices (for Maui) also make us pause and wonder about the mark-up at Whole Foods. Head toward the back to find a food counter, which gets them their ONO. Huge salad bar, hot dinner entrées, sandwiches and wraps all ready to go. Especially tasty and filling are the breakfast burritos that come out every morning. Near the cashiers are some baked goods that surpass all expectations. **$5–$15**.

Maui Coffee Roasters
444 Hana Hwy. • 877-2877

(ONO) Kahului—An excellent place for coffee and a muffin in the morning. They also have breakfast sandwiches, eggs Benedict and various bagels. They get their baked goods elsewhere, and the results are flavorful. Lots of coffee flavors and coffee drinks, and it's the only place we can think of that sells coffee for around a buck. The coffees taste freshly roasted—not surprising since they do their own roasting next door. Lunch is tasty sandwiches and wraps at a good price. Near Dairy Road next to Marco's. **$2–$7**.

Pa'ia Fish Market
100 Hana Hwy. • 579-8030

(ONO) Pa'ia—One of the better eateries in town. They have a very nice selection of fish, chicken, tacos, salads, sashimi, pasta, fajitas and burgers. The tacos and the fish 'n chips are excellent, and they seem to use a very good grade of fish. Seating, but no table service—order and wait for them to call. Beer and wine available. An easy place to recommend and pretty popular, so you may have to wait during busy hours. **$10–$25** for lunch and dinner. On the corner of Baldwin Avenue.

CENTRAL MAUI CHINESE

Dragon Dragon
70 E. Ka'ahumanu Ave. • 893-1628

Kahului—A simple Chinese restaurant with great dishes and a passable dim sum menu. You should never judge a dish by its price, but the $10 shark's fin soup made us a bit curious as to the ingredients. (In China it can cost up to $175.) Everything else seems reasonable, and the stir-fried eggplant is great. Not many spicy dishes, but they're flexible. **$9–$30** for lunch and dinner. In the Maui Mall across from IHOP.

CENTRAL MAUI ITALIAN

Flatbread Company
89 Hana Hwy. • 579-8989

(ONO) Pa'ia—They have the best pizza on the island and it's an easy place to love. Flatbread pizzas (thin, slightly chewy crust) with outrageously delicious results. You may find yourself clearing more pizza surface area than you anticipate. ingredients are organic with chemical-free meats and produce from local suppliers. Their selection goes from fairly traditional to uniquely their own, and the attention to quality is obvious. How they make it healthy yet sinfully good is beyond us, but we wish all of the islands had one. Great drink menu (a simple gin and tonic becomes so refreshing with mint and cucumber), friendly service and a casual, inviting, loud and festive atmosphere at dinner. If you ain't happy here, you must be having a bad day. Sorry to sound slobbering, but we're big fans. You may have a wait. Only ding is it gets hot inside, and there's no a/c. **$10–$20** for lunch and dinner.

Marco's Grill & Deli
444 Hana Hwy. • 877-4446

Kahului—An Italian restaurant set in a loud '50s-style diner. Pizza, pasta, sandwiches and salads are all heavily overpriced ($10 for a grilled cheese and tomato sandwich). The food tends to be bland. Stick with the salads. Italian hospitals probably serve more flavorful chicken parmigiana than Marco's. If you insist on eating this food, avoid the amazingly uncomfortable booths. **$10–$20** for breakfast, **$12–$30** for lunch and dinner. On the corner of Dairy Road.

Pizza in Paradise
60 E. Wakea Ave. • 871–8188

Kahului—Formerly called Two Fat Guys from Boston Pizza (who sold it because their "crane business was too good"), the pizza isn't the best you'll find on Maui, but it's a really good value for the money. The price is reasonable, and the portions are generous (by-the-slice is a very good deal). Two people can get a couple of slices and a Coke for around $12, which is a pretty good price for Maui. The oven-baked subs are pretty good. **$4–$12** for lunch and dinner. Between Puunene (Hwy 311) and Hukilike Street. Closed Sundays.

CENTRAL MAUI JAPANESE

Wow Wee Maui Kava Bar & Grill
333 Dairy Rd. • 871–1414

Kahului—First of all, it's not really Japanese. It's really more American with burgers and sandwiches. But they *also* have a sushi bar which, frankly, is the only reason to stop here. (Their separate phone number is 871–5050.) The sushi's fresh and reasonably priced. Avoid the standard fare menu which reads better than it tastes. At the Dairy Road Center near Alamaha. **$6–$15** for lunch and dinner.

CENTRAL MAUI LOCAL

Ba-Le
270 Dairy Rd. • 877–2400

Kahului—You can forget classifying this place. They call themselves a French Sandwich and Bakery, but serve mostly Asian dishes, huge portions with flavorful results, very cheaply. Vietnamese plate lunches, French sandwiches, local entrées—and you'll probably spend about **$5**. In the Kau Kau Food Court in Maui Marketplace. **$4–$7** for lunch and dinner.

Cary & Eddie's Hideaway
500 N. Pu'unene Ave. • 873–6555

Kahului—Imagine a lu'au without all the song and dance. Their daily Hawaiian buffet includes most items you would find at a traditional lu'au: kalua pork and cabbage, lau lau, lomi lomi salmon and, of course, poi. The lunch buffet and Sunday brunch are **$13**, and the dinner buffet adds ribs, chicken and seafood for **$22**. The best seats are in the back with a view of Kahului Harbor and 'Iao Valley. In Hawai'i we say, "Don't eat till you're full; eat till you're tired." And this is a place to do it. Behind First Hawaiian Bank at Puunene and Kaahumanu.

Tasty Crust
1770 Mill St. • 244–0845

Wailuku—Let's start by saying the place is kind of dumpy. And it's not as...kempt as we'd like. But if you're looking for very cheap and very hearty, this is the place. Their pancakes are known island-wide. Light, soft and large with a good texture, they even serve peanut butter with them, if you want. (I know how it sounds, but you'd be surprised how well the flavor combination works.) Portions are large, but the plate is too small to negotiate the syrup transfer. (That's pancake tech-talk.) They also have limited omelettes, loco moco (a local-style cholesterol lover's best friend, described on page 251) and eggs. In the traditional local way, Spam or vienna sausage available with breakfast. (Locals *love* Spam.) Lunch is saimin, pork chops, spare ribs and burgers. This place is a long-time local restaurant that lasts because they serve large portions at a good price, and they do what they do well. *That's* why we gave them an ONO. $3–$6 for breakfast, $5–$9 for lunch and dinner (add some pricier steaks at night). No credit cards. From Hwy 32, go right on Central to the end. Turn right on Mill. Opens at 6 a.m. Our review hasn't changed in years, because neither has the place.

CENTRAL MAUI MEXICAN

Amigo's Authentic Mexican Food II
333 Dairy Rd. #110B • 872–9525
Kahului—A mixed bag, though an acceptable place to eat. There's a large and diverse menu of Mexican and non-Mexican items, probably something for everyone. It's a simple setting with a smattering of tables next to the Akaku Center parking lot. Portions are generous on some items like the burritos, standard on others such as the enchiladas. Good salsa and chips, the food's reasonably good—not great—and flies can be a problem. They have a fairly good selection of tequilas, including my favorite, Don Julio. But prices ain't cheap for what you get. $9–$18 for lunch and dinner.

Las Piñatas
395 Dairy Rd. • 877–8707
ONO Kahului—This is the place to go for a quick bite, but you still want to sit down and eat reasonable quality, relatively inexpensive Mexican

food in acceptable surroundings. (If that sounds less than glowing, it's because *you aren't paying* for a glow at this place.) Burritos are large and most are around $6–$8. The Kitchen Sink burrito is a massive collection of ingredients. Chicken enchiladas are pretty tasty. Mostly Mexican beers. Between Hana Hwy and Maui Marketplace next to Kinko's. And yes, they do have lots of piñatas hanging from the ceiling. $7–$12 for lunch and dinner.

Milagros
3 Baldwin Ave. • 579–8755
ONO Pa'ia—The food alone qualifies them for an ONO, but what really impressed us was their reverence for tequila and margaritas, which they call *Da Kine Ritas*. You won't find Jose Cuervo here. The bar is raised a bit higher than that, and you will be more involved in how your *rita* is concocted. Oh, yeah. And for the food, lunch is an accommodating menu of fresh fish, Mexican items and ½-pound burgers. At dinner try the fajitas; they're sweet, smoky and delicious. Their ahi taquitos and burritos are equally amazing. Most seating is outside, making it a perfect place for observing the diverse population of Pa'ia. At the stoplight on the Hwy. $8–$12 for breakfast, $12–$16 for lunch, $14–$25 for dinner.

CENTRAL MAUI THAI

Bangkok Cuisine
395 Dairy Rd. • 893–0026
ONO Kahului—The atmosphere is not much to speak of, but the food really shines. Outstanding flavors with some of the best green curry on the island. Good phad Thai, too. Summer rolls are just OK, but most items will please. Portions are ample and the ingredients fresh. Between Hana Hwy and Alamaha. $15–$30 for lunch and dinner.

Saeng's
2119 W. Vineyard St. • 244–1567

Wailuku—At Saeng's *hot* means *hot,* and they'll hurt you if you ask them nicely. Too often Thai restaurants try to save you from yourself if you tell them to turn up the heat. Not here. Most items are under $10. We like the pad Thai. The Pad Ped sauce is good with anything, such as their slipper lobster tails, which are small but tasty. You can't go wrong with the curries, either. Most of the seating is open air, so bring something warm for the cold nights. (You Green Bay residents can stop laughing now.) On Vineyard between High and Church streets. $6–$14 for lunch and dinner.

CENTRAL MAUI TREATS

Home Maid Bakery & Deli
395 Dairy Rd. • 877–8779

Kahului—Large selection of baked goods, some breads and tasty hot malasadas (a Portuguese donut). But that's not why you're here. You came because it's a good place to get sandwiches at the crack of dawn (well, at 5 a.m.) for your long trip to Hana. The menu is basic deli offerings, (with thicker cuts of meat than we usually like) and portions are ample. One sandwich might do for two people. The food will taste better the farther you get from civilization. $2–$5 for pastries, $8–$18 for lunch. Near Alamaha Road.

Maui Specialty Chocolates
180 E. Wakea Ave. • 871–1222

Kahului—Pretty good chocolates for the price made on the premises. You can get an assorted 8-ounce box for under $9. On Wakea at Hukilike Street.

Moana Bakery & Café
71 Baldwin Ave. • 579–9999

Pa'ia—Expensive but very good baked goods from their French pastry chef. The chocolate eclairs (when they have them) and the chocolate macs will send you into orbit. They also have a good lunch with wraps, sandwiches (made from their breads) and some salads. Dinner is pasta, fresh fish, lamb, steak and sashimi. $7–$13 for breakfast (they open at 8 a.m.), $9–$15 for lunch, $12–$33 for dinner. Live music some nights. Overall, pricey but good.

Stillwell's Bakery & Café
1740 Ka'ahumanu Ave. • 243–2243

Kahului—Lots of sandwiches made on their own bread, but be specific about what you want. There are no condiments on the tables. Also some salads and soups. Baked goods are what they do best. Try the crème brûlée or the chocolate eclairs. $5–$9 for entrées, $2–$4 for baked goods. If you're there around Christmas, check out their homemade gingerbread houses; everything's edible. On Hwy 32 on the right side just before you enter Wailuku.

CENTRAL MAUI VIETNAMESE

A Saigon Café
1792 Main St. • 243–9560

Wailuku—One of the more exciting restaurants on Maui, their food is outstanding. The menu is vast and contains an enviable array of foods, many from other Asian countries. Their garden delight summer rolls are a *great* way to start it off. The shrimp pops (ground shrimp pasted on a stick of sugar cane, steamed and grilled) are also a novel appetizer. Consider the garden party shrimp (with or without a shell), tofu with curry and lemongrass, or the mahi mahi and rice in a clay pot—just make sure you stir it as soon as it hits the table. Service is either a bit rushed or friendly and playful. $10–$20 for lunch and dinner. It's tricky to find. Coming down Hwy 32 into

Wailuku (as if you're going toward the Iao Needle), turn right onto Central, quick right onto Nani, right onto Kaniela, then it will be on your left side at Kaniela and Main. At press time there was no sign out front (and hadn't been for years) because the owner, who has the signs, is "waiting for the right day to put them up" and has been "too busy." This is a popular place with locals; reservations recommended.

UPCOUNTRY DINING

Rather than create separate categories with only one entry, we're lumping all Upcountry restaurants in one section and labeling them.

Casanova
1188 Makawao Ave. • 572–0220
Italian—Dinners are their weakest point here. Some portions (especially the pathetic salads) are too small, and the raviolis are simply horrible. Their thin 12-inch pizzas make good appetizers if you can split them with others. (It's their best offering.) Breakfast and lunch are served in their deli. Egg sandwiches, coffee drinks and baked goods for breakfast, tasty sliced pizza and sandwiches for lunch. **$5–$11** for breakfast, **$11–$20** for lunch, **$14–$38** for dinner. In Makawao. Live music Fridays and Saturdays.

Colleen's Pizza & Bakeshop
810 Haiku Rd. • 575–9211
American—Located in Ha'iku at the Haiku Marketplace, the baked goods are very tasty. Definitely worth the stop. A bit less sweet than most bakeries. Breakfasts are good. Their Hangover Cure breakfast is a great deal and lives up to its name. Lunches offer sandwiches, burgers and wraps. The pizza, however, is marginal. Served only at night, it has decent crust, but the toppings are bland and pizzas are too cheesy. (But

they sure do stay hot a long time. The Earth's core cools faster than their pizzas.) **$8–$18** for breakfast, **$10–$20** for lunch, **$13–$34** for dinner, which includes steak, pasta and salads.

Grandma's Coffee House
9232 Kula Hwy. • 878–2140
American—A good place to stop if you're coming 'round the mountain from Kaupo after the long Hana Hwy drive or if you're coming down from a Haleakala Sunrise. The coffee is a bit weak but they have a good breakfast selection and it's a popular local hangout, so expect lots of chit-chat in the mornings. Good coffee cake and other sweets. On Hwy 37 between the 16 and 17 mile marker south of Kula. Open 7 a.m. to 5 p.m. **$5–$10**.

Hali'imaile General Store
900 Hali'imaile Rd. • 572–2666
ⓞⓝⓞ Pacific Rim—The location for this somewhat upscale restaurant is unexpected. You have nowhere, then you have Hali'imaile, which is 3 miles south of nowhere. The food is very good, if overpriced given the location, especially at dinner. Small lunch menu of salads, shrimp tacos, ribs and kalua pork enchiladas. ($14 for enchiladas is pretty pricey, huh?) Lunch during the week only, and they tend to rush you. Dinner brings items such as mac nut-crusted fish, ribeye steak and coconut seafood curry. Desserts are rich enough to make you sweat. Their ads mention the names of all the celebrities who have eaten there. Well, maybe overpaying for dinner doesn't bother Michael Jordan or Dustin Hoffman, but it irritates mere mortals like us, and we grumble giving them an ONO, given their remoteness. But the food really is well-conceived. **$12–$20** for lunch, **$30–$45** for dinner. Between Baldwin Avenue and Haleakala Hwy. (37). See map on page 115.

Hana Hou Café
810 Haiku Rd. • 575–2661

ono Local—Probably the best food in Haiʻku. It's local style with plate lunches, fish and chips (which is delicious), dry mein (one of their cheapest items, and it's hearty and good), burgers and salads. At dinner it gets more expensive when they add steak and seafood and a luʻau plate with items like kalua pig, lau lau, etc. You'll eat at their semi-outdoor tables. Not a high-end atmosphere, but the food's worth stopping for. **$8–$12** for lunch, up to **$20** at dinner. At the corner of Haiku Road and Kokomo at the Haiku Marketplace. Open at noon for lunch Thursday–Sunday.

Komoda Store & Bakery
3674 Baldwin Ave. • 572–7261

ono Treats—Who would expect that in this uninspiring, little, semi-dumpy building would reside some of the best bakers on Maui? Their cream puffs are legendary around the island (more like éclairs). Stick donuts, malasadas (Portuguese donuts) chocolate croissants; we've liked almost everything we've tried here. (And we're quite diligent in reviewing them every time we're in the neighborhood.) They've been here since the island rose from the sea. (OK, OK, since 1916.) Service is either friendly or indifferent, and the price is very reasonable. As at most bakeries, before noon is best. In Makawao just off Makawao Avenue. **$2–$4**. Closed Sun. and Wed.

Kula Lodge
15200 Haleakala Hwy. • 878–1535

ono American/Pacific Rim—An easy place to like. The views and ambiance are glorious. With sweeping views down the mountain, you can see South Maui, West Maui mountains and Kahului. An all-glass wall takes full advantage of the views. During spring and summer, some outdoor tables near an incredible stone and brick oven are available. They also use that oven for pizzas. The food is usually excellent. Steak and seafood. Prices are high, even for lunch, but it's a treat worth splurging for, at least once, for the view. Early dinners are best, and you can get some unbelievable sunsets from up here. Desserts can be rich and decadent but sometimes miss the mark. Breakfasts are expensive, but the food's good, and the view with the sun behind you is unbeatable. **$12–$20** for breakfast, **$15–$25** for lunch, **$28–$40** for dinner. On Upper Highway (377) before 378 in Kula.

Polli's Mexican Restaurant
1202 Makawao Ave. • 572–7808

Mexican—They've improved a lot since our last edition, but the experience is filled with *althoughs*. Tostadas are flavorful, *although* they're much more generous with the greens than the pricier meats. Burritos are large and served enchilada style, *although* the temperature might not be as warm as it should. Prices aren't bad, *although* appetizers are pricey and chips are extra. Service is friendly and the ambiance is nice, *although*…no, that's it. BBQ and burgers also available. Check for specials, which can be a good deal. **$11–$17** for lunch, **$12–$22** for dinner. Located on Makawao Avenue in Makawao. Their motto is, "Come in and eat, or we'll both starve."

Serpico's
7 Aewa Pl. • 572–8498

ono Italian—A likeable menu of thin crust pizza, several parmigianas (including shrimp), pastas such as baked and raviolis, hot hoagies and salads. It ain't fancy and you certainly won't drive all the way to Pukalani to eat here, but it's solid and comforting food after a hard day exploring Haleakala, and portions seem generous. Polish it off with their brownie sundae. On Old Haleakala Hwy and Aewa Place in Pukalani. **$6–$20** for lunch and dinner. (See map on page 115.)

Smokin' Island Tacos
810 Haiku Rd.
Mexican—A stand in the Haiku Marketplace in Ha'iku that serves reasonably good chicken, pork, fish and veggie tacos with a gruff *can't-you-read-the-sign* attitude. The tortillas are undersized, so eating the tacos can be difficult. Those expecting spotless conditions need not apply. But in the end, the $4 tacos are tasty enough to satisfy.

Stopwatch Bar & Grill
1127 Makawao Ave. • 572–1380
American—In a town that prides itself on its cowboy heritage, it's surprisingly hard to get a decent burger in Makawao. The burgers are pretty decent (though they may cook them more than the medium-well they claim—consider telling them medium or medium-rare). They also serve fish and chips, fresh fish, Thai stir fry, steak, and sandwiches. Not much healthy stuff in this noisy sports bar; head down the road for that. **$9–$20** for lunch and dinner. Good views. Our biggest complaint applies to all Makawao restaurants. After prolonged rains, they are sometimes invaded by irritating gnats, which can make things miserable. In Makawao, southwest of Baldwin Avenue.

ISLAND NIGHTLIFE

The sun has set and the scenery faded, but you don't want the day to end. If you're a night owl, you'll find that Maui probably has enough to keep you happy, but don't expect Las Vegas. This is still a relatively quiet island, especially in South Maui.

Nightlife is something that's ever-changing. Many restaurants are constantly bringing in new musicians and trying new things. We hate to pass the buck, but by definition, nightlife is something that changes all the time. Different establishments do different things, sometimes every week. No one covers this week's action as well as an insert in Thursday's *Maui News* newspaper called *Maui Scene*. Grab a copy to see what's shakin' this week. It includes special events, concerts, movies, stage plays, resort entertainment, galleries, and it has coupons.

For **movies**, the best theaters are in Kahului. (West and South Maui's theaters are small and unimpressive.) Call 249–2222 for showings.

West Maui Nightlife
Lahaina is the center of West Maui nightlife. One of the most effective ways to feel out the nightlife in Lahaina is to walk along Front St. and see what strikes your fancy. One popular spot to be is **Moose McGillycuddy's** (667–7758) at 844 Front Street, which is usually a pretty happenin' place with music every night. Especially popular with the 21- to 25-year-old crowd.

In **Ka'anapali**, watching the cliff diver mentioned on page 50 is a good way to start off an evening. Several of the beachside path restaurants there often have live music. Most of the resorts also have goings-on.

South Maui Nightlife
Nightlife in South Maui has improved the last few years. The hub is the **Kihei Kalama Village**, locally known as **The Triangle**. Bars like **Life's a Beach**, **South Shore Tiki Lounge** and **Lulu's** are hopping most nights of the week. **Kahale** (875–7711) is a watering hole in the Triangle with reliably bad live music. **Mulligan's on the Blue** (874–

1131) at the Wailea Old Blue Golf Course, mauka of the Fairmont Kea Lani Resort, has live music every night and often sports one of the most festive atmospheres you'll find, especially when the Celtic band is playing on Sunday nights. **Willie K**, a master guitar player and vocalist, kills the place on most Wednesdays and some Thursdays. **Fred's/Moose McGillycuddy's** (891–8600) at 2511 S. Kihei Rd. is a lively place for the younger crowd. Their *Taco Tuesday* has cheap tacos and boozy margaritas.

Nightlife Elsewhere

In **Hana**, find a bright light and watch the geckos eat night bugs—you crazy party animal, you. Actually, the **Travaasa Hana** (248–8211) often has some pretty good local musicians at their bar.

Upcountry isn't a nightlife mecca either. Might want to wander around Makawao and see what's shakin'. **Casanova** (572–0220) has a dance floor and lively music on weekends and Wednesdays. **Willie K** plays here a few Tuesdays each month. Sometimes **Stopwatch** (572–1380) has live performers on Fridays with karaoke on Saturdays.

In **Pa'ia**, **Charley's** (579–8085) has music Thursdays through Saturday with occasional drop-ins from local celebs like Willie Nelson.

In **Kahului**, the **Maui Arts & Cultural Center** is on Kahului Beach Road. Call 242–7469 to see what's happening there. Their Castle Theatre is a great place for a movie or play. The two rows of balconies provide excellent vantages.

LU'AU

We've all seen them in movies. People sit at a table with a mai tai in one hand and a plate of kalua pig in another. There's always a show where hula dancers bend and sway to the beat of the music, and sometimes a fire-knife dancer twirls a torch lit at both ends. To be honest, that's not far from the truth. A lu'au can be a blast, and, if your time allows, are highly recommended. The pig is baked in the ground all day, creating succulent results when prepared right. Shows are usually exciting and fast-paced. Maui's lu'au have all you can eat and drink (including alcohol) for a set fee. If the mai tais they are serving don't satisfy you, they have an open bar to fill your needs. Remember that piece of info when you pick up your first complimentary (and sometimes watery) mai tai. The bartender will season it for you or serve you whatever you want. Since lu'au are usually held outdoors at night, you might want to consider spraying mosquito repellent on your legs before the show or wear slacks.

A lu'au will usually cost you **$86–$110**, and the better ones are at the higher end. Book them in advance. If you want to know what lu'au foods are like, see page 251.

Different resorts hold their lu'au on different nights. These change with the whims of the managers, so verify the days listed here before making plans. Here's how they stack up in order of preference.

One thing you need to know is that many of the lu'au on the island are all put on by the same production company, **Tihati**. This means their shows are all similar so they can interchange personnel, right down to the same MC jokes. The shows are less personal and more of a commodity.

West Maui Lu'au

West Maui's **Old Lahaina Lu'au** (667–1998) is your best bet. We've reviewed virtually all the neighbor island lu'au, and we can say that Old Lahaina has the most professional crew we've yet encountered. Competent, friendly and always up, they

eel very welcome. The organi-
quality top to bottom. The grounds, next to but not *on* the shore, have an assortment of thatched hale. Free drinks, served almost all night, come from their accommodating bar. The food is above average with some items that are hard to find elsewhere.

The show strives for a more authentic Hawaiian feel than the others, achieving good results most of the time. No lounge lizard MC singing *Tiny Bubbles* or *Hukilau,* no shiny foil shirts. Other things missing from the more typical shows, however, include fire-knife dancers (because that's Samoan, not Hawaiian) and the Maoris wandering through the audience threatening you. Also missing is the part where they haul people from your table up onstage to embarrass them. (Which, truth be told, can be a hoot to watch when done right.) All of these are omitted since they are considered unauthentic. We *really* miss the fire dancers and Maoris (they can be lots of fun to watch), but that's the price you pay for authenticity. Perhaps the stage could be a bit higher so all 500 visitors could see better, but this is minor quibbling. They fill up most of the time, so book well in advance if you can. In Lahaina on Front Street across from Lahaina Cannery. $98.

Next in our preference for a West Maui lu'au would be the **Sheraton Maui** (877–4852). It's right next to Ka'anapali Beach with Black Rock for a backdrop. It's a **Tihati** show with great food. We like how they grill their steaks on the lawn rather than pile up precooked meat. Seating is spacious and the servers attentive. There's an open bar throughout the night, but avoid the mai tais. You could water your lawn with them and never give the worms a buzz. $99 on Mondays and Wednesdays.

The **Hyatt Lu'au** (667–4420) in Ka'anapali. It's a Tihati production but one of their bigger venues with a bigger, less cramped stage. (But the same Tihati show.) The food's OK, nothing special. It's located next to the beach, but you can't see the ocean from your table. Actually, our biggest complaint is that they make you stand in line for up to half an hour in the hot sun before bringing you in. As with most lu'au, you might want to pass on the watered-down mai tais and consider the free open bar (though it's poorly stocked with exceptionally cheap well drinks). Nightly, it's $105 or $130 for reserved seating.

Westin's Wailele Lu'au (661–2992) comes next for us. They've got some positive things going on: You get table service instead of lining up for a buffet. (Don't hesitate to ask for more if your table runs out of something you like.) And the food is good. The lit palm trees behind the stage provide an alluring backdrop long after the sun goes down. They have the best open bar. And they have a great fire knife finale. On the negative side, there is nothing for you to do other than sit at your table, you'll have to pay an extra $15–$20 to park at Whaler's Village, and the 2-foot-tall stage is so low that you may end up seeing nothing but the back of other customers' heads instead of the show unless you pay the extra $20 for premium seating. $105.

Our last choice in West Maui (heck, in all Hawai'i, for that matter) is the **Royal Lahaina Resort** (661–9119). The show has some good dancers and a good MC. That's about the only thing positive we can think of. You're packed into a table-filled gravel pit like sardines. And the food is simply bad. (*Promise* us you won't eat the mac salad.) When the chicken nuggets are among the best things you can eat, you *know* you've arrived at a really bad lu'au. $98.

It's not your typical lu'au, so we put it at the end, but it's the classiest of the bunch. **Feast at Lele** (667–5353). No pig ceremony, no waiting in lines. Each party has a private table. This is an aptly named feast with an absolutely killer location: right next to a beach in Lahaina with slightly tiered tables, so everyone gets a view. The food is *incredible* with dishes from Hawai'i, New Zealand, Tahiti and Samoa. The variety is fantastic. (Anyone who can serve us squash and have us begging for more gets our respect.) The service has seemed stretched a bit thin lately, and you may find yourself begging for another mai tai (which are exceptionally sneaky—you don't taste the rum...but it's there). The accompanying hula show is adequate— not their strongest point—but the backdrop of the show against the setting sky is beautiful. So what's the catch? The price. It's a wallet-choking $115, and you may have to book well in advance during busy times. If you can stomach the cost, it's highly recommended. They seat 150 max.

South Maui Lu'au

In South Maui it's between the Marriott and the Grand Wailea. We prefer the Marriott (**Te Au Moana** at 873–8001). The show is better with some audience participation, the mai tais might *taste* watered down but...they weren't. The food was the better of the two and the pig you saw come out of the ground is the pig you eat. $98.

As for the Grand Wailea lu'au (called **Honua'ula** at 875–7710), the location is wonderful, like the Marriott's, but other areas are lacking. They ask you to be there early (first come first serve) but you'll have to wait around before going in. The show is reasonably good, but it's not as chummy with the audience—good fire knife dancer, though. The food is average, but we noticed during the imu ceremony that the pig was already in the serving trays. When we asked, they confided that the pig they take out of the ground *isn't* for you. *Your* pig is from *yesterday's* ceremony. And what if there *was no* ceremony yesterday? Oh, then they simply serve oven-baked pork. Sort of kills the whole reason for an imu ceremony, huh? $100. Overall not a bad lu'au, but not as good as the Marriott's.

DINNER SHOWS

Lahaina has several night-time attractions that you should consider. Two are traditional dinner shows. One is sort of a dinner show...without the dinner.

The best is **Warren & Annabelle's** (667–6244), probably the most amazing show in all Hawai'i. Put simply, our jaws never stop dropping the whole time. After the first time we saw it, we were so impressed we told everyone we knew on Maui, "You gotta go see this." Most said, "Oh, I don't really like magic shows." Doesn't matter. It's not the kind of magic show you're thinking of. It might sound corny, but the whole evening's magic. Every person we've ever sent to this show has come back a raving fool. (Now the island is populated with raving fools. We're sorry to be the ones responsible.) You enter the theater in a unique way. (We won't give it away.) Then you're in an incredibly beautiful parlor, elegant in every way. You spend some time inside having tasty (though pricey) pupus and absolutely killer desserts or cocktails while their resident ghost (Annabelle) plays at the piano. You call out a song, and she probably knows it. (Hey, wait a minute. If the ghost has been dead for 150 years, how come she knows the theme to *Cheers*?) Then it's into the cozy 78-seat magic theater for—we promise you—the most amazing show you'll ever see. No smoke and mirrors, no elaborate props. Don't think David Copperfield or anything like that. Just a close-up view of a very engaging (and hilarious) man doing the absolute impossible. And we mean that literally. In fact, the first time we saw the show, we away that we were con- ...at some of the audience members had to be plants. After the two-hour show, we told Warren our suspicions. I told him, "I've seen great magicians, but *nobody's* that good." He proceeded to do some of the same things for us. (We didn't tell him who we were that night—just viewers.) We don't want to give anything away, but we can tell you that Warren does things that have literally kept us awake at night. It's simply not possible, and we've come to the awkward conclusion that Warren is simply not of this world. We've seen lots of magicians and even taken one to see Warren. But none of us has ever seen anything like it, and we've since seen the show several times.

If you only see one show on Maui, this is it. $59 per person, plus whatever you eat (gourmet appetizers which can be a meal) and drink from the full bar before the show. Book in advance. Though the act is "clean," it's age 21 and over.

The other magic show is **Kupanaha** (667-0128) at the Ka'anapali Beach Hotel. The magic is totally different from Warren and Annabelle's and not as impressive. It's mostly prop-driven and is often the same trick several different ways. (Somebody in a box, a curtain or panel goes up and when it comes down they're gone or have changed into someone else. Impressive at first, but a bit repetitious as the night wears on.) Some tricks are excellent, but we advise you not to look *too* closely. Also, the magicians' attempts at humor are a bit spotty.

The food is fairly good, though they suffer from a common dinner show ailment—it's hard to serve everyone at once and keep the food hot. (And some portions—like the tiny steak and two shrimp—could be increased.) Overall, the food is their strongest point, and they are admirably efficient in serving it. Intermixed with dinner is hula and a heavy dose of black lights. Mai tais, beer and wine are included, but other drinks cost extra, and the bar closes when the show starts. (This is an early event, starting at 4:30 and ending at 7:30 p.m.) Overall, if you're looking to be wowed by magic, stick with Warren & Annabelle's. If you really have your heart set on a dinner show, Kupanaha isn't a bad show, and kids are allowed—in fact, they are catered to. $79–$89.

When **Cirque Polynesia** (667-4540) came out, we have to confess that our expectations were probably too high. The name and their ads gave the impression that this was on the order of Cirque de Soleil (the smashing Vegas act). Think of this as a mini Cirque…more like micro. No vast staging areas and feasts for the eyes. And virtually no Polynesian performers. In truth, they have about 45 minutes of good material and 90 minutes to perform it. The best acts are high above the stage, as well as the balancing guy who will make you squirm as you worry about him falling. Snacks and beverages for sale. Don't get the "dinner show" option, which merely steers you to the Hyatt's restaurant before the show. Seats are $65–$75.

The last show, **'Ulalena** (661-9913), is the biggest, most elaborate show ever to take place on Maui. This 700-seat theater in Old Lahaina Center was specially created for musical shows. 'Ulalena is a 90-minute Hawaiian opera about life in Hawai'i before and after western contact, and about the gods and their deeds. The theater is state of the art with booming sound and excellent lighting. The show is sung entirely in Hawaiian; there is no dialogue, but the English narration helps orient you a bit during the show. The music and percussion throughout are effective, and the dancers are disciplined. The show was actually written by Canadians and, as a result, the story shows a pretty shallow view of Hawaiian life. The Hawaiians are shown to be happily toiling away in peace, harmony and innocence until the evil westerners arrive. (Actually, the 200 years preceding western contact were the bloodiest in Hawai'i's history.) And Captain Cook is portrayed as the Prince of Darkness, complete with black hat and mask, who literally walks on the backs of the trusting natives. (See page 17 for the real skinny on Cook, who they fail to mention was killed by the Hawaiians.) In this story, westerners bring only guns, sickness and sadness. But all this is mostly forgotten with some *very* creative scenes, such as the dazzling waterfall scene where the actress/spirit dangles from the falls. And the last three scenes are so beautiful and uplifting, you can't help but leave smiling. 'Ulalena may not be the best show on Maui (we prefer Warren & Annabelle's), but it's fun and entertaining. Cost is $60, $70 or $80. They don't serve dinner, but you can get packages that include meals at nearby restaurants, and they have popcorn and beverages in the lobby.

DINNER CRUISES

Not all the Hawaiian islands offer these, but Maui's often placid evening waters make dinner cruises a delight.

In West Maui the **Maui Princess** (667–6165) is a huge 120-foot yacht that feeds over 100 passengers at dinner. $75 per person includes prime rib, chicken or vegetarian, three drinks, live entertainment and dancing. While the brochure may show a cozy table for two, there are, in fact, four people seated at each table— just so you know. Tables are all on the open top deck: half along the railing, half in the middle. If the anemic mai tais are too tame for you, don't hesitate to take them to the bar and have them *seasoned* for you; it's all free. The crew is good, and, while you may expect glorified airline food for such a large crowd, the food is better than we expected. Even the desserts are

good. The slow cruise during the sun's golden hour creates pretty views of Lahaina and Ka'anapali. After dinner there's dancing below decks. You don't feel as crowded on this boat (except during boarding) as you may think. The boat is very smooth, and they stay out from 5:30– 8 p.m., leaving from Lahaina Harbor.

Pacific Whale Foundation (249–8811) has a dinner cruise for $80 for up to 80 people.

There are also lots of sunset **cocktail cruises**. Most include the open bar in the price. Out of Lahaina the smallish **Scotch Mist** (661–0386) does a good job on their 50-foot sailboat for $60. No bar, just champagne, beer, wine and soft drinks. Out of Ka'anapali Beach the **Teralani** (661–1230) has a 2-hour $60 trip. From Ma'alaea **Pride of Maui** (242–0955) has a 2-hour trip. Heavy pupus and an open bar, but we've seen them run out of food in only 30 minutes. The crew's pretty unenthusiastic, and it seems overpriced at $70. **Pacific Whale** has a cocktail cruise for $60.

From Lahaina, the **Spirit of Lahaina** (662–4477) is a very mixed bag. In some respects it's everything a dinner cruise *shouldn't* be. The bright spot, however, is the crew. Unfortunately, they're saddled with a boat that's ill-equipped for this purpose and an organizational system that makes it worse. We've seen more passengers than seats, forcing them to cram too many people at the tables. Even when it's not too crowded, it's indoors and so loud that conversations are very difficult. Long waits, cold food, insanely slow service getting drinks at dinner and poor food (except the tasty steaks) make the experience similar to cattle being led to slaughter. But after dinner the crew, which exudes *tons* of aloha, takes you upstairs and puts on a show that includes audience participation, and they go a long way toward bringing smiles to the grumpy diners. It's $79 for the 2½-hour cruise with up to 149 people.

That's it...we're not leaving...ever!

Your selection of where to stay can be one of the more important decisions you'll make in planning your visit. To some, it's just a place to sleep and rather meaningless. To others, it's the difference between a good vacation and a bad one.

There are three main types of lodgings on the island: hotels, condominiums and bed and breakfasts. The overwhelming majority of visitors stay in one of the first two types. Hotels offer more service but lack kitchens. Condos usually have full kitchens and more living area but usually lack daily maid service. Many condos have minimum stays—usually three to seven nights. This varies between different rental companies. There is a list of **rental agents** on page 292 who represent many of the condos on the island.

CONDOS

When describing condos **(shown in purple)**, three-bedroom/two-bath units are described as 3/2, two-bedroom/one-bath units are described as 2/1, etc. Differentiation between half baths and full baths is not made. The price spread for rooms of a given size is due to different views, different locations within the resort and sometimes seasonal fluctuations. So when you see that a 2/2 unit rents for $190–$250, you should figure that $250 is the high season rate or units have a better view or are closer to the water. The terms Ocean Front, Ocean View and Garden View are used rather capriciously in Hawai'i, so we often avoid them. Unless otherwise noted, all condos come with telephones, complete kitchens, coffee makers, lanais (verandas), cable TV, coin-op laundry facilities and ceiling fans and have cribs available upon request. No condos have a/c, maid service is not included unless otherwise noted, and local calls are free. Cleaning and some *annoying* booking fees or registration fees may be added to your costs, so read the fine print carefully. Many condos told us that they will book less than their listed minimum night stay, but you may have to pay a hefty cleaning fee.

All condos are non-smoking. Some allow you to smoke on the lanai; some don't want you smoking any place on property. If you smoke, you will want to check the rules before you book. We saw some high "cleaning fees" if you smoke on property and get caught— like *$500!*

The important thing to remember about renting condos is the fragmented nature of the market. Each unit usually has a different owner, they all use different rental agencies to manage them, and it changes all the time. (Spreadsheets, blinding headaches and blurred vision are all necessary to figure it out.) Therefore, when we review them, we may look at 10 units and get 10 winners. *You* may rent one and get a dump because the owner is using furniture from a landfill and carpet from the finish line at the Maui Marathon. An individual owner may opt not to participate in the community hot water, instead giving you a tiny, underpowered hot water heater, while all the other units bask in hot water. Or a resort may be scrupulously maintained, but an individual unit (yours) may have a recurring problem with marauding ants or roaches. The owner may use a different cleaning service, leaving you

in a squalid mess. You truly never know what you're going to get. Internet images only show the condos in the best of times, so keep that in mind. There's no way to take into account the individuality of units, so to a certain extent, you are playing the odds with many condos.

HOTELS

As for hotels (shown in green), unless otherwise noted, all *do* have air conditioning, telephones, small refrigerators, lanais, coin-op laundry facilities, cable TV and cribs available. None have room service unless we mention it. But if they *do* have room service, watch for built-in tips. It's easy to double tip, and you can bet that no one will point it out to you. Rooms are generally smaller than condos since they don't have kitchens and usually don't have a separate bedroom. Hotels are non-smoking, but *may* allow smoking in certain areas.

A FEW GROUND RULES

All prices given are RACK rates, meaning without any discounts. Tour packages and travel agents can sometimes get better rates. Many places offer discounts for stays of a week or more, and some will negotiate price with you. Some won't budge at all; others told us *no one* pays RACK rate. Also, be aware that these prices are subject to taxes of around 13.5%.

 The gold bar indicates that the property is exceptionally well priced for what you get.

SOLID GOLD VALUE

The gem means that this accommodation offers something *particularly* special, not *necessarily* related to the price.

A REAL GEM

WHERE ARE THE REST?

We ran into a *big problem* when we tried to do this section. What worked on the other islands—printing in-depth reviews of nearly every place to stay other than B&Bs—was *impossible* here. There are over 140 hotels and condo complexes on the island. Our book would have been as heavy as a phone book if we tried to print them all. We had two choices: Give the bare bones info on all of them, or do detailed reviews on a small fraction. Neither choice seemed palatable.

So we came up with a third way: List minimal info on all, print detailed reviews on some, and post full reviews of the rest on our website, **www.wizardpub.com**. After all, most people use this section *before* they come to the islands. And with the Web (which has infinite space available), we could do more, such as post larger aerial photos of the resorts with specific buildings labeled when appropriate, offer constant updates when necessary, and put links to the various rental agents or hotels right in the review, allowing you to go to their sites and get more photos of the rooms. You should remember, however, that resorts post photos to lure you in, and some aren't above posting modified or overly flattering shots when they were new and sparkling.

We've seen many websites that have virtual tours of properties. This really helps you get an idea of what your condo experience will be like, from the view to the bathrooms. However, having actually *been in* many, many condos at each property, then looked at their virtual tours, we've found that the Web images do not *always* match reality. It's kind of like Internet dating; you just never can be sure of what you are *really* getting.

Remember, those photos were taken on the unit's *best day ever* and details may not be visible, such as mold in the shower, stains on the sofa or sagging mattresses. If you have booked through one of our suggested contacts at each property, don't be afraid to ask for another unit. The agents we list *want* you to be happy.

Our aerials (which we took ourselves) don't lie and are designed to give you a feel for their ocean proximity (does oceanfront *really* mean oceanfront?), so you'll know what kind of view to expect from a given location within the resort. Resorts whose reviews are posted on our website are identified with Web Review.

Please remember that all these reviews are *relative to each other.* We'll repeat that later because it's so important. Even staying at a dump right on the ocean is still a *Golly!* experience. In other words, *Hey, you're on the ocean in Maui!* So if we sound whiny or picky in critiquing a resort, it's only because their next door neighbor might be such a better experience. It doesn't mean you'll be miserable, it just means that *compared to another resort,* you can do better.

Also be aware that we don't review long-term condos or apartments or resorts that are all or nearly all timeshare. Unfortunately, we also don't review **B&Bs** or **vacation rentals**. The county of Maui has cracked down on unpermitted vacation rentals and B&Bs. (And nearly all are unpermitted since it would be easier to get a permit to carry a loaded *bazooka* than it is to get a vacation rental permit.) Our website has links to the permitted vacation rentals that are available on Maui.

We're describing the resorts geographically from the top of West Maui to the bottom of South Maui with others, including Hana, at the end. All resorts (except Maʻalaea) are shown on the various maps. If you have trouble seeing some things on the aerial photos, go to our website where the photos are larger.

WHERE SHOULD I STAY?

Resorts are concentrated in a dozen regions on Maui. Each has its pluses and minuses.

Kapalua resorts are few and in the extreme far north of West Maui. Weather is poorer here than any other resort area, featuring strong winds much of the time and more passing drizzly showers. It's a long drive to off-site attractions, but many people like the relative seclusion. Kapalua Beach is a great swimming (but not snorkeling) beach. Restaurants are few.

Napili accommodations are mostly mid-'60s buildings and are clustered around wonderful Napili Bay. Restaurants are farther south.

The area from **Kahana** down to (but not including) Honokowai, includes the strip of condos and hotels that line the shoreline, most built in the '70s. Some are good values. The biggest problem is that, with few exceptions, most have no beach or the water may have seaweed. We don't want to overstate the seaweed problem. (In fact, the water quality has been improving lately.) It comes and goes. It's just that you may not find the crystal clear water available in other parts of the island, and we don't want you to be surprised when you find yourself swimming around.

Resorts in **Honokowai** are in a different category than the ones directly north of here. The condos have hotel services and hotel prices. The sandy beach here is the northern part of Kekaʻa Beach, not the beach traditionally known as Kaʻanapali. It's cleaner (not

much seaweed) than the beach patches north of here, but the nearshore waters are a bit rocky. The beach is not anywhere near the caliber of Kaʻanapali Beach. There's a grocery store nearby for condo users.

The resorts on **Kaʻanapali Beach** are all about living on this fantastic beach. Water is usually clean and clear, and the beachside path along much of the beach makes for great walking. There are tons of restaurants in the resorts and shopping center backing the beach.

When visiting West Maui, people usually speak of staying in **Lahaina**. The irony is that relatively few people actually *stay* in Lahaina because there are limited choices available. Nearly all West Maui accommodations are north of Lahaina, in Kaʻanapali, Honokowai, Kahana, Napili and Kapalua. If you do stay at one of the few accommodations here, you will be within walking distance to plenty of shops and restaurants.

Staying in **Maʻalaea** is an interesting choice. It's the windiest place to stay on Maui and possibly in the whole state. Dust and sometimes smoke from sugar operations creates an environment so dusty, you can't even leave your lanai furniture outside when not in use unless you want to sit on filthy chairs. And dining choices are very limited. In the past we were pretty hard on this area because of the trade-offs. So for this edition we decided to live in Maʻalaea for five months to get a solid feel for what life is like here. In the end we came to realize that, as long as you understand the downside, staying here can be pretty darned convenient. There's never any traffic coming in or out. You have access to a beach that, after the last condo, stretches for miles without development. And you can experience both West Maui and South Maui equally with a 20-minute drive. Prices are cheaper, too.

We separate **north Kihei** from south Kihei for a simple reason. The ocean and beaches in part of north Kihei suffer from the quality problems we mention on page 158. South of Cove Park, however, Kihei's beaches are lovely. Also, the extreme northern part of Kihei (Sugar Beach area) often has wind, dust and possibly seaweed on the beach (mentioned in the reviews). It also has a bad smell after rains from the ponds upwind. We're not trying to portray north Kihei properties as bad places. In fact, some are wonderful places to stay. But remember, our job is to review accommodations *relative to each other.*

The beaches in **south Kihei** are usually clean and clear. Enjoy the water. There are lots of restaurants, as well as Kihei's main nightlife area, called the Triangle.

Many people consider **Wailea** the most desirable place to stay on Maui. Gorgeous beach after gorgeous beach along with almost perfect weather make it a vacationer's paradise. The only downside is the price. If you look around for packages, however, paradise can be had even if your last name isn't Gates.

Past Wailea is **Makena** and its single resort. It's the most isolated part of South Maui.

There are really only two reasons to stay in **Kahului**: cheap rooms and closeness to the airport. Few would come here to lounge around the pool. Both of the large hotels here are located on Ka'ahumanu Avenue.

Staying in **Hana** has changed. We're sorry to have to report that we had to pull most of the property descriptions out of the Hana section. Staying in Hana has usually meant staying at a vacation rental or at one of the inns. But the county has been cracking down on "illegal" rentals, and almost all of them in Hana were not permitted. The county isn't *making* us do this, but owners who still rent are trying to stay under the radar and we don't want to contribute to their woes by highlighting them here. We'll review the ones with a county permit and leave it at that. If you want to sniff out any on the Internet, that's between you and the owners.

Rental Agents

AA Oceanfront Rentals & Sales	(800) 488–6004 or (808) 879–7288
Ali'i Resorts	(866) 284–2544 or (808) 879–6284
Bello Realty	(800) 541–3060 or (808) 879–3328
Chase 'n Rainbows (*charges no cleaning fees*)	(800) 367–6092 or (808) 667–7088
Classic Resorts	(877) 316–6126 or (808) 667–1100
Coldwell Banker Island Properties	(800) 808–3138 or (808) 879–2700
Condominium Rentals Hawai'i	(800) 367–5242 or (808) 879–2778
Destination Resorts Hawai'i	(800) 367–5246 or (808) 879–1595
Kumulani Vacations	(800) 367–2954 or (808) 879–9272
Ma'alaea Bay Realty & Rentals	(800) 367–6084 or (808) 244–5627
Maui Beachfront Rentals	(888) 661–7200 or (808) 661–3500
Maui Condominium & Home	(800) 822–4409 or (808) 879–5445
Maui Lodging.com	(800) 487–6002 or (808) 669–0089
Paradise Vacations	(800) 927–7672 or (808) 874–7672
Sullivan Properties, Inc.	(800) 332–1137 or (808) 669–0423
Whaler's Realty	(800) 676–4112 or (808) 661–3484

Resorts: Hotels in Green Condos in Purple	Region of Maui	Solid Gold or Real Gem	Phone(s)	Page Number or Web Review
Aina Nalu Resort	Lahaina		(800) 688–7444 or (808) 667–9766	Web Review
Banana Bungalow	Wailuku	🏠	(800) 846–7835 or (808) 244–5090	Web Review
Fairmont Kea Lani	Wailea	💎	(800) 441–1414 or (808) 875–4100	Web Review
Four Seasons Resort Maui	Wailea	💎	(800) 334–6284 or (808) 874–8000	302
Grand Champions	Wailea	🏠	(800) 367–5246 or (808) 879–1595	Web Review
Grand Wailea Resort Hotel & Spa	Wailea		(800) 888–6100 or (808) 875–1234	Web Review
Hale Hui Kai	S. Kihei	🏠	(800) 809–6284 or (808) 879–1219	302
Hale Kai	Honokowai		(800) 446–7307 or (808) 669–6333	Web Review
Hale Kai o Kihei	N. Kihei		(800) 488–6004 or (808) 879–7288 / (800) 367–5242 or (808) 879–2778	Web Review
Hale Kama'ole	S. Kihei	🏠	(800) 367–2970 or (808) 879–1221	Web Review
Hale Mahina Beach Resort	Honokowai		(800) 367–6092 or (808) 667–7088	Web Review
Hale Maui	Honokowai	🏠	(808) 669–6312	Web Review
Hale Napili	Napili	💎	(800) 245–2266 OR (808) 669–6184	297
Hale Ono Loa	Honokowai	💎	(800) 367–6092 or (808) 667–7088	Web Review
Hale Pau Hana	S. Kihei	💎	(800) 367–6036 or (808) 879–2715	Web Review
Hana Kai Maui	Hana		(800) 346–2772 or (808) 248–8426	305
Hololani	Kahana	🏠	(800) 367–5032 or (808) 669–8021	Web Review
Hono Kai	Ma'alaea		(800) 367–6084 or (808) 244–5627	Web Review
Honokeana Cove	Napili		(800) 237–4948 or (808) 669–6441	Web Review
Honua Kai Resort & Spa	Ka'anapali		(888) 718–5789 or (808) 662–2800	Web Review
Ho'olei	Wailea	💎	(877) 324–7088 or (808) 856–2000	Web Review
Hotel Wailea Maui	Wailea	💎	(800) 800–0720 or (808) 874–0500	Web Review
Hoyochi Nikko	Honokowai	🏠	(800) 487–6002 or (808) 669–8343	Web Review
Hyatt Regency Maui	Ka'anapali	💎	(800) 233–1234 or (808) 661–1234	298
Inn at Mama's Fish House	Ku'au		(800) 860–4852 or (808) 579–9764	Web Review
Island Sands	Ma'alaea		(800) 367–5242 or (808) 244–0848	300
Ka'anapali Ali'i	Ka'anapali	💎	(877) 316–6126 or (808) 667–1400	Web Review
Ka'anapali Beach Club	Honokowai		(877) 988–6284 or (808) 661–2000	Web Review
Ka'anapali Beach Hotel	Ka'anapali	🏠	(800) 262–8450 or (808) 661–0011	Web Review
Ka'anapali Ocean Inn	Ka'anapali	🏠	(800) 222–5642 or (808) 661–3611	Web Review
Ka'anapali Royal	Ka'anapali		(800) 676–4112 or (808) 661–3484	Web Review
Ka'anapali Shores	Honokowai		(877) 997–6667 or (808) 667–2211	Web Review
Kahana Outrigger	Kahana		(800) 367–6092 or (808) 667–7088	Web Review
Kahana Reef	Kahana		(800) 367–6092 or (808) 667–7088	Web Review
Kahana Sunset	Kahana		(800) 669–1488 or (808) 669–8700 / (800) 332–1137 or (808) 669–0423	Web Review
Kahana Villa	Kahana		(888) 661–7200 or (808) 661–3500	Web Review
Kahana Village	Kahana	💎	(800) 824–3065 or (808) 669–5111	297
Kaleialoha	Honokowai		(800) 222–8688 or (808) 669–8197	Web Review
Kama'ole Beach Royale	S. Kihei	🏠	(800) 421–3661 or (808) 879–3131	Web Review
Kama'ole Nalu	S. Kihei		(800) 767–1497 or (808) 879–1006	Web Review
Kama'ole Sands	S. Kihei		(800) 367–5004 or (808) 874–8700 / (866) 582–0766	Web Review
Kana'i A Nalu	Ma'alaea	💎	(800) 367–6084 or (808) 244–5627	Web Review
Kealia Condominium	N. Kihei		(800) 265–0686 or (808) 879–0952	301
Kihei Akahi	S. Kihei		(800) 822–4409 or (808) 879–5445	Web Review

(Continued on next page...)

See all Web Reviews at: www.wizardpub.com

Resorts: Hotels in Green Condos in Purple	Region of Maui	Solid Gold or Real Gem	Phone(s)	Page Number or Web Review
Kihei Bay Vista	N. Kihei	⌂	(800) 927–7672 or (808) 874–7672	Web Review
Kihei Beach Resort	N. Kihei		(866) 284–2544 or (808) 879–6284	Web Review
Kihei Kai	N. Kihei	⌂	(888) 778–7717 or (808) 891–0780	Web Review
Kihei Kai Nani	S. Kihei	⌂	(800) 473–1493 or (808) 891–0049	Web Review
Kihei Sands	N. Kihei		(800) 882–6284 or (808) 879–2624	Web Review
Kihei Surfside	S. Kihei		(800) 451–5008 or (808) 879–5445	301
Koa Lagoon	N. Kihei	⌂	(800) 367–8030 or (808) 879–3002	301
Koa Resort	N. Kihei		(800) 541–3060 or (808) 879–3328	Web Review
Kula Lodge	Kula		(800) 233–1535 or (808) 878–1535	304
Kulakane	Honokowai		(800) 367–6088 or (808) 669–6119	Web Review
Kulana Kai	N. Kihei	⌂	(808) 879–2806	Web Review
Kuleana	Honokowai		(800) 487–6002 or (808) 669–2166	Web Review
Lahaina Inn	Lahaina		(800) 669–3444 or (808) 661–0577	Web Review
Lahaina Roads	Lahaina		(800) 367–6092 or (808) 667–7088	Web Review
Lahaina Shores	Lahaina		(877) 316–6126 or (808) 661–4835	Web Review
Lauloa	Ma'alaea		(800) 367–6084 or (808) 244–5627	Web Review
Leina'ala	N. Kihei		(800) 488–6004 or (808) 879–7288	Web Review
Lihi Kai Cottages	S. Kihei	⌂	(808) 879–2335	Web Review
Lokelani	Honokowai	⌂	(866) 303–6284 or (808) 669–8110	Web Review
Luana Kai	N. Kihei		(800) 669–1127 or (808) 879–1268	Web Review
Ma'alaea Banyans	Ma'alaea		(800) 367–6084 or (808) 244–5627	Web Review
Ma'alaea Kai	Ma'alaea		(800) 367–6084 or (808) 244–5627	Web Review
Ma'alaea Surf	N. Kihei	◈	(800) 423–7953 or (808) 879–1267	Web Review
Mahana at Ka'anapali	Honokowai		(877) 997–6667 or (808) 661–8751	Web Review
Mahina Surf	Honokowai		(800) 367–6086 or (808) 669–6068	Web Review
Makai Inn	Lahaina		(808) 662–3200	300
Makani A Kai	Ma'alaea		(800) 367–6084 or (808) 244–5627	Web Review
Makani Sands	Honokowai		(800) 227–8223 or (808) 669–8223	Web Review
Makena Beach & Golf Resort	Wailea		(800) 321–6284 or (808) 874–1111	Web Review
Makena Surf	Wailea	◈	(800) 367–5246 or (808) 879–1595	Web Review
Mana Kai Resort	S. Kihei		(800) 525–2025 or (808) 879–1561	Web Review
Maui Banyan	S. Kihei		(877) 997–6667 or (808) 875–0004	Web Review
Maui Beach Hotel	Kahului		(888) 649–3222 or (808) 877–0051	Web Review
Maui Coast Hotel	S. Kihei		(800) 716–6199 or (808) 874–6284	Web Review
Maui Eldorado	Ka'anapali		(800) 688–7444 or (808) 661–0021	Web Review
Maui Hill	S. Kihei		(877) 997–6667 or (808) 879–6321	Web Review
Maui Ka'anapali Villas	Ka'anapali		(866) 817–7018 or (808) 667–7791	Web Review
Maui Kai	Honokowai	⌂	(800) 367–5635 or (808) 667–3500	298
Maui Kama'ole	S. Kihei		(800) 822–4409 or (808) 874–8467	Web Review
Maui Lu	N. Kihei		(877) 997–6667 or (808) 879–5881	Web Review
Maui Oceanfront Inn	S. Kihei		(800) 263–3387 or (808) 879–7744	Web Review
Maui Parkshore	S. Kihei		(800) 822–4409 or (808) 879–5445	Web Review
Maui Sands	Honokowai		(800) 367–6092 or (808) 667–7088	Web Review
Maui Seaside	Kahului		(800) 560–5552 or (808) 877–3311	304
Maui Sunseeker	N. Kihei	⌂	(800) 532–6284 or (808) 879–1261	Web Review
Maui Sunset	N. Kihei		(800) 233–3310 / (800) 367–2954 or (808) 879–9272	Web Review
Maui Vista	S. Kihei		(800) 488–6004 or (808) 879–7288	Web Review

See all Web Reviews at: www.wizardpub.com

See all Web Reviews at: www.wizardpub.com

See all Web reviews at: **www.wizardpub.com**

KAPALUA

Ritz-Carlton Kapalua
(800) 262–8440 or (808) 669–6200
1 Ritz-Carlton Dr.

463 rooms (including 107 1- or 2-bedroom residential suites), pool and 2 spas, keiki pool and playground, health spa, 6 restaurants, an *awesome* 24-hour fitness center (with trainers), valet parking, 37- or 42-inch flat screen TVs, 24-hour business center, resort-wide Wi-Fi, 13 conference rooms, 4 tennis courts, basketball court, environmental and cultural programs, 24-hour room service, laundry is valet only, maid service is *twice* daily, coffee makers with free daily coffee daily, wedding coordinator. The resort underwent a $180 million renovation in 2008 with great results. The overall feeling is now very Hawaiian and calming with rich wood tones and warm color schemes. The resort is expensively furnished with lots of artwork spread about the grounds. The buildings and the hotel itself are handsome. The staff is eager to please and will get you anything you need. They show a large amount of aloha to each and every guest—even small children.

A REAL GEM

They have an on-site program called "Jean-Michel Cousteau Ambassadors of the Environment" for guests 3 years old and up where you learn about sea creatures, take underwater pictures, go on hikes, etc. Prices for those range from $70 for kids 3–18 and $90 for adults.

They also offer a "kids' night out" where they'll help your keiki make pizzas and gaze at the stars or do other activities for $70. There is a cultural adviser who offers tours and programs—many of which are included with the resort fee. Their new 17,500 sq. ft. spa is very nice with co-ed areas available and showers off the treatment rooms.

The rooms are 440 sq. ft. (plus lanai), a full 160 sq. ft. smaller than a Four Seasons room (their biggest competitor), but all are nicely furnished. There are separate showers and tubs in the bathrooms. There's a *mandatory* $25 per day resort fee that mostly covers things other expensive resorts give away free, such as charging privileges *(gee, thanks)*, use of fitness center, ground shuttle services, Wi-Fi access, local and toll-free telephone calls, discounted golf fees and preferred tee times and a few other things. Self-parking is an *additional* $10, valet parking is $18 per day. The swimming pool is 3-tiered and shallow (3.5–4 feet deep) but open 24 hours. They have covered cabanas next to the pool for $100 *per day* and luxury cabanas, which are *$300 per day* and include a flat screen TV, sofa, private attendant, fruit, water, etc. These are very large and can easily fit a family of 8. (You can get a room at some places for that much!) Their Club floor rooms have their own private lounge with free goodies, like top-shelf liquor and breakfast. Their residential suites are one or two hotel-type rooms joined by a main living area with complete kitchen (except an oven).

The resort is as far north as you can get in West Maui. Allow extra time when planning off-site activities. Due to the Hawaiian sacred site adjacent to its grounds, it is set farther back from the ocean than many other large resorts. Their beach doesn't stack up well against other island hotels, and they erect a

*See all Web reviews at: **www.wizardpub.com***

BEACH CLOSED sign often, especially in the winter since it's more susceptible to high surf here. Also, weather is not as good in Kapalua as the other resort areas on the island. Very strong winds are common (we often see people by the pool covered with towels to ward off a chill), as are passing drizzly showers.

However, the remoteness of this resort may also be its charm, and the Ritz works for us. Rooms (440 sq. ft.) are $399–$909, club rooms (440 sq. ft.) are $719–$1,109, residential suites (900–1,510 sq. ft.) are $629–$1,509, suites (900–2,560 sq. ft.) are $579–$10,509.

NAPILI

Hale Napili
(800) 245–2266 or (808) 669–6184
65 Hui Dr.

18 units, daily maid service, BBQs, free Wi-Fi, free room safes and free laundry room. A dreamy location on Napili Beach with clean, comfortable rooms, and an *extremely* warm staff make you feel at home. In fact, they often greet guests saying, "Welcome home." As with many Napili resorts, most visitors are long-time repeats, and they can book out a year in advance. Layouts and furnishings are amazingly variable, but most are nice,

A REAL GEM

clean, and most face the ocean. Baths have showers only. All have full kitchens. It was built in 1965 and is not plush, but Hale Napili is an easy place to like—and an easy place to return to. Studios (approx. 500 sq. ft.) are $160–$215. 1/1s (approx. 700 sq. ft.) are $260. 3-night minimum. Discounts on longer stays.

KAHANA

Kahana Village
(800) 824–3065 or (808) 669–5111
4531 Lwr. Honoapiilani Rd.

42 units, pool, spa, maid service mid-week (weekly stays), BBQs, free room safes, washer/dryer in the units, free hi-speed Internet access. Wonderfully spacious rooms, high-grade appliances and a great oceanfront location. The grounds are very lush. Units have lots of glass and an open feel, but they are still private if you want. The ground floors are massive 1,600 sq. ft. 3/2s with wet bars, nice kitchens, and the additional bedrooms are equally large. The shoreline from the "prime" (ocean front) units seems delectably close. They changed their classifications, and now units 7–18 are called "ocean front," which we feel might be a little generous since the pool and lawn front your view. But maybe we're just being a bit picky. Upstairs units are 1,200-sq.-ft., 2/2 townhouse-type units with the second bedroom as a loft-type—not quite as desirable as the lower

A REAL GEM

See all Web reviews at: www.wizardpub.com

units. All units have nice, large lanais. They have three categories: standard, deluxe and luxury (the latter completely upgraded). Since the overall quality at the property is *very* high, you will probably be just as happy in a standard unit for less money. And here's a treat: They have *free* long distance phone calls (even if you're calling Mongolia). Kahana Village is a good value for the price and a place that you will want to come back to again and again. 2/2s (1,200 sq. ft.) are $260–$500, 3/2s (1,700 sq. ft.) are $460–$740. The reason for the price spread is due to the individual unit's quality rating. 5-night minimum.

HONOKOWAI

Maui Kai
(800) 367–5635 or (808) 667–3500
106 Ka'anapali Shores Pl.

80 units, pool, spa, BBQs, central air conditioning, free hi-speed Internet access, free room safes, Ping-Pong, daily maid service. Though the building is old (1969) and the exterior relatively unimpressive, this one's a winner and the best priced in this area. They are impossibly close to the ocean—around 25 feet!—so rooms look almost straight down into the water. Their sandy beach is narrow but gets wider next door. The pool obviously wouldn't fit on the ocean side,

SOLID GOLD VALUE

so it's tucked away on the mountain side and has no view, but there's a computer for you to use, free Wi-Fi and a kitchen at the pool to cook your meals. There's a grocery store across the street. Units vary *a lot,* but we didn't see any we wouldn't want to stay in. They added DVRs and iPod docking stations to the rooms, so you won't miss your favorite shows or tunes. Some of the studio units have pull-down wall beds—get out of bed, pop it up and you have the whole room. Corner units offer particularly tasty views. If you're staying on the Ka'anapali Beach Club side of the building, you may hear their nightly poolside events. Free morning coffee in the lobby. All in all, it's an excellent deal. Studios, which they call Jr. Suites (500–550 sq. ft.), are $199–$249, 1/1s (750–800 sq. ft.) are $259–$319, 2/2s (1,200 sq. ft.) are $289–$349. 2-night minimum.

KA'ANAPALI

Hyatt Regency Maui
(800) 233–1234 or (808) 661–1234
200 Nohea Kai Dr.

806 rooms, 2 pools, spa, 3 restaurants, 4 tennis courts, 24-hour room service, coin-op laundry, 10 conference rooms, business center, hi-speed Internet access and Wi-Fi in rooms and resort-wide, 37-inch HD flat screen TVs, 24-hour fitness center and day spa, numerous shops, lu'au, valet parking, empty refrigerator, child care program. Wow, where do we start? This is one of the biggest resorts on Maui, consisting of three 8- and 9-story buildings among 40

A REAL GEM

See all Web reviews at: **www.wizardpub.com**

acres of spacious and exotic grounds. The two outstanding pools are large with waterfalls, and one has a fast 150-foot waterslide (you must be at least 4-feet tall), swinging bridge and a swim-up bar inside a cave. Little ones can enjoy a shorter waterslide, a sand-lined lagoon and synchronized fountains. Between the two is a poolside bar filled with the roar of the artificial waterfalls. The lobby is next to the huge atrium, which, in the mornings, is filled with the sound of wild birds there to steal some food.

They have tours of the wildlife strewn about the grounds (such as the warm weather penguins, swans, flamingos and parrots), and there's a nice oceanside state-of-the-art fitness center. Their Spa Moana has all the bone-melting fixin's. (They'll even treat your child at the spa and offer services such as the M & M manicure—a different color for every nail.) They charge $25 ($15 for kids) for the guided rooftop astronomy demonstrations with their 16-inch scope, and you get a *Milky Way* or *Starburst* afterwards. There are two restaurants, including Son'z at the Swan Court. Downstairs near the pool is the cheaper food court-style area called the Umalu. Feel free to wear your bathing suit there. Watch for the thieving birds who'll rob you blind if you turn your back.

The Hyatt has a lu'au (the oceanfront rooms in the Lahaina Tower are exposed to the sound until 8–8:30 p.m.). We only have two dings with this resort. One is the *mandatory* $25 resort fee that covers things such as local calls, room safe, fitness center, daily coffee, etc. Valet is an *additional* $18. The other ding is that their part of Ka'anapali Beach *occasionally* gets seaweed blooms, especially in front of the Napili Wing. And there's more reef in the nearshore waters, so you can't frolic in the shallow waters without

water shoes, or you may tear up your feet. They have ocean activity booths where you can rent water toys such as boogie boards and snorkel gear at normal resort prices (meaning expensive). Cabana chairs are $50 per day.

Hyatt's keiki program (called Camp Hyatt) is $45 or $80 per day. They haven't left out adults with pampering treats such as massages by the ocean and dinners under the stars for $495 per couple (includes tip). You can even rent your own thatched hut by the ocean for $150 per day, and they'll bring you just about anything for a price, of course.

In all, the Hyatt does a very good job, and the staff is very warm and professional. The place radiates the dreamy warmth that you want from a fantasy resort. It's especially pretty at night. Rooms are nicely furnished and are a respectable 451 sq. ft. costing $259–$569. Regency Club rooms (marginally nicer but more amenities—namely free continental breakfast in a private lounge—not worth the upgrade) are $409–$649. Suites (554–2,500 sq. ft.) are $659–$4,449.

The Whaler
(877) 997–6667 or (808) 661–4861
2481 Ka'anapali Pkwy.

360 units, pool, spa, BBQs, air conditioning, sauna, elevator, fitness center, 24-hour business center, free hi-speed Internet access in units, daily maid service. This

See all Web reviews at: www.wizardpub.com

1975-built property consists of two 12-story towers on delicious Ka'anapali Beach. The services for a condo resort are admirable. The daily maid will even do your dishes if you want. The resort is well-run and friendly. Staff is excellent, many of them long-term. The pool courtyard was redone in 2009 and looks very dreamy now with large koi ponds. However, this property lost its REAL GEM rating because many of the rooms didn't have the polish you'd expect at this price, and on this visit many still lacked that GEM feel to us. Rooms do have a great layout with a bedroom and living room sharing the view. We debated which ocean views were best and lean toward north-facing views because Moloka'i looks better than Lana'i from your large lanai. Oceanfront has the best views, of course, but the extra money is pretty painful. Some of the ocean view (3rd floor and above) rooms get less desirable the further back you go in the buildings. Regardless, consider the 1/2s instead of the 1/1s. Extra full bathrooms are about $30 more (a good deal). You have signing privileges at some other Ka'anapali properties. It's $12 a day to park. They have a *mandatory* $10 amenity fee that includes daily coffee, Internet and some other items. Studios are relatively spacious at 640 sq. ft. (and some have pull-down beds, offering more usable room for up to 3 people) at $329–$519. 1,114 sq. ft. 1/1s are $479–$649. At 1,118 sq. ft. the 1/2s are $399–$809, and 1,952 sq. ft. 2/2s are $575–$1,219. 2-night minimum.

LAHAINA

Makai Inn
(808) 662-3200
1415 Front St.
18 rooms, free Wi-Fi, lanais in 4 front units, a/c in 6 units that are not ocean

front. A small, quiet (and they like it that way) oceanfront inn north of downtown Lahaina. It's not a bad place to stay considering the proximity to the ocean, the kitchen and the price. Pretty basic. No a/c, no TV, no phones. Maid service "as needed." Decor is old-style Hawaiiana. We wish it was a bit cleaner and more updated, but the garden is pretty. 1/1s (400 sq. ft.) are $105–$180. 2/1s (800 sq. ft.) are $180. That price includes tax.

MA'ALAEA

Island Sands
(800) 367-5242 or (808) 244-0848
150 Hauoli St.

84 units, pool, a/c, washer/dryer in units, free Wi-Fi in some (computer in lobby), BBQs, elevator. A 6-story 1970s building with most units facing the ocean. Condos are clean, but not remarkable. There is a nice big lawn by the ocean, but no beach. It's a short walk to a sandy beach. 1/1 units (683 sq. ft.) at $165–$205. 2/2 units (802 sq. ft.) are $200–$265. 4-night minimum. Discounts on longer stays and some packages available. Ma'alaea Bay Realty & Rentals also has units here for less money.

*See all Web reviews at: **www.wizardpub.com***

NORTH KIHEI

Kealia Condominium
(800) 265–0686 or (808) 879–0952
191 N. Kihei Rd.

50 units, pool, a/c, washer/dryer in units, free hi-speed Internet or Wi-Fi in units, lanais, BBQs. elevator. A 6-story institutional-looking building. It's real windy and dusty here, but they do a good job of keeping up with the problem and spend a lot of time on pre-cleans. Most of the units have been nicely upgraded, so ask for one, but they still feel small to us. The 2/2 units are by the ocean and have good views. The studios face the street and park, and what little ocean you see is partially blocked by large trees. Some of the 1/1s can only accommodate two people. The pool area is nice and you're on the beach. Attentive staff here. Ultimately, you can get more space for the money elsewhere. Studios (420 sq. ft.) are $115–$130, 1/1s (556 sq. ft.) are $150–$190, 2/1s (730 sq. ft.) are $215–$250. 4-night minimum.

Koa Lagoon
(800) 367–8030 or (808) 879–3002
800 S. Kihei Rd.
42 units, pool, BBQs, a/c, washer/dryer in units, free hi-speed Internet access, free long distance to mainland, elevator.

What a steal! Though the building isn't overly impressive from the outside, the

SOLID GOLD VALUE

mid-'70s concrete walls hide an incredible find (and block the sound, as well). Exceptionally stunning oceanfront views, with West Maui as part of the backdrop. Rooms are impeccably clean, comfortable and large. Six floors; the upper ones have some palm tree crowns in the view. The beach isn't a good swimming beach, but it's pretty. This is one of the best deals in North Kihei with one caveat: There may be some seaweed in the water and on the beach; however, they scrape the beach each morning. Deluxe units cost an extra $10, but they're probably not worth it since the overall quality of the rooms is already so high. The on-site agent we list will take great care of you if you rent your unit directly with them. 1/1s (697 sq. ft.) are $140–$170, 2/2s (979 sq. ft.) are $170–$200. 5-night minimum.

SOUTH KIHEI

Kihei Surfside
(800) 451–5008 or (808) 879–5445
2936 S. Kihei Rd.
84 units, pool, BBQs, shuffleboard, hi-speed Internet access, washer/dryer only in 2/2s (the rest use coin-op), elevator. A 6-story semi-circular building with nice views north up the coast, especially rooms ending with 01 or 02. Though built in 1974, it's clean, tidy, and they

See all Web reviews at: www.wizardpub.com

have nice extras such as a good front office, huge lawn area, putting green and games such as croquet and bocce ball. It's a short walk to Keawakapu Beach. Three room layouts: 1/1 D units (500 sq. ft), 1/2 B & C units (650 sq. ft.) and 2/2 A units (950 sq. ft.). Those square footages include the lanais. B & C units are the best deal. Rooms ending in 03–06 overlook the pool, which may be a bit noisy. Overall, it's a very nice place to stay because of the price and location, not because of the rooms themselves, which are acceptable but not remarkable. 1/1s are $231–$289, 1/2s are $264–$326, 2/2s are $330–$433. 4-night minimum.

Hale Hui Kai
(800) 809–6284 or (808) 879–1219
2994 S. Kihei Rd.

40 units, pool, elevator, free Wi-Fi. A great location on Keawakapu Beach. Most units are 850 sq. ft. and have a very roomy feel and pleasing layout. The 3-story complex is clean and surrounds a pretty atrium. The

SOLID GOLD VALUE

bedrooms on the atrium side may be noisier and have less privacy. The oceanfront units are 1,250 sq. ft. and have awesome views overlooking the superb beach. Ground floor units *may* get a bit buggy. Only units 301–303, 305 and 313 have a/c. Rates for the 2/2 units are $185 for low-season garden view to $395 for their best oceanfront during high season (units ending in 11, 12 and 13). No credit cards. 5-night minimum.

WAILEA

Four Seasons Resort Maui
(800) 334–6284 or (808) 874–8000
3900 Wailea Alanui Dr.

380 rooms, 3 pools (including a keiki pool and adult pool), 4 spas, day spa, 24-hour

A REAL GEM

fitness center, valet-only parking, child care program, 2 lighted tennis courts, game room, hi-speed or Wi-Fi in rooms and resort-wide, 3 restaurants, 5 shops, 24-hour business center, 8 conference rooms, 24-hour room service, wedding coordinator. Oh, my, where do we start? We're fearful of sounding like drooling stooges for the Four Seasons, but this is our favorite resort in Wailea. When you walk in, you can actually feel the tension falling from your limbs. It soon becomes evident why. Here, they did everything right. The resort is immaculate and lovingly cared for. The smallest details seem to have been anticipated. The grounds are impeccable. No dead leaf or blade of grass in sight. The staff here is the

See all Web reviews at: **www.wizardpub.com**

most professional we've seen and seem genuinely concerned about your happiness. There are 2¼ employees for every room. (It's getting harder and harder to find those ¼ employees.) While you're at the pool, they'll come by and spritz you with Evian water, offer chilled towels, fresh fruit, popsicles and even wet the beach sand with water so you don't toast your tootsies. The pool area doesn't feel as packed as some other Wailea resorts. Their adult-only pool has bubble loungers (a flat area to lie on with jets under your body) and a swim-up bar. Also, *private* permanent cabanas (for up to 4 people) at pool's edge with flat screen TV, sofa and fridge are truly the ultimate in luxury—albeit at $350–$450 *per day!* Oh, yes, you have arrived, and you'll weep when you have to leave. The number of complimentary services is way too long to list, but includes a *free* child care program that goes from 9 a.m. to 5 p.m. (you only pay for their lunch), free cabana chairs (4 chairs under cover) and casabella chairs (2 chairs with a folding cover) at the beach and main pool (other resorts charge up to $350–$395 *per day* for those simple cabanas), free snorkel gear for an hour at the beach each day, free SCUBA demos, free daily aerobics and yoga classes, free access to their indoor-outdoor fitness room, free Kona coffee in rooms, rooms safes, etc. They even have a free game room with free video games, billiards, etc. It goes on and on. It's clear that they've made a decision to not nickel and dime their guests. We were a bit surprised that they charge $20 for valet-only overnight parking (that used to be free), that Internet access is extra (but they have free computers sprinkled around the resort) and local calls are a buck. Laundry services are valet only. They have an excellent collection of contemporary Hawaiian or Hawaiian-influenced artwork and a tour is available.

Rooms are very large (600 sq. ft.) and the bathrooms are fit for a king—lots of marble, deep tub, separate shower and tons of wiggle room. Rooms are elegantly furnished in keeping with the rest of the resort. They were renovated in 2007 with very pleasing results. The housekeeping staff would make an operating room nurse proud. Dirt is simply not tolerated and is dispatched with extreme prejudice.

Their beach, Wailea Beach, is one of the best on the island, an absolute dream.

The Four Seasons doesn't give many discounts, but they do offer promotional rates and package throughout the year. Their RACK rates start lower than most of their competition in the area, and with all the freebies it's actually a good deal. Rates are $485–$1,395. Suites (1,000–3,700 sq. ft.) are $995–$15,000. The $485 mountain side rooms are actually a very good deal as the rates increase *a lot* with better views.

Polo Beach Club
(800) 367–5246 or (808) 879–1595
4400 Makena Alanui Dr.

71 units, pool, spa, a/c, BBQ areas, daily maid service, washer/dryer in unit, elevator, free hi-speed Internet access in rooms. The location sure is amazing—right next to Polo Beach. In fact, because it's so close to the water and also so close to where you park your car, it's popular with folks who don't want to walk much. The 8-story building is shaped in a series of notches, so if you get an oceanfront unit, ask for one of the notch-

A REAL GEM

See all Web reviews at: *www.wizardpub.com*

es closest to the water. (The front notches are called Prime Oceanfront and are the priciest.) Layouts are pleasing with both living room and the master bedroom next to the ocean, so you get to live and sleep to the sound of the ocean. Ocean view units are farther back, but the angling of the building allows for good views from most units. There may be some stairs in your unit. No one will accuse the Polo Beach Club of being a bargain, but its location and spacious, well-furnished units certainly qualify for the gem rating. Many people don't rent cars here (we hope you're not one of them) and just lie on the beach the entire time.

The main rental agent, Destination Resorts, has extra services such as grocery shopping before you arrive, massages, and rental cars are available for $29 per day and up.

2/2s (1,186–1,321 sq. ft.) are $465–$810. 3-night minimum. They add a 5.2% "resort fee" to your room rate.

KAHULUI

Maui Seaside
(800) 560–5552 or (808) 877–3311
100 Ka'ahumanu Ave.

190 rooms, pool, restaurant, Wi-Fi. This local chain always has clean, tidy rooms and grounds served with lots of aloha, and this location is no exception. The rooms, though very dated, always have spotless bathrooms with polished chrome fixtures (wish we knew their secret—ours always get pitted with rust). Their RACK rates listed

should be taken with a grain of salt. Nearly everyone gets discounted, and they have lots of packages. Staff is friendly. Parking is $7; no room safes, but they have free ones at the front desk. Local calls are 50¢. Larger rooms are in the tower building, and its even-numbered rooms have better views. Rooms (168–378 sq. ft.) are $125–$135, poolside rooms are $170, kitchenettes (when available) are $180.

ACCOMMODATIONS ELSEWHERE

Kula Lodge
(800) 233–1535 or (808) 878–1535
15200 Haleakala Hwy. (Route 377)
5 rooms, free coffee daily. Located up Haleakala at the 3,200 foot level, this is the place to stay if you're hankering to be close to Haleakala Crater, you want to stay where it's cool, or you just want to get away from it all. No phones, no TV, no Internet and maybe no cell phone reception, but some expansive views. Rooms have gas stoves since the winter temps dip into the low 60s (summer gets into the *upper* 60s). Hey, that might not be chilly where you come from, but it's considered the Arctic to Maui residents. Rooms are simple and quaint if a bit overpriced at $125–$220. No laundry facilities on site. On Hwy 377 between the 5- and 6-mile markers.

HANA

Travaasa Hana
(855) 868–7282 or (808) 248–8211
5031 Hana Hwy.
70 rooms, 2 pools, 2 spas, 3 restaurants, room service, 2 tennis courts, day spa, valet parking, coffee maker with free fresh ground coffee daily, free Wi-Fi access in club room, croquet, bocce ball. This resort has been though

A REAL GEM

See all Web reviews at: **www.wizardpub.com**

quite a lot. Built as a high-end getaway for the well-to-do, in the late '90s it fell into disrepair. Three owners later it has reclaimed much of its former glory and now exudes an old-world feel. (But it was for sale again at press time, so it's hard to say where it's going.) It's impossible to stay here and not feel relaxed—unless you contemplate the bill that awaits you at the end.

Tranquil green hillside grounds, fairly large rooms, and a good staff make this a GEM. Special touches are available like in-room massages, private spas in some of the rooms (for extra) and a concerted effort not to nickel and dime you. Free local calls, free room safes, free fitness room, free laundry facilities, free items from the in-room fridge and free valet parking (though you don't need it) and use of some of the day spa facilities (treatments are extra). They have a 3-hole putting green and have free bikes for use. They offer a lu'au show with buffet and special chef-inspired dinner buffets with wine pairing on some nights. Every guest gets a welcome basket of fresh fruits and banana bread, and champagne is added for honeymooners.

Rooms are very comfortable, and many have nice ocean views. No TVs or alarm clocks and no a/c. (You can request a fan if you're hot, particularly at night.) This is Hana, and you're not supposed to *care* what's on TV or what time to get up. Some of the cottages have their own hot tub on the deck.

Travaasa Hana is expensive, but it's the kind of place that will soothe your soul. It captures the essence of Hana's unique place in Hawai'i. They often run inclusive packages that add extras like spa packages and meals. Rooms (543–835 sq. ft.) are $400–$780 (that $780 rate is for the Sea Ranch Cottages and includes breakfast for two). Suites (942–1,475 sq. ft.) are $880–$980 (breakfast for two included). The Sea Ranch Cottages only allow guests 16 years and older.

Hana Kai Maui
(800) 346–2772 or (808) 248–8426
4865 Uakea Rd.

18 units, daily maid, BBQs, free Wi-Fi, free laundry (when resort is not using it). This place has really improved since our last visit, and we were happy to see so many rooms updated. The bedding has all been redone with high thread count Egyptian cotton sheets. The grounds have been carefully tended, are very tropical and include a lovely koi pond with waterfall. Good Hana Bay views from most units (except two first floor studios). They have phones in all the rooms and local calls are free (important because your cell phone may not work), but no TVs. Since this is a small property, you may hear your neighbors if adjacent rooms are occupied. The lanais are spacious (about 300 sq. ft.) and tend to be very private. You won't get tired of sitting on them and watching the ocean. Studios are a decent deal. All rooms have complete kitchens. Studios (300–400 sq. ft.) $195–$260, with 1/1s (550 sq. ft.) $205–$275, 2/2 (890 sq. ft.) are $425. The oceanfront units have a 2-night minimum.

Island Dining Index on page 248, Where to Stay Index on pages 293–295.

Island Dining Index on page 248, Where to Stay Index on pages 293–295.

INDEX

Island Dining Index on page 248, Where to Stay Index on pages 293–295.

Island Dining Index on page 248, Where to Stay Index on pages 293–295.

Island Dining Index on page 248, Where to Stay Index on pages 293–295.

Island Dining Index on page 248, Where to Stay Index on pages 293–295.